Vern —

Happy Birthday!

Good luck & Best Wishes.

Your friend,

Van

9/27/2021

Cover Photo - the author at the gravesite of Col. John Singleton Mosby (CSA), in Warrenton, VA, holding Mosby's Colt 45 revolver, courtesy of the Stuart-Mosby Civil War Cavalry Museum in Centreville, VA. One of the thrilling things that happens when you travel and make new connections is that you get to hold history in your hands!

Photo by Gwen Wyttenbach

Title: Civil War Travels with Ms. Rebelle

ISBN: 9781985391963

Published by
Bull Run Civil War Round Table, Centreville, VA

Kindle Direct Publishing Platform
2020

Civil War Travels

with

Ms. Rebelle

A Guide to Civil War Gravesites
North and South

Janet L. Greentree

by

Janet L. Greentree

Dedicated...

...to my late father, Alan R. Schrader, for instilling in me as a child a love of Civil War history, travel and photography. We shared many happy years as he took our family to battlefields and historical places associated with the Civil War, and his appearance as a re-enactor with the 13th Virginia at the time of the 1961 Centennial Anniversary reenactment of Bull Run/First Manassas is one of my fondest memories of him. He had such an impact on my life.

At right: visiting the Lee Museum at Gettysburg, which - in 1863 - served as Conf. Gen. Robert E. Lee's head-quarters. This was Ms. Rebelle's first trip to Gettysburg, about age 5. She is the little girl by the cannon. Behind are her mother, grandmothers, aunts and uncles. Photo taken by her father, Alan R. Schrader.

At left: Lookout Mountain in Tennessee; standing is Mom, Esther Schrader (left); sister Kathe, age 3 (seated, left) and myself, age 9. My family is aprecious part of my memory of this very dramatic land-scape. Traveling with my family to Civil War sites always made the history there more personal.

i

Acknowledgements

Ed Bearss, Chief Historian Emeritus of the National Park Service, for being my biggest fan. He urged me for a long time to compile my stories into a book.

James Wirth, my late 8th grade history teacher at Annapolis Junior High School. He made the Civil War come alive through his teachings. He took our class to Gettysburg on a field trip – an early indication to me of its great importance in history.

The Bull Run Civil War Round Table for publishing my book, and, over the years, including over 94 of my articles in their newsletter, *The Stone Wall*.

The Greater Boston Civil War Round Table (Al & David Smith) for letting me join their tour of Richmond in 1997, and then urging me to join a round table in my area.

Nadine Mironchuk of Boston, for being a great friend, travel companion, my biggest cheerleader, and current editor of Bull Run Civil War Round Table's newsletter, *The Stone Wall*. It is she who put this book together for us.

My sister, Kathe Fernandez, for being my best travel companion – together, we have roamed all over this beautiful country of ours. She has trekked through many cemeteries along the way, helping me finding graves.

My children Lisa, Mark, Gregg, and Melanie - even though they kid me about being in a "cult." My oldest daughter, Lisa Tully, and her husband Paul, Gettysburg residents, were always willing to take pictures of markers and other monuments for inclusion in my articles (even though I received off-the-wall photos from them too!). My son, Mark, and his family (Wendy, Sarah, and Katerina) took me to cemeteries in Illinois, Missouri, and New York. My son, Gregg, the English teacher - for his advice and support. My daughter, Melanie, for accompanying me to find Col. John Singleton Mosby's grave in Warrenton, VA, my very first famous grave.

My first cousin, Alan Norris (my father's sister's son) and his wife Carol, for all of our Gettysburg trips together, and for accompanying me on many walks through cemeteries. His family joined my family (plus grandmothers) in visits to Gettysburg when I was only 4 or 5 years old (see Dedication page photo of Lee's Headquarters, taken on one of these jaunts).

My www.findagrave.com friends - the late Joe Ferrell, whose wife, Pam, gave me all of Joe's cemetery maps from all over the country. Burl Kennedy, for providing me with help on Southern cemeteries. The late Art Loux, for sending me two huge binders full of cemetery information on Civil War general's graves.

Saundra Cox, former editor of the newsletter *The Stone Wall*, who ran my first article and who urged me to continue writing my stories.

Nancy Anwyll, for being my first cemetery travel companion, and for helping me find a lot of the 420 graves I have found.

Gwen Wyttenbach and her daughter, Debbie, for being travel companions on our West Point trip to see what we called "military Disneyland," and finding all 28 generals' graves.

Alan Smolinski of the Greater Boston Civil War Round Table, who shared his love of taking pictures of general's graves with me, and for his wonderful tour of Mount Auburn Cemetery in Cambridge, Massachusetts.

Members of the Bull Run Civil War Round Table, who have told me they love my articles and read them first. President Mark Trbovich, for wanting to publish my book. The late John McAnaw, for encouraging me to make the articles into a book. Jim Lewis, for his help with ideas for the book. E.B. Vandiver, for profiling me in his Meet the Member series in *The Stone Wall* newsletter.

Jim Tipton, developer of www.findagrave.com, for the great job they do with profiling Civil War generals and others, most including pictures of grave markers. Back in 1998, Jim had me send him my pictures of famous graves and scanned them onto the site. Without this wonderful site, people would be walking and driving around cemeteries forever, searching for gravesites. They have also allowed me to post 546 photos of mostly Civil War general's graves, 9 biographies, and 165 memorials to their site.

Happy Travels Make BFFs

Nadine Mironchuk and Janet Greentree

Alan Smolinski and Dave Smith

Janet Greentree and Al Smith

Nancy Anwyll and Janet Greentree

Paul and Lisa Tully

Ed Bearss and Janet Greentree

Ms. Rebelle (right) with children (left to right): Gregg Greentree, Lisa Tully, Melanie Greentree, and Mark Greentree.

Gwen Wyttenbach

Carol and Alan Norris

Kathe Fernandez and Janet Greentree

Some of the great BFFs that make traveling to Civil War sights so enjoyable, and whom I would like to thank for being there - adding to my knowledge of history - throughout the years.

~

Table of Contents

Table of Contents (con't)

Table of Contents (con't)

Foreword

With the publication of this book, one of my long-time goals has been achieved. For many years, I have urged Janet Greentree to make her accounts of Civil War travels available to a wider audience. Janet has led an assortment of relatives and friends on trips to the burial sites of Civil War generals. They visit the graves of the Blue and the Gray; famous, infamous, and forgotten, throughout the United States. Sometimes there is just one, sometimes there are many. A few are not generals, but interesting all the same. She photographs their markers and sometimes houses and possessions and provides brief biographical sketches.

The articles, "Civil War Travels with Ms. Rebelle," are published in the superb monthly newsletter, *"THE STONE WALL,"* of the Bull Run Civil War Roundtable (BRCWRT), a leader in Civil War education and preservation in Northern Virginia; an organization of which I am proud to be a member.

National Park Service Historian Emeritus Edwin C. Bearss (right) submits his Foreword to Janet Schrader Greentree, happy to have encouraged her to compile her essays into a book that might encourage others to visit the places of Civil War history.

Over many years, she has visited the gravesites of over four hundred Civil War generals and a few other characters from that war. These were documented in over 60 separate articles, many of which are included in this book.

All of those seriously interested in the history of our great national conflict will find this book both fascinating and rewarding reading. I have certainly found the articles to be this, looking forward each month for the latest. Well done, BRCWRT, for publishing this. Very well done, Janet Greentree.

Edwin C. Bearss

Edwin C. Bearss
Historian Emeritus, U.S. National Park Service

So – Who is This Ms. Rebelle, Anyway?

by E. B. Vandiver, III

Janet Greentree joined the Bull Run Civil War Round Table when we still met in the auditorium at the Manassas Battlefield Park Center. She has had a lifelong interest in Civil War history but didn't learn of our round table until she signed up for a Virginia battlefield tour of Richmond with the Greater Boston Civil War Round Table. They suggested she join a local round table; some internet research found us, and she joined. Nine years later, she became Ms. Rebelle – but more about that later.

Her father, Alan Schrader, was an avid Civil War amateur scholar (sounds better than a Civil War nut!) who visited and photographed sites, studied genealogy, and participated in the 1961 Centennial Reenactment of the First Battle of Manassas. Janet had an eighth-grade history teacher, James Wirth, who really ignited her interest in history, especially by taking the class on a field trip to the Gettysburg Battlefield. She has been visiting Civil War sites ever since.

Janet was born, raised, and attended public school in Annapolis, Maryland, where her father worked as a mechanical engineer for the U.S. Navy. Janet's younger sister Kathe (Fernandez) faithfully accompanies Ms. Rebelle on her cemetery jaunts and other historical site explorations.

Janet Schrader Greentree – AKA "Ms. Rebelle."

Janet had two great-grandfathers in the Civil War, one from Virginia with the Confederate Army, and another from Ohio serving in the Union Army. She visits the gravesites of both Confederate and Union generals, photographing and writing of them in her "Civil War Travels with Ms. Rebelle" feature in the Bull Run Civil War Round Table newsletter, *The Stone Wall*. Her pronounced Southern leanings gave rise to her nom de plume of Ms. Rebelle, conferred by a friend.

A Confederate ancestor (a maternal great-grandfather) George Washington Baker from Augusta County, Virginia, served with the 23rd Virginia Cavalry Regiment. This unit was formed in April, 1864, when seven companies of the 41st Virginia Cavalry Battalion were combined with two companies of O'Ferrall's Battalion. Originally, the 41st conducted operations in Western Virginia and the Shenandoah Valley. When reorganized as the 23rd Virginia Cavalry Regiment, it was assigned to Imboden's Brigade, participating in the defense of the Shenandoah Valley until the war ended and they disbanded. An older brother, John Baker, in the 12th Virginia Cavalry, also served in the Shenandoah Valley in 1864 with Gen. Jubal Early's Army. They were eventually both captured (but at different times), interred at Camp Chase, Ohio, repatriated to Virginia, and finally migrated back to Ohio to farm. Janet says that today George Washington Baker's farm is covered by an upscale housing development near Columbus, Ohio.

Another maternal great-grandfather served in the Union Army, joining the 18th U.S. Infantry Regiment, the second Battalion of which was organized at Camp Thomas near Columbus, Ohio in the summer of 1861. It became part of the Regular Amy Brigade of the Army of the Ohio, serving all its campaigns and battles in Kentucky, Tennessee, and Georgia. After the fall of Atlanta, it moved to Chattanooga, Tennessee area, remaining there until July 1865. He was medically discharged in January 1864 and returned to Ohio to farm (also in the Columbus/Westerville area). Today, that farm is being overrun by suburban housing developments.

Janet's first tour with our Round Table was to Arlington National Cemetery, which piqued her interest in the final resting places of Civil War generals. The first gravesite visited was that of Col. John Singleton Mosby in Warrenton, Virginia (hey, he wasn't a general, but he did more damage than most of them did!) with her youngest daughter Melanie. Ms. Rebelle now makes an annual trip with her younger sister (who lives in California and attends our Round Table when visiting

Janet), with each trip resulting in one or more "Civil War Travels with Ms. Rebelle" articles in *The Stone Wall*.

To date, there have been over 80 articles documenting many of the hundreds of gravesites visited (of the 1,003 Civil War generals North and South), and a few other interesting individuals who were not generals. One such attractive figure is Lt. Colonel Myles Keogh, who died fighting with Custer at Little Big Horn. She found his battlefield death marker after a harrowing hike on rattlesnake-infested *trials*, and later visited his grave at Fort Hill Cemetery in Auburn, New York. Her favorite general's grave is that of Gen. William Tecumseh Sherman at Calvary Cemetery in St. Louis, Missouri. She admires the crossed flags and other symbols on his elegant tombstone. Her son took her on this visit on a beautiful sunny day, creating an indelible and cherished memory.

Here, now, the Round Table will publish a volume of all her articles to date, for leisurely winter fireside reading.

Janet's children are grown, so she now shares her home with a Maine Coon cat named Charlotte. She never misses coming to our monthly round table meetings (only two or three unavoidable absences in 20 years), enjoying the fellowship of the speaker's dinner beforehand. She loves learning about the war and especially enjoys the tours. She never missed any of John McAnaw's frequent local tours. She plans continuing the travels of Ms. Rebelle.

Ms. Rebelle says her #1 fan, Ed Bearss, has long urged this. I know I would buy one.

Keep it up Ms. Rebelle: you only have 588 generals to go!

NOTE: Ms. Rebelle's hobby is traveling the country finding and honoring the graves of our 1,008 Civil War generals. So far, she has located and photographed 420 - 169 Confederate and 251 Union. Each person visited has a unique life story, and each visit provides an opportunity to learn more about America's most profound event—the Civil War.

E.B. Vandiver, III is the author of "Meet the Member" profiles of long-time, devoted members of the Bull Run Civil War Round Table.

About the Sponsor of this Book - The Bull Run Civil War Round Table

The Bull Run Civil War Round Table meets every second Thursday of the month, and each meeting features a speaker who is knowledgeable about some aspect of the Civil War.

For 27 years, the BRCWRT has followed these precepts:

Purpose: To stimulate member and general public interest in the study of the American Civil War-era, including the Antebellum and post-war Reconstruction periods. These studies include the military, political, economic and social history of both the United States and the Confederacy. In coordination with those studies, the organization seeks to promote strong and robust programs that support a better understanding of Civil War issues, battlefields, memorials, sites, buildings and artifacts through the following goals.

Education goal: The Round Table promotes the study of Civil War history and raises member and public awareness of the era's issues, battlefields and sites. It accomplishes this through lectures, tours, newsletters, the development of historical signage, and supporting selected Civil War events and ceremonies. Electronic communication also supports the effort via Web site and social media.

Preservation goal: The Round Table promotes the preservation of nation-defining Civil War sites and causes by raising awareness of threats to the integrity of local and national Civil War battlefields, memorials, and sites to the local authorities. These efforts are supported through research, attendance and testimony at government symposia and hearings, and financial donations.

General Membership meetings are held at 7 p.m. at the Centreville Regional Library, 14200 St. Germain Drive, Centreville, VA 20121-2255. For specific meeting dates and information, please visit the Web site: http://bullruncwrt.org.

Captain/Brevet Lt. Col. Myles Walter Keogh

"Unsurpassed in dash" is the way the late historian Brian Pohanka described Myles Keogh. According to Keogh's citizenship papers, he was 6' ½" tall, blue eyes, brown hair, and had a florid complexion. It seems that Brian had a lifelong interest in both Keogh and the Battle of Little Big Horn.

Ms. Rebelle and her sister recently went to the Little Big Horn Battlefield. Visiting Little Big Horn was on my bucket list, and if you haven't been there, it should be on your bucket list, as well. The terrain remains unchanged from that fateful day of June 25, 1876, when Custer's 7th U.S. Cavalry attacked a village of hostile Indians camped along the Little Big Horn River.

My goal was to find Keogh's death marker site on the battlefield and to place a flag there. It turned out to be more of a challenge than I thought it would be. Keogh's Company I was positioned between Calhoun Hill and Last Stand Hill. He and his men died in a cluster at the bottom of a hill. First Sgt. Frank Varden, Cpl. John Wild, trumpeter John Patton, and others would die around Myles. Even though it had been 103 degrees the day before our visit, it was cold, windy, and rainy on the day we took to the field.

Lt. Col.. Myles Walter Keogh

We took a bus tour offered by the Crow Native Americans. Our tour guide was a Crow woman who told the story of what happened during the battle, and she also used Indian sign language to tell the story. She was very interesting, extremely knowledgeable, and you could tell she knew the

Janet Greentree makes her way through the snakes to flag Lt. Col. Myles Keogh's death site at Little Big Horn.

Photo by Kathe Fernandez

oral history from her people. When I told her that I wanted to walk down to Keogh's marker, she said it would be a good day to do it, as the rattlesnakes would not be out. A park ranger had previously tried to discourage me from doing this. Nonetheless, Ms. Rebelle walked down the long, winding path, passing many markers of the unknown dead, until I got to the far right on the path, and there it was. Someone a long time ago had placed a 7th Cavalry flag on his marker; it had become very ragged. Myles Keogh now has a new U.S. flag on his marker. My sister wasn't as brave as me, and remained towards the top of the path. I must say, I walked very fast up and down that hill "just in case."

Myles Keogh was born March 25, 1840, in Leighlinbridge, County Carlow, Ireland, to a well-to-do family. Myles had seven sisters and was the youngest of five boys. The potato famine in Ireland didn't have an effect on his family, as they farmed barley, and had land and money. His father died at an early age.

In 1860, when Myles was 20 years old, he fought in the Papal Wars in Italy. After the war, Keogh was invited to be a member of the Vatican Guard. He was awarded the Order of St. Gregory and the Agnus Dei (Lamb of God) medals for his Papal War service. His mother died in 1862. During that year, Secretary of State William Seward went to Europe to recruit members of the Papal Army to fight in our American Civil War. Myles and two Irish and Papal Army friends, Joseph O'Keefe and Daniel Keily, were recruited, and came to America.

Keogh and Keily set sail on March 17, 1862, from Liverpool with first class accommodations on the steamer Kangaroo. O'Keefe joined them a week later in New York City. All three men went directly to Washington to sign up for the Union Army and were given the rank of captain. They were all assigned on April 9, 1862, to the staff of Gen. James Shields. Their first battle on June 9, 1862, was at Port Republic, VA, where the Union forces very nearly captured Gen. Thomas "Stonewall" Jackson. Keogh was briefly on the staff of Gen. George B. McClellan, where he met George Armstrong Custer and his good friend, Andrew Alexander. Keogh was assigned to the personal staff of Gen. John Buford on July 31, 1862.

In researching Keogh, I came across a possible connection to Gen. Philip Kearny, Jr. at the Battle of Ox Hill/Chantilly. There is a very likely possibility that Keogh was sent down to Difficult Run with the 9th New York Cavalry to receive the Confederate ambulance bearing the body of Gen. Kearny. Bull Run Civil War Round Table (BRCWRT) Member Ed Wenzel and I are still working to verify this fact with the National Archives, but it is interesting to know that Keogh perhaps had a connection to the battle at Ox Hill/Chantilly.

Keogh fought at 2nd Manassas with Gen. John Buford, Jr.; he was on the staff of Gen. McClellan at Antietam; fought at Fredericksburg; Brandy Station; Upperville; and was on Buford's staff at Gettysburg; fought at Funkstown; Williamsport; Bristoe Station; Kennesaw Mountain; the Atlanta Campaign; and marched in the Grand Review in Washington. He was assigned to Gen. Stoneman's staff after the death of Gen. Buford on December 16, 1863. In 1864, he and Stoneman were captured trying to liberate Andersonville Prison and were sent to the Charleston, South Carolina, city jail. Gen. Sherman facilitated their release. After the war, Keogh was assigned to Gen. Stoneman in Knoxville, TN, where he shared quarters with Emory Upton. He also did court-martial duty in Nashville.

Keogh's friend, Joseph O'Keefe, was wounded at Brandy Station and then wounded again at Five Forks. O'Keefe died at Providence Hospital in Washington on May 30, 1865, with Keogh by his side. His friend, Daniel Keily, would die in Louisiana of yellow fever in 1867.

On May 4, 1866, Keogh was commissioned a 2nd lieutenant in the 4th Texas Cavalry, but did not serve with them. Instead, he received a commission as captain of Co. I, 7th U.S. Cavalry, under Brev. Maj. George Armstrong Custer.

The Crow woman who gave us the bus tour at Little Big Horn said Keogh was the bravest of the brave. Many Indian accounts have Keogh fighting to the end with tenacity and bravery. Most of his (and Custer's) men shot their horses and used them for cover in the midst of the massacre. Keogh did not kill his horse, Comanche. There are reports that Keogh took cover between Comanche's front legs and died with the reins in his hand. Even though he

GUSTAVE KERN WITH COMANCHE

was stripped naked by the Indians, his body was not mutilated like the others. Since he had the reins of his horse in his hand and his Papal medal around his neck, the Indians believed it would be a bad omen to desecrate his body. Comanche was found with bullet wounds and seven arrows in his body. He was the only survivor of Little Big Horn, other than the Indians.

Comanche was taken to Fort Lincoln and cared for by Gustave Kern, who would later die at Wounded Knee. Comanche had seven scars – four to the back of his shoulders, one on each of his hind legs, and another through a hoof. Gen. Samuel Sturgis, whose own son James was killed at Little Big Horn, wrote a three-paragraph General Order No. 7 detailing the care of Comanche. He was never to be ridden again, never to work, was to live in a comfortable stable fitted for him, and would be saddled, bridled, and draped in mourning with boots reversed and paraded at special events and on the anniversary of Little Big Horn.

Comanche would die at Fort Riley, Kansas, on November 7, 1891, when he was around 29 years old. His remains are now preserved and on display at the University of Kansas in Lawrence, where he has 120,000 visitors a year. He is one of only two horses to be put to rest with full military honors. The other horse honored was Blackjack, the caparisoned, riderless horse of the 3rd U.S. Infantry Regiment - The Old Guard, which took part in the funerals of Presidents Hoover, Kennedy, Johnson, and hundreds of others in the Armed Forces held at Arlington National Cemetery.

Keogh seemed to have a keen sense of humor, as evidenced by the pictures taken of him. One is taken on the front steps of Custer's home at Fort Lincoln, where Keogh sits on the front porch holding a ladies fan in his hand. Another has him with Gen. Andrew Alexander while he is tugging at Alexander's beard. There is a picture of him standing on the very edge of Lookout Mountain with a group of soldiers. He also lent one of his Papal medals to one of his coterie, a Wadsworth sister, both of whom donned the uniforms of Tom Custer and W.W. Cooke. Emma and Nellie Wadsworth both had medals on in the picture, along with Tom Custer's two Medals of Honor. Myles loved the ladies, but never married.

Libbie Custer, pictured on the steps of her home in Fort Abraham Lincoln, North Dakota, sits beside the standing Mrs. Margaret Calhoun, her husband's sister. To Margaret's right is Bloody Knife, a skilled Arikara scout and favorite of Gen. Custer. On the steps beneath him sits two-time Medal of Honor recipient and brother to Gen. Custer and Margaret Calhoun, Capt. Thomas Custer. In front of the opposite post is Margaret's husband, Lt. James Calhoun, described by Custer as "the Adonis of the 7th." The man with legs crossed in the bottom center is Irish-born Capt. Myles Keogh.

Myles Walter Keogh was disinterred from his burial site at Little Big Horn in 1877, and is buried at Fort Hill Cemetery in Auburn, New York, between his two friends, Generals Andrew Alexander and Emory Upton. His wishes were to be buried in Auburn, as he spent many happy times with the Throop Martin and Alexander families at Willowbrook. The inscription on his stone reads: "Sleep Soldier! Still in Honored Rest, Your Truth and Valor Wearing; The Bravest are Among the Tenderest! The Loving are the Daring!"

Keogh's stone became discolored over the years. Brian Pohanka asked permission to clean it in 1989. Brian also had Keogh's marker at Little Big Horn moved 65 feet, after archaeological digs found the base of his original marker. Keogh's medals were said to have been secured by Frederick Benteen after the battle and sent to his family in Ireland. Keogh had taken out a $10,000 life insurance policy on himself in October of 1875. The money was also sent to his family in Ireland.

Along with Brian Pohanka's interest in Myles Keogh, the late Gene Autry owned several items belonging to Keogh, which are displayed in the Gene Autry Western Heritage Museum in Los Angeles. There is also a stained-glass window dedicated to Keogh in St. Joseph's Church in Tinryland, County Carlow, Ireland.

His family still lives at Clifden Castle, which Myles gave to his sister Margaret.

Above, left: Keogh's monument at Fort Hill Cemetery in Auburn, NY; above, right: Army personnel view the marker noting Myles Keogh's burial place on the Little Bighorn battlefield.

"Tiger" John McCausland -
the Unreconstructed Rebel

"Burnt by Rebel Cavalry" are the words etched in concrete above the door of the Franklin County Courthouse in Chambersburg, Pennsylvania. To be more specific, the words are: Built 1842, Burnt by Rebel Cavalry, July 30, 1864, Rebuilt 1865. There is no mention of the name of Gen. John McCausland, who under orders from Gen. Jubal A. Early, asked for a ransom of $100,000 from the town of Chambersburg, PA. If no ransom was paid, he would burn the town in retaliation for the burning of the Shenandoah Valley by Union Gen. David Hunter, and especially in McCausland's mind, Hunter's burning of the Virginia Military Institute in Lexington, Virginia.

On my first visit to Chambersburg, there was a historical sign in the town Diamond saying about the same thing as the attached photo, but without the name of Gen. McCausland. On subsequent trips, a new historical sign does mention the name of McCausland. There is also a monument stone in the Diamond that does not mention his name. Feelings ran deep in Chambersburg for many years after the burning of the town. However, on the 100th anniversary of the burning in July, 1964, the general's grandson, Dr. Alexander McCausland, from Roanoke, VA, was asked to be present at a memorial event. Dr. McCausland, son of John III, accepted and was treated very kindly by the citizens of Chambersburg.

My interest in Gen. McCausland was started by correspondence between a fellow graver and findagrave.com contributor, the late Joe Ferrell, and Ms. Rebelle, about the whereabouts of Gen. McCausland's grave in West Virginia. Joe lived in Charleston, WV, and had been to McCausland's grave, which is located in the Smith Family Cemetery atop a "mountain" in Henderson, WV. Joe kindly offered to show Yankee Nan (BRCWRT member Nancy Anwyll) and me where his grave was located. Little did we know that, nine years ago, we would be climbing that mountain (no roads) to view that grave. Not only did Joe help us find the grave, he found the grandson of the general, Smith McCausland, who was willing to show us Grape Hill, the general's home in Pliny, WV. Both of us so enjoyed talking to Smith, who was very humble, soft spoken and extremely proud of his ancestor. Smith still farms the

Plaque above door of Franklin County Courthouse in Chambersburg, PA.
Photo by Janet Greentree

Historical monument in town center Diamond of Chambersburg, PA.
Photo by Janet Greentree

land his grandfather owned; he is the son of Alexander McCausland.

Grape Hill is a huge, 19-room stone house with an octagonal belvedere on top of the roof. McCausland had installed dumb-waiters in the house, as well as a central collection device for collecting ashes from the fireplaces. The house was built in 1885 and he had one of the first telephones in Mason County. After the war, when McCausland bought the land in Mason County, it was swampy. Using his engineering skills learned at VMI, he designed tiles to divert the water,

McCausland's Grape Hill in Pliny, W.V.
Photo by Janet Greentree

which are still in use today. McCausland built the house after he married Charlotte Hannah. They met at the Greenbrier Hotel during a reunion with Gen. Fitzhugh Lee. They had four children: Samuel, Charlotte, John, and Alexander.

John McCausland, Jr. was born to John & Harriet McCausland in St. Louis, Missouri, on September 13, 1836. His neighbors were the Dent family. Julia Dent would later marry Ulysses S. Grant. His father devised a tax system for the city of St. Louis which is still in use today. In 1843, he became an orphan when his parents died within a month of each other. He was taken by his Uncle Alexander to Henderson, WV, to live with his maiden aunt, Jane Smith. When he was 16, he entered the Virginia Military Institute and graduated first in the class of 1857. He became an assistant professor at VMI, alongside future Gen. Thomas "Stonewall" Jackson. Jackson, McCausland, and a group of VMI Cadets, acting as guards around the scaffolding, witnessed the execution of John Brown in Charles Town in 1859.

When the Civil War began, McCausland was commissioned a colonel and commanded the 36th Virginia Infantry Regiment. His men gave him the sobriquet of "Tiger John." Most of McCausland's time was spent in western Virginia with faceoffs between him and Gen. David Hunter. When Gen. Albert Gallatin Jenkins died at Cloyd's Mountain, McCausland was given command of the Confederate forces. He was instrumental in saving the city of Lynchburg from Gen. Hunter. The city gave him a gold sword inscribed "The City of Lynchburg to Gen. John McCausland, June 18, 1864." He was given a new horse, accoutrements, and solid silver spurs. The city sent him telegrams for years on his birthday, in appreciation. On the 61st anniversary of the battle, the mayor of Lynchburg sent the following telegram: "On this sixty-first anniversary of the attack on Lynchburg, which you so ably repelled with troops under your command, permit me to remind you of the grateful remembrance of our people and express the wish you are this day enjoying the satisfaction that must be yours through having served God and your fellowmen."

McCausland during the Civil War, and later in life.

McCausland was also with Gen. Jubal Early in July 1864, in Early's attempt to take Washington. McCausland got as close as Georgetown and could see the unfinished dome of the Capitol.

Now we come back to Chambersburg. Gen. Early ordered him to go north into Pennsylvania, demand $100,000 in gold or $500,000 in greenbacks from the prosperous town of Chambersburg, in retaliation for Hunter's burning of the Valley. He arrived about 8 a.m. and set up headquarters at the Henry Greenawalt house west of town. He ate breakfast with his staff at the Franklin Hotel, while the town's elders decided what to do. The elders thought the ransom demand was a joke and said they would not pay.

The town was torched, destroying 550 buildings, including 278 homes and businesses, 271 barns, stables, and outbuildings. Two thousand inhabitants were left homeless. The residents hid where they were able, including the local cemetery. The entire center of town was destroyed. Only one local resident died, and three

Henry Greenawalt House – McCausland's HQ – Chambersburg, PA.

Photo by Janet Greentree

Confederates. The monetary loss to the town was estimated to be $915,137.24, which is enumerated on the monument stone on the Diamond. Gen. Winfield Scott Hancock issued an order: "The President directs that you cause the rebel Gen. McCausland to be arrested and held until application is made for this person by the civil authorities of Pennsylvania." New York papers called him the "Hun of Chambersburg."

He also fought at Fort Donelson, the Valley Campaign (3rd Winchester, Fisher's Hill, Cedar Creek), the Siege of Petersburg, and the Battle of Five Forks. He was present at Appomattox. When he asked Fitzhugh Lee what was happening, Lee replied, "Uncle Bobby has surrendered." Like Col. John Singleton Mosby, rather than surrender, he and his men left Appomattox and disbanded in Lynchburg. He became known as the "Unreconstructed Rebel." When asked about his sons becoming soldiers, he said: "I rather see my boys dead, than to wear the blue uniform."

Gen. McCausland surveying his work of arson in Chambersburg, PA.

Above, Joe Ferrell (left) and Smith McCausland (right) were generous tour guides for our McCausland adventure. Below, Janet Greentree and Nancy Anwyll are delighted at having reached the object of the day's travels.
Photo by Janet Greentree

With a price on his head at age 29, he left the country and traveled in Europe and Canada. He carried letters of introduction from prominent friends and the faculty of VMI. Gen. Ulysses S. Grant declared in 1867 that Chambersburg should be forgotten and forgiven. McCausland returned to West Virginia, but remained a recluse and farmer the rest of his life. His grandson Smith told us the story of Pres. Grant stopping by his house on the Great Kanawha River and wanting to visit. McCausland declined to see him.

McCausland died of a stroke on January 22, 1927, at the age of 90 in his rocking chair at his home in Pliny. Due to the swollen condition of the Great Kanawha River, his coffin was floated down the river on a large barge to Henderson, and then pulled on a sled up the mountain to the Smith Family Cemetery for burial. The Daughters of Confederacy handled the funeral. The coffin was draped with the Confederate Stars and Bars. He was the next-to-the-last Confederate general to die. Gen. Felix Robertson of Texas would survive him by 13 months.

All my thanks to the late Joe Ferrell and his wife, Pam. This trip would not have been possible without him. Pam kindly sent me all of Joe's cemetery maps for finding generals after his death, which I am still using to this day.

As a complete non sequitur, the "Legend of the Mothman" was confabulated in Point Pleasant, West Virginia, and this sculpture commemorating the 1966 paranormal event is an example of some of the weird and wonderful things that you get to see when you travel along the byways of this great country.
Photo by Janet Greentree

Gen. William Tecumseh ("Cump") Sherman

Many people over the years have asked me which grave of all that I have found is my favorite. My answer is always Gen. William Tecumseh Sherman's grave at Calvary Cemetery in St. Louis, Missouri.

The general's grave monument is a 10-foot obelisk with two large crossed knotted and fringed flags. Above the flag is a square with Gen. Sherman's name with three columns of written material. Below that is an arrow pointing to the right, a triangle below that, and a shield with a star on top of that, with 40 rounds inside the star. An acorn is hanging at the bottom of the shield. The 40 rounds is a reference to the XV Corps and the acorn references the XIV Corps at Chickamauga. Three of his dying words, "faithful and honorable," are inscribed at the bottom of the monument. I have not been able to find out what the symbolism of all this means. If anyone knows, please let me know. All I know is that it is a very beautiful monument.

William Tecumseh Sherman was born in Lancaster, Ohio on February 8, 1820. His father gave him the middle name of Tecumseh after the Shawnee Indian chief. Sherman was known as "Cump." He was one of eleven children of Charles & Mary Sherman. Sherman's father was a Supreme Court justice in Ohio when he died in 1829. With eleven children and limited finances, the children were farmed out to relatives and friends. Sherman was sent to live next door with Thomas Ewing, a family friend, who was a senator from Ohio.

Other than the person buried in Grant's Tomb, this general's grave monument is the most impressive to Ms. Rebelle.

Photo by Janet Greentree

Gen. Sherman's boyhood home (above) in Lancaster, Ohio. Below, the Ewing house next door.

Photos by Janet Greentree

At age 16, he was appointed to West Point, where he excelled in academics and graduated with the class of 1840. He graduated sixth in his class. Eleven future generals also graduated in his class – Union: Stewart Van Vliet, George Thomas, George Getty, and William Hays – Confederates: Richard Ewell, James Martin, Bushrod Johnson, William Steele, Paul Hebert, John McCown, and William Henry Whiting.

Unlike most of the West Point graduates, Cump did not fight in the Mexican War. He was stationed in California. He married Eleanor Boyle Ewing in 1850, who was the daughter of his foster father, Charles Ewing. Resigning his commission in 1853, he worked as a banker in California and then went to Kansas to practice law. In 1859, he was headmaster of the Louisiana Military Seminary, which is now Louisiana State University. He resigned when the Civil War began and was made a colonel in the 13th U.S. Infantry. His first action was at the battle of Bull Run. His headquarters was on a hill overlooking the Stone Bridge there. It is now the site of the Winery at Bull Run, profiled in last month's *Stone Wall* by BRCWRT member Chuck Mauro. Sherman was quick to make brigadier general, being appointed to that position by President Lincoln on August 7, 1861. He was then transferred to the Western Theatre, fighting at Shiloh, Vicksburg, Jackson, Chattanooga, Meridian Campaign, Atlanta Campaign, Savannah Campaign (his famous 'March to the Sea'), and the Carolinas Campaign.

Sherman's March to the Sea carved a 40-60 mile swath through the state of Georgia from Atlanta to Savannah, burning and destroying everything in his path. He wired President Lincoln on December 21, 1864, giving him an early Christmas present – the city of Savannah. His next target was Columbia, South Carolina, since that state seceded first from the Union. He captured the city on February 17, 1865, firing up entire sections of the city. On April 26, 1865, he accepted Gen. Joseph Johnston's surrender. His military strategy was known as "total war."

Gen. Sherman on his horse, "Old Sam," at the trenches during the battle for Atlanta.

After Columbia, his path went north to Cheraw, which Yankee Nan (Nancy Anwyll) and I visited quite a few years ago. The small town was so charming to Sherman that he did not burn it. The town has over 50 beautiful and well-maintained Victorian houses.

Two of Sherman's famous quotes were: "I am tired and sick of war. Its glory is all moonshine. It is only those who have neither fired a shot nor heard the shrieks and groans of the wounded who cry aloud for blood, for vengeance, for desolation. War is hell." When he declined to run for the presidency, he said: "I will not accept if nominated, and will not serve if elected."

He made the rank of full general after the Civil War and was general-in-chief of the army from 1869-1883. In 1869, he was sent out west to protect the railroad construction from hostile Indians. In February, 1884, he retired from the army and lived in New York City at 75 West 71st Street. Looking up that address on Google maps, the building is a large gray one with Harry's Burritos on the ground floor. The building is now a condo and overlooks Central Park.

Gen. Sherman died in New York City on February 14, 1891, at 1:50 p.m. at the age of 71. His illness came on suddenly on Febru-

Above, Sherman's 'March to the Sea.' Below, the burning of Columbia, S.C.

ary 4th when he caught a chill after going to the theatre. His strep throat, complicated by his asthma, turned into pneumonia. His family was at his side, except for his son, Jesuit priest Father Thomas Sherman. Father Sherman arrived five days later and officiated at the funeral. His friends Generals O.O. Howard and Henry Slocum were in an adjoining room. Generals Kilpatrick and Ewing were present as well.

Sherman predicted his death earlier to a friend when participating in talk of planning a celebration for the anniversary of Gen. Grant's birth in April. He stated that "I shall be dead and buried by that time." The general did not want a grand funeral, as his good friend Grant had. His wishes were not honored, as he had a funeral in New York City as well as one in St. Louis where he lived after the Civil War (at 912 North Garrison Avenue). At that time, it was the largest funeral St. Louis had ever had, and still may be.

The private New York city funeral was held in Sherman's house on 71st Street. The general was dressed in full uniform. His coffin was covered by two fringed United States flags. Gen. Butterfield led the procession, leading his coffin to the train station. Honorary pallbearers

Top - Gen. William T. Sherman at the time of the Civil War, and later in life.

were: Generals Henry Slocum, Joseph Johnston, Grenville Dodge, Montgomery Corse, Wager Swayne, Horatio Wright, John Moore, and Steward Woodford. A riderless horse with the general's saddle and accoutrements was covered in a long black velvet drape, with his boots reversed. A total of 30,000 soldiers marched in the procession, including cadets from West Point. Gen. Joseph Johnson refused to wear a hat, became sick himself, and died ten days later.

The funeral train reached the city of St. Louis, where the streets had been washed and cleaned and black draping was placed on the buildings. Guns were fired when the train came into the station and continued firing until the final car stopped. President Roberts of the Pennsylvania Railroad had lent his personal car to the family of Gen. Sherman. A riderless horse with Sherman's saddle and accoutrements was led by Sergeant Rothgeber of the 7th Cavalry. There were seven local pallbearers and six honorary military pallbearers: Beckwith, Smith, Turner, Warner, Barriger, and Commander Cotton of the U.S. Navy. Gen. James Forsyth led the procession to the cemetery. A new caisson with four black horses led by Sergeant John Cahoon was brought from Fort Riley.

Thirteen of the original Wounded Knee troops accompanied the caisson. Six companies came from Fort Leavenworth. The 7th Cavalry Bugle Corps was followed by Gen. Wesley Merritt and six carriages of family. Former President Rutherford B. Hayes, Generals Schofield and George Stannard, were in the third carriage, followed by Generals Howard and Slocum, and then Colonel William McCrary, the general's bodyguard.

Gen. Sherman is buried in the family plot next to his wife, Ellen Ewing Sherman, who died earlier in 1888, and his daughter Mary Elizabeth Sherman. His beloved young son Willie, who died in 1863 in Memphis, is buried to the right of his mother. Other family members are buried there as well.

The gravesite monument of Sherman's dear son, Willie, features a draped drummer boy motif.
Photo by Janet Greentree

This article has taken a village to write, so my sincere thanks go to Nancy Anwyll for the loan of two Sherman books and the photo of Sherman's boyhood home in Lancaster, Ohio, and to Nadine Mironchuk, our illustrious editor, for help with the New York Times copyrighted articles on the funeral and obituary, as well as trying to decipher what the symbols mean on Gen. Sherman's grave. I would also like to thank my son Mark for taking me to Calvary Cemetery when he lived in Illinois. Some material from the New York Times Archives from February, 1891 was used in the writing of this article.

Thanks to also go to BRCWRT member Rich Sherwood, for providing information on the puzzling stone carvings on Gen. William Tecumseh Sherman's grave marker. It seems that our Gen. Sherman designed his own marker. He wanted a simple shaft with draped stone flags on its face, and between them, the insignia he had drawn in 1868 to symbolize the unity of his armies – at the top of the swift arrow, badge of Blair's 17th Corps; hanging from it the shield of Schofield's 23rd; on the shield the star of Slocum's 20th; dangling below, the acorn of David's 14th Corps but standing out at the very heart of the design, the badge of the 15th Corps; and a cartridge box bearing the words that a ragged private had hurled one cold marching day in Tennessee: "Forty Rounds."

This information came from a posting on the genealogy site Rootsweb from the book by Lloyd Lewis: "Sherman: Fighting Prophet."

Brig. Gen. States Rights Gist, CSA

After listing 24 odd first names of generals in the Civil War in the June-July, 2017 issue of The Stone Wall, it is time to profile one of those with a very different name. States Rights Gist was my choice to be featured in this month's article.

States Rights Gist, known as States, was born on September 3, 1831, on Wyoming Plantation in Union, South Carolina, to Nathaniel and Elizabeth Lewis McDaniel Gist. States Rights was the 7th son and 9th child of his parents. Wyoming Plantation is about three miles from Jonesville, SC. The home still stands, but is privately owned. The current owner moved the house about a half-mile from its original spot.

The house on Wyoming Plantation where S. R. Gist was born.

State's great-great grandfather, William Gist, was a brother to Gen. Mordecai Gist of the Revolutionary War, who fought in the battle of Camden in 1780 and also the battle of Combahee. He was present when Gen. Cornwallis surrendered in Yorktown in 1781. Mordecai was also credited with saving the life of George Washington twice when they were both surveying in Ohio. Mordecai named two of his children Independence and States Rights, so States Rights was a family name before it became my subject's name. Our States Rights' brother, Nathaniel Jr., had a vision of his brother's death on the battlefield while on his own deathbed in 1864.

Young States was first educated at Mount Zion Academy in Winnsboro, SC, learning Latin, Greek, Algebra, Geometry, and Physics. He graduated from South Carolina College, now known as the University of South Carolina, in 1852. He attended Harvard Law School, but did not graduate. He instead went back to Union, SC, passed the bar, and partnered with William Munro in the practice of law. He married Jane Margaret Adams on May 6, 1863. Her father was James Hopkins Adams, a governor of South Carolina from 1854-56.

S. R. Gist became active in the secession movement, served in the state militia as a captain; an aide-de-camp of Governor Hopkins, and in 1856 became a brigadier general in the South Carolina Militia. In 1858, his cousin Governor William H. Gist appointed him as an "especial" aide-de-camp. During this time, S. R. lived in the Governor's mansion with his cousin. In October of 1860, Governor Gist sent States to visit six other Southern governors to seek support for secession, just prior to Abraham Lincoln being elected president on November 6, 1860.

In December, 1860, South Carolina's new governor, Francis Pickens, appointed States as state adjutant and inspector general. He also acquired weapons for South Carolina, and men for the Confederate Army. After the fall of Fort Sumter, Gist accompanied Gov. Pickens and Gen. P.G.T. Beauregard for the raising of the South Carolina flag and the Confederate flag over the fort.

Gen. Patrick Cleburn's uniform coat, on display at the former Museum of the Confederacy in Richmond, VA.
Photo by Janet Greentree

Markers note the participation of Gist in several battles, including (upper left) Winstead Hill, TN; (upper right) Vicksburg, MS; and (lower left) the place where he fell in Franklin, TN.

In July 1861, he was under the command of Gen. Joseph E. Johnston; he served as an aide-de-camp to Gen. Barnard Bee. Gist took over for Gen. Bee after he was killed at First Manassas. Gist was slightly wounded during that battle, as well.

On March 20, 1862, he was appointed a brigadier general on the recommendation of Confederate Sen. James Chestnut. He commanded the James Island Military District and was responsible for the coastal defenses of South Carolina. He fought at Vicksburg, where there is a statue of him; also at Chickamauga, Chattanooga, Atlanta (where he was wounded in his hand), and at Franklin, where his life ended.

Gen. Gist is one of six generals who died either on the field or in a field hospital at Franklin. Four of them were laid out on the porch of the house at Carnton Plantation, which was being used as a hospital – Generals John Adams, Patrick Cleburne, William Granberry, and Otho Strahl. Gen. John Carpenter Carter was also killed at Franklin. Inside Carnton are pictures of the six generals killed at Franklin on November 30, 1864.

Ms. Rebelle has come across four versions of Gist's death - account no. 1 states: two men from his staff, Captain H.D. Garden and Lt. Frank Trenholm, stated that "he rode to the front after ordering a charge and waving his hat to the 24th, rode away in the smoke of battle, never more to be seen by the men he commanded on so many fields. His horse was shot, and he was leading the right of the brigade on foot when he fell, pierced through the heart."

Carnton Plantation (and the historical plaque there), Franklin, TN.

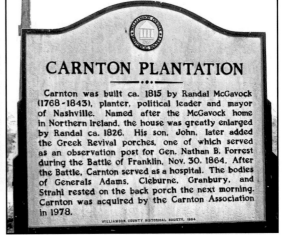

Another account states: "He was killed leading his brigade during a charge on the field at Franklin during Hood's desperate attack on the city in November of 1864… Gen. Gist's horse was wounded and Gist dismounted. He led his men forward and was shot several times. He was carried from the battle to a field hospital and died later that evening."

The third version comes from the book Five Tragic Hours, the Battle of Franklin, by James Lee McDonough and Thomas L. Connelly. The authors uncovered an account of Gist's body servant; according to the enslaved man, "Uncle Wiley" Howard of South Carolina: "The wounded general was taken to a field hospital on the far left of the Confederate line. Gist died there on the night of November 30th. The next morning, the faithful servant remained with the corpse as it was taken to the residence of William White, where Gist was buried in the yard under a large cedar tree."

According the authors: "The house where Gist died was on the far western side of the battlefield, almost two miles west of the Carter house. The William White home fronted on the Boyd Mill Road."

The last version is etched in stone at a marker for Gen. Gist at Winstead Hill in Franklin (see above). The marker reads: "Having his horse shot from under him, Gist sprinted for the locust abatis in his front. Advancing to within a few yards of the abatis, Gist went down with a bullet to the chest. He died the next morning at The Harrison House. He was buried, first in a private cemetery in Franklin, then and finally, at the Trinity Episcopal Church in Columbia, South Carolina."

To show how long news took to get to soldiers' homes, the Macon Telegraph of December 19, 1864, had a small article stating: "Gen. S.R. Gist – The Columbian Guardian says: 'In the list of officers reported killed in the battle near Franklin, we notice the name of Brigadier-Gen. S.R. Gist. We caution our readers not to put too much confidence in the report. It seems probable that if it were true, some information of the fact would have been received by his relatives and friends here.'"

A partial funeral announcement was published in the South Carolina Magazine of Ancestral Research; it reads as follows: "The friends and acquaintances of States Rights Gist, deceased and the Members of the Society of the Cincinnati, and of Union Kilwinning Lodge No. 4, are requested to attend his funeral 3

Gen. Gist's gravesite in Trinity Episcopal Church Cemetery, Charlestown, SC.
Photos by Janet Greentree

o'clock, this afternoon, at the late residence of the deceased, No. 5 Meeting Street (Charleston, SC). The Members of the State Society in Cincinnati, are invited to attend as Mourners the Funeral of States Gist Esq. from his late residence No. 5 Meeting Street at 3 o'clock this afternoon."

The interesting thing about all this is that Gist was first buried in Franklin. He was then disinterred and his body taken to Charleston for his funeral. Subsequently, his body was taken to Columbia, SC, by some unknown means for interment in the Trinity Episcopal Church Cemetery.

It is always amazing how many

An illustrated view of the works at the Battle of Franklin, TN.

times people of the Civil War era, especially KIA, were disinterred and reinterred. Columbia is 115 miles from Charleston. Gen. Gist was 33 years old when he died; left no direct descendants.

Harriet Tubman

Harriet Tubman was not an actual military general, as are most of the personalities highlighted in this column; however, the famed "Moses of her people" who escaped slavery and then led many dozens more to freedom was called "General Tubman" by the abolitionist John Brown. In Tubman's own words, she said "I was conductor of the Underground Railroad for eight years, and I can say what most conductors can't say – I never ran my train off the track and I never lost a passenger." Tubman will soon be honored as the first woman ever to appear on U.S. paper currency. Her image will be placed on the $20 bill, as announced by the U.S. Treasury Department on April 20, 2016.

A colorized version of a photo of Harriet Tubman helps to make her more lifelike to us, instead of like just a character out of a child's book.

Trump administration Secretary of the Treasury has "postponed" the production of the Tubman $20 bill, saying it has to review all of the currency for security against counterfeiting, but one would think the $20 bill—the most frequently used currency - would be reissued first after review, with the new imagery in place.

This article will be a collaboration with our illustrious editor of The Stone Wall – Yankee Girl Nadine Mironchuk. She will incorporate the Eastern Shore trip we took searching out the Underground Railroad while she was here in June 2016 for our 25th Anniversary Meeting.

To begin with, a tour of the Eastern Shore of Maryland in search of the important sites associated with the African-American icon requires preparation, as the markings and preservation of her life and times while enslaved, as well as the telling of slavery in that area of ante-bellum Maryland, is "under construction," as they say – literally.

A new Harriet Tubman National Museum has now been constructed by the federal government; a collection of artifacts and documents relating to Tubman that had been available for viewing has been boxed up and moved from its former home in a small storefront museum in downtown Cambridge to the new site, located in the midst of the landscape of swamplands and forests of Tubman's imprisonment. This new facility opened in April of 2017.

The site of the Brodess plantation, where Harriet Tubman was born and lived until her escape as a young adult, is pictured above.. The historical marker is one of the few along the driving route that assist a tourist in identifying the places important to Tubman's life and history. The expanse of land pictured is only a part of the size of the plantation. The house within the yellow circle is not the original house, but a modern residence; the structure is, however, in the same location as the site of the original Brodess plantation house.

Photo by Nadine Mironchuk

To search for Tubman's early history on the Eastern Shore, one must get a map of a driving tour that has been outlined for Tubman enthusiasts from the Eastern Shore Visitor's Center, and then hope you can manage directions by way of GPS coordinates that are the only locational information included. If not, then you need to come prepared with printouts from internet sites that list addresses and estimates of location, as well as follow your GPS unit's directional information.

Keep your eyes peeled for the few markers along the way (as you zip past them, and then either back up or "bang a U-ie," as they say in Boston). Only by triangulating these references can you judge the locations of unmarked areas that you will want to visit.

Harriet Tubman was born a slave in Dorchester County, Maryland possibly in 1822.

She really didn't know what year or date her birthday was or how old she was. Some people think she was closer to 100 than the 91 years she is credited for. Tubman said she was born in 1825, her death certificate lists 1815, and her tombstone lists 1820. She was born Araminta Ross and went by the name of Minty. Her parents were both slaves, Ben Ross and Harriet (Rit) Green. Her mother was a cook and her father was a skilled woodsman. She had eight siblings. The plantation was owned by the Brodess family. Her maternal grandmother was brought to the U.S. on a slave ship from Africa. She was told she was of the Ashanti lineage from Ghana.

Her mother was feisty too. Edward Brodess sold three of the family daughters and wanted to sell Rit's youngest son, Moses. Rit hid him for a month. When Brodess and another planter came to take him, Rit said: "You are after my son; but the first man that comes into my house, I will split his head open." Brodess did not go forward with the sale. Some of Tubman's biographers think this is when she started believing in the power of resistance.

As a child of six or seven, she worked for and her owner was paid by another planter, James Cook, checking muskrat traps in the marshes and swamps of Dorchester County. This job also helped her skills with the topography of the land and the marshes. Imagine having to walk for hours into freezing water in the dead of winter with no coat, shoes or gloves – just a shawl to keep the howling wind from your face and form, to wrangle dead animals from traps. When she grew older she did field work, plowing and driving oxen. Her mother told her Bible stories, and she had a strong faith in God.

When she was a teenager, sometime between 1834 and 1836, she was sent to the Bucktown store, a fair walk from her home, for supplies. An overseer from a neighboring farm was there looking for a slave boy who had left the fields without permission. Harriet was hit in the head with a two-pound counter weight thrown at the boy by that overseer. The brain injury that she sustained was so severe that she was unconscious for two days, and a scarf she had wrapped around her hair that morning had embedded itself into the cracked-open skull wound. As soon as she awoke, and with blood collecting in her hair, she was sent back to her work. She would endure headaches, seizures and sleep-like trances for the rest of her life.

Ms. Rebelle stands at the entrance to the Bucktown Store, where Harriet Tubman sustained a brain injury severe enough to impair her for the rest of her life. Ms. Rebelle enjoyed one of her most meaningful adventures when she followed the trail of Harriet Tubman's early life, enslaved on Maryland's Eastern Shore.

Photo by Nadine Mironchuk

In fact, the peculiarity of her falling into unconsciousness every 20 minutes - to - every few hours gave her mission to escape, and to later free others, a dangerous aspect that makes her achievements even more amazing. Tubman credited the brain injury and its accompanying seizures with giving her an almost supernatural insight while on the run, which she believes saved her many times from imminent capture. As with many epileptics, she had visions, or 'epiphanies,' of having spoken directly with God. She believed that God had particularly directed her many times out of danger.

The Bucktown Store can today be visited, being located in its original spot, but was rebuilt after burning down prior to the Civil War. The current structure there pre-dates the war. The Meredith family has continually owned the store for several generations. It continued operating into the 1930's, when it was closed at the death of the great-grandfather to the latest generation of Merediths. It has since been refurbished and is kept as an original 18th-century general store. The family is hoping that, through its non-profit status, they can make it a true link to the life and heroism of Harriet Tubman.

If you are visiting this location, at 4303 Bucktown Road in Cambridge, MD., you are urged to call the curators at: 410-901-9255; they are sometimes available to open the store and answer questions you may have about the Tubman incident. As we found out by taking a chance and calling, you may meet one of the family, whose history as plantation owners is closely interwoven with the history of enslavement in that area.

One famous incident connected with them involves the flight of the "Dover Eight," which made national headlines on March 8, 1857 when eight slaves (two owned by the Merediths) escaped from Dorchester County. The group first sought help from Rev. Samuel Green in East New Market. Then they found assistance from Harriet Tubman's father, Ben Ross. They soon found their way to Thomas Otwell, a black Underground Railroad conductor in Delaware. Tubman trusted Otwell with the group's safety. Instead, he lured them to the Dover jail so he could collect the $3,000 reward for their capture. With quick thinking and a show of force, the group successfully broke out of the jail and fled to Wilmington, then Philadelphia, and finally to Canada.

Matt Meredith, a charming young man, answered our call with a warm welcome and an enthusiasm for his family's story, as it related to the Tubman association. He opened the store, and discussed the incident of the counter weight being flung at and injuring the young slave. He had on hand such a weight (used to weigh goods for sale), handing it to us, so that we could feel the devastating impact it would have had.

We happened to mention that author Kate Clifford Larson, who has produced the most serious biography on Tubman in the last 60 years (Bound for the Promised Land: Harriet Tubman: Portrait of an American Hero), was a speaker north of Boston recently, and had mentioned that a priceless treasure of historic importance to the Tubman story had been recovered in recent times, when a home in the area was being sold out of an original family's ownership and the contents being dumped into a dumpster by the contractor. Neighbors rushed to save the many antique quilts, albums and memorabilia being discarded; they knew that such a trove is rarely just scattered to the winds for the taking and preserving. The old cartons of newspapers produced the only original copy ever found of the "runaway ad" that was published locally when Tubman "stole" herself from her owner, running away from the Brodess farm, never to return.

"That was ME!" cried Matt! "I'm the one who found it," he exclaimed, with pride and joy.

Matt explained that, when he was much younger, he and his Dad saw the house in downtown Cambridge being cleaned out, and wondered why no family members wanted the many items that a family would want to keep, such as albums and records. There were beautiful old quilts and antiques, and boxes and boxes of saved documents, records and photos. Every night, they would sit at the table and read the old newspapers that they had rescued. One night, Matt saw the ad for a runaway slave named "Minty."

"Hey, Dad," he said, "wasn't Harriet Tubman named Minty?" he asked. Dad (Jay Meredith) was dumbfounded, and called all the historical societies he could. This matchless item of history –

THREE HUNDRED DOLLARS REWARD.

RANAWAY from the subscriber on Monday the 17th ult., three negroes, named as follows: HARRY, aged about 19 years, has on one side of his neck a wen, just under the ear, he is of a dark chestnut color, about 5 feet 8 or 9 inches hight; BEN, aged aged about 25 years, is very quick to speak when spoken to, he is of a chestnut color, about six feet high; MINTY, aged about 27 years, is of a chestnut color, fine looking, and about 5 feet high. One hundred dollars reward will be given for each of the above named negroes, if taken out of the State, and $50 each if taken in the State. They must be lodged in Baltimore, Easton or Cambridge Jail, in Maryland.

ELIZA ANN BRODESS,
Near Bucktown, Dorchester county, Md.
Oct. 3d, 1849.

☞The Delaware Gazette will please copy the above three weeks, and charge this office.

Above - as absurd as it seems to us today that someone's property can run away from them, and then be returned to them via an advertisement in the local paper, the tiny graphics of black travelers decorating this ad is the height of absurdity.
Photo by Nadine Mironchuk

Matt Meredith (right) shares his once-in-a-lifetime historic find with Nadine Mironchuk.

Photo by Janet Greentree

a first source – was the only exact reference existing that verified the date of her run to freedom; even Tubman never could recollect the exact day she had fled enslavement. Such a priceless item was saved by a ten-year-old who thought it was neat to read old newspapers with his Dad!

Matt was happy to run next door to his family's house (also having passed out of his family a few generations ago, only to be re-acquired by Jay and preserved). He came back with the actual newspaper ad to show us and have us photograph. Jay Meredith has made it his life's work to re-purchase the properties his family owned, and to donate lands (like the store) to the historical community for preservation of this important history. Matt was very frank about his slave-holding ancestors, and agrees that the mission to contribute to the recognition of Tubman's life and struggles is a true calling.

In 1844, Harriet married John Tubman, a free black man. Even though he was free, Harriet's slave status dictated that any children born of the marriage would be enslaved. She changed her name from Minty to Harriet after her marriage. She became ill again in 1849 and was unable to work. Her owner, Brodess, tried to sell her again but he died before that happened. His wife Eliza also tried to sell the family slaves at her husband's passing, and the sales to itinerant slave purchasers was decided. These slavers roamed the Eastern Shore in waves, knowing that the timely increases in enslaved families required some owners to divest of their "property," if they could not maintain growing families of slaves. This is when Harriet determined to run away.

"I freed a thousand slaves. I could have freed a thousand more, if only they knew they were slaves."
- Harriet Tubman

Harriet had been hired out to another plantation, so Eliza didn't realize that she was gone. Harriet took her two brothers Ben and Henry with her. She escaped with them on September 17, 1849. Most likely, her route was along the Choptank River, through Delaware, and then north into Pennsylvania. The route was about 90 miles from her home, in Dorchester County. She was helped by free and enslaved blacks, abolitionists, and Quakers. She followed the North Star and had to be constantly on the alert for slave-catchers. When she came to Pennsylvania, she said: "When I found that I had crossed that line, I looked at my hands to see if I was the same person. There was such a glory over everything; the sun came like gold through the trees, and over the fields, and I felt I was in Heaven."

In 1851, Tubman returned to Dorchester County to find her husband. Unfortunately, he had remarried, was happy with the new wife, and didn't want to leave. She started ferrying slaves from Dorchester County up to Canada. The Fugitive Slave Act, which the South had insisted be part of the Compromise of 1850, demanded that northern-states authorities assist in recapturing runaway slaves who fled the South. Therefore, Tubman could not, nor could any escaped slave, settle in the north and chance that they would not be found, caught, and sent back into slavery. Most people escaping slavery went along the Underground Railroad directly into Canada.

This one piece of legislation was the determining factor in energizing the North for the abolition of slavery; while they may not have been offended by the institution of slavery as it existed before 1850, they were quite angry to now be under threat of being jailed if they did not participate in the enforcement of slavery by turning in or helping detain slaves who ran from their Southern masters.

The Auburn, NY, house William Seward, sold to Harriet Tubman. The building is now a museum dedicated to Tubman, who lived her life in the North quite poor but always reached out to assist formerly enslaved people who needed help, having been kept ignorant and destitute in their captivity.
Photo by Janet Greentree

Tubman's last trip to aid in the escape of slaves was in November, 1860. All in all, she risked her freedom accomplishing 13 rescue trips, freeing about 70 slaves, including quite a few family members. She carried a gun and would threaten to shoot them if they decided to go back. Children were given paregoric to keep them quiet. Most of her trips were in the winter, since the nights were so long. She planned her rescues to coincide with holidays or weekends, when runaway ads could not appear in publication until after a day or two had passed without notification being posted.

Traveling through the Eastern Shore where her early life was spent toiling in the swamps and felling trees alongside her father – she a slave piling up profits for her owner – he a free man, making his own meager living in the black community that sustained itself outside the plantations of Eastern Maryland – you can sense the isolation and weary toil that inflicted such misery on so many people who were born into life as packhorses... abused animals... just property that an owner could profit from, tear from their family in desperation for capital, or extinguish at will, given "sufficient" cause.

Above, the burial of Harriet Tubman Davis in March of 1913. Below, her headstone marks the resting place of a true American hero.

Harriet became friends with Frederick Douglass, John Brown and William Seward, who lived in Auburn, NY. She was active in abolitionist activities with all of them. Her knowledge of swamps and topography led her to be the first woman to lead an armed assault by Union troops during the Civil War against plantations along the Comabahee River in South Carolina on June 1-2, 1863. More than 750 slaves were liberated during this raid.

In 1859, William Seward sold her a piece of land in Auburn, New York where her house still stands. Later, she was able to bring her aging parents and several family members to New York to live with her. The house became a haven housing former slaves and others looking for a better life. One of her boarders was a Civil War veteran, Nelson Davis. They fell in love and were married on March 18, 1869. He was 22 years younger than her. In 1874, they adopted a baby girl, Gertie.

Harriet Tubman-Davis' stone in Fort Hill Cemetery, Auburn, NY. From an enslaved girl to "The General," Minty did all that she could to affect her condition and aid others at the same time.
Photo by Janet Greentree

Harriet's seizures and headaches continued to plague her for the rest of her life. In the late 1890s she had brain surgery at Massachusetts General Hospital. She requested no anesthesia and instead bit down on a bullet like the Civil War soldiers did. She died of pneumonia in 1913 and was buried with semi-military honors at Fort Hill Cemetery in Auburn, NY. There, she shares her final resting place with William Seward and his family; Captain Myles Keogh, and Generals Emory Upton and Andrew Alexander. The city installed a memorial plaque on the Courthouse in Auburn dedicated to Tubman. Booker T. Washington gave the keynote address.

Her home was abandoned in the 1920s, but the AME Zion Church renovated it. It now stands as a museum and education center. It took a lifetime for Harriet to travel so far and wide, and accomplish so much, not just for her own people, but for all Americans who could then live in a better, more perfect society, freed from the terrible requirements of oppression, through emancipation.

If you embark on the tour to the Eastern Shore, follow her life there and comprehend the enormous scope of her heroic accomplishments and how they contributed directly to our nation, you will then understand why she is worthy of appearing on our currency, as other great Americans do.

Lunch with Fitzhugh Lee

As has been her custom on the way home from the North Carolina beaches, Ms. Rebelle stops and has lunch at her favorite cemetery - Hollywood Cemetery in Richmond - dining with Gen. Fitzhugh Lee and Pres. Jefferson Davis. There is a nice bench facing the graves of Davis and Lee, with a view of the James River on the left and a very beautiful (and sad) angel on the right. It is a very peaceful place to have lunch.

Talk about famous ancestors and family, Confederate Gen. Fitzhugh Lee certainly has some. His uncle was general of the Confederate Army Robert E. Lee; he is the grandson of Gen. "Light Horse Harry" Lee; nephew of Gen. Samuel Cooper; cousin of George Washington Custis Lee; Rooney Lee; and Robert E. Lee, Jr. Fitzhugh's father, Sydney Smith Lee, is Robert E. Lee's brother; Sydney served under Commodore Matthew Perry in Japan. His mother, Anna Maria Mason Lee, is the granddaughter of George Mason and sister of Sen. James Murray Mason. To say he was "connected" is quite an understatement!

Gen. Fitzhugh Lee's grave in Hollywood Cemetery, Richmond, VA.

Photo by Janet Greentree

Gen. Fitzhugh Lee

Fitzhugh Lee was born locally in Fairfax County, at Clermont. The actual site of the house is now under the Beltway in the Alexandria area. He graduated near the bottom of his class from West Point in 1856, as a second lieutenant in the 2nd Cavalry Regiment. Unlike his Uncle Bobby, Fitzhugh had many demerits. The regiment was commanded by Col. Albert Sidney Johnson, and his Uncle Bobby was the lieutenant colonel. In May 1860, he took a position at West Point as an instructor of cavalry tactics, but quickly resigned his position when the Civil War began in 1861.

Fitzhugh was a staff officer to Gen. Richard Ewell at First Manassas and was then promoted to lieutenant colonel of the 1st Virginia Cavalry under Colonel J.E.B. Stuart. He was promoted to brigadier general on July 24, 1862.

He got into some trouble by arriving late to a raid occurring on Stuart's headquarters, where Union cavalry captured Gen. Stuart's plumed hat and cape. He later made up for that when he captured the headquarters tent of Union Gen. John Pope and "captured" his dress uniform. The uniform was presented to Stuart by Fitzhugh.

Fitzhugh Lee fought in the Maryland Campaign of 1862 at South Mountain, delaying the Union Army's advance to Sharpsburg, and also at Kelly's Ford, where he captured 400 men and 150 horses, losing only 14 men, himself. His skill at Chancellorsville allowed Gen. "Stonewall" Jackson's successful flanking attack. Due to an attack of rheumatism, he missed Brandy Station, but accompanied Gen. Stuart on his ride around the Union Army prior to Gettysburg. He was with Stuart at Gettysburg on

Gen. Fitzhugh Lee's HQ at Appomattox (still standing).

the East Cavalry Battlefield, facing Gen. George A. Custer. Fitzhugh Lee guarded the rear and flanks of the Confederate Army on their way back to Virginia.

His major general promotion came on August 3, 1863. Stuart's comment about his performance was: "He was one of the finest cavalry leaders on the continent, and richly [entitled] to promotion.

Lee fought in the Overland Campaign and at Petersburg, the defense of Fort Pocahontas, the

Shenandoah Valley, and Third Winchester, where three horses were shot out from under him; he was severely wounded in the thigh by a rifle ball. Lee assisted Gen. Joseph E. Johnston in North Carolina; he was with J.E.B. Stuart when Stuart was mortally wounded at Yellow Tavern on May 12, 1864; and fought at Trevillian Station, Virginia, with Wade Hampton. Lee was named commander of the cavalry on February 11, 1865. He led the last Confederate charge on April 9, 1865, at Farmville.

Fitzhugh Lee was at Appomattox where he heard his Uncle Bobby was going to surrender. He left for Lynchburg with his men, rather than surrender then and there. He did not return until three days later, finally surrendering.

Fitzhugh, along with his Uncle Bobby, his cousins Custis and Rooney Lee, and 33 Confederate and civilian personnel were indicted for treason after the war. The charge was withdrawn in February, 1869. Fitzhugh was granted a government pardon.

After the war, he was a farmer in Stafford County, Virginia. He and five of his brothers were in business together with a gristmill, stud farm, and a fishing pier. At age 35, he married 18 year-old Ellen Bernard Fowle of Alexandria. The couple had seven children, including two sons who later joined the 7th Cavalry. All of his daughters married officers in their brothers' regiments.

Fitzhugh also wrote a book in 1894 about his famous uncle, entitled simply "General Lee." He was also the author of Cuba's Struggle Against Spain, published in 1899.

In 1885, he was elected the 40th governor of Virginia. Leaving office in January, 1890, the Richmond Dispatch stated that "Virginia never had a governor who was more beloved or tried more consciously to do his duty."

Fitzhugh had a variety of jobs after the war. President Grover Cleveland appointed him collector of revenue in the western district of Virginia in 1895. In 1896, he was appointed the United States consul general in Havana, Cuba. Due to the turmoil on that island, Lee recommended against sending the U.S.S. Maine there. The battleship exploded and sank in Havana harbor on February 15, 1898, killing 26 American sailors. On April 9, 1898, Lee was the last American to evacuate Cuba before the U.S. declared war on Spain.

Lee put on the blue uniform once more when the U.S. declared war on Spain and was in command of the 7th Army Corps. In November 1900, he was sent to the Department of the Missouri in Omaha, Nebraska, where he retired as a brigadier general on March 2, 1901.

Gen. Fitzhugh Lee visiting the site of the wounding of Gen. "Stonewall" Jackson (at Chancellorsville), after the Civil War.

Fitzhugh Lee attended the Battle of Bunker Hill centennial in Boston in 1875. In 1885, he was

William Jennings Bryant (left) with Gen. Fitzhugh Lee at Camp Cuba Libre, Jacksonville, FL .

a member of the board of visitors at West Point. At President Cleveland's inaugural parades of 1885 and 1893, Lee commanded the third division. In 1899, he was appointed military governor of Havana and Pinar del Rio. He spent his final years in Charlottesville and died on a business trip to Washington, D.C., on April 28, 1906.

Doing research on my subjects turns up many interesting pictures. I came across a picture of Fitzhugh sitting with Col. William Jennings Bryant at Camp Cuba Libre; his campaign posters; an advertising poster for cigars; a picture of him in a carriage at the Jackson Monument at Chancellorsville while he was governor; he and his staff in the Spanish-American War; the house, still standing, that was his headquarters at Appomattox; and an engraving of the Last Council of War, with Generals Robert E. Lee, John Brown Gordon, and James Longstreet.

Ox Hill/Chantilly Generals
Philip Kearny and Isaac Ingalls Stevens

Since the Battle of Ox Hill/Chantilly is so local to the members of the Bull Run Civil War Round Table, I thought I would do an article on Union Generals Philip Kearny and Isaac Ingalls Stevens, who were killed at the Battle of Ox Hill/Chantilly on September 1, 1862. This article is dedicated to our BRCWRT member, Ed Wenzel, who along with Brian Pohanka and Bud Hall, who practically single-handedly saved what is left of this battlefield. I must say, there were a few "Oh My God" moments researching the life of Gen. Phil Kearny. To say he was an interesting subject is putting it mildly.

Philip Kearny was born into a very wealthy family in New York City on June 1, 1815, the son of Philip Kearny and Susan Watts. John Watts, his mother's father, was the last Royal Recorder of

New York City. The position of Royal Recorder was begun in the year 1683. Duties included being judge of the Court of Gen. Sessions, deputy mayor and vice resident of the Board of Alderman. Watts had interests in mills, factories, investment houses, ships, and banks. Kearny's father owned a brokerage firm and was also one of the founders of the New York Stock Exchange. Kearny's mother died at a young age, so his Grandfather Watts had a huge influence on his life and future.

A career in the military was Kearny's dream but his grandfather had other ideas for him. Watts sent him to Columbia College to earn his law degree. Kearny graduated in 1833. Three years later in 1836, Watts died, leaving Phil an inheritance of over $1 million dollars. He became one of the richest men in America. Since he was now a free man, Kearny chose to join the military and was assigned to the 1st U.S. Dragoons as a second lieutenant of cavalry. The adjutant of this unit was Jefferson Davis. Kearny was sent to France to study cavalry tactics in 1839. Already an accomplished horseman from the age of eight, he learned to ride his horse with his sword in his right hand, his pistol in his left hand, and the reins in his teeth. The French nicknamed him "Kearny le Magnifique" (Kearny the Magnificent).

Gen. Philip Kearny (above) during the Civil War; and (below) in 1859 in Paris, France.

After returning to the U.S., he wrote a cavalry manual for the Army. In 1849, his father died as well, leaving him another large inheritance.

Kearny was assigned to the staff of Gen. Winfield Scott and became his aide-de-camp. He complained that "honors are not won at headquarters, and I would give my arm for a brevet." These are certainly words that would haunt him later. He resigned his commission in 1846 but within a month returned to the army when the Mexican-American War broke out. Due to his wealth he spared no expense outfitting his command. He bought 120 matched dapple gray horses for his men. Kearny became a captain in December 1846. Company F fought in the battles of Contreras and Churubusco with Kearny leading a cavalry charge where he was wounded with grapeshot in his left arm. Future president Franklin Pierce (a general at the time) held him down as his arm was amputated. Gen. Scott called him "a perfect soldier and the bravest man I ever knew." Kearny returned to duty in a short time.

Kearny's personal life was interesting as well. He married Diana Bullitt in 1841. He was sent to Washington, D.C., after requesting a field assignment in the west. Mrs. Kearny adored her role as a society hostess. He was so unhappy in Washington that he described himself as "a highly placed flunky." Finally, in 1844, he was transferred to Fort Leavenworth. Diana Kearny had no intention of leaving Washington for frontier life with small children. Kearny went to Kansas alone. Later, Kearny decided he had enough of army life and settled with the family in New York City. The marriage failed, and Diana left after eight years of marriage; she filed for divorce in New York. One of the stipulations Diana had entered in the divorce decree was that Kearny could never marry again as long as she was alive. Kearny was 36 years old, very rich, and took off on a world tour. In Paris, he met Agnes Maxwell, and they began living together. Since Kearny's attorneys interpreted the decree to only mean he could never re-marry in New York, he and Agnes married in New Jersey and lived there.

When the Civil War began, Kearny tried to rejoin the army but, having only one arm, he was rejected. Pres. Lincoln appointed him as a Brigadier General of Volunteers, placing him in command of the New Jersey brigade. He was sent to Alexandria, Virginia. Again, using his wealth, he made sure his men were well-fed and clothed. He and Gen. George B. McClellan clashed, as Kearny wanted McClellan to attack Richmond.

Kearny was appointed commander of the 3rd Division in 1862. He fought at Williamsburg, the Peninsula Campaign, 2nd Manassas, Groveton, and finally at Ox Hill/Chantilly, where he rode into the Confederate line and was killed by a single bullet in his spine.

Gen. Kearny's body was released under a flag of truce at Difficult Run and was brought back to Washington. He laid in state at Bellegrove, his home in New Jersey, before burial at Trinity Church in New York City. In 1912, his body was moved to Arlington National Cemetery. His grave is one of only two with equestrian statues in the cemetery.

The Kearny Patch (of scarlet cloth) evolved into the Union Army Corps identification insignia. The Kearny medal was created by his troops after his death and awarded to officers who served honorably under him. The Kearny Cross was awarded as a cross of

Above, an illustration of Gen. Phil Kearny conducting his fatal charge at Ox Hill/Chantilly, September 1, 1862.

Above, the commemorative stone memorials for the two generals killed at the battle of Ox Hill/Chantilly, VA - Union Maj. Gen. Phil Kearny and Confederate Brig. Gen. Isaac Ingalls Stevens. Below, the park area has been expanded and commemorative events are held on the anniversary of the battle. Thanks are extended to Ed Wenzel and his volunteers for fighting to preserve the battleground.

Bottom photo by Janet Greentree

Gen. Kearny's gravesite memorial in Arlington National Cemetery.
Photo by Janet Greentree

At left, the Kearny Cross; at right, the Kearny Medal of Honor.

valor to enlisted men in his old division. The town of Kearny, New Jersey was named in his honor.

Isaac Ingalls Stevens was born March 25, 1818 in North Andover, Massachusetts. He attended Phillips Academy, was appointed to West Point and graduated with the class of 1839, first in his class. He served in the army with the Corps of Engineers during the Mexican War, seeing action in Vera Cruz, Cerro Gordo, Contreras, and Churubusco. He was brevetted for bravery at the Battle of Chapultepec, becoming a major. He was severely wounded in the Battle of Mexico City. After the Mexican War, he supervised fortifications on the New England coast, from 1841-1849. He then headed the coast survey office in Washington, D.C. Pres. Franklin Pierce named him the first governor of the Washington Territory and Superintendent of Indian Affairs. In 1853, on the way to his new job in the Washington Territory, he used his engineering skills and mapped and surveyed a railroad route across the U.S.

Gen. Isaac Ingalls Stevens

Stevens was a controversial governor. He forced and intimidated Native American tribes of Washington Territory to sign treaties that handed over their land and rights to the government. He was elected to Congress in 1857, serving the Washington Territory until 1861.

Stevens was commissioned as a colonel of the 79th New York Volunteers (Cameron Highlanders), serving under Gen. John Pope in the Northern Virginia Campaign. He was promoted to brigadier general in September 1861; he then fought at Secessionville and 2nd Manassas. Stevens was awarded the rank of major general posthumously in March, 1863. Like Kearny, Isaac Stevens was killed at the Battle of Ox Hill/ Chantilly on September 1, 1862, when he picked up the flag from his old regiment shouting, "Highlanders, my Highlanders, follow your general." Stevens was struck in the temple by a bullet and died instantly. The general's son, Capt. Hazard Stevens, was also injured in the battle. Young Hazard was awarded the Medal of Honor for capturing Fort Huger, Virginia. Both father and son are interred at Island Cemetery in Newport, Rhode Island.

An illustration of the death of Gen. Stevens at Battle of Ox Hill/ Chantilly, VA.

Gen. Stevens' grave monument at Island Cemetery in Newport, RI.
Photo by Janet Greentree

Stevens County, Washington and Stevens County, Minnesota, Fort Stevens in Washington, D.C., and also in Oregon are all named for him. Also named for him are Stevens Hall at Washington State University, Lake Stevens, Washington, and the town of Stevensville, Montana. Stevens was the author of several books.

Maj. Gen. James Lawson Kemper, CSA

Sometimes, while doing historical research, you just have to request access to important sites to achieve the desired result, even if where you want to go is on private property. This story goes

Maj. Gen. James L. Kemper

quite far back to June 2003, when the late Bev Regeimbal, Nancy Anwyll and I were out in Orange County, riding around. On Route 15, just north of Orange, there's a historical marker at the approach to the bridge over the Rapidan River stating that "a mile south" is the grave of Gen. James Lawson Kemper. Don't you just love the vague "near here" markers?!

Not having my book *Generals at Rest* containing directions to all the Confederate graves with me, we took off on a road looking for where he may be buried. The first road wasn't the right one, and that fact was verified by a neighbor who told us where the estate of James Kemper is

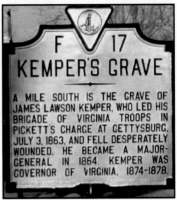

The roadside marker that is "near" a historical site - in this case, near Gen. Kemper's gravesite.
Photo by Janet Greentree

located. We drove down a long and winding dirt road and came upon a large plantation home named Walnut Hills. Several barking dogs came running into sight, so we weren't sure we even wanted to get out of the car.

A lovely woman came down the steps, and when we told her what we were looking for, she invited us into her home for some sweet tea. She showed us Kemper's clock and other items associated with him. She told us to walk through several pasture gates to find the Kemper Family Cemetery behind the house.

James Lawson Kemper is another one of my Gettysburg generals. His shield marker on West Confederate Avenue is located five markers down on the right side from Gen. Lee's statue. I have to thank my daughter Lisa Tully again for my never-ending photo requests to her of Gettysburg monuments and locations.

Kemper was born June 11, 1823, on his family plantation, Mountain Pro-

The façade of the lovely home Walnut Hills, which has the Kemper Family Cemetery attached to the rear of the property. At right, some Kemper memorabilia inside.
Photos by Janet Greentree

spect, in Madison County, Virginia. His parents were William and Maria Allison Kemper. Kemper was the sixth of eight children. His father's family immigrated to Virginia from Siegen, Germany, during the 17th century. Governor Alexander Spotwood's Germanna colony had recruited Kemper's great-grandfather as a miner for the colony. Kemper has quite an interesting ancestral lineage. Colonel John Jasper Stadler, his maternal great-grandfather, served as a civil engineer on George Washington's staff and engineered fortifications in Maryland, Virginia, and North Carolina during the Revolutionary War. John Stadler Allison, his grandfather, was an officer in the U.S. Army during the War of 1812.

His father and Henry Hill of a neighboring plantation started the Old Field School on Mountain Prospect to educate the children in the area. One of James' classmates was future Gen. A.P. Hill, who became a lifelong friend. Kemper attended both Locust Dale Academy and Washington College, and also took engineering courses at VMI. Kemper graduated Washington College first in his class and gave the commencement address in 1842. The subject of his speech was "The Need of a Public School System in Virginia." He returned home after college and read the law under George W. Summers of Kanawha County. Kemper earned a Master's Degree in June 1845, and was admitted to the Virginia Bar on October 2, 1846.

That same year, the Mexican War began. Kemper was appointed as quartermaster and captain under Col. James F. Hamtramck in the First Regiment of Virginia Volunteers. His unit arrived after the battle of Buena Vista, and he maintained defenses in the Coahuila province. After being discharged from the U.S. Army in August 1848, Kemper returned to Madison County to practice law. He became interested in politics, proclaiming his platform as being pro-slavery, anti-abolitionist and pro-states rights. He was elected to the Virginia House of Delegates in 1853. In 1861, he became Speaker. By 1858, he was a brigadier general in the Virginia Militia.

In 1853, Kemper married Cremora "Belle" Cave who was 11 years his junior. They would have seven children.

Jimmy Kemper started out at the Civil War's outbreak as a colonel of the 7th Virginia. He led the 7th under Jubal Early at First Manassas (at Blackburn's Ford). He and his friend A.P. Hill were both assigned to Gen. James Longstreet in June of 1861. He fought at the Battle of Seven Pines and the Seven Days Battles. He became a division commander when the Confederate Army was reorganized by Gen. Robert E. Lee. He fought at the Second Battle of Manassas and against Burnside at Antietam. Old friend, A.P. Hill, saved the day by coming up from Harper's Ferry to assist Kemper.

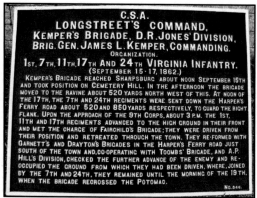

In top photo, the historical marker above describes the activity of Kemper's Brigade as part of Longstreet's command at Antietam. Below, Kemper's Brigade shield at Gettysburg, noting the chaos of Pickett's charge on the third day of the battle; Kemper was wounded just before reaching the "high water mark" at the stone wall on Cemetery Ridge.

Gettysburg photos by Lisa Tully

Kemper missed the action at Chancellorsville, as he was with Longstreet in Suffolk. He was with Gen. Richard B. Garnett at South Mountain with only 800 men; Union Gen. Abner Doubleday reported (erroneously) that he had engaged 4,000 to 5,000 men there with his force of 3,500 men.

At Gettysburg, he was assigned to Pickett's Division. The 1st, 3rd, 7th, 11th, and 24th Virginia Infantry arrived in Gettysburg in the evening of July 2nd and camped at Spangler's Woods. His brigade was one of the main assault units on the right flank of Pickett's Charge on the 3rd of July. Fifty-six were killed and 673 wounded or missing in that iconic charge. The brigade made it across

The July 3, 1863 charge of Confederate troops at Gettysburg is depicted here, when withering fire broke down the offensive just as the stone wall was being breached.

the Emmitsburg Road and was on the right of the copse of trees when Union Gen. George J. Stannard's Vermont men flanked him. Kemper urged the men forward and shouted: "There are the guns, boys, go for them." Kemper himself would be wounded by a bullet that traveled through both his groin and abdomen. He encountered Gen. Lee while being carried on a stretcher and told Lee that he thought the wound mortal. Kemper asked Lee to "do full justice to this division for its work today."

Kemper would be captured by the Union Army on the retreat to Hagerstown, survive his wounds and spend three months in a Union prison. His wife was told that she would not be able to see her husband, even though Kemper was badly wounded, because the Confederates had previously refused a Union officer's wife the right to see him. He was exchanged on September 19, 1863, for Gen. Charles K. Graham when Union surgeons surmised it would be unlikely that Kemper would recover and rejoin the fight. Recover he did, however, but would endure groin pain the rest of his life as the bullet could not be removed safely.

Kemper spent the remainder of the war commanding the Virginia Reserves, since he was too ill for combat. He was promoted to major general on September 19, 1864.

After the war, he went back to the practice of law in Madison, Orange and Culpeper Counties. He was elected the first governor of Virginia after Reconstruction, serving from 1874 to 1878. He was known for his strong position on civil rights, public transportation and the public school system.

Kemper's house in Madison, VA, where he set out in life with his family after the Civil War; he purchased it in 1868, a year after his wife's death, from her mother.

Photo by Janet Greentree

In 1882, he bought Walnut Hills in Orange County. He used a small log cabin behind the main house at Walnut Hills for his law office. He also raised sheep there. His beloved wife Belle died in 1867 at age 33 after giving birth to her 7th child. Kemper stayed in the log cabin at night after she died because he couldn't stand to be in the house without her.

Kemper's health deteriorated in later years; and he died in his sleep at Walnut Hills on April 7, 1895. He was one of the longer surviving Confederate generals, even though his wound at Gettysburg was determined to be mortal at that time.

Ms. Rebelle is not advocating trespassing on private property, but this time it did work out.

At right, the headstone of Gen. James Kemper's grave at the Brush Hill family cemetery, behind Walnut Hills in Orange County, VA.

Photo by Janet Greentree

West Point, Orbs & Connections

Fellow BRCWRT member Gwen Wyttenbach, her daughter Debbie, and I made our journey to West Point June 24-26. Gwen has coined the phrase "it was military Disneyland." What an apt description. It was like Disneyland for all of us. Debbie is into World War II so there are lots of things to see pertaining to that. She devoured the museum running up and down the stairs to make sure she saw everything. She was especially interested in Gen. George S. Patton, Jr. Patton's statue and his memorabilia in the museum. Gwen and I were in awe of all the Civil War connections, and of course, the twenty-eight Civil War generals buried in the West Point Cemetery. We had never been in the presence of so many great men in one spot before. Every man's grave we came to was more famous than the last. Kevin Anastas loaned us his favorite movie, "The Long Gray Line." We recognized many places from the movie and even found Marty Maher's grave. My plan for writing this month's article was to be dedicated entirely to Gen. George Armstrong Custer, but we had some amazing things happen to us in the cemetery, so my article is about the connections of the men and the orbs we found on our pictures when they were uploaded to our computers.

An orb is a round or oblong white spot colored around the edges in rainbow colors. Supposedly, the orbs are spirits who are showing themselves to you in this manner. A couple of years ago, my good Boston friend Nadine Mironchuk and I went to Devil's Den in Gettysburg after dark to "find" ghosts. Little did we realize that we probably did find some, because on a very dark night, there were many orbs in my photos. One has to be somewhat skeptical, but there is no other way to explain these circles of light on a dark night.

At left, orb appears floating above the Devil's Den at Gettysburg battlefield. Photo by Janet Greentree. Below, an orb appears at the left knee of Ms. Rebelle (pointed out by arrow) while she was honoring Gen. John Buford with a flag at his grave in the cemetery at West Point, NY. Photo by Gwen Wyttenbach.

The three of us, however, arrived at West Point around 4:30 p.m. It was summer and daylight savings time was in effect. It was somewhat cloudy, but it was very much still light outside. In all my years of going to cemeteries, I have never had orbs appear in my pictures before. In thinking about these orbs over and over, perhaps it is me that may be the connection to these orbs at West Point. If you read my article of February 2010 in the *Stone Wall*, my trip was to Auburn, New York, to find the graves of Colonel Myles Keogh (who died with Custer at Little Big Horn), Gen. Andrew Alexander, plus Gens. Emory Upton and William Seward. There is no connection with the latter two but there is a definite connection with Keogh and Alexander. The first orb appeared while I was placing a flag on the grave of Gen. John Buford. The orb is next to my left knee and quite large. Buford has always been my favorite Union general. Myles Keogh was on Buford's staff. Gen. Buford was staying at the house of Gen. George Stoneman in Washington, in December 1863 when he died in the arms of Myles Keogh. Captain Keogh accompanied Buford's body to West Point for burial. Keogh was so distraught that he transferred out west after the Civil War and was assigned to the 7th Cavalry under Custer. Pres. Lincoln appointed Buford a major general for meritorious service at the Battle of Gettysburg while Buford was on his deathbed. When Gen. Andrew

Col. Myles Keogh and Gen. John Buford in 1863.

29

Alexander gave Buford his commission, Buford replied, "It is too late, now I wish I could live." Gen. Buford died December 16, 1863.

Next to the grave of John Buford is Lt. Colonel Alonzo Cushing, who held Buford's high ground at Gettysburg. Cushing was born in Wisconsin in 1841 and graduated from West Point with the class of 1861. On June 30, 1863, Alonzo wrote some exciting news to his Navy lieutenant commander brother William "Will" that he and his unit, Battery A of the 4th New York Artillery, were getting ready to march to Pennsylvania as part of the Gettysburg Campaign. Gwen, Nancy Anwyll and I had just been to the Naval Academy in Annapolis and found the grave of William Cushing on a hill overlooking the Severn River. Alonzo and Will are the only two family members to be buried in the service academies of West Point and Annapolis. Alonzo stayed on the high ground with his guns even though he was terribly wounded during Pickett's Charge. His last earthly act was to fire his cannon. He was then struck in the mouth by a bullet killing him instantly. Cushing died July 3, 1863.

A second orb at the cemetery at West Point (shown by arrow) appeared on Col. Benjamin F. "Grimes" Davis' gravestone, as Gwen Wyttenbach honors Lt. Col. Alonzo Cushing.
Photo by Janet Greentree

Just left of the grave of Alonzo Cushing is buried Colonel Benjamin Franklin "Grimes" Davis. Gwen is kneeling next to Cushing's grave placing a flag there. On Davis' maker is another orb. Davis was killed on June 9, 1863, at the Battle of Brandy Station in the Gettysburg Campaign under Gen. Buford's command. Davis was a southerner born in Alabama and raised in Mississippi. He graduated from West Point with the class of 1854. When the Civil War broke out, he chose to stay with the Union, and was colonel of the 8th New York Volunteer Cavalry. Davis was one of the most skilled and aggressive cavalry commanders in the Civil War. While rallying his regiment, he was shot off his horse by Lt. Owen Allen of the 6th Virginia Cavalry and died instantly. Sadly, Davis' men mistook Sgt. John Stone for Allen and split his head with a saber blow. Now there are three connections to Gen. Buford – Keogh, Cushing, and Davis.

Gwen looked through her pictures for orbs and found a very large orb in a tree over the grave of Gen. Robert Anderson, the Union general who surrendered Fort Sumter. In researching Anderson, I have not come up with a connection to Buford, Cushing, or Davis but his orb is the biggest one we have captured. Perhaps it is Gen. Custer wondering what we are doing. Gwen has been to Little Big Horn. Custer's grave is very near Anderson's marker. Perhaps they all wonder why I spend my time going around the country placing flags on graves to honor these men who fought so valiantly in the Civil War. It certainly is a lot to think about. It so happens that we were at West Point on June 25, 2011, exactly 135 years from June 25, 1876, when Gen. Custer and Col. Keogh were killed at Little Big Horn. Now that gives Gwen and me the chills.

Not to digress too far, John Buford was born a southerner near Versailles, KY, on March 4, 1826. The family soon moved to Rock Island, IL, when John was 8 years old. Buford's father was a Democratic opponent of Abraham Lincoln. The family has had a long military tradition. Buford's grandfather and his great uncle both served in Virginia regiments during the Revolutionary War. His half-brother, Napoleon Bonaparte Buford, was a major general in the Union Army. His cousin, Abraham Buford, was a Confederate general. (Abraham Buford is one of my Confederate graves in Lexington, KY.)

Gen. Buford first attended Knox College in Galesburg, IL, and then transferred to West Point, graduating with the class of 1848. He graduated 16th out of 38 graduates and was commissioned a brevet second lieutenant

Brevet Lt. Col. Myles Keogh

in the 1st U.S. Dragoons, and then later the 2nd U.S. Dragoons. He served in Texas, fought the Sioux, kept the peace in Bleeding Kansas, and fought in the Utah War. He was stationed at Fort Crittenden, Utah, from 1859-1861.

When the Civil War began, even though he was a southerner, he chose to stay with the Union. Many of his relatives fought for the Confederacy. In July 1862, he was given the rank of brigadier general of volunteers after serving several months in Washington. He fought with Gen. John Pope at Second Manassas and was wounded in the knee by a spent bullet. After recuperating, he served as chief of cavalry for Gens. McClellan and Burnside. During the Maryland Campaign, he fought at South Mountain and Antietam. After Chancellorsville, Gen. Alfred Pleasanton was given command of the cavalry. Buford led his 1st Division of Cavalry at the Battles of Brandy Station and Upperville. At Gettysburg, Buford was promoted to command the 1st Division and arrived in Gettysburg on June 30, 1863. He knew right away that it was imperative to hold the high ground from the Rebels. After Gettysburg, Buford was sent to Emmitsburg to resupply. His division pursued the Confederates to Warrenton and was engaged in many operations in central Virginia. He also fought in the 1863 Bristoe Campaign.

John Buford became ill with typhoid fever in November 1863, after the Rappahannock Campaign. He died at age 37 on December 16, 1863. His last words were: "Put guards on all the roads, and don't let the men run to the rear." Buford's pallbearers included Gens. Silas Casey, Samuel Heintzelman, Daniel Sickles, John Schofield, Winfield Scott Hancock, Abner Doubleday, and Gouverneur K. Warren. His friend, Gen. George Stoneman, led the procession that included Buford's old white horse, Grey Eagle, whom he rode at Gettysburg. Pres. Lincoln was among the mourners.

In addition to seeing Grant's Tomb in New York City, we stopped briefly at Oakland Cemetery in Yonkers, NY, to find two graves of men connected to the Lincoln assassination. A very kind woman at the cemetery, Katie Hoffnagle, left me a map Scotch-taped to the door, giving me the exact location of the graves. We found Gen. Thomas Ewing, Jr., who represented the conspirators Dr. Samuel Mudd, Michael O'Laughlen, and Samuel Arnold in the conspiracy trial. The second grave was Dr. Charles Augustus Leale, the first doctor to reach Pres. Lincoln in the box at Ford's Theatre.

Even though many of you saw my PowerPoint presentation of West Point, I do hope this article explores other interesting things that happened to the three of us at West Point. It was a most exciting trip for us, and we can't stop talking about the chain that went across the Hudson during the Revolutionary War, twirling Gen. Sedgwick's spurs, the museum, the new cadets, the beauty of the Hudson River, and of course, all the famous people buried in the cemetery, a most hallowed ground. This visit brings my total to 355 Civil War generals' graves located. Unfortunately, I missed two generals while at West Point, even though I had section lists and photos of all the graves. Just too much excitement. It was AWESOME!

~

Polish-born engineer Thaddeus Kosciusko was charged with building West Point - not to fire on ships, but to defend the chain from assaults by land. The chain was strung between West Point and Constitution Island at a bend in the Hudson River; it prevented the British from sailing to to attack New York City from the north.

U.S. Military Academy legend has it that a cadet who spins the rowels (photos at right) of the spurs on boots of Gen. Sedgwick's West Point statue, at midnight, while wearing full parade dress gray over white uniform under arms, and the gets back to their room undetected will have good luck on his or her final exam.

Unusual Burial Structures in West Point

Walking in the back gate of the West Point Cemetery with BRCWRT member Gwen Wyttenbach and her daughter Debbie, we passed by two very unusual structures in the cemetery. The first one was an Egyptian pyramid complete with two sphinxes in front. Inside is a recumbent statue of Union Gen. Egbert Ludovicus Viele. To the left of Viele's structure was a huge white gazebo in memory of Union Gen. Daniel Butterfield.

Ms. Rebelle has done research on Gen. Viele but has been unable to find out why he is buried in a pyramid. His is the third grave that I've seen in the form of a pyramid. John Core, one of Mosby's Rangers, is buried in an even bigger pyramid in Norfolk, VA. When walking through Magnolia Cemetery in Charleston, SC, I saw one there as well. The interesting thing that I discovered is that the general was extremely afraid of being buried alive. That seemed to be a common fear in the 19th century. He had a buzzer and light installed in his coffin that connected directly to the caretaker's house on the premises. The second interesting thing is that this buzzer was connected for twenty years after his death. Unfortunately for the general, he did not revive and never rang the buzzer.

Union Gen. Egbert Ludovicus Viele

Gen. Viele was born on June 17, 1825 in Waterford, NY. He was the son of State Senator John L. Viele. After graduating with honors from the Albany Academy, he entered West Point and graduated 30th in the class of 1847. Classmates included Union Gens. Romeyn Ayres, Ambrose Burnside, John Gibbon, and Orlando Willcox. Confederate Gens. Henry Heth and A.P. Hill were also in the class of 1847. He was commissioned a brevet second lieutenant in the 2nd United States Infantry. After serving in the Mexican War, he established Camp Crawford in Laredo, Texas. In 1853, he resigned from the Army and became the state engineer of New Jersey in 1855. One of his first jobs was to survey the area of Central Park in New York City and submit a design for the park. His original design had four roads going into the park. In 1856, he was appointed engineer-in-chief of Central Park and submitted plans for Prospect Park in Brooklyn, NY.

Gen. Egbert L. Viele

In 1860, he re-entered the Army with the 7th New York and became a brigadier general of U.S. Volunteers in 1861. He was in command of the all Union forces during the siege of Fort Pulaski in Savannah, GA. Later, in 1862, he was appointed Military Governor of Norfolk. He resigned again from the army in October 1863 to work as a civil engineer in New York City. One of Viele's greatest accomplishments is the *"Sanitary and Topographical Atlas of the City and Island of New York,"* published in 1874. This map is still called the Viele Map and used today by engineers building new buildings in the city. It was used at the World Trade Center site when it was constructed in 1973. The map shows his surveys of the steams, marshes, and the coastline of the city. Over the top of the colored map is the street grid of the city. Engineers today state that the map will probably never be updated, as it would be practically impossible to trace all the streams today. Viele also developed plans for the subway system in New York.

Gen. Viele's unusual grave monument at West Point, NY.
Photo by Janet Greentree

Gen. Viele helped design the Post Cemetery at West Point. His grave, even though in the back of the cemetery, is very prominent. The general's wife thought the pair of sphinxes guarding the mausoleum were too buxom, so they were thrown in the Hudson River. More modest new sphinxes were made, per his wife's request. Someone rescued one of the sphinxes and it

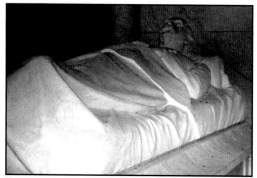

The recumbent Viele sarcophagus within his pyramid monument at West Point, NY.
Photo by Janet Greentree

resides behind one of the quarters at West Point. The general died in New York City on April 22, 1902.

Union Gen. Daniel Butterfield

Daniel Adams Butterfield's final resting place is below an elaborate gazebo at West Point. The curious thing about his burial is that he never went to West Point. He was a Medal of Honor winner, so most likely that is the reason he is buried there.

Butterfield was born October 31, 1831, in Utica, NY. He graduated from Union College in Schenectady, NY, in 1849. He was originally employed by the American Express Company, founded by his father, John Warren Butterfield. The elder Butterfield was also the owner of the Overland Mail Company, telegraph lines, and two different modes of transportation, including stagecoaches and steamship lines.

Gen. Daniel Butterfield

On April 16, 1861, shortly after Fort Sumter fell, Butterfield joined the Army in Washington, DC, as a first sergeant. He was given a commission as a colonel in the 12th New York Militia, later becoming the 12th New York Infantry. His unit was the first to cross the Long Bridge into Virginia. In July 1861, he commanded a brigade and was appointed a brigadier general in September 1861. He joined Gen. George McClellan in the Peninsula Campaign and fought at the Seven Days Battles at Gaines Mill, where he was wounded seizing the colors of the 83rd Pennsylvania Volunteers. In 1892, he was awarded the Medal of Honor. His citation reads: "Seized the colors of the 83rd Pennsylvania Volunteers at a critical moment and, under a galling fire of the enemy, encouraged the depleted ranks to renewed exertion."

While recuperating from his wounds at Harrison's Landing, VA, Butterfield experimented with bugle calls and is credited with the composition of Taps. Taps was written to replace the firing of three rifle volleys at the end of burials during battle. Shortly thereafter, both sides used Taps, and it is still in use today as the official bugle call.

The incredible gazebo monument marking the grave of Gen. Butterfield, at West Point, NY.
Photo by Janet Greentree

Butterfield was a brigade commander at Second Bull Run and Antietam, and became a division commander and V Corps commander at Fredericksburg. His corps went through the city of Fredericksburg, taking fire from Marye's Heights. In January 1863, when Gen. Joseph Hooker became the commander of the Army of the Potomac, Butterfield became his chief of staff. He was promoted to major general in March 1863. Hooker and Butterfield became close friends. Butterfield was disliked by many of his colleagues. After Hooker was replaced by Gen. George Meade before the battle of Gettysburg, Meade retained Butterfield as his chief of staff, even though Meade distrusted him.

Butterfield was again wounded by a spent artillery shell at Gettysburg on the third day of battle. Meade removed him as his chief of staff. When he returned to duty as Hooker's chief of staff, he then commanded II Corps in the Army of the Cumberland at Chattanooga. He led the 3rd Division of the XX Corps in Sherman's Atlanta Campaign, then was sent to Vicksburg, and later commanded the harbor forces in New York before the war ended.

Pres. Ulysses S. Grant appointed Butterfield as assistant treasurer of the United States. He was involved in the Black Friday gold scandal during the Grant administration in 1869. Gen. Butterfield died in Cold Spring, New York on July 17, 1901.

The Last 3 Generals in Arlington National Cemetery

A real sense of satisfaction made my day recently as I have now found the graves of the last of eighty Civil War generals buried in Arlington National Cemetery. My trek to find these illustrious gentlemen began back in 1999 on my first excursion to Arlington National Cemetery with the Bull Run Civil War Round Table. Over the years, I have been back on numerous occasions and tours, and have always managed to find several graves per trip. These last three, especially Gen. Crittenden's, were very elusive. The other two were tucked away, but were at least within plain site – Gens. Alexander S. Asboth and John F. Miller. Out of the 80 generals buried there, only two are Confederates; Gen. Joseph Wheeler, buried in front of Arlington House, and Gen. Marcus Joseph Wright, buried in Jackson Circle at the Confederate monument there.

Arlington is the final resting place of some very big names in the Civil War, such as George Crook, Abner Doubleday, John Gibbon, Rufus Ingalls, Philip Kearny, Montgomery Meigs, John Rawlins, James Ricketts, William Starke Rosencrans, John Schofield, Philip Sheridan, Daniel Sickles, and Frank Wheaton.

Union Gen. Alexander Sandor Asboth

Gen. Asboth was born in Keszthely, Hungary, on December 18, 1811, and is one of several Hungarians reaching high ranks in the Union Army. He graduated from the academy at Selmecbanya as an engineer and worked in various parts of Hungary before joining the Hungarian Revolt of 1848 with Lajos Kossuth. Both Asboth and Kossuth fled Hungary after the revolt to the United States aboard the U.S.S. Mississippi. After becoming a naturalized citizen, he went back to his career of engineering and surveying, in New York City. While there, he developed a new method of asphalt paving, and also did the original surveys for New York's Central Park.

Asboth served in the Union Army from 1861-1865, starting out with Gen. John C. Fremont in Missouri. He led the cavalry advance into Benton and Washington Counties before the Battle of Pea Ridge, in Arkansas. He captured Fayetteville and occupied the headquarters house. Asboth fought heroically on the first day of the battle, incurring a serious wound to the arm. Without him, the Union Army may have collapsed, as they were outnumbered. Gen. Asboth prevailed over Confederate Gen. Van Dorn, whose troops were running low on supplies. After Pea Ridge, he served in Mississippi, Tennessee and Kentucky in a variety of roles.

He was also one of the officers who recommended Phil Sheridan to the rank of brigadier general. Asboth was sent to Florida and seriously wounded in his left cheek and left arm during the Battle of Marianna, Florida, on September 27, 1864. He was operated on by both Union and captured Confederate surgeons but would carry the bullet in his cheek

Gen. Asboth's grave marker in West Point's cemetery, placed there by the country's Hungarian-American community. Below, Asboth is depicted again with a loyal dog accompanying his master on a battlefield charge.

Photos by Janet Greentree

Gen. Alexander S. Asboth, with dog (undated).

until after the war when it was removed in Paris, France. The wound ended his field service, and he was mustered out in August 1865.

After the war, he was minister to Argentina and Uruguay. He died January 21, 1868, in Buenos Aires, Argentina, and was buried there in the British Cemetery until 1990. The official cause of death was listed as wounds incurred in the Civil War. He was considered a hero in Hungary, and through efforts of Hungarian Americans, his body was brought back to the United States to comply with his wish to be buried at Arlington National Cemetery. So, on October 23, 1990, Gen. Asboth was buried with full military honors, including the horse-drawn caisson and a riderless horse. President George H.W. Bush's written eulogy was read during the ceremony. The general's great-great-grandson, Sandor Asboth, attended the ceremony and was given the folded U.S. flag that had been draped on his coffin.

Gen. Asboth, serving the USA in less flamboyant dress.

Union Gen. John Franklin Miller

Gen. Miller was born on November 21, 1831, in South Bend, Indiana. He received his law degree in 1852 from New York State and National Law School. He practiced in South Bend but later moved to Napa, California, for health reasons. He lived there for three years before returning to South Bend to resume his law practice. He was elected to the Indiana State Senate in 1860. On August 27, 1861, Governor Oliver P. Morton of Indiana commissioned him a colonel of the 29th Indiana Infantry. His regiment was assigned to Gen. Don Carlos Buell's Army of the Ohio and went to Tennessee. Miller fought at Shiloh, Cornith, pursued Braxton Bragg through Kentucky, and commanded a brigade under Gen. James S. Negley during the fighting at Stones River. He was wounded in the neck at Stones River.

Gen. John F. Miller (above) during the Civil War, and (below)

During the Tullahoma Campaign, Miller commanded a brigade under Gen. Alexander M. McCook in the XX Corps. During this action, he was severely wounded and lost his left eye in June 1863 in a minor fight at Liberty Gap. The general was out of action for almost a year recuperating from the loss of his eye. He returned to the field in December 1864, commanding both 12 regiments of infantry and 14 artillery batteries at the Battle of Nashville. He was brevetted a major general on March 13, 1865.

After the war, he resigned his commission and returned to California. President Andrew Johnson appointed Miller as collector of customs at the Port of San Francisco, where he served until 1869. He then served 12 years as president of the Alaska Commercial Company, which controlled the fur industry on the Pribilof Islands. Miller bought a "wilderness" area

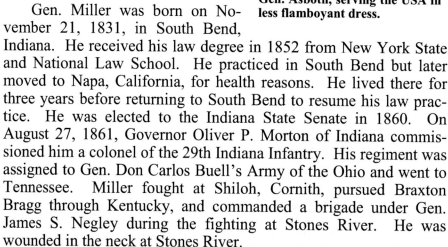

Gen. Miller's impressive grave marker at Arlington National Cemetery, VA.

Photo by Janet Greentree

35

in Napa Valley in 1869, which was part of Rancho Yajome. The area now is the home of the Silverado Country Club.

Miller then returned to politics and was a member of the 1878-79 second state constitutional convention. He was elected to the U.S. Senate in 1880, representing California. He was very outspoken about several bills limiting the influx of Chinese immigrants. He also was a member of the Committee to Revise the Laws of the United States and the Committee on Foreign Relations.

Sen. Miller died in Washington, D.C. on March 8, 1886, and was interred in the Laurel Hill Cemetery in San Francisco. The cemetery later closed, and he was reinterred at Arlington National Cemetery on May 5, 1913, in Section Two.

Union Gen. Thomas Turpin Crittenden

Gen. Crittenden's grave took at least three visits to find. Even with pictures of the stones and maps, some time it is very difficult to find the graves. He is buried in Section Seven.

The general was born October 16, 1825, in Huntsville, Alabama. His family moved to Texas shortly after his birth. He is the nephew of Sen. John J. Crittenden of Kentucky, and a first cousin to Gens. George B. Crittenden, CSA, and Thomas L. Crittenden, USA. It sounds like his family was definitely caught up in 'brother against brother' fighting.

Crittenden received his law degree from Transylvania College in Lexington, Kentucky. He was practicing law in Missouri when the Mexican War started. Joining in that fray, he was a 2nd lieutenant in a Missouri regiment. After this war, he moved to Indiana. Only five days after the attack on Fort Sumter, he volunteered and was commissioned a captain in a company of the 6th Indiana Infantry.

Crittenden led his regiment into (now) West Virginia and fought at Philippi in the first land battle of the Civil War. His unit was reorganized, and it was the first Union regiment to enter Kentucky. They entered the Battle of Shiloh on the second day's action.

In April 1862, he was commissioned a brigadier general. Crittenden took command on July 13, 1862, in Murfreesboro, Tennessee, and his command was captured by Confederate Gen. Nathan Bedford Forrest. This incident virtually ended his career, and after his release in October 1862, he saw no further important service. In 1868, Crittenden

Gen. Thomas T. Crittenden

moved to Washington, D.C. In 1885, he moved to San Diego, California, where he became a real estate developer. He died while on vacation in East Gloucester, Massachusetts on September 5, 1905.

Editor's Note: Our most distinguished guest speaker, Ed Bearss, paid Ms. Rebelle quite a compliment. When he arrived at dinner before the meeting last month, he sat down and asked who Ms. Rebelle was, not realizing she was sitting right next to him. Ed said that, whenever he receives our newsletter, he looks for her column first. Way to go Janet ... uh ... Ms. Rebelle!

At left: Gen. Crittenden and wife Elizabeth repose with daughter Lucy and her husband, Navy Captain Albert A. Ackerman.

Photos by Janet Greentree

A Gathering of Eagles

The Three Musketeers of Civil War events (Gwen Wyttenbach, Nancy Anwyll and me) were invited by our own Gen. Richard S. Ewell (Chris Godart) to attend the Gathering of Eagles event held in Winchester, VA, on June 2nd. The event is held in the 1840s Winchester Courthouse Civil War Museum located on Loudoun Street in the city. It turned out to be a beautiful day, so it was just perfect to watch the action of the reenactors making "their" generals come alive. The three of us just sat there absolutely enthralled with the event.

Chris told me later than there is no script for the event. The members are given a year before an event to prepare. This year's event was the year 1862. The action began with Gen. Ewell reading a copy of Harper's Weekly. A reporter from Harper's Weekly started asking questions of the generals on various topics relating to 1862. Some of the generals were seated in the center of the Courtroom, while others were in the gallery on either side, or on the bench behind.

Gen. Richard S, Ewell (Chris Godart) starts his day reading Harper's Weekly while attending the Gathering of Eagles.
Photo by Janet Greentree

Gen. George B. McClellan was asked many questions. Then the others started making pithy comments, so it was a lot of back and forth with the discussion. Chris tells me that, sometimes, it gets very animated, and there is shouting back and forth between the Union and Confederate officers. We didn't get to see any outright arguments, but there were some heated discussions.

In looking at my pictures from the event, it seems there were more Confederate generals than Union. One of our favorites was Gen. William Tecumseh Sherman (Jim Opdenker). This is the first time I have ever seen anyone portray the general. He was sitting in the Courtroom with his rakish red hair in a slouched position that made you believe it really was Gen. Sherman before you. Afterwards, the general told us that he has never lit a fire (along the march through Georgia), but people come up to him all the time and give him matches.

Gen. William T. Sherman (Jim Opdenker) relaxes amongst his fellow officers.
Photo by Janet Greentree

It was a treat to see Loudoun's own Col. John S. Mosby (Jimmy Fleming), Col. Heros von Borcke (R. J. Cicero) and Gen. J.E.B. Stuart (Bill Frueh) there. Bill Frueh has been to the Bull Run Civil War Round Table before. He lives outside of Denver, CO, and several years ago, Nancy and I saw him in the Denver airport in full Stuart regalia, including his sword, getting ready to travel. Colonel von Borcke had his blunderbuss with him. He also presented a Confederate coat to Gen. "Stonewall" Jackson (Greg Randall), replacing his Union coat that he wore as a Union officer at First Manassas. Mosby, von Borcke and Stuart walked 'round and 'round the Courtroom singing "Riding Around McClellan" while Gen. McClellan sat in the Courtroom.

The ladies had a tea and sewing circle, at which they discussed the war and the hardships they had to endure because of it. It turns out that one of the ladies had a

Left to right: Col. John Mosby (Jimmy Fleming), Gen. J.E.B. Stuart (Bill Frueh) and Col. Heros von Borcke (R. J. Cicero) hanging out at the Gathering of Eagles.
Photo by Janet Greentree

Barry Meadows offered a fine impression as Gen. Ulysses S. Grant, champion of the Union,
Photo by Janet Greentree

birthday on June 2nd, so Gen. George Pickett (Niles Clark) sang to her. He has a marvelous voice and sang a cappella.

During intermission, I approached Gen. John F. Hartranft (John Schlotter) and asked him what it was like to read the death sentence on the gallows to the Lincoln Conspirators. He said they were very respectful of Mary Surratt. I told him I had found the grave of his aide, Col. William Henry Harrison McCall, in Prescott, AZ, several years ago. We talked about the poor state of the Norristown, PA, cemetery, where he and Gen. Winfield Scott Hancock are buried. Gen. Hartranft's marker has bullet holes in it, as do several others in the cemetery. In "real" life, John Schlotter is the postmaster of Gettysburg.

The great Al Stone (Gen. Robert E. Lee) is head of 'Lee's Lieutenants.' Al is very believable as Gen. Lee. The three of us joined him at lunch at Blenheim once, and he stood, while we sat down. Wow! Al headed up the event and got all the reenactors together for pictures at the end.

At left, Gen. Robert E. Lee (Al Stone) chats strategy with Gen. J.E.B. Stuart (Bill Freuh) while Union general staff encroaches on the Winchester Courthouse.
Photo by Janet Greentree

I enjoyed talking to Gen. James Longstreet (Gene Pennell), Gen. Isaac R. Trimble (David Trimble), Lewis Armistead (Dennis Cole), Maxcy Gregg (Tony Virando), Gen. Ulysses S. Grant (Barry Meadows) and Gen. George Sears "Pap" Greene (Paul Bourget). Tony Virando looked so much like Gen. Gregg. His beard was really something. Our 'Extra Billy' Smith (Dave Meisky) and Col. Brett H. Venable (Mark Whittenton) were also in attendance.

In all my years of going to Civil War events, this was by far my favorite. These men absolutely made the Civil War come alive with their portrayals of the generals. I would heartedly recommend this event to all of you. The Lee's Lieutenants Web site is: leeslieutenants.com, and the Federal generals' Web site is: federalgeneralscorp.com.

The Blue & the Gray turned out for the Gathering of Eagles in Winchester. At front, left of the Union contingent is the French-born Marie Tepe earned the nickname 'French Mary,' while traveling with her husband, in the 114th Pennsylvania Zouaves. Marie, dressed in her blue Zouave jacket, and red skirt worn over trousers, would travel with the army selling tobacco, hams and contraband whiskey to the troops. Marie served from August 1862 until war's end. Wounded in the heel at Fredericksburg while attending to the wounded, she once again came under fire at Chancellorsville. At the latter, her uniform was riddled with bullet holes as she carried water to the wounded. For her bravery at Chancellorsville, she received the medal of valor, the Kearny Cross. Forty years after the war, crippled by the pain of her war wound, Marie committed suicide. The actual Marie Tepe is inset in center.
Photo by Janet Greentree

Connections from Fredericksburg to Savannah

Ms. Rebelle was recently in Fredericksburg for her "17th" Four Days in May tour with the Greater Boston Civil War Round Table. Great tours are given by this group, and they would love to have anyone from the Bull Run Civil War Round Table join them. Next year's tour will be Petersburg and Appomattox. The following year a tour to North & South Carolina is in the planning stages. Our tour guide was Scott Walker, owner of Hallowed Ground Tours in Fredericksburg. He was a very good guide and was constantly talking about connections and obscure information which is what I find extremely interesting.

Driving around Fredericksburg, Scott was constantly pointing out interesting things to us. We drove by the Hugh Mercer Apothecary Shop, where he talked about the Savannah connections, so I knew I had my subject for this month's article.

Hugh Mercer was a physician in Fredericksburg. Physicians disbursed herbs and potions back in the 1700s, and he opened his Apothecary Shop in downtown Fredericksburg.

Hugh Mercer's apothecary in downtown Fredericksburg, VA. Photo by Janet Greentree

Colonial Gen. Hugh Mercer

One of his clients was Mary Washington, mother of our first president, George Washington. George and Hugh became close friends. Washington sold Mercer his childhood home, Ferry Farm. Both of them fought in our American Revolution. Mercer received a letter in 1776 that was signed by John Hancock, then in the Continental Congress appointing him a brigadier general. On January 3, 1777, as Gen. Mercer, along with 350 men, were on their way to Princeton, NJ, they encountered two British infantry regiments and also cavalry. A fierce fight broke out. The British, thinking Mercer to be George Washington, surrounded him and ordered him to surrender. Mercer chose to fight it out with his saber. He was beaten to the ground, bayoneted seven times, and left to die with a saber in his chest.

His body was taken to a white oak tree nearby; the tree then became known as the Mercer Oak. The Mercer Oak is part of the seal of Mercer County, NJ. Mercer died nine days later, on January 12, 1777, at the age of 35, at the Thomas Clarke house on the eastern end of the battlefield. Artist Charles Wilson Peale did a painting "Washington at the Battle of Princeton, January 3, 1777." The painting shows Gen. Washington in the foreground with Gen. Mercer mortally wounded, lying in the background. Dr. Benjamin Rush is supporting Mercer, with Maj. George Lewis holding the American flag. Fortunately for my story, Mercer married Isa-

Gen. Hugh Mercer's monument in Fredericksburg, VA. Photo by Janet Greentree

bella Gordon and fathered five children before the Revolution. His son, Hugh Tennant Mercer, is the father of Civil War Gen. Hugh Weedon Mercer.

Gen. Huge Weedon Mercer, CSA

Gen. Hugh Weedon Mercer

Hugh Weedon Mercer was born in Fredericksburg, Virginia at "Sentry Box" on November 27, 1808. He was named for his grandfather, Hugh Mercer, a Revolutionary War general, referenced above. Mercer graduated from West Point third in a class of 33 cadets in 1828. After graduating, he served in Georgia as an aide to Gen. Winfield Scott. He was also stationed at Fortress Monroe, with the artillery school. He served in the Army from 1828-1835. He was an artillery officer in the Georgia militia as well.

After resigning from the Army, Hugh married Mary Stiles Anderson from Savannah, and settled there, working as a bank cashier at the Planter's Bank. Mercer was first married to Bessie Steenberger of Virginia and had one child with her, Alice. Most likely, Bessie died, as Mercer remarried. Hugh and second wife Mary had six children together.

The Mercer House in Savannah, GA.
Photo by Janet Greentree

Construction of Mercer House in Savannah was started by him in 1860, but the beginning of the Civil War interrupted the further building of the house. For those of you who have read the book or seen the movie, Midnight in the Garden of Good & Evil by John Berendt, Mercer House was featured in both venues. No Mercers ever lived in the house, but it has retained the name all these years. The house was completed in 1868. The house is located at 429 Bull Street. It is now the Mercer-Williams Museum.

Mercer enlisted in the Confederate Army in 1861, became the colonel of the 1st Georgia Infantry; he was promoted to brigadier general in October 1861. He was instrumental in getting slaves and free blacks into the Confederate Army. [Editor's Note: these black men were "impressed" or coerced/kidnapped into servitude to Confederates, they were not enlistee soldiers; See: Wikipedia Biography.]

Mercer left Savannah for service in the Atlanta Campaign with the Army of the Tennessee. He fought at Dalton, Marietta, Kennesaw Mountain, and Atlanta. His son, George, was wounded at Kennesaw Mountain. Being 56 years of age (in 1864) as the war wore on was hard on his body; he became ill and was sent back to Savannah under Gen. William J. Hardee. He then was in charge of the defenses of Savannah. Mercer and Hardee left the city before Gen. William T. Sherman arrived, but

This picture, most likely taken in the winter of 1862, shows some of the officers of the 48th New York Volunteer regiment on top of the rampart of Fort Pulaski. Accompanying one of the officers is a pet dog; ahead of him is Col. William Barton, commander of the regiment, and his wife. Photo courtesy of the National Park Service, Fort Pulaski National Monument.

Mercer returned later. He was imprisoned briefly at Fort Pulaski, a fort which he had commanded. He was relieved of duty for physical inability on August 31, 1864.

After the war ended, he returned to the banking profession. In 1869, he moved to Baltimore, MD, and worked as a commission merchant. Still having health problems, he moved to Baden Baden, Germany, staying for five years, trying to find a cure for his illness. Try as I may, I cannot find out what that illness was, or what he died from. He died in Baden Baden on June 9, 1877. Most likely (but there is some speculation that it wasn't), his body was returned to Savannah for burial in Bonaventure Cemetery. Mercer is buried in Section F, Lot 19, and grave #7. The records in the Baden Baden cemetery where he was first interred do not show that he was ever disinterred. His marker in Savannah may be a cenotaph.

It is interesting how everyone named their homes in earlier times. The Sentry Box house where Hugh Weedon Mercer was born is just below the middle pontoon bridge site on the

Rappahannock River. The home was heavily damaged during the battle of Fredericksburg on December 13, 1862. There is a historic marker at the corner of Dixon & Caroline Streets noting that the home Sentry Box was located near there. The home was owned by Gen. George Weedon (Revolutionary War) and his wife Catherine. After Gen. Hugh Mercer was killed at the Battle of Princeton, Catherine Weedon invited the Mercers to live with them at Sentry Box.

If you have never been to Bonnaventure Cemetery in Savannah, it is a beautiful place to visit. It

The Sentry Box, used in Three Wars to give Alarm of the Approach of the Enemy

sits along the Bull River with Spanish moss hanging from the trees. The address is 330 Bonnaventure Road, Thunderbolt, GA. In addition to Gen. Mercer (maybe) resting there, five other Confederate Civil War generals are buried there: Robert Houston Anderson, Francis Stebbins Bartow, Henry Rootes Jackson, Alexander Robert Lawton, and Claudius Charles Wilson.

One of the most interesting things about the Mercer family is their descendants. In addition to Gen. Hugh Weedon Mercer, direct descendants are John Mercer Patton (Governor of Virginia), Lt. Col. Waller T. Patton (mortally wounded at Pickett's Charge), Col. George Smith Patton (Waller's brother, Civil War), Gen. George S. Patton, Jr. (World War II), and the songwriter/lyricist Johnny Mercer. Johnny Mercer is buried near Gen. Mercer at Bonnaventure Cemetery.

At left - counter-clockwise: Colonial Gen. Hugh Mercer's gravestone, Laurel Hill Cemetery, Philadelphia, PA; Gen. Hugh Weedonn Mercer's gravestone, Bonnaventure Cemetery, Savannah, GA; Johnny Mercer's grave memorial, also Bonnaventure; and the grave marker for the songmeister.

Photos by Janet Greentree

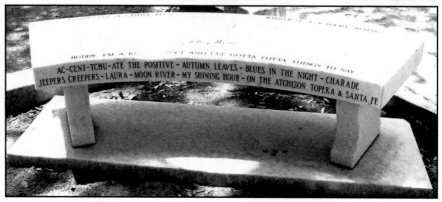

Brig. Gen. Lewis Addison Armistead, CSA

Sometimes it just takes a village to find my Civil War generals' graves. Lewis Addison Armistead - it took diligence and a key to a locked cemetery in Baltimore (shades of Gen. Benjamin Butler in Massachusetts with *The Stone Wall* editor Nadine Mironchuk) to find his grave. Supposedly, in the dead of night, Armistead's body was brought to Old St. Paul's Cemetery in Baltimore, MD, to be buried next to his famous uncle, George Armistead, the hero of Baltimore at Fort McHenry in the War of 1812.

My late friend, Joe, had given me a map and a phone number for the Rector of St. Paul's Church, who put me in touch with the caretaker of the cemetery. Yankee Nan (Nancy Anwyll) and I met up with him one Saturday morning after wondering the whole trip up to Baltimore if he would show up. Thank goodness - show up he did. The first thing the caretaker wanted me to do was to drive through the gate after he opened it - a gate made for buggies, not cars. I worried whether my side mirrors would be ripped off in the effort. My worries were for naught, as my car really did fit through the gate.

The caretaker took us to Armistead's grave and gave us a tour of the cemetery. Several famous people are buried there including Samuel Chase, signer of the Declaration of Independence; several Congressmen; a Maryland governor; a Revolutionary War Officer; and we also viewed a cenotaph placed for Francis Scott Key. The caretaker was very proud of "his" cemetery.

Armistead died after the Battle of Gettysburg, following his mortal wounding on July 3, 1863, at the 'High Water Mark' of Pickett's Charge. He died two days later, around 9 a.m., even though the surgeon pronounced that his wounds were not of a serious nature.

The grave of both Gen. Lewis A. "Lo" Armistead and his uncle George, a hero of the War of 1812.

Photo by Janet Greentree

Narrow gate or not – Ms. Rebelle is sure to gain the objective in her Civil War grave searches.

Photo by Janet Greentree

He was wounded in the shoulder and below the knee. There is speculation that, at the age of 46, he perhaps had undiagnosed medical problems which contributed to his death.

Dr. Daniel Brinton, chief surgeon of the XI Corps, 2nd Division Union field hospital at the George Spangler Farm, stated that his death "was not from his wounds directly, but from secondary fever and prostration." The heat of his heavy wool uniform, temperatures in the high 80s, anxiety, a heart attack or stroke, an infection, lack of sleep, or depression over his two wives' death (and the deaths of two children) all could have contributed to his death.

Prophetically, he said of his dear friend, Union Gen. Winfield Scott Hancock, that "if ever he (Armistead) would raise a hand against him, he wanted God to strike him dead." Armistead knew very well that Gen. Hancock was in command near the Copse of Trees.

As I have stated before, there always seems to be connections. After shouting to

Armistead urging his men on at the stone wall at Gettysburg. Image is a National Park Service holding.

his comrades crossing the wall "Boys, give them the cold steel," with his hat held aloft on his sword, he reached Lt. Colonel Alonzo Cushing's guns and placed a hand on one of those guns. Was it Cushing's gun? Was Cushing killed and Armistead wounded at the same time? Did they see each other? A 1906 newspaper account about survivors attending a Pickett's Charge reunion, men of the Philadelphia Brigade stated that both Cushing and Armistead were killed/wounded at the same time.

Marker noting the spot at which Armistead fell, at the "high water mark" of the Battle of Gettysburg, just at the stone wall.
Photo by Janet Greentree

An aide to Gen. Hancock and a fellow Mason, Capt. Henry H. Bingham, approached the general as he lay wounded. Armistead then gave the Masonic sign (at the time) "My poor mother is a widow." He gave his Masonic watch to Bingham and asked that his Bible be given to Cornelia Hancock, the general's wife. Bingham later reported that the general was "completely exhausted, and seemingly broken-spirited." Gen. Abner Doubleday sent an aide to ascertain Armistead's rank. Armistead said "Tell Gen. Doubleday in a few minutes I shall be where there is no rank." When Armistead fell, command of his brigade went to Col. William R. Aylett, a grandson of Patrick Henry.

Ms. Rebelle's award-winning photo of the 'Friend to Friend Masonic Civil War Monument.'
Photo by Janet Greentree

On August 21, 1993, a statue of Armistead and Bingham called the 'Friend to Friend Masonic Civil War Monument' was erected in front of the Gettysburg National Cemetery. Ms. Rebelle's picture of the statue won third place in the Civil War Trust Photo Contest, Close-up Division, in 2006 - my first entry into their contest - and another connection.

Lewis Addison Armistead, known as "Lo" to his friends (for Lothario, the classic lover), was born on February 18, 1817, at the home of John Wright Stanly, his great-grandfather, in New Bern, North Carolina. His parents were Walker Keith Armistead and Elizabeth Stanly. His grandfather, John Stanly, was a U.S. Congressman and his uncle, Edward Stanly, was the military governor of North Carolina during the Civil War. Like many of our Civil War generals, his family fought for our country in the War of 1812 and had ties back to colonial America. His father, joined by his four brothers, fought in the War of 1812. His uncle, George Armistead, has a large statue at Fort McHenry. There is a statue of George Armistead on Federal Hill in Baltimore as well.

Armistead was appointed to West Point in 1834 but resigned after he broke a plate over the head of future Gen. Jubal Early. Speculation surrounds his resignation, in that he may have had trouble with French language

Left, Lt. Col. George Armistead, hero in the War of 1812 and uncle of Lewis Armistead. At right, the monument near Ft. McHenry in Baltimore dedicated to George Armistead.

43

studies, or other academic difficulties. His father was instrumental in obtaining for him the rank of second lieutenant in the 6th U.S. Infantry, on July 10, 1839.

After marrying his first wife, Cecelia Lee Love, a distant cousin of Robert E. Lee, he served in Arkansas, Fort Washita, and the Mexican War, where he was wounded at Chapultepec. His daughter, Flora Love, died at Jefferson Barracks in St. Louis in April 1850. He then lost his wife in December 1850 in Mobile, Alabama. He married his second wife, Cornelia Taliaferro Jamison, in Alexandria, VA, on March 17, 1853. Their first child, Lewis B. Armistead, died on December 6, 1854, and is buried next to his half-sister Flora Love at Jefferson Barracks. He then lost Cornelia on August 3, 1855, at Fort Riley, Kansas, during a cholera epidemic.

Above, at left - Gen. Lewis A. Armistead; at right - Gen. Winfield S. Hancock; below - a depiction of the final moments of Gen. "Lo" Armistead.

When the Civil War began, he resigned from the U.S. Army and was made a major in the Confederate Army on March 16, 1861. He commanded the 57th Virginia. He achieved the rank of brigadier general, under Gen. Benjamin Huger, on April 2, 1862. Armistead fought at Seven Pines, Seven Days Battles, Malvern Hill, 2nd Bull Run, Antietam, Fredericksburg, and Gettysburg. At Gettysburg, he urged his men "to remember what you are fighting for – your homes, your friends, your sweethearts."

Capt. Henry Bingham wrote a letter to Gen. Hancock on January 5, 1869, saying in part: "I think I found you in about fifteen minutes after I got Armistead's messages and effects. When I found you, you were on the ground wounded… I did not give you the message on the field but gave it to you at the Hospital in the woods, where you were lying in the ambulance….

He continues, "I met Armistead just under the crest of the hill, being carried to the rear by several privates. I ordered them back, but they replied that they had an important prisoner and they designated him as Gen. Longstreet… I dismounted my horse and inquired of the prisoner his name, he replied Gen. Armistead of the Confederate Army. Observing that his suffering was very great I said to him, General, I am Capt. Bingham of Gen. Hancock's staff, and if you have anything valuable in your possession which you desire taken care of, I will take care of it for you. He then asked me if it was Gen. Winfield S. Hancock and upon my replying in the affirmative, he informed me that you were an old and valued friend of his and he desired for me to say to you "Tell Gen. Hancock for me that I have done him and done you all an injury, which I shall regret or repent (I forget the exact word) the longest day I live." Then I obtained his spurs, watch chain, seal and pocketbook. I told the men to take him to the rear to one of the hospitals."

The general's only surviving son, Walker Keith Armistead (from his first marriage) served as a courier to Gen. J.E.B. Stuart, and also on his father's staff. Walker married Julia Frances Appleton, a granddaughter of Daniel Webster.

You just can't make this stuff up!

Capt. Henry H. Bingham, who tended to Armistead on the field, and carried his last messages to Gen. Hancock. Capt. Bingham was awarded the Medal of Honor for his services at the Battle of the Wilderness on May 6, 1864.

The *H. L. Hunley*

Ms. Rebelle had the distinct pleasure of driving to Charleston, South Carolina with my sister Kathe Fernandez and bff Gwen Wyttenbach over Easter weekend to see this beautiful city, and all the Civil War history we could fit in during our three-day visit. This was my third time visiting the city. We spent much time driving up and down Meeting and East Bay Streets to see all the sights. The houses on the Battery are truly beautiful. We stayed on the Mount Pleasant side of town and ended up crossing and re-crossing the Arthur Ravenel, Jr. Bridge, which has to be an engineer's dream.

Prior to the trip, we bought tickets for visiting the Warren Lasch Conservation Center, formerly the Charleston Navy Yard, to see the recently-recovered Confederate submarine. This turned out to be a really good decision, as the facility was extremely crowded. Seeing the *Hunley* was the highlight of our trip. The submarine is now upright in a tank of water, relieved from its original condition of listing to the right (starboard) on the sea bed, following its demise on the night of February 17, 1864.

The *Hunley* is in this container to help clean it from encrustations and to keep the vessel from rapid decomposition in the air, is observed by looking down on it from a platform. Unfortunately, NO pictures are allowed to be taken of the submarine. Our tour guide told me that National Geographic owns the rights to all the photos. Another docent told me that people had dropped cameras and cell phones into the tank so the no-photography rule went into effect. We are just going to have to remember the way it looked. It was actually in remarkable condition.

A replica of the *Hunley* serves to astonish visitors with its peculiarity.

Photo by Janet Greentree

Prior to entering the room where the *Hunley* is displayed, there is a replica of the submarine. We were surprised how very small and narrow it was. It was 40 feet long and the highest point of the hull was 4' 3". There is another mockup where a visitor can sit inside the submarine and turn the crank to make the submarine "go." What an incredibly hard thing that was to do - it takes every muscle in your body to turn the crank. I can't imagine how hard that must have been when in the water or submerged under it.

There is also a display showing how small the hatches were – 14" by 15 ¾". Some people, mostly children, tried to fit inside the hatch. The taller men must have really had a tight fit in the small sub-marine. Some of the crew actually were relatively tall: Lieutenant George E. Dixon (KY, 5'9"), Arnold Becker (Germany, 5'5"), C. Lumpkin (European born, 5'10"), Frank C. Collins (Fredericksburg, VA, 6'), J.F. Carlsen (Germany, 5'8"), J. Miller (GA, 5'10"), James A. Wicks (NC, 5'10"), and Joseph F. Ridgaway (Talbot Co., MD, 5'10").

Dixon's crew was the third crew to pilot the Hunley. Both prior crews (21 men) died, as well the most recent crew, except for four men from the first crew who escaped while it was being tried out. All three crews are buried in Charleston's Magnolia Cemetery, along with the creator of the submarine, Horace L. Hunley.

Janet Greentree (r) with fellow shipmates Gwen Wyttenbach (c) and unidentified youngster (l) aboard replica Hunley, showing that, although she can be 'cranky,' it's all in good fun!

Photo by Kathe Fernandez

Horace Hunley also died along with his second crew. Dixon had to work to convince Gen. P.G.T. Beauregard to allow him to try once again to pilot the *Hunley* after such a fatal record of service. Dixon said his (the third) crew was the best he ever had.

The Hunley was built in Mobile, Alabama and launched July 1863. It was shipped by rail on August 12, 1863, to Charleston. It sunk the first time out during a training exercise on August 29, 1863. It sank again on October 15, 1863. The *Hunley* was raised both times and returned to service. The sub had two watertight hatches, forward and aft, two short conning towers with portholes, and triangular cutwaters.

The *Hunley* set sail at night on February 17, 1864, and rammed her long metal-barbed spar, loaded with a 135-pound torpedo containing 90 pounds of black powder, into the *U.S.S. Housatonic* in Charleston Harbor off of Sullivan's Island. After ramming the spar into the *Housatonic*, the men of the *Hunley* were to back up the sub and pull away from the scene, but there is speculation that a 150' rope was still attached to the *Hunley* from the spar when the *Housatonic* blew up. The men were found inside at their stations when it was raised and opened, and most likely died either from the impact of the explosion, sinking of the *Housatonic*, or a loss of oxygen with suffocation that followed. Some say the *Hunley* was only 20 feet from the *Housatonic* when the ship exploded. Witnesses on the *Housatonic* claim that the sub was 100 feet away. The sub did manage to surface and flash their blue magnesium light to their crew on Sullivan's Island. There is also a possibility that the *Hunley* was unintentionally rammed by the *U.S.S. Canandaigua*, which was aiding the *Housatonic*. The *Hunley* was the first submarine to sink an enemy ship.

A cabinet displays the facial reconstructions of crewmembers. Left to right are: George Dixon, Arnold Becker, C. Lumpkin and Frank Collins. Further reconstructions have been done and joined these figures in the museum.
Photo by Janet Greentree

Dixon was found with a misshapen $20 gold coin close to his body, given to him by his sweetheart, Queenie Bennett. The coin was in his pants pocket at Shiloh when a bullet struck the coin, saving his life and his leg. Dixon had the coin engraved "Shiloh April 6, 1862 My Life Preserver G.E.D." A diamond ring and broach were also found on his body. All three are displayed in the museum.

Following the Civil War, efforts were made to find the *Hunley*. P.T. Barnum offered $100,000 as a reward to anyone finding the *Hunley*. It was not until 1995 that Clive Cussler found the *Hunley*, buried in silt. The sub was found 100 yards from the *U.S.S. Housatonic* in 27 feet of water. It had been protected by several feet of silt for over 100 years.

On August 8, 2000, the *Hunley* was raised from the Atlantic Ocean, 3.5 miles from Sullivan's Island. The sub broke the surface of the sea at 8:37 a.m., 136 years after it went down. The sub was rotated to its upright position in June 2011.

On April 17, 2004, a large funeral was held in Charles-

The *Hunley* is lifted from its watery seabed on August 8, 2000.

ton for the eight member crew of the *Hunley*. The funeral cortege proceeded 4.5 miles from East Bay Street on the Battery to Magnolia Cemetery. Six thousand reenactors and 4,000 civilians wearing period attire were in the procession. There were color guards from all five branches of the U.S. armed services also participating in the procession. The coffins were covered with the 2nd Confederate flag. All crew members were buried with full Confederate military honors.

Lieutenant Dixon's caisson was first in the procession, followed by a caparisoned riderless horse with boots turned.

The funeral for the crew of the *Hunley* makes its way down East Bay Street in the Battery, Charleston, SC, on April 17, 2004.

Each caisson was pulled by four horses, two ridden, and two riderless, and a mounted escort. Following each caisson, a reenactor carried the individual's Medal of Honor on a red pillow. When the procession arrived at Magnolia Cemetery, all eight men were buried side-by-side in a large plot. The pallbearers for each man were retired submarine veterans. Lieutenant Dixon had full Masonic last rites before his burial. Dixon belonged to Mobile, AL Lodge #40.

There was a 50-cannon salute and Freeman's Battery, Forrest's Artillery, fired an 1862 Howitzer. Before the funeral, all eight men lay in state on the *U.S.S. Yorktown*; John Wesley United Methodist Church; Cathedral of St. John the Baptist; and Church of the Holy Communion. Descendants of Frank Collins, James A. Wicks, Joseph F. Ridgaway, and Queenie Bennett were honored guests.

Of course, no trip is complete without a visit to a local cemetery, so Gwen and I went to Magnolia Cemetery to visit the *Hunley* graves. All three of the crews are buried together. Dixon and his crew are buried in a row in the order they were found. Horace L. Hunley is buried there as well. It is a very impressive site. We also visited the grave of Micah Jenkins.

A gentleman in Ireland had previously been in contact with me through www.findagrave.com and asked if I could find and photograph the grave of

The graves of the *Hunley* in Magnolia Cemetery, Charleston, SC.
Photo by Janet Greentree

his ancestor, Captain John C. Mitchel, located at Magnolia Cemetery.

Mitchel was the commander of Fort Sumter on July 20, 1864, dying on the parapet during the bombardment. Ms. Rebelle placed a Confederate flag on his grave at his descendant's request. Mitchel's last words are etched on the stone: "I willingly gave my life for South Carolina. Oh! That I could have died for Ireland." He was in the 1st Regiment, South Carolina Artillery.

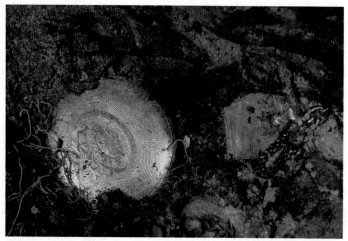

Ornate gold pocket watch recovered on May 30, 2002 during the excavation of the *H. L. Hunley*, the world's first successful combat submarine lost at sea during the Civil War after destroying the *USS Housatonic* on February 17, 1864. The watch, which belonged to the Confederate Hunley commander Lt. George Dixon, is a standard Liverpool English fusee watch with a lever escapement, gold chain and marine fob.

- http://www.hunley.org

47

Charleston – Part Two

As promised, Ms. Rebelle is continuing with the descriptions of the visit my sister Kathe, Gwen Wyttenbach and I made to Charleston, South Carolina, at the end of March. Our first big outing was by car to Fort Sumter from the Point Pleasant side of Charleston. It is a much shorter trip than the boat that leaves from the downtown Charleston area. The first view of the fort is of all the flags blowing in the wind. What a spectacular sight. The fort is, sadly, in ruins from all the shelling in the Civil War. Our trip was pretty close to the April 12, 1861, anniversary date of 152 years. On April 11, 1861, Gen. P.G.T. Beauregard sent three aides, Col. James Chestnut, Jr., Capt. Stephen D. Lee and Lt. A.R. Chisolm to demand the surrender of the fort. Negotiations failed; Union Maj. Robert Anderson held the fort for 34 hours before surrendering to the Confederates. We know that the Confederates fired the first shot at the fort, sparking the Civil War, but Capt. Abner Doubleday, who was second in command to Anderson, fired the first shot in defense of the fort.

Adversaries at Ft. Sumter - above, left: Union Maj. Robert Anderson; above, right: Confederate Gen. P.G.T. Beauregard. At right: Edmund Ruffin, a leading "fire-eater," or great agitator for secession.

Edmund Ruffin took credit for that first Confederate shot, but Lt. Henry S. Farley *actually* fired the first shot, from Morris Island, at 4:30 a.m. Since the Union was ill-equipped to return the fire, consistent firing wasn't begun for two hours. The fort was surrendered on April 13, 1861. Gen. Anderson retained possession of the Union flag that flew over the fort when he left. It is now displayed in the museum on the premises. Union soldiers evacuated on April 13th, boarding the *Star of the West,* headed for New York City. It took the Union four years to take the fort back.

The fort was built following the War of 1812. Construction started in 1829 and was still unfinished in 1861, when the shelling began. New England exported 70,000 tons of granite to build up a sand bar at the entrance of Charleston Harbor. The brick structure is five-sided, with walls five feet thick.

Unfortunately, the National Park Service doesn't allow a lot of time to look at everything in the fort. Only an hour was allotted to see the inside, the small museum, and walk the grounds. Park Rangers give talks on the aspects of the fort and answer questions. There is a small museum on the premises, as well a gift shop.

Above: undated photo of destroyed Ft. Sumter; below: Ft. Sumter as one visits it today.
Photo by Janet Greentree

Then and Now in Charleston

Touring around Charleston we came across several really old and beautiful buildings. The first one is

the City Market and Hall. The market was first established in 1692, encompassing four city blocks, from Meeting Street to Church Street. It was original called the Beef Market Building and was redesigned by Edward B. White in the early 1840s, after burning down in 1796. If anyone has read Gone With the Wind, Scarlett O'Hara liked to go to the market to socialize and find out the gossip of the day. The building is all open-sided, with many stalls inside.

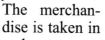

The merchandise is taken in and out every day. There is just about anything you might want to buy sold in the building, including a wide variety of food. The most famous item offered there is the Gullah baskets, woven by local African American Charleston women using a modi-

Then and Now - photos at left on page: the Market Hall, Charleston, SC. Above: The Market Building. Later photos by Janet Greentree

fied spoon to weave the designs. Bring your wallets with you, though, as they are quite expensive. The Confederate Museum is located on the Meeting Street side, at 188 Meeting Street. City Hall is another beautiful building, located at the corner of Meeting and Broad Streets. This intersection is called the Four Corners of Law, as the four buildings represent state, federal, municipal, and ecclesiastical law. Almost everything interesting is on Meeting Street in Charleston.

The second floor of the grand building is still utilized as city government offices. Also, on the second floor, is a huge oil painting of Gen. Pierre Gustave Toutant Beauregard. The general's sword is on display, as well as some other items belonging to him. The building was designed between 1800-1804 by Gabriel Manigault in the Adamesque style. The round basement windows are unique to his style of design. The Calhoun Mansion is also located "guess where?" You've got it – 16 Meeting Street. The 35 - room mansion was owned by Vice President John C. Calhoun, who is buried at St. Philips Episcopal Church Cemetery at 142 Church Street in Charleston.

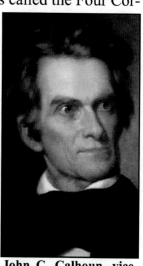

John C. Calhoun, vice president of the United States from 1825 to 1832, and a staunch defender of slavery.

John C. Calhoun's mansion in Charleston, SC, where some of the TV mini-series *North and South* was filmed.

Photo by Janet Greentree

John Calhoun is one of six or more famous people buried there, including Charles Gadsen; James Gadsen; Daniel Huger; also brothers Charles C. (a signer of the Declaration of Independence) and Thomas Pinckney; and Edward Rutledge (also a sign-

Then and Now - St. Michael's Church in downtown Charleston, SC.

Later photo by Janet Greentree

er of the Declaration of Independence). Even though John C. Calhoun accomplished quite a bit in his life, he was not eligible to be buried in the church side of the cemetery. Only people born in Charleston were eligible to be buried on the church side. Calhoun was born in Clemson, so he is across the street from the church. The Calhoun Mansion was used in the TV mini-series *North and South* as the home of George Hazard, portrayed by James Read. The movie *The Notebook* was also filmed there.

St. Michael's Episcopal Church is located at 17 Broad Street at the intersection of Meeting Street. The steeple of the church is 186 feet above the street and is visible in many of the old photos of Charleston during the Civil War. The weathervane atop the steeple is 7 ½ feet tall. The clock in the tower has kept the time for Charleston since 1764. George Washington worshipped there in May 1791 in pew No. 43 (the Governor's Pew), a large double pew in the center of the church. Gen. Robert E. Lee worshipped there in the same pew in the 1860s. The eight famous bells made in England in 1794 were sent to Columbia during the Civil War but were cracked in a fire there in 1865.

Remnants of the bells were salvaged from the fire and sent to England to be recast. The bells still ring in Charleston. The pulpit is original, and there are several beautiful stained-glass windows in the sanctuary. The chancel's stained-glass window was crafted by Louis Comfort Tiffany in 1905, in the design of a blue sky with gold stars and a starburst.

Boone Hall Plantation is located in Mount Pleasant, SC, at 1235 Long Point Road, a short distance from Charleston. The original house was included in a land grant to Maj. John Boone in 1681. The current house was built in 1936 and was patterned after the original house, which burned down many years ago. One of the most interesting things about Boone Hall is its long driveway, with live oak trees, bending towards each other, and the hanging Spanish moss on them.

Those of you who love *North and South* can just visualize the late actor, Patrick Swayze as Orry Main, riding down the lane at a full gallop. Gwen, my sister Kathe and I spend most of the

Boone Hall Plantation, Mount Pleasant, SC. This was another site for filming of *North and South*. In 1743, the son of Major John Boone planted live oak trees, arranging them in two evenly spaced rows. This spectacular approach to his home symbolizes southern heritage and will take root in your memory for many years to come. It would take two centuries for the massive, moss-draped branches to meet overhead, forming today's natural corridor. The economic success of such a large working plantation (which eventually grew to over 1,000 acres) depended on the widespread use of African slaves for labor — initially cultivating rice, then indigo, cotton, and pecans.

Photos by Janet Greentree

day there, just enjoying this most beautiful place.

The Battery on East Bay Street is one of the most beautiful parts of the city. The mansions overlook Charleston harbor and have a view of Fort Sumter, as well. Following the Civil War, Union Gen. John Porter Hatch assumed military command of the city of Charleston and had his headquarters on South Battery Street from February-August 1865. I am proud to say that he is "one" of my 385 graves visited and decorated; he is buried in Arlington National Cemetery.

One of our last visits in Charleston was to The Citadel, incorporated in 1842. The campus is located at 171 Moultrie Street, along the Ashley River. It reminded us a lot of the Virginia Military Institute in Lexington, VA. The building that resembles VMI the most has a red-and-white checkerboard inlaid on the courtyard of the building. I asked permission to walk inside, but in true Southern tradition, a cadet must escort females into the diamond, as they call it. So, a nice young cadet took my arm and escorted me inside. Pretty impressive, I must say. The photograph below shows the checkerboard pattern underneath the class ring for 2013.

Above: Union Gen. John Porter Hatch's HQ at the Battery in Charleston, SC, at the close of the war. Below, Hatch's officers at the headquarters.

Later photo by Janet Greentree

Four Confederate Civil War generals graduated from the Citadel – Ellison Capers, Micah Jenkins, Evander Law and John Bordenave Villepigue. The Federal army took possession of the Citadel in 1865 and held possession of it until 1879. The Citadel reopened in January 1882. One hundred eighty-nine Cadets reported to the newly reopened Citadel on October 2, 1882.

The places listed above are just a few of the many things to see and do in Charleston. The three of us did pretty well, seeing all we could in two days, with two travel days down and back. If you go, you have to have some of the wonderful low country food – shrimp and grits come fast to my mind. We ate at the Hominy Grill, which was wonderful. We had the best motel in Point Pleasant – the Quality Inn. The chef made such a spread every morning for breakfast, including a large pan of grits and fresh biscuits or scones, with everything else in between. It was wonderful. Ms. Rebelle had grits every day in Charleston. The motel prices are a little more reasonable across the Ravenel Bridge, and there are no parking fees, with quick access back into the city.

Gen. John Porter Hatch

The Citadel, Charleston, SC.
Photo by Janet Greentree

51

Gen. A.P. Hill, CSA

April 2, 2015, marked the 150th anniversary of the death of Lt. Gen. Ambrose Powell Hill, CSA, during the Petersburg campaign. He was killed near the modern-day intersection of Route 1 (Boydton Plank Road) and Sentry Hill Court in Petersburg, VA. A monument stands on the spot, aptly stating: "Spot Where A.P. Hill was Killed."

Gen. Hill went through the war and almost made it entirely through, until the approach to its end at Appomattox on April 9, 1865. Just returning from sick leave on April 2nd, he rode out along the defensive lines at Petersburg trying to rally his troops; he came across a patrol of Union soldiers. Hill demanded their surrender, but Cpl. John W. Mauk, Co. F, 138th PA Infantry, instead fired the fatal

shot. Mauk had no idea who he had killed until he was later told.

Being contained by the Union Army, Hill's men were unable to have his remains buried in Hollywood Cemetery in Richmond (preferred and available all through the war for worthy personages), so he was placed in a pine box and was buried hastily in the Winston family cemetery in Chesterfield, VA.

In September, 1867, he was disinterred and reburied in Hollywood Cemetery with no marker, and only the words: "Lt-Gen A.P. Hill" carved into the curb in front of his grave. Not destined to remain in Hollywood long, he was again disinterred and reburied under a monument honoring him in a traffic circle on Laburnum Avenue and Hermitage Road in Richmond on July 1, 1891.

If you wish to visit the marker, please be advised that it is a very busy intersection, and you definitely take your life in your own hands if you try to take a picture of the marker.

Statue of Gen. A.P. Hill, in the center of a Richmond, VA traffic circle. Photo by Janet Greentree

Did you know that Hill had red hair and hazel eyes? The colorist who recently colorized his picture definitely got it wrong. He was 5'8" or 5'9" and weighed around 160 pounds, unless he was fighting in a battle, during which time he would drop 20 pounds or so.

Hill was a roommate to George McClellan at West Point. He also courted and was betrothed to Ellen Marcy, McClellan's future wife. It was said that he fought harder if he knew McClellan was on the other side. Her parents were against the marriage, and so the engagement was broken. He contracted gonorrhea during his junior year at West Point and had to drop out for a year. He returned to graduate 15th in his class of 1847. He was known as Powell, Little Powell, and A.P. to distinguish him from Gen. D.H. Hill.

Ellen Marcy, A.P.'s lost love - lost to George B. McLellan, his future battlefield nemesis.

Hill was born in Culpeper, Virginia, on November 9, 1825. His house still stands at 102 North Main Street in Culpeper. He was the youngest of seven children of Thomas and Fannie Baptist Hill. Powell was named for his uncle, Ambrose Powell, an Indian fighter; friend of President James Madison; legislator; explorer; and sheriff. As a young boy, his father taught him to be a perfect horseman. He was especially close to his mother, being the youngest child.

Colorized photos of A.P. Hill have not been all that illuminating.

Hill was a voracious reader, devouring everything from Shakespeare, the Bible, to books on Napoleon. He was sent to the private boarding school Black Hills Seminary three miles northwest of his home in Culpeper. In 1842, at age 17, he was appointed to West Point. He became good friends with Henry Heth and Ambrose Burnside during his attendance there.

After graduating, Hill served in the Mexican War but did not see action in any major battles. From 1855-1860, he worked for the United States Coastal Survey. In 1857, while attending a party at the Willard Hotel in Washington, he met Kitty Morgan. She was blue-eyed, petite, vivacious and stylish, with light brown hair; she could sing like a bird. Her Mammy called her Dolly, because she looked like a doll.

On July 18, 1859, in Lexington, KY, Hill married the young widow Kitty (Dolly) Morgan McClung, whose husband had died suddenly. Dolly's brother, John Hunt Morgan, was Hill's best man at the wedding.

Dolly and Powell had four children, all girls: Henrietta, Frances Russell, Lucy Lee, and A.P. Hill. Their last child, Ann Powell Hill, was born two months after the general died (on June 6, 1865). Gen. R. E. Lee was godfather to Lucy Lee. Dolly traveled with Powell as much as she could during the war, but would depart several

The young and dashing A. P. Hill and the "vivacious" Kitty (Dolly) Morgan McClung, Hill's wife on the rebound. Dolly was a great supporter of "the cause," apparently doing a little spying between bearing four children.

times just moments before impending danger. Kitty wasn't above doing some spying for information, either. She also used her beautiful silk wedding gown to make a battle flag for the 13th Virginia.

When the Civil War began, Hill resigned his U. S. Army commission and was appointed colonel of the 13th Virginia Infantry Regiment. His regiment was transported by railroad as reinforcements at the First Battle of Manassas. He was appointed brigadier general on February 26, 1862, and, after his performance in the Peninsula Campaign in 1862, was appointed major general. At the Battle of Seven Pines, Hill began referring to his division as the Light Division. His men said the name was applicable, since they often marched without accoutrements other than their weapons and haversacks. Hill wanted his men to have a reputation for speed and agility.

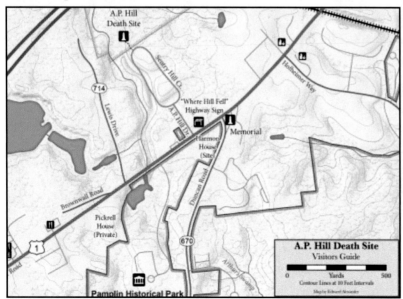

Actor Patrick Falci, who portrayed Gen. A.P. Hill in the movie "Gettysburg," yearly portrays the general at the commemoration of Hill's death.
Photo by Janet Greentree

After both the Seven Days Battles and at Malvern Hill, A.P. Hill became embroiled in a dispute with James Longstreet, in reference to several disparaging newspaper articles appearing in the Richmond Examiner. Longstreet's charges of military malfeasance came to the point where Hill was arrested; he challenged Longstreet to a dual. Gen. Lee stepped in and sent Hill's division to Gordonsville.

At the Battle of Antietam, after receiving a call for assistance from Gen. Lee, Hill marched his men at the double quick to reach the battlefield in time for a counterattack against Gen. Burnside. Lee's army was undefeated because of Hill coming up in time to assist Lee. Later, at Fredericks-

Above - the Cashtown Inn, where Gens. Hill and Lee held a confab about taking the Union Army at Gettysburg; below, a depiction of Hill and Lee's earlier meeting in Chambersburg Diamond on June 26, 1863.

burg, Hill's division suffered 2,000 casualties – almost two-thirds of the casualties in Stonewall Jackson's corps. Jackson later had Hill arrested and charged him with eight counts of dereliction of duty. Nothing came of this as they were too busy fighting the war to pause for a court of inquiry. Later, Jackson was mortally wounded in Chancellorsville in May, 1863, with Hill also being wounded in his calves. J.E.B. Stuart was tapped to replace Hill while he recuperated.

Hill was promoted to lieutenant general on May 24, 1863 – the fourth highest-ranking general of the time - and placed in charge of the Third Corps. We all remember actor Patrick Falci portraying Gen. Hill in the movie "Gettysburg," standing in front of the Cashtown Inn talking to Gen. Lee. Did you know that Lee and Hill met in the Chambersburg, PA, diamond prior to that, too? Hill led the Third Corps at Gettysburg. Two-thirds of his corps were in force at Pickett's Charge. Hill's Corps suffered the most casualties in Gettysburg.

Hill had said that he had no desire to witness the collapse of the Confederacy. His desire became reality when he was shot dead on April 2, 1865. A newspaper account from June 27, 1867, in the San Francisco Bulletin states as follows:

"Death of A.P. Hill—But now, before 8 o'clock, all the network of exterior defenses had been swept by the Union troops, who rapidly advancing, drove their exhausted opponents far back to the last strong chain of works, which immediately girdled Petersburg. At this time, within the city, Gen. Lee, Gen. A.P. Hill, and Gen. Mahone were talking over the perils and prospects of the day at the headquarters of the former officer. As the firing drew near and ominously nearer the front, Gen. Lee, listening, said to Hill, "How is this, General? Your men are giving way." Instantly Gen. Hill mounted his horse and dashed down the road to the front. Gen. Lee's words were true; the Union forces were already crossing the lines at all points. As Hill rode along, he suddenly came upon two or three men in blue uniform, who, taking position behind a tree, leveled their pieces at him. "Throw down your arms," cried the General. The men were staggered for an instant by the very audacity of the demand, but, recovering, gave back their answer from their rifle's mouth; and A.P. Hill, who had fought throughout Virginia, from the first hour of Bull Run to the last hour of Petersburg, fell from his horse, dead." Gen. Lee remarked after hearing the news of Hill's death – "He is at rest now, and we who are left are the ones to suffer."

Gen. Pierre Gustave Toutant-Beauregard, CSA

Of all the generals Ms. Rebelle has studied, Pierre Gustave Toutant-Beauregard is the one who I would have liked to have heard speak. He had to have had a French Creole way of speaking, since he was a New Orleans native.

Departing from my usual modus operandi, I did not go to New Orleans to find his grave. My daughter and her husband, Lisa and Paul Tully, went to New Orleans on an "empty nester" trip. Lisa asked if I would like her to find any generals for me. Beauregard has been on my list forever, so I said: Beauregard. Unfortunately, she didn't know what she was getting into, trying to find a grave in a big cemetery without a picture. The good general is buried in a locked mausoleum underneath the Army of the Tennessee Monument. The statue on top of the monument is not even Gen. Beauregard. The statue is of Gen. Albert Sidney Johnson, who was briefly buried within that mausoleum. Johnston's grave is now in Austin, Texas.

Gen. Pierre Gustave Toutant-Beauregard

The Army of Tennessee Monument where Beauregard is interred.
Photo by Lisa Tully

Beauregard was second in command of the Army of the Tennessee. There are 48 slots in the mausoleum and Beauregard is the most famous of those interred there. The Tullys must have gotten in the spirit, though, as they found Gen. Harry Thompson Hays on a tour they took, which started in Lafayette No. 1, the cemetery where Hays is interred.

Walking around the city, they stumbled upon the Beauregard-Keyes House located at 1113 Chartres Street in the French Quarter. This house is where the general and his second wife spent their wedding night. Later, he would live in the house from 1866-1868. In the year 1925, the current owner of the house wanted to tear it down. The Beauregard Memorial Associates was formed by local women, and the house was saved. Today, the house is open for touring and also for special events such as weddings.

Above, Gen. Beauregard's remains are identified inside with a plaque on the sarcophagus. Photo by Bill Gardner.

At right, the mausoleum where Beauregard is resting, with dozens of other lesser-known folks.

Pierre G.T. Beauregard was born on May 28, 1818, in St. Bernard Parish, Louisiana, at his family's sugar cane plantation, Contreras, about 20 miles north of New Orleans. Later in his life, he would fight at the battle of Contreras in the Mexican War. His parents were Jacques Toutant-Beauregard of French and Welsh ancestry and Helene Judith de Reggio, of French and Italian ancestry. His mother was a member of an Italian noble family. He had three brothers and three sisters.

As a young child P.G.T. had playmates who were slaves on the plantation. P.G.T.'s wet nurse was a Dominican enslaved woman. Until the age of 12, P.G.T. spoke only French. At age 12, he was sent to Freres Peugnet School in New York City, a French school, where he learned to speak

Beauregard-Keyes House, today (left) and in 1900 (right).

Photo at left by Lisa Tully

English. Prior to that, he was educated in New Orleans private schools. He was appointed to West Point and graduated second in his class in 1838. While at West Point, he dropped the Pierre from his name and went by G.T. One of his instructors was Robert Anderson, who he would later face at Fort Sumter. His classmates were: Edward "Allegheny" Johnson, William Hardee, Irvin McDowell, Robert Grander, Henry Hopkins Sibley, Carter Stevenson, Andrew Smith, and Alexander Reynolds (a grave I recently found in Zanesville, OH). His classmates had several nicknames for

Marie Antoinette Laure Villere

him: Bory, Little Frenchman, Little Creole, Felix, and Little Napoleon.

Most people thought Beauregard had a foreign appearance, even though he was born in the U.S. He had dark eyes, an olive complexion, very black hair and considered very handsome. Later during the Civil War, his hair would turn gray due to the unavailability of black hair dye during the blockade. People thought he resembled Napoleon III. His thoughts were that he more resembled Napoleon Bonaparte. He was mostly reserved, but would sometimes be abrupt with people who displeased him. It was said he would sometimes go months without smiling.

G.T. married his first wife Marie Antoinette Laure Villere in 1841. She was a member of one of the most prominent French Creole families owning sugar cane plantations in Plaquemines Parish. Her paternal grandfather, Jacques Villere, was the second governor of Louisiana. She and G.T. had three children, Rene Toutant, Henri Toutant, and Laure. Marie died in March, 1850, while giving birth to her third child, Laure. In 1860, G.T. married Marguerite Caroline Deslonde, daughter of another sugar cane planter. The couple had no children together. Marguerite was ill from 1861-1864 and died in Union-occupied New Orleans on March 2, 1864. Union Gen. Nathaniel Banks arranged for a steamer to carry her body back to her parish. Six thousand people attended her funeral.

Like most of his classmates, he fought in the Mexican War and was wounded twice. He fought in the battles of Contreras, Churubusco, Mexico City, and Chapultepec. He fought under Gen. Winfield Scott and was one of the first soldiers to enter Mexico City. After the Mexican War he was in charge of the Engineer Department defending the Mississippi River and the lakes of New Orleans. He invented a self-acting bar excavator to be used by ships crossing over sandbars. He also stabilized the foundation of the U.S. Custom House in New Orleans that was sinking into the ground. The structure had been built in 1848.

Pierre's brother-in-law John Slidell (through his 2nd wife's family) was influential in getting him the position of superintendent of West Point on January 23, 1861. Unfortunately, G.T. served five days in that position. When the Civil War began, his superintendent position was revoked by

An illustration of Beauregard (mounted) issuing orders at the battle of First Manassas, or Bull Run.

the War Department. He protested to the War Department, stating "that their revoking of his position has put improper reflection upon his reputation or position in the Corps of Engineers." Coming back to New Orleans after being dismissed as superintendent at West Point, he enrolled as a private in the Orleans Guards. Again he used his influence with John Slidell and President Davis to obtain a senior position in the Confederate Army. He was appointed the first brigadier general of the Confederate Army on March 1, 1861. Only four months later, he was promoted to full general, and was one of only seven to make that rank.

G.T. was assigned to Charleston on March 3, 1861. His former instructor, Maj. Robert Anderson, was in charge of Fort Sumter. Not wanting to fire on his former instructor to take the fort, he sent several cases of whiskey, brandy, and boxes of cigars to Anderson and his officers. All gifts were refused and returned to him. On April 12, Anderson, his officers, and men endured 34 hours of shelling from Beauregard's troops. Maj. Anderson surrendered the fort on April 14. This is where G.T. earned the sobriquet of "Hero of Fort Sumter." He was given a hero's welcome in Richmond after his accomplishment.

Next came the First Battle of Bull Run, the first major battle of the Civil War. He and others held the line against the Union, chasing them back to Washington City. G.T. earned the rank of full general on the date of the battle – July 21, 1861.

Did you know that generals Beauregard, Joseph Johnston and Quartermaster John Cabell met in our own Fairfax City and designed the Confederate battle flag? Confederate women donated silk from their dresses for three flags to be given to Beauregard, Johnston, and Earl Van Dorn.

There is an historical marker on Main Street not too far from Kamp Washington (intersection of Main Street and Fairfax Boulevard) going west on the right side of the road near a new condo complex. It's not easy to pull over and read, but Beauregard was there.

Article researchers/photographers Paul and Lisa Tully.

The Fairfax marker denoting the location of the meeting in Fairfax City where the Confederate battle flag was designed.
Photo by Janet Greentree

During his career, Pierre clashed with Pres. Jefferson Davis and Gen. Robert E. Lee. He was transferred to Tennessee to become 2nd in command to Gen. Albert Sidney Johnson. He fought at Shiloh, Corinth, Charleston Harbor, Fort Wagner, 2nd Charleston Harbor, 2nd Fort Sumter, the Bermuda Hundred campaign, Petersburg, and Bentonville.

At the war's end, he was reluctant to seek amnesty, but generals Lee and Johnston urged him to do so. He swore to an oath of loyalty in front of the Mayor of New Orleans on September 16, 1865, and was pardoned by President Andrew Johnson on July 4, 1868.

After the war, he sought a position in the Brazilian Army

in 1865, but then thought better of it. The armies of Romania and Egypt also pursued him for a position in their armies, but he refused. He said, "I prefer to live here, poor and forgotten, than to be endowed with honor and riches in a foreign country." He was a champion of civil rights and for giving the right to vote to former slaves. He was active in the Reform Party and a lifelong Democrat. Like many other former Civil War generals, he worked in the railroad business as chief engineer and general superintendent of the New Orleans, Jackson, and Great Northern Railroad. He was promoted to president of the railroad in 1866. He served until 1870, when a hostile take over occurred. In 1877, he was a supervisor of the Louisiana Lottery. Gen. Jubal Early worked with him. His friend, Gen. John Bell Hood, was offered the position but declined. Gen. Beauregard wrote several books – *Principles and Maxims of the Art of War*, *Report on the Defense of Charleston*, and *A Commentary on the Campaign and Battle of Manassas*.

When his his friend Gen. Hood and Hood's wife both died in 1879 from yellow fever, leaving 10 children, Beauregard stepped in and formed the Hood Relief Committee to have Hood's memoirs published (*Advance and Retreat*), with all proceeds going to the children. When the cornerstone of the Lee Monument was laid in Richmond, Beauregard was the grand marshal of the festivities. He was asked in 1889 to lead Pres. Jefferson Davis' funeral but declined, saying: "We have always been enemies. I cannot pretend I am sorry he is gone. I am no hypocrite." (Harsh, for sure.)

The Hero of Fort Sumter died in his sleep in New Orleans on February 20, 1893, of heart disease and aortic insufficiency. Gen. Edmund Kirby Smith, the last surviving full general of the Confederacy, served as the chief mourner. Pierre's funeral was held on February 23rd. The parade included State militia of the first military district, all veteran Confederate organizations, the fire department, and many civic associations. *The Virginian Pilot* newspaper reported: "The City Hall is being very elaborately decorated this morning, both exteriorly and interiorly. The columns of the portico have been heavily draped in black and a catafalque is being constructed in the chamber itself…. Tomorrow will be observed as a general holiday…. Steps are already being taken to raise a fund for a monument to the deceased. It will not be a costly shaft, but it will be representative of the strong affection which Louisiana has for the memory of the dead soldier."

The statue was erected in 1915 and removed on May 16, 2017, in the dead of night. The *Sacramento Bee* stated: "The funeral of General P.G.T. Beauregard ranked with that of Jefferson Davis for magnificence in display, number of participants and general evidences of mourning. The doors of City Hall were not closed during Wednesday night, and the chamber of mourning was never without visitors. From dawn till the hour of the funeral on Thursday many thousands passed by the bier and viewed the body." The *Boston Herald* listed the pallbearers as: "Gen. Wright Schaumberg, Gen. John Glynn, Col. Lyman and Capt. Domoreaulle. The honorary pallbearers were city officials, state judges, leading journalists and prominent citizens."

Charleston, South Carolina, loved Gen. Beauregard, as well. The city displays Beauregard's sword and a huge portrait of him, in a government office building downtown. The general even stipulated that the city would receive the sword in his will: "I give to the city of Charleston, S.C., if acceptable, to it, the sword which was presented to me by some ladies of New Orleans in 1861, for the capture of Fort Sumter (illustrated below)."

"Devil Dan"
The Scandalous Life of Maj. Gen. Dan Sickles

Before Ms. Rebelle starts this article, our Editor Nadine Mironchuk is back. As you can see by her quote, after I told her who my subject was for this issue, this is what she said: "Yes, Sickles was responsible for a Chelsea [MA] soldier being killed on that stupid salient he went out at on July 2nd. If he wasn't already dead, I'd kill him!" So glad you finally got better from your illness Nadine. We missed you so much. A great big thanks to Saundra Cox who stepped in without hesitation to take over for Nadine.

Maj. Gen. E. Daniel Sickles

After reading about the life of Gen. Hugh Judson Kilpatrick, I thought he was the most scandalous person in the Union Army. However, Gen. Sickles could easily be called "the bad boy of the 1800s." He even had the trial of the century in April 1859.

One of many, many interesting things about Sickles is his choice of a marker for his grave in Arlington National Cemetery. He has a government marker, very understated and like most all of the graves in Arlington. Knowing his personality, it seems like he would have had a marvelously large, over-the-top marker, like so many Civil War generals. Sickles is buried in Section 3, Grave #1906. It seems his second wife, Carmina Creagh Sickles, wanted him to be buried by the New York Memorial in the Gettysburg National Cemetery. Permission was granted, but when the general was close to death, he decided to be buried at Arlington National Cemetery instead.

The very simple stone marking the grave of one of the flashiest characters ever to people the American landscape.
Photo by Janet Greentree

In 1993, a New York man, the late Richard H. Davis, contacted Gettysburg National Park Service Superintendent John Latschar for permission to have Gen. Sickles removed from Arlington and reburied in Gettysburg. Davis went as far as to find a great-great-nephew of Sickles, John V. Shaud, who gave his permission. The Sickles family agreed to pay the costs, but the general is still in Arlington. Sickles comment about being buried in Gettysburg was: "The entire battlefield is a memorial to Dan Sickles."

Daniel Edgar Sickles was born to wealthy parents George Garrett Sickles and Susan Marsh Sickles on October 20, 1819, or possibly on the same date in 1825 in New York City. Even Sickles was vague about the date. More about that later. His father was a patent lawyer, politician, and was also in the printing business. Young Dan attended private school in Glen Falls, NY. At first, he learned the printing trade but then went to the University of New York (now New York University). After graduation, he studied law in the firm of future Union Civil War Gen. Benjamin Butler. Sickles opened a law office even before passing the bar, in 1846. He was elected to the New York State Assembly in 1847. He was part of the Tammany Hall political network - he was elected to the U.S. House of Representatives in 1857 and served until 1861. Dan was described as being handsome and very articulate. He romanced many ladies.

At the age of 32, he married Teresa Da Ponte Bagioli on March 2, 1853, in New York City, against the wishes of both families - when she was 17 and pregnant. Hence, the need to make himself younger than his real birth year of 1819. Teresa was a beautiful young woman and spoke five languages. They had met when Sickles was studying French and Italian so that he could be in the diplomatic corps. He had been friends of her parents for years. Their daughter, Laura, was born

Teresa Da Ponte Bagioli Sickles

in 1854. Sickles spent a lot of time away from home, continuing to romance the ladies and ignore his wife.

Mrs. Sickles then met Phillip Barton Key, son of Francis Scott Key, at the 1857 inaugural ball of Pres. James Buchanan. Key was a friend and legal assistant to Dan Sickles. The Sickles lived on the west side of Lafayette Square in a rented house just across from the White House. The Stockton mansion rented for $3,000 per month. Key rented a house across the street from the

An illustration (left to right) of Dan and Teresa Sickles, and Phillip Barton Key.

Sickles, also on Lafayette Square, which became a liaison point for their romance.

Key would tie a string to the shutters to signify to her that he was at home. In February 1859, Sickles received an anonymous letter from "RPG" informing him of the affair between Teresa and Key. He confronted his wife, who admitted to the affair. She also confessed to liaisons in the Sickles house and rendezvous in Congressional and Oak Hill Cemeteries. Sickles made Teresa write out a confession and had her ladies' maid sign the document as a witness. The next morning, Sickles saw Key in the street, signaling with a white handkerchief to his wife. Sickles grabbed two derringers and a pistol and

went out into the street to kill Key. There were at least a dozen people in the street when Sickles confronted Key.

Sickles said: "Key, you scoundrel. You have dishonored my home. You must die." His first shot only grazed Key. A struggle ensued, and Key tossed his opera glasses at Sickles. Sickles then fired another shot that struck Key in the groin. Key fell to the ground and leaned against a tree shouting: "Don't shoot me!" and "Murder." Sickles next shot misfired. His last shot hit Key in the chest mortally wounding him. Sickles fired another shot at his head, but the gun misfired again.

Key was taken inside the Benjamin Ogle Tayloe house (or the Cosmos Club

Above, left, the mansion that Sickles rented in Lafayette Square; above, right, the Benjamin Ogle Tayloe house, in front of which Key was shot and killed.

Photos by Janet Greentree

next door – old newspapers indicated both) where he quickly died. Sickles said: "Of course I killed him. He deserved it." A White House page, J.H.W. Bonitz, was one of the twelve people

An illustration of the deed being done.

An illustration of the "honorable" Dan Sickles lamenting his situation in prison, not that he took the life of another man.

present. He ran back to the office of Pres. Buchanan and told him what happened. Buchanan gave him money, told him to go on a long indefinite leave, and go back to North Carolina. (Hmmmmm!)

After the deed was done, Sickles turned himself in at Atty. Gen. Jeremiah Black's home, which was only a few blocks away on Franklin Square. Before going to jail, he was allowed to first stop at his house to pick up a few items. One of the items he took was the wedding ring off his wife's finger – she was laying on the floor, crying. He was placed in a cell at the Washington jail at Fourth & G Streets. The cell was small, dark, filthy, and full of bed bugs. Sickles had so many visitors that he was transferred to the jailor's office, where he slept on a cot, had visits from his 6-year-old daughter, meals from home, visits from his dog, and visits from politically connected friends. He was also allowed to keep his personal weapon.

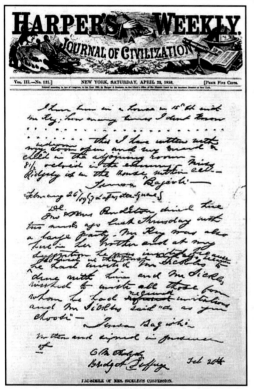

Just so everyone got the picture, Sickle's "Dream Team" of lawyers leaked the written confession of Theresa Sickles' affair with Barton Key to major press outlets, such as Harper's Weekly.

He was charged with murder. The charge read: "Daniel E. Sickles, late of the county of Washington, in the year of our Lord 1859 [had] feloniously, willfully and of his malice afterthought, did make an assault...upon the body of one Phillip Barton Key [with] a pistol of the value of two dollars...by force of the gun powder [and] leaden bullet(s) discharged and shot off [and] did strike, penetrate, and wound [Key]..upon the left side...a little below the 10th rib [with] one mortal wound... the depth of 10 inches and of the breadth of half an inch, of which he...then and there instantly died."

Sickles hired Edwin M. Stanton and James T. Brady as two of his attorneys. Like O.J. Simpson's trial of the century, he also had a team of eight attorneys. Sickles was the first person to use the temporary insanity plea. Stanton pleaded that Sickles had been driven insane by his wife's infidelity and was thus out of his mind when he shot and killed Key. Sickles himself leaked his wife's confession to newspapers, who published it in full. The confession was inadmissible in court, however. One of the witnesses, Congressional Clerk George B. Wooldridge, testified that: "Two days before the slaying, he (Sickles) showed the anonymous note about the affair to him and then Sickles put his hands to his head and sobbed in the lobby of the House of Representatives." The trial of the century lasted 20 days. Sickles was acquitted of murder in 70 minutes. The newspapers of the day said that Sickles was a hero for saving all the ladies of Washington from this rogue named Key. Sickles later forgave his wife but rarely was at home with her or spent any time with her. She contracted tuberculosis and died at the age of 31.

The Civil War was looming in Sickles' immediate future. As it commenced, he raised volunteer units from New York, was appointed colonel, and then, in September 1861, he rose to brigadier general of the Excelsior Brigade. They fought in the Peninsula Campaign, Seven Days, Fredericksburg, and Gettysburg. Sickles was a close friend of Gen. Joseph Hooker. It was said that their Army headquarters were like a rowdy bar and bordello. Pres. Abraham Lincoln nominated Sickles for major general in November 1862. The commission did not get approved until March 1863. Sickles was now in charge of the III Corps, the first commander of a corps not to have graduated from any military academy.

At Gettysburg on July 2nd, Gen. George Meade ordered Sickles to take position at the southern end of Cemetery Hill. He wasn't happy with his orders to connect up with Gen. Winfield Scott Hancock by occupying the space on the ridge that dipped low and marched his men almost a mile in front of Cemetery Ridge, instead, creating a salient that could be fired on from multiple sides. Meade held a meeting with his Corps commanders that Sickles missed. Meade and Gen. Gouverneur K. Warren rode out to see why he took the position he did. Sickles offered to withdraw, but Meade said no. Now Sickles was in the direct line of Gen. James Longstreet's attack. Sickles was wounded near the Trostle Barn by a cannon ball that mangled his right leg. Refusing to risk lowering his men's spirits by seeing him incapacitated, he was carried on a stretcher sitting up puffing on a cigar and grinning.

Sickles was taken to the Daniel Schaeffer farm on Taneytown Road, where his right leg was removed above his knee by surgeon Thomas Sims. He and the amputated leg were evacuated to Washington. The leg was later sent in a small coffin-shaped box to the National Museum of Health and Medicine, where it still resides today. The attached card said: "With the compliments of Major Gen. D.E.S." Sickles went to visit his leg for years on the anniversary of the battle. The farmhouse where Sickles' leg was amputated at 259 Baltimore Pike, not Taneytown Road.

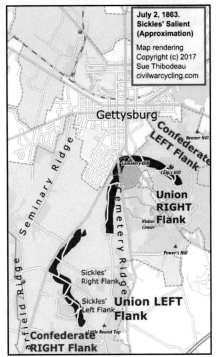

Thirty-four years after the battle, Sickles received the Medal of Honor. The citation stated: "that Sickles displayed most conspicuous gallantry on the field, vigorously contesting the advance of the enemy and continuing to encourage his troops after being himself severely wounded."

Sickles wanted to continue serving in the Army, but Gen. Ulysses S. Grant would not let him return to combat. He commanded the Department of South Carolina, Department of the South and the Second Military District. In 1869, he retired with his major general rank.

In 1869, he was appointed U.S. Minister of Spain and served to 1874. It was rumored that he had an affair with the deposed Queen Isabella II. He met and married a second time in Spain to Carmina Creagh on September 27, 1852. They had two children – Stanton and Eda. In 1888, he became president of the New York Board of Civil Service Commissioners and sheriff of New York County in 1890. In 1893, he was elected to the 53rd Congress. He was the chairman of the New York Monuments Commission but got into another scrape when $27,000 was found to be missing from the monument fund. Gen. Longstreet's widow

Gen. Sickles' ill-advised salient caught the Third Division in a storm of chaos, as enfilading fire was poured onto his troops from three sides when the portion of the Union line managed by him was brought out so far in front of the main Union position on July 2nd, 1863, at the Battle of Gettysburg.

Helen, in 1913, offered to raise money for Sickles. She said it was Longstreet's fault he was wounded and lost his leg, and wanted to help. His wife Carmina even pawned $8,000 of her jewelry in 1912 to help with the monument scandal, but Sickles would not take the money. The monument to the Excelsior Brigade was erected on July 2, 1893 at Gettysburg, on Excelsior Field. The monument was to have a bust of Gen. Sickles inside the five pillars, but that didn't happen because of the money scandal. He attended the 30-year reunion at Gettysburg on July 2, 1893, posing for pictures with fellow Confederate and Union generals, and at the Trostle barn where he was wounded. He was also heavily involved getting the Gettysburg battlefield saved and made into the Gettysburg National Military Park. The black wrought iron fence that surrounded Lafayette Square when he killed Phillip Barton Key was pro-

At far left, a large rock marks the spot near the Trostle Farm where Sickles was brought and laid down when wounded. At near left, the cannon shot damage to the Trostle barn is testament to the battle that raged and made many casualties that day.

Left to right: Gen. Joseph B. Carr, Gen. Dan Sickles and Gen. Charles K. Graham meet after the war at the site where Sickles was wounded.

Carmina Creagh Sickles

The Excelsior Brigade monument at Gettysburg.

cured by Sickles and now surrounds the Gettysburg National Cemetery.

There are so many stories about Dan Sickles. He had a mistress, Fanny White, who was a well-known madam in New York City. He took her to London in the 1850s while newly married to the pregnant Teresa. He introduced Fanny to Queen Victoria, using the alias last name of a political rival. He was also censured for bringing Fanny into his chambers at the New York State Assembly. When he returned to Teresa, Fanny was so angry, she followed him into a hotel where she attacked him with a whip.

Another story included Mary Todd Lincoln. She and the president visited with Sickles' division in 1862. Sickles tried to cure the president's melancholy by having several young women start kissing Lincoln on the face. Mrs. Lincoln was not amused.

Rumors that he was near death circulated in March 1913. When a reporter telephoned his home to inquire as to his health, Sickles said: "Yes, this is Gen. Sickles. Am I ill? Nonsense, I was never better in my life. There's nothing to that story. It's all a lie." Sickles died on May 3, 1914, at his home at 23 Fifth Avenue in New York City, at age 94, of a cerebral hemorrhage. The house is now the Rubin Hall Dorm and part of New York University. Although he had been estranged from his second wife and children for 29 years, his wife Carmina and son Stanton were at his bedside when he died. It seems that his wife would not come to his home until his secretary, Miss Eleanora Wilmerding, moved out of the house. The general had been ill for about two weeks.

Major Gen. Daniel E. Sickles' funeral was held at St. Patrick's Cathedral. The *New York Times* reported: "The body will be escorted to the Cathedral.... By the Twelfth Regiment, New York National Guard, of which Gen. Sickles was once a member, two troops of cavalry, and the First Battery, Field Artillery. Members of the Phil Kearny Post, G.A.R. will also be in the escort." From the May 8, 1914 *New York Times:* "Fifteen of the forty surviving members of the Phil Kearny Grand Army Post...will be the pallbearers in a more ceremonious memorial procession from the Sickles home to St. Patrick's Cathedral...." The body was escorted to Pennsylvania Station for the train ride to Washington, D.C.

At left, scenes of the funeral of Gen. Daniel E. Sickles, who killed his wife's lover while womanizing for years; was both court-martialed and awarded the Medal of Honor for his Gettysburg actions, and who never spent a dull moment in his 94 years.

The Cashtown Inn

Ms. Rebelle's first cousin is Alan Norris, our Ohio family member. His very lovely wife, Carol, is the sweetest person ever, and she loves the study of the Civil War, too. My father and his mother were brother and sister. My family's annual vacation was to go to Ohio and stay with the Norris family. Alan is the middle son and has an older brother Jim and a younger brother Dave, who is my age. Alan is also named for my father, our family's first Civil War enthusiast. President Ronald Reagan appointed Alan as a Federal Judge and he sits in Cincinnati.

The author's cousins Alan and Carol Norris from Ohio.
Photo by Janet Greentree

At a very sad occasion, his Mom's funeral, we discovered we had this mutual Civil War interest. Somehow, I think his Mom arranged that. They have been coming out East here for quite a few years now, mostly making Gettysburg their headquarters and branching off on other trips around the area, including the Booth escape route. That's another one of Alan and Carol's passions. Since I had been on several Booth escape route tours, I mapped out the roads for their tour. Alan is a diligent researcher, and I'm sure could have done it all on his own. For my help though, they knew I had always wanted to stay at the Cashtown Inn outside Gettysburg, so they gave me a free overnight stay there.

For my stay at the renowned (and haunted) Cashtown Inn, outside Gettysburg, PA, I was able to book the Gen. John Daniel Imboden Room. Imboden was my Confederate ancestor's commanding officer, so I requested that room. It fronts on the Cashtown Pike, and my room was on the left, second floor corner. One of windows looks right up the road where Lee came down with his troops to converge on Gettysburg. If you close your eyes, you can almost see the dust and troops coming down that road in late June of 1863. The only thing different is that it is paved now. It was truly a thrill to stay there. The Inn is now a bed-and-breakfast, run by Jack and Mary Paladino. Mary does the greeting and business end, and Jack is the excellent cook. He made a fantastic breakfast for me the next morning.

Two views of the Cashtown Inn - modern-day (photo by Janet Greentree) and an antique card view.

The Inn has been there since 1797. The innkeeper in June of 1863 was Jacob Mickley. He said it looked as if the entire force under Lee had passed within twenty feet of his barroom. Gen. A.P. Hill made the Inn his headquarters. Gen. Henry Heth stayed there too. A.P. Hill's room was next to mine in the front. Gen, Hill was under the weather when he arrived at the Inn. There is a spring that runs through the cellar that was supposed to be very healthy for those who are sick. The cellar also had two very large brick ovens where the Confederates baked bread. The waitress at breakfast said she hates to go down in the cellar, as it is very, very creepy.

The name Cashtown came from the first innkeeper, Peter Marck, who insisted on only cash payments for the services, goods, and tolls he collected. The current Innkeeper says the cellar is also the site of the first death in the Gettysburg campaign. It seems that locals Henry Hahn and David Powell drew a line across the Cashtown Pike at Gallagher's Knob, daring any Rebs to cross over the line. They laid in wait for the Rebs. One of Jubal Early's Georgia boys came over the line, was mortally wounded and died, and then was taken to the Cashtown Inn. The publication Blue and Gray, however, claims the man died in the A.P. Hill room, upstairs.

After the battle, Gen. Imboden made the Inn his headquarters for the march back to Virginia. The 17-mile-long wagon train began at the Cashtown Inn, departing at 4:00 p.m. on July 4th.

The Inn was featured in the movie "Gettysburg". Several of the actors stayed there during the filming, including Gen. Buford, a/k/a Sam Elliott. There are several pictures in the front room from the movie. I'm sure you remember the scene shot there with A.P. Hill, a/k/a Patrick Falci, coming out of the Inn in his red shirt to greet Gen. Lee. The Inn was also featured in Mark Nesbitt's book Ghosts of Gettysburg and a cover story in the Blue and Gray.

The view out the window in the Imboden Room, where you can imagine Lee's troops tromping up and passing by to get to Gettysburg.
Photo by Janet Greentree

Ms. Rebelle spent somewhat of an uneasy night there. There is no TV, so I decided to read the journals left in the room. Everyone writes something about their stay in the room. I must say, some of the things are a little suspect, but some are downright spooky.

All the time there, I kept smelling roses. There was no potpourri in the room. I had a very strange dream that I've never had before and woke up saying "You're not going to do that to me." Whatever 'it' was, stopped when I woke up. I felt as though I were covered in a sheet of blue gauze and was swatting at it as I awoke.

The next morning Innkeeper Jack said there is a woman Mary that haunts that room. The smell of roses comes from her. She was there during the battle trying to protect her family. He said a lot of people wake up feeling like someone is patting them or smoothing out their hair. I asked him if he had had any experiences there, but he says he's not susceptible to those things. He did say he was standing in the bar area once and felt someone push him. He turned around and no one was there. Lots of people wrote of the creaking floors and stairs, of things falling off tables in the

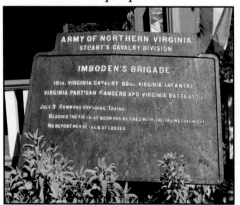

A marker noting Gen. Imboden's movements in the Cashtown area during the Gettysburg campaign is outside the Cashtown Inn.
Photo by Janet Greentree

room, the feeling of someone walking back and forth at the end of the bed, and the strange closet that won't open in the room. It was an OK experience in a haunted inn, and a most interesting adventure for Ms. Rebelle. I would stay there again.

One of cousin Alan's passions is the list of "140 Things every Battlefield Guide Should Know." He has found 55 of the 140 already. Every time we get together, and sometimes with Yankee Nan, a/k/a Madame President Nancy Anwyll, we try to find some of the things on the list. This time, we cousins found the name A.C. Coble, 1st NC Reg., etched in a rock on Culp's Hill at Gettysburg. Alan and Carol's research found that Coble created the only carving by a Confederate soldier on the battlefield. He was a private in Company E and was the unit's color-bearer at the battle. The rock marks the spot where he held his regiment's colors .

I absolutely couldn't wait to get home to send the photo to our round table's tour guide Kevin Anastas to see if he knew where that was. He did. We were all crestfallen! We got Kevin on another one though. Gen. John Rutter Brook carved an "X" in a rock in another area of Culp's Hill. We found that one, and Kevin didn't know about it! He said he's adding it to his tours now. If I can ever get Alan and Carol out here on a meeting date, Alan would be an excellent speaker. He does a presentation for his fellow judges and Civil War enthusiasts of all his tours when he returns home from his many travels. It's pretty neat to have relatives with whom to share Civil War interests and information. We have such fun together.

Maj. Gen. Lunsford Lindsay Lomax, CSA

This story could have been tragic, but Fate was looking out for Ms. Rebelle and - fortunately - the story turned rather funny instead. Early on in my travels to find Civil War generals' graves, I ran into Don Hakenson in Herndon and asked him if he knew where Gen. Lunsford Lomax's gravesite is located in the Warrenton Cemetery. He hand-drew a map for me showing that the general's burial site is located in the middle of a hedge that has overgrown the site, not too far from the grave of Col. John Singleton Mosby.

All alone (which is never a good way to visit cemeteries), I drove through the cemetery until I saw a very large hedge totally surrounding his grave, except for about a 4" opening. In addition to having only 4" to get inside the hedge, insects were flying all over the place. I decided that, since I was there and he was right there buried inside, I would just push quickly through the opening. Well, unbeknownst to me, a foot marker jutted out of the ground just inside the hedge. I tripped on it and fell flat on my face inside the hedge. Being the photographer that I am, I was very grateful my camera didn't get broken.

Maj. Gen. Lunsford Lomax during the Civil War. He was known as 'The Black Knight' for his jet-black hair, and choosing pure black horses to ride on the field.

Thank goodness the good Lord was looking out for me that day, as I came very close to hitting my head on the general's marker, and, who knows when or if I would have been found. Once inside, I got my picture, but then I had to push back through the hedge to get to "freedom." Luckily, for all of you who today may be searching for his grave, the terrible hedge has since been removed.

Above: the Lomax marker in Warrenton Cemetery, with the hedge surrounding site (photo by Janet Greentree); below, Dan Carr, a reenactor portraying Gen. Lomax at the grave, minus hedge (photo by Gwen Wyttenbach).

Lunsford Lindsay Lomax was born into the First Families of Virginia in Newport, Rhode Island, on November 4, 1835, while his father was stationed at Fort Walcott. His father was Major Mann Paige Lomax, who served in the 3rd U.S. Artillery as an ordnance officer. His mother was Elizabeth Virginia Lindsay, a descendant of Captain Lindsay, who commanded a company under 'Light Horse' Harry Lee in the Revolutionary War.

Lomax received his early education in both Richmond and Norfolk, Virginia. He was appointed "at large" to West Point, since he didn't have a direct Congressional sponsor. He graduated West Point 21st out of 49 in the class of 1856. His best friend at the Point was future Confederate Gen. Fitzhugh Lee. Upon graduation, Lomax was assigned to the Second Cavalry upon graduation and served on the plains of Kansas and Nebraska. He resigned his commission as first lieutenant on April 25, 1861, after the Civil War commenced.

He rose to captain in the Virginia Militia and served as adjutant general under Gen. Joseph Johnston. His next assignment was serving on the staff of Gen. Benjamin McCulloch in the Western theater. When McCulloch was killed at Pea Ridge, he served on the staff of Gen. Earl Van Dorn as lieutenant colonel. He returned to Virginia in February, 1863 when he was appointed colonel of the 11th Virginia Cavalry. After reorganization of JEB Stuart's Cavalry, he was promoted to brigadier

Photo of Gen. Benjamin McCulloch's Staff – Gen. Lunsford Lomax seated, at left; Gen. Francis Crawford Armstrong is standing behind Lomax, and the others in the photo are not known.

Unidentified illustration of Gen. Lomax riding in battle.

general on July 23, 1863. At Gettysburg, he served under Gen. William E. Jones; he fought in the battles of Brandy Station, Winchester, Rector's Crossroads, Upperville, and Buckland — leading up to Gettysburg.

Later, he served with his friend Fitzhugh Lee and commanded three regiments – the 5th, 6th, and 15th Virginia Cavalry. These units fought at Culpeper Courthouse, Morton's Ford, Todd's Tavern, Wilderness, Cold Harbor, Yellow Tavern, Reams Station, and Trevalian Station. At Yellow Tavern, Lomax was holding off the Union forces of Gen. Wesley Merritt when Gen. JEB Stuart arrived and subsequently was mortally wounded.

Lomax was promoted to major general in August 1864. He fought under Gen. Jubal Early in the Valley at Third Winchester, Fisher's Hill and Cedar Creek. He led the attack against Col. Charles Russell Lowell when Lowell was mortally wounded at Cedar Creek. Lomax was captured at Tom's Brook by Gen. Torbett's Cavalry on October 9, 1864, but within three hours, he overpowered his captors and escaped. On March 29, 1865, Lomax commanded the troops in the Shenandoah Valley and supervised intelligence gathering services for Col. Mosby. Following Appomatox, his command surrendered on April 25, 1865 in Greensboro, North Carolina with Gen. Joseph Johnston.

After the War, he returned to Warrenton, became a farmer and married Elizabeth Winter Payne in 1873 in Fauquier County. He had a rather interesting life after farming, featuring many different forms of employment. He was Superintendent of Fauquier County Schools and served as Superintendent of the Stationary Department at the U.S. House of Representatives, but was removed from office in 1882; he was in charge of river and harbor improvements in St. John's, Florida; and was the 4th president of the Virginia Agricultural and Mechanical College (later Virginia Tech), from 1885-1890. He also worked in Washington, D.C., on the Official Records of the Civil War. Lomax's final position before retiring was as commissioner of the Gettysburg National Military Park between 1905 and 1913.

According to the 1910 census of Gettysburg, he lived with his wife and daughters at 289 Carlisle Street in Gettysburg. Enlisting my daughter Lisa Tully once again as researcher, she checked out

Elizabeth Winter Payne Lomax

whether there was a house still standing at that address on Carlisle Street; her visit to the locale highlighted some street-numbering confusion. Present-day Google Maps fixes 289 in the middle of Stevens Street, near the corner of Carlisle Street, even though the number is not enumerated at the location. The house is now a sorority house for Gettysburg College. The house number may have changed, as happens over the years.

In a newspaper column published in 1920 in the *Baltimore Sun* published some time after Col. Mosby's death in 1916, Col. Mosby is quoted as having said the following about Lomax: "Lomax had also arranged for me to begin independent operations in Loudoun County to the North.... At that time I only had a few men, less than a dozen but we soon expanded and trained the men we had. We never were a large group nor were we designed to be a large fighting force. We had to form up and dissolve into the

Former Lomax residence in Gettysburg, PA.
Photo by Lisa Greentree Tully

Gen. Lomax (sixth from left - slightly behind) with the committee members who were managing the establishment of the Virginia monument at the Gettysburg battlefield, on Seminary Ridge, recognized as the equestrian statue of Gen. Robert E. Lee.

countryside in a few minutes. Secrecy was our greatest ally. We didn't drill like regulars and we had no permanent camps to provide that camp drudgery so disliked by regulars. We used dinner bells and whistles to signal with and to cause assembly...." Lomax and Mosby were close friends.

Gen. Lomax died May 28, 1913. The Washington Post published his obituary on May 29, 1913. It notes his passing as follows: "Confederate General Succumbs to Injuries Received from a Fall – General Lunsford Lindsay Lomax, aged 78 years, a Confederate soldier died at Providence Hospital yesterday morning as the result of a fall sustained two weeks earlier while visiting his daughter in Warrenton, Virginia. He broke his hip. Funeral services will be held today at his home in Warrenton, VA. He was the oldest major general of cavalry in the Confederate Army living and was one of the three commissioners of the Gettysburg National Military Park. The Honorary Pallbearers for his funeral will be Gen. Richard Loder of NY, Major Holmes Conrad of Winchester, Gen. Marcus Wright and Major Robert Coward of Washington, Eppa Hunton and Judge L.L. Lewis of Richmond, Gen. Thomas Smith, Moses Groom, Dr. Robert Hicks of Warrenton, and Col. Robert (Preston) Chew of Charles Town, WV. The active pallbearers will be Robert E. Lee, grandson of the Confederate general, Dr. Edgar Snowden, Henry Robinson, George B. Stone and William Meredith of Washington, Granville Gaines and Dr. Douglas of Warrenton, and Frank R. Pemberton of NY." Note: Gen. Eppa Hunton died in 1908, so, the Eppa Hunton mentioned above must be a son.

Gen. Lomax shares space in the Warrenton Cemetery with Col. John Singleton Mosby and Gen. William Fitzhugh Payne. His name is listed backwards, as Lindsay Lunsford Lomax, on his marker (at right).

Gen. Lomax's marker at Warrenton Cemetery, Warrenton, VA.
Photo by Janet Greentree

The Confederate Spy Buried in Wisconsin

Sooooo, who do you think it is? First clue – it is a woman. Is it Rose O'Neal Greenhow – no, she is buried in Oakdale Cemetery in Wilmington, NC. Is it Antonia Ford – no, she is buried in Oak Hill Cemetery in Washington, D.C. Second clue – she is practically a local girl. Is it Laura Ratcliffe – no, she is buried in Herndon, VA, in front of the Holiday Inn. Could it be Elizabeth Van Lew (Crazy Bet) – no, she is buried in Shockhoe Cemetery in Richmond, VA. Although Van Lew lived in Richmond, she was a Union spy.

Do you all give up? It is the ultimate spy - Belle Boyd - who was on a speaking tour when she died in Wisconsin Dells, WI, formerly known as Kilbourne City. She was at a Grand Army of the Republic Hall talking about her book "Belle Boyd in Camp and Prison" when she died of a heart attack, on stage. It is totally amazing to me, given the number of times people were buried, disinterred, and moved elsewhere after an initial burial, that she was left in Wisconsin, instead of being brought back to Virginia, her home state.

After reading that people brought Virginia dirt to her grave in Wisconsin, Ms. Rebelle took a small package of dirt to put on her grave, along with a Confederate flag, denoting her allegiance during the war. Luckily, TSA didn't confiscate either item from me. There have been pictures I've seen of her grave with many Confederate flags on it. When I arrived, there was only the 1st National. I'm sure my little flag won't stay there long, but I put it there for her.

Ms. Rebelle at the gravesite of the notorious Belle Boyd, holding the native Virginia soil she sprinkled around the site. The fact that Boyd is located so very far away from the center of her exploits doesn't seem right, says the author.

Photo by Kathe Schrader Fernandez

Isabella Maria, a/k/a Belle Boyd, was born on September 9, 1844, in Martinsburg, VA (now WV), to Benjamin Reed Boyd and Mary Rebecca Glenn Boyd. The Boyds were a very prosperous family with strong Southern ties. Belle's father was a soldier in the Stonewall Brigade. Several members of her family were convicted of being Confederate spies. Belle described her childhood as idyllic. She was quite a tomboy; strong-willed, high-spirited, and the oldest of her siblings. She loved riding horses. She once rode a horse into her home when her parents told her she was too young to attend a party they were having. Her house still stands in Front Royal, next to the Warren Rifles Museum. She was educated at the Mount Washington Female College in Baltimore, Maryland. She had her coming-out party as a debutante in Washington, D.C.

Belle Boyd in her Confederate regalia, playing her part as a Rebel spy to the hilt.

Belle, at age 17, had just returned home from Baltimore on July 4, 1861, when Union soldiers came to the hotel in Front Royal that her father ran. They had heard that she had Confederate flags in her room. In retaliation, they hung the Union flag outside her home. The Union soldiers cursed at her mother. Belle stated: "I could stand it no longer… we ladies were obliged to go armed in order to protect ourselves as best we might from insult and outrage." At one point, Belle pulled out a pistol she had hidden in her skirts, fired upon a Union soldier, and killed him. She was exonerated from punishment, but guards were positioned around her house to keep track of her activities. She was extremely good at flirting and charmed the Union men. She watched all that was going on, and sent the information to generals Stonewall Jackson and P.G.T. Beauregard.

In May 1862, at a local hotel, she hid in a closet, hollowed out a knothole and listened to Gen. James Shields and his staff discussing tactics. Belle mounted a horse and rode to Gen. Turner Ashby to tell him the information. When Jackson's men advanced to Front Royal on May 23, 1862, she rode to meet the troops, incurring bullet holes in both her skirt and purse from enemy fire. She told Jackson "the force was very small, and he could charge right down and he will catch them all." Gen. Jackson gave her the rank of a captain, an honorary aide-de-camp designation, and the Southern Cross of Honor.

Jackson also gave her a pass to go through his lines. An historical marker, located in Front Royal, references her ride. Her favorite outfit was a gray frock coat, butternut kepi, and a velvet headband with the seven stars of the Confederacy. To complete her outfit, she added a pair of shoulder straps with her "rank" - Lt. Col., Fifth VA Regiment, Confederate Army.

Belle Boyd was arrested on July 29, 1862, after being reported by her lover as a spy. She was sent to the Old Capitol Prison. Secretary of War Edwin Stanton had issued a warrant for her arrest. She was far from a model prisoner, and waved Confederate flags from her window, sang Dixie, and concocted a scheme to communicate with her supporters below. A rubber ball was shot into her cell by a supporter. Belle would sew messages inside the ball and throw it back outside. There must have been some pretty lax guards guarding her.

Old Capitol Prison—where Belle Boyd made a general pain of herself to federal authorities.

Another inquiry was later held, and she was kept at the prison until August 29, 1862, when she was exchanged at Fort Monroe. In June 1863, she was released after contracting typhoid fever.

Following her recovery, she attempted to travel to England, but was stopped by a Union blockade and sent to Canada. At the time, she was carrying letters from Pres. Jefferson Davis. She flirted with and distracted Union Naval Officer Samuel Wylde Hardinge; he took her as prisoner, but allowed the Confederate captain of the boat in which she had arrived to escape capture. Hardinge was court-martialed and discharged from the Navy. She was then sent to Boston, where she stayed at the Tremont Hotel. She was ordered out of the country and told never to put her foot on United States soil again or she would be shot without trial. Hardinge and Belle later married in England. She had one child with him, a daughter Grace. Hardinge died in 1866.

Belle Boyd later in life.

She married her second husband, John Swainston Hammond, in 1869, in New Orleans. They had four children – two boys - Arthur and John - and two girls - Byrd and Maria Isabelle. They divorced in 1884, and Belle married her third husband, Nathaniel Rue High, in 1885. They had no children; she was married to him until her death.

After the Civil War, Belle became an actress, traveling the country giving dramatic lectures about her exploits as a spy during the Civil War. She wrote a two-volume book entitled: "Belle Boyd in Camp and Prison," which she discussed at her lectures. She billed her show as "The Perils of a Spy."

While in Kilbourne City (now Wisconsin Dells), at a Grand Army of the Republic Hall speaking about her book, she had a heart attack on stage and died at age 55 on June 11, 1900. She is buried in Spring Grove Cemetery in Wisconsin Dells. Members of the local GAR served as her pallbearers. The monument on her grave says: "Belle Boyd, Confederate Spy, Born in Virginia, Died in Wisconsin and was buried in Spring Grove Cemetery, Erected by a Comrade."

During her Civil War days, she was known as 'the Cleopatra of the Secession,' 'the Siren of the Shenandoah,' 'La Belle Rebelle,' 'the Rebel Joan of Arc,' and 'Amazon of Secessia.'

Boston, Mount Auburn Cemetery and Gen. Benjamin "Beast" Butler

First of all, I must say that I LOVE the Civil War Round Table of Greater Boston. My sister, Kathe, and I toured the New England states which included three days in Boston. Six of their members, Al Smith, Dave Smith, Marilyn Greenfield, Alan Smolinski, Joyce Kelly, Ingeborg Reichenbach, and Nadine Mironchuk (our driver through the maze of Boston streets and traffic) all turned out to greet us. They treated us to many historical sites in the Boston area and many good meals together. What a fun group they are.

Our tour started in Stoughton, MA. One wonders if it was named for Union Gen. Edwin Stoughton, captured by Col. John Singleton Mosby, but the general was born in Vermont. Our first stop on the agenda was a visit to the GAR (Grand Army of the Republic) Hall and Museum in Lynn, Massachusetts, where the Gen. Lander Civil War Round Table, and (occasionally) The Civil

The Grand Army Hall in Lynn features many historic items, including (in foreground) the capstan from the *U.S.S. Kearsarge*. In background, at left, are the ceremonial chairs, and surrounding the walls are the faces of the 1,200 men who fought and later met to share their memories of the Civil War, and to aid their brethren in difficulty following the war.

Photo by Greg Mironchuk

War Round Table of Greater Boston meets. What an absolutely amazing place this is. I kept saying how much the BRCWRT members would love to see this place. The Hall was built in 1885 and is one of many in the country. There are 210 GAR Halls alone in Massachusetts. The main hall on the third floor is 56' x 46' and has original furnishings and photos of the veterans line every wall. There are many historical artifacts in the Hall, which is now a museum, including a large frame filled with carte de visites of all the Lincoln assassination conspirators, President and Mrs. Abraham Lincoln, and Boston Corbett who killed John Wilkes Booth. There is a signed note from Lincoln to Secretary of War Stanton, the last Confederate flag to fly over Richmond, and many, many more very interesting things.

The hall is named for Gen. Frederick W. Lander, who was wounded at Ball's Bluff and later died from illness in Paw Paw, VA. His funeral procession through Washington, D.C., was led by Pres. Lincoln. On May 7, 1979, the Lynn GAR Hall was added to the National Registry of Historic Places.

Alan Smolinski gave all of us a wonderful tour of Mount Auburn Cemetery in Cambridge, MA. Joyce Kelly was his able assistant. There are ten Civil War generals buried in the cemetery – George Andrews,

Members of the CWRT of Greater Boston at Mount Auburn Cemetery, Cambridge, MA. L to R - Dave Smith, Alan Smolinski, Al Smith, Nadine Mironchuk, Kathe Fernandez (Ms. Rebelle's sister), and (front,) Joyce Kelly.
Photo by Janet Greentree

71

James Carleton, Robert Cowdoin, Charles Devens, Jr., Henry Eustis, Edward Hincks, Albion Howe, Charles Russell Lowell, Charles Paine, and Thomas Stevenson. In addition to the generals, many historic figures are also buried in the cemetery including Edwin Booth, Dorothea Dix, Mary Baker Eddy, Edward Everett, Oliver Wendell Holmes, Julia Ward Howe, Ernest Longfellow, a memorial monument to Robert Gould Shaw, and Charles Sumner.

At every stop, Alan gave us a narrative of the person's accomplishments and connections to the Civil War. We also stopped at other notable's graves with Civil War connections. Hollywood Cemetery in Richmond is patterned after Mount Auburn. The cemetery was founded in 1831. The founders of the cemetery believed that burying and commemorating the dead was best done in a tranquil and natural setting. The cemetery is full of ornamental plantings, beautiful old trees, flowers, fences, and fountains. It was a joy to finally see this as I've heard Alan and Joyce talk about it so much over the years.

Our able driver, Nadine, gave us a tour of downtown Boston stopping at the Robert Gould Shaw Memorial on the edge of Boston Commons. The sculpture was done by Augustus Saint-Gaudens and Stanford White. It was begun in 1885 and not completed for another fourteen years. The memorial was commissioned by a group of Bostonians to honor Colonel Shaw and the 54th MA. He rides erect with his regiment. There is a winged female figure hovering over Shaw and his troops. She has poppies in her hand, the traditional emblem of death and remembrance, plus an olive branch for victory and peace. The monument is very beautiful. In 1982, 62 names of the gallant soldiers of the 54th MA who gave their lives in the war were inscribed on the back of the monument. Shaw's story was made into the movie Glory in 1989. The poet, Robert Lowell made reference to Shaw and the memorial in his poem "For the Union Dead." The Shaw neighborhood in D.C. was also named for Robert Gould Shaw.

The iconic Robert Gould Shaw Memorial in Boston, MA.

Photo by Janet Greentree

A warm October day in Boston took us out in the Boston Harbor for a boat ride to George's Island and Fort Warren. Fort Warren is a star fort built in 1833. It protected the shipping channels and was named for Dr. Joseph Warren, a patriot, who deployed Paul Revere and William Dawes to alert Lexington and Concord on the night before the Revolution began. Dr. Warren was killed at the battle of Bunker Hill. It is much larger than Fort Sumter and Fort McHenry. The fort defended Boston Harbor from 1833 through the end of World War II. During the Civil War the fort served as a prison for Confederate officers and government officials. Among the many notable Confederates held there were Gens. Richard S. Ewell, Isaac Ridgeway Trimble, John Gregg, Adam Rankin "Stovepipe" Johnson, Simon Bolivar Buckner, and Lloyd Tilghman. Vice President of the Confederacy Alexander Stephens and Confederate Postmaster General John Henninger Reagan were also held there. A very kind Park Ranger showed us an area of the fort that is similar to where Alexander Stephens was

Fort Warren on George's Island in Boston Harbor was the site of the imprisonment of Conf. Vice Pres. Alexander Stephens.

Photo by Janet Greentree

held. The song '*John Brown's Body*' was written at the fort, incorporating an old Methodist camp song. Julia Ward Howe heard the song while in Washington, D.C. She wrote new words for the song at the Willard Hotel, and it was then called The Battle Hymn of the Republic. The song is one of the most remembered songs of the Civil War era. My friend Nadine knows of my interest in finding the graves of Civil War generals around the country. When asked what things we would like to see in the Boston area, the grave of Gen. Benjamin Butler came up.

His grave, however, is in the Hildreth Family Cemetery in Lowell, Massachusetts, and is locked to the public. Nadine (who says she's a member of a Secret Cemetery Society) found

The author gains access to the private Hildreth family cemetery where Gen. Benjamin Butler is buried, in Lowell, MA.

Photo by Nadine Mironchuk

someone to contact for the key, so Ms. Rebelle was able to personally unlock the cemetery gate to get into Butler's locked cemetery. Of course, it wasn't entirely easy as the first cemetery address we came to had a lock that our key wouldn't fit. A woman across the street saw what we were trying to do and pointed us to the cemetery gate just adjacent to the other one. There were two huge locks to open before we could actually access the correct cemetery. Butler has a huge stone noting his accomplishments. Butler's daughter Blanche was married to Gen. Adelbert Ames, who is also buried in the cemetery.

We all know of Butler's General Order No. 28 made in New Orleans proclaiming that if any woman should insult or show contempt for any officer or solider of the United States, she shall be regarded and shall be held liable to be treated as a woman of the town plying her avocation, i.e., a prostitute. This is dedicated to my late friend and BRCWRT member, Bev Regeimbal, who had a chamber pot with Butler's face at the bottom of it.

Another first for me was visiting a cemetery at night. Gen. Frederick West Lander is buried in Salem, MA. After attending an evening 2nd South Carolina String Band concert in Beverly with Nadine, we went to Salem to find the general. By that time, it was dark, but there was open access to the cemetery. Unfortunately, his brass marker has been stolen, but I have a picture of where it used to be! Lander is famous out West as a trailblazer in Wyoming prior to the Civil War. He is one of many Civil War generals to have married an actress, which is odd, since they were held in such ill repute. Maybe because his wife was a famous New York celebrity, it passed muster.

President Dave Smith of the CWRT of Greater Boston also showed us Gen. Nathaniel Prentiss Bank's grave in Waltham, MA.

All in all, my sister and I traveled 2,500 miles through 12 states to see the sites and fall color. We hit every single New England state, and I have twenty-five more generals' graves to add to my total.

L to R: Gen. Ben Butler; Gen. Adalbert Ames; Gen. Frederick Lander; Jean Davenport Lander; Gen. Nathaniel Banks.

Gens. Gouverneur K. Warren & Joshua L. Chamberlain

Before arriving in Boston, Massachusetts, and enjoying the trip I told you about in last month's Stone Wall, my sister and I started our New England tour at West Point. John Milton Brannan and Eugene Asa Carr, the two generals I missed on the West Point trip in June with Gwen Wyttenbach, were found this time. These two bring the total of Civil War generals' graves I located at West Point to 28. We crossed over the Hudson River to Beacon, NY, and found Gen. Henry Eugene Davies at St. Luke's Church. The next general to be found was Joseph K. Fenno Mansfield, in Middletown, Connecticut. Our next stop was Island Cemetery in Newport, Rhode Island. What a beautiful and charming little town Newport is. The ocean is so blue and the mansions along the ocean are truly spectacular.

Gen. Gouverneur K. Warren

Island Cemetery has three generals buried there – Gen. Thomas West Sherman, Isaac Ingalls Stevens and Gouverneur Kemble Warren. Gen. Warren, known as the Hero of Little Round Top at the Battle of Gettysburg, was born January 8, 1830, in Cold Spring, New York, on the Hudson River, just across from West Point. Warren was named for Gouverneur Kemble, a local congressman, industrialist and diplomat. He entered West Point at the age of 16 and graduated in 1850, second in his class out of 44 cadets. He was commissioned a second lieutenant in the Corps of Topographical Engineers.

Before the Civil War, he worked on the Mississippi River, did transcontinental railroad surveys and - in 1857 - created the first map of the United States west of the Mississippi. He also surveyed the Minnesota River Valley. The River Warren in Minnesota was named in his honor after his death.

When the Civil War began, he was a mathematics professor at West Point. He raised a local regiment and was appointed lieutenant colonel of the 5th New York Infantry in May, 1861. His regiment saw their first combat at Big Bethel. Assisting Gen. Andrew Humphries, he commanded his regiment at the Siege of Yorktown in 1862, in the Peninsula Campaign. Warren drew detailed maps of the peninsula for the army to follow. He was wounded in the knee at Gaines Mill and refused to be taken from the field. His brigade stopped the attack by the Confederates at Malvern Hill near Richmond. He was promoted to brigadier general in September 1862.

Warren's star shone at Gettysburg. He quickly realized the importance of the position of the left flank of the Union Army on Little Round Top, which was left unoccupied. He instructed Col. Strong Vincent to occupy the position just minutes before being attacked and saved the small hill. Warren assumed command of the V Corps after Gen. Winfield Scott Hancock returned from medical leave. Warren's statue by Karl Gerhardt has a commanding presence on a rock on top of Little Round Top at Gettysburg. The statue was dedicated in 1888. In addition to Gettysburg, Warren saw action at Fredericksburg, Bristoe Station, the Wilderness, and outside Petersburg.

Gen. Phil Sheridan and Warren clashed at the battle of Five Forks on April 1, 1865. Sheridan believed that Warren moved too slowly in the attack. Sheridan relieved Warren of his command immediately. After being humiliat-

Gen. Warren will forever examine the expanse between Little Round Top and Seminary Ridge at Gettysburg, as he did on July 2, 1863, helping Gen. George Meade avoid defeat by repairing the lines on Cemetery Ridge and preventing the Rebel onslaught from overtaking artillery situated on Little Round Top.
Photo by Janet Greentree

Gen. Gouverneur K. Warren (fifth from left) shown with his 5th Corps staff outside Petersburg.

ed by Sheridan, Warren resigned his commission, on May 27, 1865.

Warren served as an engineer for 17 years following the war, building railroads, and the Rock Island Bridge (over the Mississippi); and making harbor improvements along the Mississippi, the Atlantic Coast and the Great Lakes. Warren unsuccessfully tried to have Gen. Ulysses S. Grant exonerate him for charges related to Five Forks. Warren's requests were either refused or ignored.

The marble slab covering the grave of Gen. Warren in Island Cemetery, Newport, RI, reads: "Gouverneur K. Warren, Major General, U.S.V.; He Has Written His Own Epitaph with Sword and Pen."

Photo by Janet Greentree

Later, during the administration of Pres. Rutherford B. Hayes in 1879, another court of inquiry was held. This time, Warren's dismissal by Gen. Sheridan was deemed unjustified.

Sadly, Warren died of acute liver failure related to diabetes in Newport, Rhode Island, on August 8, 1882, at the age of 52. The favorable results of the inquiry were not published until after his death. Warren was buried in civilian clothes and without military honors, per his request. The last words he uttered were: "The flag! The flag." Warren left an extensive collection of papers, maps and letters.

Of the 25 generals' graves found on this trip, Gen. Chamberlain means the most to me. Gen. Warren was called the "Hero of Little Round Top," but Col. Chamberlain (at the time) was called "the Lion of the Round Top."

Joshua Lawrence Chamberlain was born in Brewer, Maine, on September 8, 1828. His father named him for sea Captain James Lawrence, who was famous for his quote: "Don't give up the ship." His great-grandfathers were soldiers in the American Revolution. His great-grandfather Franklin fought in the battle of Yorktown as a sergeant. His grandfather Joshua fought in the War of 1812 as a colonel. His father served in the Aroostook War (a non-violent confrontation with England over the Maine/Canada border) in 1839.

Chamberlain entered Bowdoin College in Brunswick, ME, in 1848. To pass the entrance exam to Bowdoin, Chamberlain taught himself ancient Greek. His professor's wife was Harriet Beecher Stowe, author of Uncle Tom's Cabin. Chamberlain graduated in 1852. He went on to study three more years at the Bangor Theological Seminary in Bangor, ME. He then returned to Bowdoin College as a professor of rhetoric. During his tenure there, he taught every subject but science and mathematics. He was fluent in nine languages: Greek, Latin, Spanish, German, French, Italian, Arabic, Hebrew, and Syriac (a literary language of the Middle East between the 4th and 8th centuries).

Gen. Joshua L. Chamberlain

Despite not having any military background, Joshua Chamberlain believed the Civil War to be just. In a letter to the governor of Maine, he said: "I fear, this war, so costly of blood and treasure, will not cease until men of the North are willing to leave good positions, and sacrifice the dearest personal interests, to rescue our country from desolation, and defend the national existence against treachery." He was granted a leave of absence and enlisted in the Union Army without telling his family or the college of his plans. Chamberlain was appointed the lieutenant colonel of the 20th Maine under Col. Adelbert Ames, after refusing to take on the colonelcy, stating he preferred to "start a little lower and learn the business first." His younger brother, Thomas, was also an officer in the 20th Maine. His brother, John, was a chaplain in the U.S. Christian Commission.

Chamberlain's 20th Maine first fought at Fredericksburg, but his unit missed Chancellorsville, due to an outbreak of small pox in their ranks. At Gettysburg, like Warren, Chamberlain's star shone. The 20th Maine was the extreme left flank of the Union Army on Little Round Top. He was told to hold the hill at all costs. The 15th Alabama, under Col. William C. Oates, charged the hill. The action went back and forth. In desperation, Chamberlain ordered a bayonet charge after their ammunition was depleted. The 20th Maine charged down the hill with their bayonets, capturing 101 of the Confederates and saving the hill. He was given the Medal of Honor for his brave charge at Little Round Top. The citation reads: "Daring heroism and great tenacity in holding his position on the Little Round Top against repeated assaults, and carrying the advance position on the Great Round Top." He was wounded several times; the most serious

Chamberlain's house in Brunswick, ME, was originally a one-story home, but as he grew in prominence, he wanted a more grand interior in which to entertain guests. He therefore had the first floor raised up on pillars and built in a new first floor that was of a higher Victorian design.

Photo by Janet Greentree

wound, received at Petersburg, would eventually end his life, but not until 1914. At the surrender at Appomattox, he was given the honor of presiding over the parade of Confederates laying down their rifles. He fought in 20 battles, many skirmishes, was cited for bravery four times, was wounded six times, and had six horses shot out from under him.

After the war, he went back to Maine and was elected and served as Maine's governor for four one-year terms. He returned to Bowdoin College in 1871 as president and kept that position until 1883, when he had to resign, due to poor health. He wrote his memoirs "The Passing of the Armies," as well as books about Maine, and education. His Medal of Honor was awarded to him in 1893. Gen. Chamberlain died in

Gen. Chamberlain's modest headstone in Pine Grove Cemetery, Brunswick, ME.

Photo by Janet Greentree

Portland, ME, on February 24, 1914, at the age of 85. His surgeon, Dr. Abner Shaw, who operated on him in Petersburg fifty years prior, was beside him when he died. The Minnie ball that wounded him in Petersburg is displayed at his home on Maine Street, across from Bowdoin College.

Lt. Col. Alexander Swift "Sandie" Pendleton

When Stonewall Jackson was asked what he thought about his young staff officers, he said: "Ask Sandie Pendleton. If he does not know, no one does." Stonewall thought of Sandie as a son. They shared the same religious convictions.

"Sandie" Pendleton early in the Civil War.

Ms. Rebelle is departing a bit from generals with this article. Sandie was an interesting young man. He was a lieutenant colonel when he was mortally wounded at Fisher's Hill in Woodstock, VA, on September 22, 1864.

Sandie was born on September 28, 1840 in Alexandria, VA, sandwiched in the middle of six sisters. His father was later Confederate Gen. William Nelson Pendleton, a minister, who called his cannons Matthew, Mark, Luke and John. The cannon still reside in front of the Virginia Military Institute in Lexington, VA. Sandie's father was the first principal of Episcopal High School in Alexandria.

When Sandie was 13 years of age, his family moved to Lexington, VA, where his father took over the pastorship of Grace Episcopal Church. Washington College offered free tuition to ministers' sons, so Sandie attended the school at age 13. He graduated in three years as one of 10 graduates in 1857 and also as one of three recipients of the Robinson Gold Medal. The medal was awarded by the faculty to graduates for outstanding student accomplishment. Sandie was the first recipient under the age of 17. He gave the oration at graduation.

After graduation, he continued at Washington College as a teacher of mathematics and Latin. He first met Stonewall Jackson when Jackson was a teacher at VMI and they belonged to the same literary society in Lexington. In 1859, he began studies at the University of Virginia to obtain a Master's Degree in Latin, Greek, Modern Languages, and Mathematics. He had completed most courses by the time the Civil War began, but did not graduate.

In 1861, he was commissioned as a second lieutenant in the Corps of Engineers in the Provisional Army of Virginia and left for Harper's Ferry to help quell John Brown's rebellion at the arsenal. He later joined the Rockbridge Artillery, a unit organized by another of my subjects, Gen. John McCausland (see April 2014 Stone Wall). Stonewall then requested Pendleton to join his staff on June 25, 1861. He became his adjutant general after Antietam.

Sandie was with Stonewall Jackson at 1st Manassas, where Jackson would get his nickname. After Sandie's horse was killed, he joined the 33rd VA, attacking Rickett's Union battery, supported by Ellsworth's Zouaves. He was wounded by a ball to the thigh. Sandie wrote most of the battle reports of 1st Manassas, earning him the rank of major.

He fought with Jackson in the Valley Campaign; Shenandoah Valley; Seven Days battles; Maryland Campaign at Antietam; Fredericksburg, and Chancellorsville. Some of Sandie's words about the battle of Antietam: "Such a storm of balls I never conceived it possible for men to live through. Shot and shell shrieking and crashing, canister and bullets whistling and hissing most fiend-like through the air until you could almost see them. In that mile's ride I never expected to come back alive."

After the battle of Fredericksburg on December 13, 1862, Jackson and his staff spent

Sandie Pendleton's overcoat on display at the American Civil War Museum at the Tredegar Ironworks in Richmond, VA. According to family tradition, this coat was sewn into a chair cushion during the Federal occupation of Lexington, Virginia, in 1865 and remained concealed until 1896.

At left, Kate Corbin Pendleton; above: Moss Neck, the site of pleasant memories for Pendleton, as he celebrated Christmas 1863 and was soon married here, near Fredericksburg, VA.

December 1862 to March 1863 at the Corbin Plantation - Moss Neck - near Fredericksburg. On Christmas Day in 1863, Gens. Lee, Stuart and Pendleton were among the guests for Christmas festivities.

It is here where he met and courted his future wife, Kate Corbin. They married at Moss Neck on December 29, 1863. Kate was the daughter of James Parke Corbin. Her sister-in- law Dianna (married to her brother - Spotswood Wellford Corbin), was the daughter of Matthew Fontaine Maury. Moss Neck still stands and is open occasionally for tours.

Pendleton was not with Jackson on the night of May 2, 1863, when Stonewall's party took ethal friendly fire from Confederate pickets. He told Jackson's wife Mary Anna that "God knows, I would have died for him." Sandie dressed Jackson's body for burial. He a companied his body on the train to Lynchburg, then on the packet boat *Marshall* to Lexington for burial. He also served as a pallbearer at Jackson's funeral. Way back in 2003, 'Yankee Nan' (Nancy Anwyll) and

Above: the packet boat Marshall, used to transfer Stonewall Jackson's body to Lexington, VA, for burial. At right: the remains of the Marshall in Lynchburg, VA.
Photo at right by Janet Greentree

I visited Riverside Park in Lynchburg. While there, we saw the remains of the Marshall's hull.

After Jackson's death, Pendleton served with Gen. Richard S. Ewell as chief of staff and was promoted to lieutenant colonel. He served with Ewell in the Gettysburg campaign. When Ewell was replaced by Gen. Jubal Early, Sandie retained the rank of lieutenant colonel with the Second Corps and continued as chief of staff.

On September 22, 1864, three days after the battle of Third Winchester, he was mortally wounded in the stomach at the battle of Fisher's Creek. He died the next day. His body was buried on the battlefield but later exhumed and sent home to his parents in Lexington. A funeral was held on October 24, 1864. Kate, who was pregnant with their only child, gave birth to a son a month later. The boy, named after his father, lived less than a year; he died of diphtheria in September 1865. Kate has been quoted as saying: "I wonder people's hearts don't break. When they have ached and ached as mine has done till feeling seems to be almost worn out of them. My

At left: the Hotchkiss map detailing the battle at Fisher's Hill in the Shenandoah Valley - Sept. 22, 1864. Hotchkiss also commented on the wounding of Pendleton:

"Our men came back in a perfect rout, and so rapidly that the enemy was crossing the railroad before the head of the column got into the pike, even. It was then getting dark. I hastened back to try and stop the mass of fugitives on the top of hill near Mount Prospect. General Gordon, General Pegram, and Colonel Pendleton with others came up. Colonel Pendleton and myself had gotten a few men to stop near a fence, there, and also two pieces of artillery, which were opened on the enemy. By the combined efforts of all a few men were induced to stop The artillery was opened on the woods where the enemy was advancing and it check the for the moment, but most of our me went on, officers and all, at breckneck speed. Wharton came along parallel to the pike and on the left, and kept some of his men together. He checked the enemy some, and a rear guard was formed from his division which made a stand at Tom's Brook, and gave the enemy a volley which made them disist from the pursuit. Battle's brigade moved to the left and came out intact. Colonel Pendleton was mortally wounded soon after we made a stand on the hill."

Ms. Rebelle at the gravesite of Lt. Col. Alexander Swift "Sandie" Pendleton, who was killed at Fisher's Hill, VA, during the last year of the Civil War, and shortly thereafter transferred to Lexington, VA, where he lies at the Stonewall Jackson Memorial Cemetery.

Photo courtesy of Janet Greentree

poor empty arms, with their sweet burden torn away forever." Kate later married John Mercer Brooke, a Confederate Naval Officer. Kate died in 1918. She and her second husband are buried near Sandie and little Alexander in the Stonewall Jackson Memorial Cemetery in Lexington.

As a side note, while researching this article, I discovered that a Corbin married into my Confederate ancestor George Washington Baker's family. A new-found cousin, Barry Williams, whose mother was a Corbin, sent me 444 pages of Corbin descendants. Our common ancestor was Mary Elizabeth Baker, George's sister. The document reads like a 'Who's Who' of Virginia history and FFVs (First Families of Virginia). The document lists names like Custis, Washington, Carter, Fairfax, Fitzhugh, Corbin, Lee, Pendleton, and many, many others. Barry is a third cousin, five times removed, from Robert E. Lee. Barry and I are third cousins, once removed. I imagine that it is pretty watered down when it gets to me, but now I know why I lean towards the Confederates.

An illustration depicting the Battle of Fisher's Hill, with the view from Strasburg, in the Shenandoah Valley.

FFVs, Stuart's Ride Around McClellan, Rooney Lee, and Gen. Williams Carter Wickham, CSA

Ashland, Virginia, was my destination to find the grave of Gen. Williams Carter Wickham, CSA. Thank goodness for my late friend Joe's hand-drawn map outlining the back roads to Hickory Hill, the plantation house that was the home of the Wickham family. Hickory Hill was one of the ten largest plantations in Virginia and had 275 enslaved workers on the property.

Williams was very much connected to the FFVs (First Families of Virginia). His father was William Fanning Wickham, and his mother was Anne Butler Carter, born at Shirley Plantation, and a sister to Anne Hill Carter Lee, mother of Robert E. Lee. Thus, Williams is a first cousin to Robert E. Lee.

Hickory Hill, one of the most distinguished properties in Virginia, located in Ashland, VA.

Photo by Janet Greentree

Above, Gen. Williams Carter Wickham; below: Anne Hill Carter Lee, mother of Gen. Robert E. Lee.

His grandfather was John Wickham, a constitutional lawyer. He is descended from the Nelson and Carter (Robert "King" Carter) families. His ancestor, Gen. Thomas Nelson, Jr., was a signer of the Declaration of Independence. Williams married Lucy Penn Taylor, a great-granddaughter of John Penn, also one of the signers of the Declaration of Independence.

Gen. Robert E. Lee was fond of visiting Hickory Hill. He wrote a note to Wickham's father stating, "I am so glad that I stopped at Hickory Hill on my return to Lexington. It has given me pleasant thoughts for the rest of my life." Williams was born September 21, 1820, in Richmond but spent most of his life at Hickory Hill. He graduated from the University of Virginia with a law degree and was admitted to the bar in 1842. He later became a justice and was elected to the Virginia House of Delegates in 1849. He was elected by Henrico County to the state convention in 1861 as a Unionist and voted against the articles of secession.

Williams' Civil War service began in March of 1861 as captain of the Hanover Dragoons at First Manassas. He later was a lieutenant colonel of the 4th Virginia Cavalry, was wounded at Williamsburg (a saber wound), fought at Second Manassas, and Boonsboro, was wounded again at Sharpsburg (by a shell fragment to his neck). He fought at Fredericksburg, Chancellorsville, Bristoe, Gettysburg (with Stuart's Cavalry), Brandy Station, and Buckland Mills. He defended Richmond during Kilpatrick's raid, was with Fitzhugh Lee in the Overland campaign; he was also in the Shenandoah Valley campaign.

In September 1863, he commanded Wickham's Brigade of

Gen. Thomas Nelson, Jr.

Fitzhugh Lee's Division. He was at the Battle of Yellow Tavern when Maj. Gen. J.E.B. Stuart was mortally wounded. Stuart's last command was, "Order Wickham to dismount his brigade and attack."

In September 1864, after the Confederate defeat at Fisher's Hill, Wickham blocked Sheridan's attempt to encircle the Confederate forces of Gen. Jubal Early. He resigned his commission in November 1864 after leading his men in 59 engagements, and took his seat at the Second Confederate Congress, to which he had been elected while serving in the field. Williams participated in the Hampton Roads Conference, in an attempt to help end the war.

After the surrender of the Confederacy, Wickham was active trying to improve conditions between the states and worked on Virginia's economy, which had been devastated

At left, New York financier Collis P. Huntington; at right, Julia Beckwith Neale Jackson, Gen. "Stonewall" Jackson's mother.

by the war. In November 1865, he was elected president of the Virginia Central Railroad, one of the most heavily damaged railroads in Virginia. The railroad was then merged with the Covington and Ohio Railroad to form the Chesapeake and Ohio Railroad. After unsuccessfully trying to get funding in Virginia for the railroad, he secured funding in the amount of $15 million from New Yorker Collis P. Huntington. The merging of the railroads ended up costing $23 million. The final spike ceremony for the 428-mile line from Richmond to the Ohio River was held on January 29, 1873, at the Hawk's Nest railroad bridge in the New River Valley near Ansted, West Virginia. (Side note here: Ansted is where Stonewall Jackson's mother, Julia Beckwith Neale Jackson

Above - the brick enclosure surrounding Wickham's grave; below, the stone marking his grave.

Photos by Janet Greentree

Woodson, is buried.) Wickham drove in the last spike. Under Wickham, a line was extended east from Richmond down the Virginia Peninsula through Williamsburg, Hampton Roads, and Newport News. Hickory Hill had its own stop for the railroad. The stop was called Wickham, and is located at C&O milepost 105.4 north of Richmond.

Wickham became a Republican and voted for Ulysses S. Grant for president in 1872. He was active politically until his death in his office in Richmond on July 23, 1888. Gen. Wickham is buried in a small brick-enclosed cemetery on the Hickory Hill plantation, within view of the house. There is a statue of Wickham done by Edward Virginius Valentine in Monroe Park in Richmond, given by the general's men and the employees of the C&O Railroad; it was dedicated on October 29, 1891. The speech for this unveiling was given by Gen. Fitzhugh Lee. The inscription reads "Soldier, Statesman, Patriot, Friend." The same four words are written on his tombstone.

While driving down the unpaved back

Like many lonely ol' roads in Virginia, this one leading to Hickory Hill is really significant - it was used by Stuart (depicted above, right) to ride around McClellan in the Peninsula campaign.

Photo by Janet Greentree

road to Hickory Hill, I realized that I had been there before. This road was the actual one that J.E.B. Stuart used on his ride around McClellan. Back in 1997, on my first trip with the Boston Civil War Roundtable, J.E.B. Stuart, IV, was our tour guide for Stuart's ride around McClellan. We stopped here to see Hickory Hill. The road looks just like it must have looked when J.E.B. Stuart rode down it many years ago in 1862.

William "Rooney" Fitzhugh Lee

Hickory Hill was also the site of an incident with Robert E. Lee's son, Rooney, when he was captured by Union forces on June 26, 1863. As was customary during the period, men would go to their family homes, or extended family homes, to recuperate from their wounds. Rooney was married to Charlotte Wickham, a cousin of Williams Carter Wickham. Rooney was wounded during the cavalry battle at Brandy Station, suffering a severe leg wound. His brother, Robert "Rob" E. Lee, Jr., came to take care of him, as did Rooney's wife, Charlotte, his mother and sisters.

Rooney was recuperating in a small building called the office on the property when three shots were heard near the outer gate. Five or six Union Cavalry came down the road and captured the injured Rooney. Just previously, Rooney had told his brother to leave the office and hide. Rob hid in the thick boxwood hedges. Later, he crawled closer to the house and hid himself under the long branches of a thick fir tree. He saw Rooney being carried out on a mattress to one of Hickory Hill's carriages and two of their horses. Rooney was taken to his White House plantation and then put on a boat to Fortress Monroe. The Yankees determined Rooney was having too many visitors, so he was transferred to Fort Lafayette in New York Harbor and exchanged in March 1864. Sadly, his wife Charlotte became ill after witnessing Rooney's capture and died in December 1863.

A second stop was planned at Boswell's Tavern, to track Gen. William McComb, CSA, but that will have to be a story for next time.

The Office, the small building in which Rooney Lee was recovering at Hickory Hill after his capture.

Photo by Janet Greentree

Camp Parole

Before Moms worked or drove cars - before second or third cars were part of families, when your Dad took the car to work - we rode the bus. Growing up in Annapolis, Camp Parole meant the end of the local bus line and the roller rink where, as junior high kids, we would go on skating parties. Eventually Camp Parole was shortened to just Parole. Then in the 60s, the site became the Parole Shopping Center, which almost put downtown Annapolis out of business, if you can believe that. Finally, in 2003, a roadside historic sign was placed across the street from Camp Parole. As with most of these signs, there is nowhere to pull over to read it. If you pull into the parking lot of Value City on Solomons Island Road, Route 2, just south of West Street, you can read the sign through the chain link fence. Maybe, just maybe, if you're tall enough, you can get a picture of it without the chain link grids over top of the sign. Now at the site, the old Parole Shopping Center has been demolished and a new, fancy shopping center/office/hotel/apartment complex is being built. It looks like a small city there now.

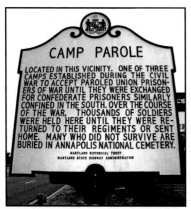

The historical roadside marker for Camp Parole - just handy enough to take a good photo of.
Photo by Janet Greentree

The name Parole came from the practice of releasing a prisoner during the Civil War, providing he promised to return to custody at a specific time, and to cooperate with the authorities. Understandably, the Army often had difficulty locating them again after they were exchanged. Often, men rejoined their units, where their status as AWOL would be changed to held as prisoner during their time missing, and their service continued. Camp Parole was a Union camp where many, many Union prisoners from the Southern prisons would come either for the hospital facilities or to just regroup, bathe, acquire clean clothes, and have a shave before being discharged to go back to their regiments or families. They came up the Chesapeake Bay on steamers to Annapolis.

The first point of business was a bath in College Creek. The soldiers would throw their clothes and boots in the creek for washing. Some 30 years later, the boots were still being picked out of the mud on the bottom of the creek. The official exchange location designated by both sides on July 22, 1862 was City Point, VA. Union soldiers were to be held in Annapolis until paroled. On the grounds of St. John's College in Annapolis, the first camp of paroled soldiers was established in 1861. At that time the camp was called College Green. By the time there were 3,000 parolees at the college, College Green became too small to hold all of them, so Camp Parole was established two miles outside of town. The camp was built on a farm southwest of Annapolis, most likely on the south side of Forest Drive between Greenbriar Lane and Bywater Road. In the six-week period after the camp was established, there were

Camp Parole outside in Annapolis, MD, in 1863.

20,000 men there. Clara Barton was also at Camp Parole, tending to the wounded and dying soldiers. Still, many died from their injuries or diseases such as smallpox, ague, dysentery, consumption, and tuberculosis.

In April 1864, Gen. Grant suspended all parole and exchange of prisoners. The Confederates at this point were unable to care for the large numbers of Union prisoners. Grant would neither send

Another contemporary depiction of Camp Parole.

supplies to the Union prisoners, nor exchange the Confederates for them. Finally, the Confederates returned Union prisoners with no hope of receiving any of their own men back.

In October 1864, the Andersonville prisoners were released and thousands upon thousands of men streamed into Annapolis. The camp was expanded again in February 1865. Union men continued to arrive there six weeks after the war ended. Camp Parole was closed by July 1865. Col. George Sangster of the 47th New York State Militia was in charge of the camp. He was highly regarded by the prisoners. During my research at the Ancestry.com site, I came across a letter written by Isaac W. Monfort, an Indiana Military Agent at the Camp. Monfort states that there were over 500 Indiana soldiers at the Camp. Most were in good spirits, all but really wanted to be back

in Indiana or be exchanged to their own regiments in the field. Monfort says that the Camp was two miles from the city of Annapolis and was the best field hospital he had ever visited. There were tents with pine doors and floors, and the place was kept very clean and orderly. The colored lithograph picture of the camp included here looks pretty impressive. Just down the street on West Street going back towards town is the Annapolis National Cemetery. Surprisingly, the cemetery only holds the remains of twenty-four of the Camp Parole detainees who weren't lucky enough to go back home or back to their regiments. These men either died at the Camp or nearby hospitals.

President Lincoln established fourteen National Cemeteries in 1862, with Annapolis being one of them. Annapolis had no land battles or Naval battles during the Civil War. Our illustrious Union Gen. Benjamin "Beast" Butler did spend some time there. Some of the 7th New York and the 8th Massachusetts camped on the grounds of the abandoned naval school, now known as the U.S. Naval Academy. The vacant buildings were used as field hospitals. By the fall of 1863, Annapolis was a major hospital center. After the war in 1871, Admiral David Porter built a Navy hospital at the Academy with a huge anchor in front, which is still there to this day.

The Annapolis National Cemetery holds some of the deceased from Camp Parole.
Photos by Janet Greentree

84

Gen. John Daniel Imboden

Did you know that Gen. Imboden had five wives? It wasn't that he divorced one and married another. All of them but his last wife, unfortunately, predeceased him. The general lived until 1895. Was it bad luck to be married to him? His first wife was Eliza Allen McCue. She bore him four children and died in 1857. He then married Mary Blair McPhail. She bore him three children and died in 1865. His third wife was Edna Paulding Porter, his fourth Annie Harper Lockett, and fifth Florence Crockett. Florence died in 1908. His daughter, Helen McGuire Imboden, was delivered by Dr. Hunter Holmes McGuire, Stonewall Jackson's physician. Her mother was Annie Harper Lockett. In total, he had nine children.

Gen. John D. Imboden

John Daniel Imboden was born on February 16, 1823, to George William Imboden and Isabella Wunderlich near Staunton, VA. His father and ancestors were farmers and of the Lutheran faith. George served in the War of 1812. Isabella's father Johann Daniel Wunderlich served in the Revolutionary War. After being educated in local schools, at age 16 he attended Washington College, now Washington & Lee University. His classmates were J. Horace Lacy, Beverly Tucker Lacy and James Kemper. All three would have ties to the Civil War. Stonewall Jackson's arm was buried at Ellwood, owned by J. Horace Lacy. Beverly Tucker Lacy was Stonewall Jackson's chaplain. And, as well, Jimmy Kemper was a Civil War general almost mortally wounded at Gettysburg. Imboden's January 1873 passport application described him at 6'2", blue eyes, black hair, high and broad forehead, large and aquiline nose, large chin and mouth, and long face. Obviously, the detailed description was before passport pictures.

Imboden did not graduate from Washington College. He worked for a time as a teacher at the Virginia School for the Deaf and the Blind in Staunton. He then read for the law, passed the bar exam, and opened a law practice with William Frazier. He was elected twice to the House of Delegates of the Virginia General Assembly. He received a commission as captain and founded the Staunton Light Artillery even though he had no military experience. Imboden's first assignment was at Harpers Ferry on April 19, 1861, commanding a unit for the capture of the town. He fought at First Bull Run, injuring his ear while firing an artillery piece, making him deaf in his left ear.

While in northwestern Virginia (now West Virginia), he and Gen. 'Grumble' Jones led a raid with 3,400 men, destroying train tracks and bridges in the Kanawha Valley. He and Jones spent 37 days covering 400 miles of the area. They destroyed eight railroad bridges, captured supplies, horses, mules, and 3,100 cattle, totaling a loss of over $100,000 to the Union Army.

Imboden left the artillery and organized the Virginia Partisan Rangers, the 62nd Virginia Mounted Infantry. Imboden's job during the Gettysburg Campaign was the rear guard for Lee's Army under Gen. J.E.B. Stuart. When they reached Cashtown, PA, Imboden stayed in the left top floor room of the Cashtown Inn, now called the Gen. John Imboden Room. Ms. Rebelle stayed in that room (see June-July 2009 Stone Wall article). There is a marker in front of the inn for the 18th VA Cavalry and 62nd VA Infantry.

Jones' Raid road marker denotes the cost to the Union Army of Imboden's actions in the Kanawha Valley of Virginia (West Virginia).

Above, the Cashtown Inn, where Gen. Imboden was billeted during the Gettysburg Campaign; below, at right, is the view overlooking the Cashtown Road from the Imboden Room.

Photos by Janet Greentree

There is also a marker on Reynolds Avenue on the south end for Imboden's unit. Their principal job was to be the rear guard. Most of their time, however, was spent in Chambersburg.

However, after the three-day battle, Gen. Imboden was chosen to command the 17-18 mile-long wagon train of the wounded and dying back to Virginia. Gen. R. E. Lee summoned him at 1 a.m. on July 4th to tell him the news. He had 2,100 Cavalry with him who had not been used during the battle. His orders were to leave Cashtown in the evening, turn south at Greenwood to avoid Chambersburg, and take the road to Williamsport, MD, where they would cross into West Virginia on their way to Winchester, VA. The journey didn't start until 4 p.m. on July 5th, because of torrential rains that had started on the 4th. One of the first wagons carried severely wounded Gens. William Dorsey Pender and Alfred Scales, both from North Carolina. Both opted to ride in the wagon train rather than be captured by the Union. General Scales would survive, but Pender did not (see Aug-Sep 2015 Stone Wall). Other wagons held the wounded Gens. Albert Gallatin Jenkins, John M. Jones, George Anderson, Paul Semmes, and Major Joseph Latimer (see June-July 2018 Stone Wall).

The roads were filled with mud. There were no cushions, straw, or springs in the wagons to aid the bumps and jolts to the terribly wounded soldiers on their way back to the south. The wagon train had been ordered not to stop until they reached their destination. They were attacked by civilians in Greencastle, who took axes and cut the spokes of the wagon wheels. Many of the men had to be left on the side of the road in hopes that the locals would take them in and nurse them. Most

A depiction of the misery-laden retreat from Gettysburg by the Confederate Army.

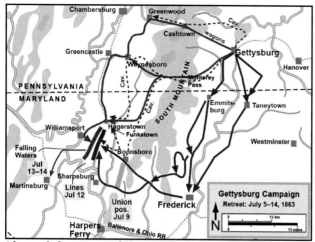

Above, left, a map of the tragic flight from the Gettysburg defeat; above, right, the river crossing at Williamsport, where Imboden accomplished the salvaging of the Confederate Army's casualties following the devastating Battle of Gettysburg.

Photo by Janet Greentree

had been without food for 36 hours. Those who were wounded, but not severely, marched behind the wagon train. There were at least 10,000 animals, too, including captured cattle. Approximately 4,000 prisoners were also being taken back to Virginia. The men were crying out "why can't I die?" "Have mercy on me and kill me." Gen. Imboden said: "During this one night I realized more of the horrors of war than I had in all the two preceding years."

The wagon train finally reached Williamsport, but was unable to cross due to high water from all the rain. Imboden occupied the town and turned it into a giant hospital. He ordered the local residents to cook for the men. The next day Union Cavalry under Gens. Buford and Kilpatrick attacked the wagon train . Imboden held them off and repulsed them when Gen. FitzHugh Lee showed up with 3,000 men. The wagons, men and animals were floated across the Potomac River on two flat-bottomed ferries pulled by wire pulleys. It took from July 5-14th for everyone to cross the river.

After the crossing, Gen. Robert E. Lee said of him: "In passing through the mountains in advance of the column, the great length of the trains exposed them to attack by the enemy's cavalry, which captured a number of wagons and ambulances, but they succeeded in reaching Williamsport without serious loss. They were attacked in that place on the 6th by the enemy's cavalry, which was gallantly repulsed by General Imboden."

After the Gettysburg Campaign, Gen. Imboden fought in the Valley Campaign of 1864. He became incapacitated by typhoid fever and spent the rest of the war in Aiken, SC, on prison duty.

He resumed his law practice in Richmond after the war and developed the coal industry in Virginia. He founded the town of Damascus, VA, in the southwestern area of Virginia and died there on August 15, 1895. He was also the author of several articles and books about the Civil War, including: *"The War of the Rebellion: A Compilation of the Official Records of the Union and Confederate Armies"* and a pamphlet *"The Coal and Iron Resources of Virginia: Their Extent, Commercial Value, and Early Development Considered."* In 1876, he was a commissioner of the Centennial International Exposition in Philadelphia. In 1893, he was a commissioner of the World's Columbian Exposition in Chicago.

Ms. Rebelle's Confederate ancestor George Washington Baker served under General Imboden in the 23rd Virginia Cavalry.

The general is buried in the Officers Section of Hollywood Cemetery in Richmond, Virginia.

Confederate Gen. Imboden's gravestone in Hollywood Cemetery, Richmond, VA.

Photo by Janet Greentree

Brevet Brig. Gen. William Jackson Palmer, USA

Above, undated photo of William J. Palmer during the Civil War; below, also undated, photo of Palmer after the war.

Ms. Rebelle and her sister rode the Durango-Silverton Narrow Gauge train from Durango to Silverton, Colorado, on our trip to Colorado last September and October. A nice young man came through the train we were on selling a small book, "*America's Railroad, the Official Guidebook*," by Robert T. Royem, outlining the history of the train. Imagine my surprise when I saw that there was a Civil War connection in Colorado. Gen. William Jackson Palmer was with the 15th Pennsylvania Cavalry, and was the founder of the Durango-Silverton Narrow Gauge Railroad.

William Jackson Palmer was born a Quaker on September 17, 1836, in Leipsic, Kent County, Delaware. His family later moved to Philadelphia, where he grew up. He became interested in railroads and went to work for the Pennsylvania Railroad, finally becoming the private secretary to the president, John Edgar Thomson.

Palmer was sent to England and France to study the railroads there. He recommended that the Pennsylvania Railroad change from burning wood to using coal, as the railroads did in England and France. The Pennsylvania Railroad became the first railroad in the country to burn coal. In 1861, when the Civil War began, Palmer was commissioned in the Union Army. His Quaker upbringing made him abhor violence, but he also believed in ending slavery in America. In August 1862 Palmer began recruiting a battalion of cavalry. He recruited nearly a thousand men from all over the state and began training them at Carlisle, PA. Palmer was assigned as a bodyguard to Gen. Robert Anderson, and the company's name became Anderson's Troop.

Palmer had quite an illustrious career during the Civil War. He remained in the war from 1862 to 1865. His unit was ordered to stay in the Cumberland Valley during the Maryland Campaign. Gen. James "Old Pete" Longstreet reported to Gen. Robert E. Lee that "had he not found swarms of Yankee cavalry in his front he would have advanced further into the State." On September 18, 1862, following the battle of Antietam, Palmer was inside enemy lines in civilian clothes scouting for Gen. George B. McClellan. He was taken prisoner on September 19, 1862, and sent to Castle Thunder prison in Richmond, VA. He was released on January 15, 1863 and rejoined his unit.

Palmer's unit saw much action during the war mostly in the Western Theater. His unit also chased Gen. John B. Hood after the battles of Franklin and Nashville. He was brevetted brigadier general on November 6, 1864. He was awarded the Congressional Medal of Honor on January 14, 1865 for his bravery at Red Hill, Alabama. His citation reads: "With less than 200 men, attacked and defeated a superior force of the enemy, capturing their fieldpiece and about 100 prisoners without losing a man."

In late April 1865, Palmer was commanding Gen. Alvan C. Gillem's Division [side note: it was on Gen. Gillem's grave on which I placed a Confederate flag, instead of a Union flag, on a trip to Nashville]; he was ordered south to participate in the capture of Jefferson Davis. His 15th Pennsylvania captured seven wagons containing $185,000.00 in coin, $1,585,000.00 in bank notes, bonds and securities, and $4,000,000.00 in Confederate money on May 8, 1865. The wagons he nabbed also contained private baggage, maps, and official papers of Gens. Beauregard and Pillow.

All captured items were sent undisturbed directly to the U.S. Government for further use.

The 15th Pennsylvania mustered out on June 21, 1865. After the Civil War, Palmer went back to railroading. He went west as the construction manager of the Kansas Pacific Railroad. Under his direction, the railroad first reached Denver, CO, in August 1870. Palmer then went on to found the Denver & Rio Grande Railroad. While riding on the train west, he met his future wife, Mary Lincoln (Queen) Mellen. They were married in Flushing, NY, and honeymooned in the British Isles, where Palmer first saw a narrow-gauge railroad.

Palmer's dream for his railroad was for it to go to Mexico. Of course, Colorado is full of mountains, so the narrow-gauge railroad would be able to navigate sharp curves and grades. Only two sections of the narrow gauge remains - the 45-mile stretch between Durango and Silverton and the 63-mile route between Cumbres, Colorado and Toltec, New Mexico, a portion of which is shown above. Palmer also founded the city of Colorado Springs. A large equestrian statue of him is located there at the intersection of Platte and Nevada in the downtown area.

Shown at right in photo, the train's route through such rugged scenery is typical of the kind of journey riders took when the railroads came to the West.
Photo by Janet Greentree

Gen. Palmer's Quaker upbringing made Colorado Springs alcohol free until the end of Prohibition in the 1930s. Limit Street was the end of the 'clean living' section and the beginning of the 'wild living' section, filled with bars and brothels.

Gen. Palmer was thrown from a horse in 1906, became an invalid, and he died March 13, 1909. He is buried in Evergreen Cemetery in Colorado Springs. Ms. Rebelle did not get to Colorado Springs, but if I do get back there, I would like to find his grave. The city of Colorado Springs staged a 100th-year anniversary reenactment of his funeral in March 2009.

Palmer's legacy includes the Denver & Rio Grande Railroad, Colorado College, International Typographical Union's Printers Home, Colorado School for the Deaf and Blind, a tuberculosis sanitarium that became the University of Colorado at Colorado Springs, and several churches. His wife, Queen, opened the first public school in Colorado Springs in 1871. Today in Colorado Springs, the Queen Palmer Elementary School is named after her. There is also a Gen. William J. Palmer High School. Palmer Hall at the Hampton University in Virginia is also named for his many contributions to the school. In 1907, Palmer hosted a reunion of the 15th Pennsylvania, held at his home, Glen Eyrie, in Colorado Springs. More than 200 of the veterans of the 15th Pennsylvania attended the reunion. What an interesting man.

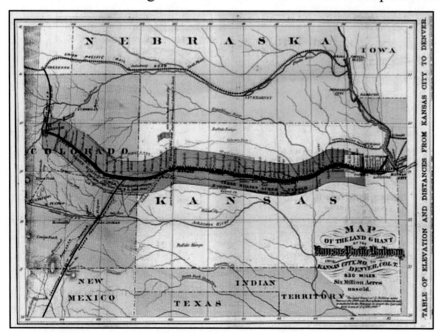

The Kansas Pacific main line shown on an 1869 map. The thickened portion along the line indicates the extent of the land grants available to settlers. At the time of the map, the line extended only as far as western Kansas (section in green). The extension to the Colorado Territory (section in red) was completed the following year.

89

Petersburg

Ms. Rebelle and Gwen Wyttenbach (the Snake Lady, per Ed Bearss) went south, yes - south - after all my northern trips, to Petersburg, for a day-and-a-half visit. The purpose of the trip was to attend a ceremony on April 2nd at the Gen. A.P. Hill death site marker in Petersburg commemorating Hill's death in 1865. The ceremony was lovely and was attended by quite a few people. Patrick Falci, who portrays the general in the major film "Gettysburg," was in attendance and did a moving tribute to Gen. Hill.

At the end of the ceremony, everyone who had a Confederate ancestor in the Civil War came up to the marker, placed their hand on the stone, and recited their ancestor's name. Ms. Rebelle cited her ancestor, George Washington Baker, of the 23rd Virginia Cavalry.

Above, the house was built in 1912 by the Eppes family, who lived in Appomattox Manor. Below, Appomattox Manor.
Bottom photo by Janet Greentree

Gwen and I previously had started out from City Point (Hopewell) at Appomattox Manor and Grant's very small cabin on the site. We found out that there was a row of cabins leading all the way down a street, to a house next to the one Grant used. From Grant's temporary housing, it was on to the City Point dock area. I wanted to try to duplicate some of "then" wharf pictures for an upcoming Civil War Trust Photo Contest (now Battlefield Trust).

At the dock, there is a huge mansion that sits on the right side of the road on a big bluff overlooking the water. Judging from old photos, I thought it most likely they were taken on this bluff. The house was called Miami Lodge. After trying to Google it, I found there was little information available on the property, so it must hold some "secret" history. It looked deserted, so we walked along the edge of the property. Gwen thinks this was the site of the Don Stivers' Supporting Victory painting of Lincoln, Sherman and Grant at City Point. It certainly looks like the view we saw.

Our next stop was Blandford Church in Petersburg, built in 1735. If you haven't been inside to see the 15 beautiful Louis Comfort Tiffany stained glass windows, it is a must stop. Gwen and I, plus the docent, were the only ones touring the church at that time. She gave us a wonderful history and an up-close view of the windows.

The Virginia window of St. John shows the velvet of his robe. The detail of seeming fabric featured in the windows is amazing. She pointed out ones that evoked silk, satin, and even watermarked taffeta robes. She told us that all fifteen windows cost $800.00. Years later, when they removed them to be cleaned and reworked, the price was estimated in the thousands. The windows were made and installed between 1901-12 and were commissioned by the Ladies Memorial Association of Petersburg.

Blanford Church, Petersburg, VA.
Photo by Janet Greentree

Memorial services for Presidents George Washington, John Adams and Thomas Jefferson were held in the church.

Ms. Rebelle also tried duplicating a "then and now" shot of the church. Some of the graves outside in the yard were damaged in the Siege of Petersburg. One near the church was the grave of Sarah Poythress, who died in October 1760. Her flat-top marker has the impression of a cannon ball on it.

Blandford Church cemetery has three Confederate Civil War generals buried on the premises - Gen. William Mahone, Gen. Cullen Andrews Battle and Gen. David Addison Weisiger. Gen. Mahone is buried in a big mausoleum with the letter "M" above the door. Ms. Rebelle knocked on the door, but the general was not receiving.

We toured the battlefield and saw the "Dictator." This was the first time I had seen this famous piece of heavy artillery. It's hard to believe it fired a shell that weighed over 200 pounds and shot it to a distance of over two miles. It took over 14 pounds of black powder to shoot a cannon ball.

During the siege of Petersburg, from June 1864-April 1865, the Union forces fired the Dictator 218 times at the city of Petersburg. The Dictator weighed 17,120 pounds and was transported by a railroad car. The train tracks are near where the Dictator now sits. It ran on the tracks from City Point to Petersburg. The weapon caused the Confederate gunners to withdraw

Above, the mausoleum at Blanford Church, Petersburg, VA. Below, Ms. Rebelle pays a call on Gen. William Mahone, but - gladly - the gentleman did not rise for the occasion.
Photos by Janet Greentree

Gwen Wyttenbach (left in bottom photo) and Ms. Rebelle demonstrate "Then and Now" at the Dictator, matching up to an undated photo during the Civil War.
Bottom photo courtesy of Janet Greentree

along the right of the Union line, it was so fearsome. The farthest point reached by the gun was Centre Hill in Petersburg, a distance of 2.7 miles (or 4,752 yards). One soldier from the 35th Massachusetts said, in reference to the Dictator being shot and the noise of the ball arriving, as being: "I'm a- coming, I'm a-coming," and then: "I'm HERE!" It made the ground quake when the shot hit home. The Dictator was cast by Charles Knapp at his Pittsburgh, PA, ironworks.

Gwen and I ran into a group of five Civil War enthusiasts from Cleveland touring the battlefield. Every place we stopped found them there, as well. Finally, we took each other's pictures at the different points. Our last meeting was at the Crater.

Before the ceremony honoring Gen. A. P. Hill started the next day, we toured around 'old town' Petersburg. Not having been there for at least 15 years, I was very impressed how much the town has improved. My first visit found all the storefronts with heavy locked gates on them. The town has been working very hard to restore everything historically important, and to make it a safe place to visit. We found the Visitors Center and ran into the same docent that gave us a tour of Blandford Church.

Ms. Rebelle had another "then and now" picture to accomplish. It was of the Union wagon train leaving Petersburg for Appomattox. It was determined that the picture was taken on West Washington Street. I must thank BRCWRT member Mike Block for telling me the city in which that picture was taken. There are two church steeples in the picture. One steeple had the top blown off, but even with new buildings in the picture, West Washington Street is the correct street. Gwen and I believe the photographer, Timothy O'Sullivan, was standing somewhere on a building's roof to get the photo, which was not possible for us, of course.

The old Courthouse is still standing, wedged between some other buildings. That was another opportunity for a "then and now" picture. On our way to the Siege Museum, we passed by Longstreet's Deli. Bet you didn't know our Longstreet had a deli in Petersburg! Inside the museum, we were shown Gen. A.P. Hill's lunchbox. It was made of sweet grass, braided for the general in intricate patterns by a local woman.

Next month's article will profile one of the three Civil War generals buried at Blandford Church - I've found some interesting things about 'Little Billy' Mahone.

'Little Billy' Mahone

Gen. Mahone's wife Otelia said of her 5'5", 100-pound husband - when she heard he was wounded in the chest at Second Bull Run - "Now I know it is serious for William has no flesh whatsoever." Even one of his men said that "he was every inch a soldier, though there were not many inches of him." Another of his men said that he was "the sauciest little manikin imaginable and the oddest and daintiest little specimen" he ever saw.

Mahone had his own distinct wardrobe, putting comfort before military uniforms. On some occasions, he wore a brown linen jacket with trousers to match; a large Panama hat, and sometimes a linen duster that was so long it covered up the tip of his sword. Pacing back and forth in his duster, his men said, "He looked like the image of a bantam rooster or gamecock." He had long hair; deep blue eyes under bushy eyebrows; a small, straight nose, and a huge mustache and beard. His voice was high - almost like a falsetto tenor. Can't you just see him?!

Gen. William 'Little Billy' Mahone.

He also had dyspepsia, so he couldn't eat anything but eggs, crackers and fresh milk. He brought his own cow and chickens with him and hung all his cooking utensils on the cow's back. He has been said to have a lot of nervous energy; a quick temper, and cussing fits. He kept a flock of turkeys outside his tent. On Christmas day in 1862, two soldiers stole one of his turkeys. The perpetrators endured 39 lashes for their crime.

After first finding his grave in Blandford Church Cemetery many years before with the Boston Civil War Round Table, the second interesting thing that I found about him was that he has a highway named for him called the Gen. Mahone Highway, Route 460, south of Petersburg, ending up in Suffolk, Virginia. The road is straight as an arrow, doesn't have much traffic and goes through Virginia's peanut country, as well as the the Great Dismal Swamp. You travel this route if you want to bypass the Newport News and Norfolk areas. For me, it was a shortcut to the North Carolina beaches.

Gen. Mahone was born December 1, 1826, in Monroe, VA, on the banks of the Nottoway River in Southampton County. The town is now called Courtland. He was the son of tavern keeper, Fielding Jordan Mahone, and his wife Martha Drew. Both of William's grandfathers were veterans of the War of 1812. Isn't it interesting how many of these Civil War generals have an ancestral connections to earlier wars?

Nat Turner's insurrection occurred in Southampton County in 1831, and William's father had a hand in quelling the insurrection. At age 17 (in 1844), William was appointed a cadet at the newly opened Virginia Military Institute in Lexington, Virginia. He graduated as a civil engineer in 1847, 8th out of 12 cadets in his class. One of his teachers was Thomas J. (later "Stonewall") Jackson. After graduation, he was a teacher at the Rappahannock Academy in Caroline County.

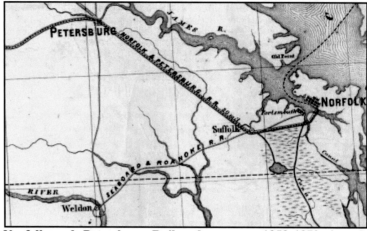

Norfolk and Petersburg Railroad map, c. 1858-1870, issued by William Mahone, President.

Mahone had a fascination for trains and was an engineer for the Orange and Alexandria Railroad. Later he was superintendent of the Norfolk and Petersburg Railroad. Using his engineering skills, he built a plank road between Fredericksburg and Gordonsville. While with the Norfolk and Petersburg Railroad, he designed a 12-mile long roadbed through the Great Dismal Swamp, between South Norfolk and Suffolk. The roadbed had a long foundation laid at right angles beneath the surface of the swamp. This roadbed is still in use today. His 52-mile long track between Petersburg and Suffolk has no curves, as well paralleling Route 460. He was also involved designing a beach community in Norfolk. The section is now called Ocean View.

Gen. Mahone was a civilian in 1861 but worked a ruse capturing the Gosport Shipyard in Portsmouth. He was able to bluff the Union troops into abandoning the shipyard when he ran a single passenger train back and forth into Norfolk with much noise and whistle blowing, creating the illusion that there were many troops arriving in Norfolk. The Union army retreated to Fortress Monroe.

Mahone next accepted a commission as lieutenant colonel in the Confederate Army. He was promoted to brigadier general in November 1861. He fought in the Peninsula Campaign; at the defenses around Drewry's Bluff; Seven Pines; Malvern Hill; Second Bull Run; Fredericksburg; Chancellorsville; Gettysburg; the Wilderness; and Spotsylvania. Mahone was regarded as the hero of the Battle of the Crater. After Pennsylvania coal miners tunneled under the Confederate line, blowing a huge crater in the Virginia landscape, Mahone repelled the attack. He was promoted to major general at this point. He was also present with Gen. Robert E. Lee at the Appomattox surrender.

After the surrender, Gen. Mahone went back to his love - the railroads. He was president of three lines: the Norfolk and Petersburg; South Side, and the Virginia and Tennessee Railroad. He also lobbied the Virginia General Assembly to form the Atlantic, Mississippi & Ohio Railroad (AM&O). The abbreviation was said to stand for

Above, left: young Otelia with her mother, Otelia Butler Mahone. Photo taken in Petersburg, circa 1870. Above, right: William Mahone, Jr., one of three surviving children of the Mahones.

William Mahone late in life.

"all mine and Otelia's" (his wife). The Mahones rode the new railroad line, naming the stops along the way: Windsor, Waverly, Wakefield, Ivor and, lastly, Disputanta. Since the Mahones couldn't agree on a name for the last stop, it was called Disputanta.

William and Otelia had 13 children with only three reaching maturity. One of their former residences on South Sycamore Street in Petersburg is part of the Petersburg Public Library. Even though Gen. Mahone owned slaves during the war, he started the Virginia Normal and Collegiate Institute for the education of former slaves and black children. The school later became Virginia State University. He also started Central State Hospital in Dinwiddie County.

Mahone was active in political life for 30 years as a delegate to the Virginia General Assembly; mayor of Petersburg; leader of the Readjuster Party (group of Republicans, Democrats, and African Americans seeking to reduce Virginia's pre-war debt); candidate for governor of Virginia, losing to Democrat Phillip W. McKinney; and as a United States senator. Virginia continued to elect Democrats as governors until 1969, when Republican A. Linwood Holton, Jr. was elected.

Mahone also worked on determining Virginia and West Virginia's share of debt from the Civil War. The case was finally settled in 1915 when the Supreme Court ruled that West Virginia owed Virginia $12,393,929.50. The final payment was made to Virginia in 1939.

A monument to the general's honor stands on the Petersburg Battlefield, near the Crater. The inscription reads: "To the memory of William Mahone, Major General, CSA, a distinguished Confederate Commander, whose valor and strategy at the Battle of the Crater, July 30, 1864, won for himself and his gallant brigade undying fame."

Little Billy Mahone died of a massive stroke in Washington, D.C. on September 8, 1895, when he was 68. He is buried in a large mausoleum at Blandford Church Cemetery in Petersburg, Virginia. I'm going to have to add him to my list of people that would have been interesting to know in person. He sounds like quite a character.

Mahone monument at Petersburg, VA.

In 1887, 57th Massachusetts veterans pose at The Crater. William Mahone, the Confederate brigadier general who led counterattacks at The Crater on July 30, 1864, is the man with the cane and long, white beard in the front row. (William Tipton | Library of Congress).

Brig. Gen. Charles Russell Lowell

Brig. Gen. Charles Russell Lowell has a connection to my last story about Gen. Lunsford Lindsay Lomax. Lomax led the charge at Cedar Creek on October 19, 1864, when Lowell was mortally wounded. Lowell also chased Colonel John Singleton Mosby for 10 months through Mosby's Confederacy, and was present at the Front Royal incident where six of Mosby's command were executed by Gen. George Armstrong Custer and Gen. Wesley Merritt's troops.

Lowell's family, including his mother's Jackson and Cabot families, were part of the First Families of Boston. [*Ed. Note*: "And this is good old Boston / The home of the bean and the cod; / Where the Lowells talk to the Cabots / And the Cabots talk only to God." – old toast chiding the '1-percent' of Boston society.]

Charles Russell Lowell, III was born in Boston, Massachusetts on January 2, 1835, to Charles Russell Lowell, Jr. and Anna Cabot Jackson. Anna was the daughter of Patrick Tracy Jackson.

Charles Russell Lowell, Sr.

Effie and Charles Lowell

Above, Capt. Charles Russell Lowell, III; below, a bust of Lowell at Harvard University.

Charles, Jr. was the son of Charles Russell Lowell, Sr., a Unitarian minister. Patrick Jackson was the founder of the city of Lowell, Massachusetts.

Lowell, Sr. spoke out about the issue of slavery, and was the editor of the Anti-Slavery Standard. Lowell, III was educated at Boston Latin School, English High School and Harvard, graduating as the valedictorian in 1854.

After college, he worked in an iron mill in Trenton, NJ; he spent two years abroad (1858-1860) trying to recoup his health after he contracted tuberculosis, and, in 1860, he was put in charge of the Mount Savage Iron Works in Cumberland, Maryland. He married Josephine (Effie) Shaw, the sister of Colonel Robert Gould Shaw, on October 31, 1863, at Staten Island.

He happened to be in Baltimore on April 19, 1861, when an angry mob set upon and attacked a regiment of Massachusetts volunteers as they changed trains for Washington. Lowell went directly to Washington and applied for a commission in the regular army. He was commissioned as a captain in the 3rd U.S. Cavalry. He later transferred to the 6th U.S. Cavalry. He served as aide-de-camp to General George B. McClellan during 1861 and 1862. He was with McClellan in the Peninsula Campaign and at Antietam.

Lowell organized the 2nd Massachusetts Cavalry under Col. Percy Wyndham (Mosby intended to capture Wyndham at one

Anna Lowell, Charles' sister, seated, with fellow nurse Miss Low, a niece of New Hampshire Senator John P. Hale and a volunteer in Ward I. Washington D.C., circa 1863. Anna learned of Charles' death two days after, directly from General Custer, another brigade leader at the Battle of Cedar Creek where Charles had been mortally wounded. Anna met with Custer at Secretary of State Edwin Stanton's offices, where she had gone in search of news about her brother.

The fatal shot to Lowell, leading the troops, at Cedar Creek, by James Taylor.

juncture in the war, but captured General Edwin Stoughton in Fairfax instead), and was appointed its colonel, a rank he held to his death . He was assigned to stop General Jubal Early's raid on Washington. He commanded a brigade of cavalry for Gen. Wesley Merritt in the Valley Campaign of 1864. He was also at Tom's Brook, fighting against General Lomax. Merritt was part of General Phil Sheridan's army and Lowell fought alongside General Custer at Cedar Creek.

Lowell was described as being 'closely knit,' with a wiry frame and a light, delicate figure; his intense vitality and exhaustless energy achieved what seemed impossible to others. There wasn't an ounce of superfluous weight on him. He had 13 horses shot from under him.

Lowell was first wounded in general fighting at Middletown, sustaining a collapsed lung and internal bleeding. He refused to leave the field. General Merritt, knowing Lowell was dying, allowed him to be strapped into his saddle to lead the charge of 3,000 cavalrymen. He was immediately shot, this time in the spine, by a sharpshooter on the roof of a house in Middletown. He fell off his horse, paralyzed. He lived through the night, dictating letters and giving orders, and died at dawn the next morning, October 20, 1864. There is a marker to him on the grounds of the Wayside Inn in Middletown. When Custer heard of his death he wept. General Sheridan stated:

"I do not think there was a quality which I could have added to Lowell. He was the perfection of a man and soldier."

Sheridan himself made sure Lowell was given his brigadier general rank on October 19th. General Merritt stated that he would give up his command if only Lowell were there to receive it.

Many of Lowell's relatives and friends were also lost during the Civil War, including brother-in-law Robert Gould Shaw; his brother, James Jackson

The Wayside Inn in Middletown, VA, site of Lowell's demise. A marker noting the location is located there.

Lowell; friends Richard Goodwin, Richard Cary, Stephen Perkins, William Sedgwick, Wilder Dwight, James Savage, and classmate Paul Revere at Gettysburg; cousins William Lowell Putnam, Warren Dutton, Cabot Russell, Samuel Storrow, and Sumner Paine. Two of his cousins survived the war - Oliver Wendell Holmes, future Supreme Court Justice and Henry Lee Higginson, who later founded the Boston Symphony Orchestra.

Lowell's body was sent back to Boston by train. The funeral was held on October 28, 1864. The people of Boston must have truly loved him. Caroline Healey Dall and several other women decorated the Harvard College Chapel for his funeral. Pine boughs, fern fronds, variegated ivy, chrysanthemums, orchids, camellias, miniature orange and lemon, geraniums, pelargoniums, and cape jasmine were used to decorate the chancel, reading desk, and pulpit. It is said the entire chapel had a heavy floral fragrance. Notables attending included Henry Wadsworth Longfellow, Ralph Waldo Emerson, Oliver Wendell Holmes, Joel Hayden (the

Gen. Lowell's grave marker at Mt. Auburn Cemetery, Cambridge, MA.
Photo by Janet Greentree

Effie and Carlotta Lowell

lieutenant governor of Massachusetts), Dr. Samuel G. Howe, Frank Stanborn, Thomas W. Higginson, General Francis C. Barlow, and Senator Charles Sumner.

His coffin rested at the Lowell residence on Quincy Street, just across the street from Harvard Yard. Just before noon, the Corps of Cadets assembled in front of the house. Pallbearers carried the coffin down the steps of the house in pouring rain to the chapel. The pallbearers were officers of Lowell's regiment. His adjutant and one of the pallbearers, Lt. Henry E. Alvord, had escorted the body back from the Shenandoah Valley. Lowell had fallen from his horse into Alvord's arms. Lowell's coffin was draped with the U. S. flag and covered with flowers. Lowell's sword, hilt, scabbard, cap and gauntlets were placed on top of the coffin, as well. His body was buried at Mount Auburn Cemetery on Fountain Avenue, Lot 323 in Cambridge, Massachusetts. My dear Boston friends gave me a tour of the cemetery, where we found his grave, plus many other notables.

General Lowell died two weeks short of his first anniversary, at age 29. His wife, Josephine, was eight months pregnant with their first child. Their daughter, Carlotta Russell Lowell, was born November 30, 1864. She lived until 1924.

Lowell (center) and Officers of the 2nd Mass Cavalry.

Gen. Edward Porter Alexander, CSA

Just imagine you are 26 years old on July 3, 1863; you are a Colonel in the Confederate Army Artillery, and chief of artillery for Gen. James Longstreet at Gettysburg. After a two-hour long cannonade using 150-170 cannon and most of your ammunition, you are ordered to tell Gen. George Pickett to then step off for 'Pickett's Charge.' How would you feel - knowing both Gen. Longstreet and you, yourself, weren't in support of the charge being ordered? That is a lot of pressure on a young person. Alexander would write in 1901: "Never, never, never did Gen. Lee himself bollox (bungle) a fight as he did this."

E.P. Alexander, or known to his family and friends as Porter, was born on May 26, 1835, in Washington, Georgia, about 100 miles east of Atlanta. His parents were Adam Leopold and Sara Gilbert Alexander. Adam lived in the low country on a plantation named Hopewell, near Riceboro, GA, south of Savannah.

After his marriage to Sara, they would live in the high country at the old Gilbert plantation named Fairfield, which is located on Alexander Drive (between North Alexander and Poplar Drives) in Washington, GA. Fairfield was not burned by the Yankees during the Civil War. Today, it is the Yawkee Wildlife Preserve. Porter would be one of eight children born there. He had a passion for hunting and fishing that would endure throughout his life. His older sister, Fredericka Louisa, would marry future Confederate Gen. Jeremy Francis Gilmer, a recent graduate of West Point. His sister Sarah

Fairfield Plantation, Washington, GA.

would marry future Confederate Gen. Alexander Robert Lawton. Gilmer convinced Porter's father that Porter should go to West Point. Future Confederate Gen. Robert Toombs would recommend his appointment to West Point.

Alexander was 5'9½" tall (and 150 pounds) when he reported to West Point in June 1853. He graduated in 1857, third in his class. He received his commission as 2nd lieutenant as an engineer on October 10, 1858. He would briefly teach engineering and fencing there. He would then be sent on the Utah Expedition under Gen. Albert Sidney Johnson. Alexander would lead the first column of six. He would fall back on his hunting and fishing skills to kill 25 buffalo from horseback, plus shooting other prey. It was on this expedition that he would meet captains Lewis Armistead and Richard Garnett, later his compatriots at Gettysburg.

Edward P. Alexander as a cadet at West Point, circa 1853, and, above, Betty Mason.

Porter returned to West Point to resume teaching and met his wife Betty Mason, a visiting 'Southern Belle.' They would marry in King George, VA, on April 3, 1860. That marriage produced five children. They would be married for 39 years; Betty died on November 20, 1899. Porter would marry again at age 66 to Betty's niece, Mary Mason.

Alexander went from graduation at West Point at age 22 to brigadier general by age 28. He fought in battles at First Manassas, the Peninsula Campaign, Antietam, 2nd Manassas, Fredericksburg, Chancellorsville, Gettysburg, Knoxville Campaign, the Overland Campaign, Richmond-Petersburg Campaign, and was present at Appomattox for the surrender.

He and Maj. Albert Myer developed the wig-wag signal flags that were used at Signal Hill in Manassas to warn Colonel Nathan "Shanks" Evans: "Look out to your left, your position is turned." At Gaines Mill, even though afraid of heights, he ascended on June 27, 1862, in the gas-filled balloon Gazelle, the silk dress balloon, to check on Gen. George B. McClellan's troop movements. Our last month's speaker, Kevin Knapp, told us that the balloon was made of silk that could have been used for ladies' dresses - adding that no Southern belle's dresses were harmed.

On November 7, 1862, Alexander became head of Longstreet's Artillery. His cannon were placed in defense of Marye's Heights at the battle of Fredericksburg. Alexander is quoted as saying to Longstreet: "General, we cover that ground now so well that we will comb it as with a fine tooth comb. A chicken could not live on that field when we open on it." His guns were instrumental in stopping the Union troops. On July 2, 1863, he provided support for the Confederate assaults at Gettysburg. On July 3rd, we all know what happened.

Smashed Confederate artillery after battle of Fredericksburg.

During the Petersburg Campaign, Alexander became convinced the Union was tunneling under Confederate lines. He would be wounded in the shoulder on June 30, 1864, by a sharpshooter at Elliott's Salient. He informed Gen. Lee of his suspicions before leaving on medical leave. In October, 1864, he was appointed brigadier general.

At Appomattox Courthouse, Alexander counseled Gen. Lee to disperse the army rather than surrender it. General Lee told him the army had endured enough. Alexander was so distraught

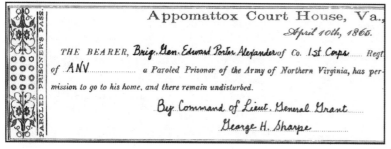

after the surrender that he briefly toyed with the idea of joining the Brazilian Army. He decided against that, though, and went on to teach mathematics at the University of South Carolina in Columbia. Alexander served on the Charlotte, Columbia & Augusta Railroad, the Savannah and Memphis Railroad, and later became president of the Louisville & Nashville Railroad. He served on the Central Railroad & Banking Company of Georgia until 1891.

He became friends with Pres. Grover Cleveland, renewing his interest in duck hunting with Cleveland at his home in Georgia. In May, 1897, Pres. Cleveland appointed him to the commission to settle the boundaries between Nicaragua and Costa Rica. He also looked into building a canal across Central America. When all was settled, Nicaragua gave him a hero's welcome with a 50-piece band, 21-gun salute and church bells ringing. He returned to the states in 1899. His first wife died shortly thereafter.

Some interesting tidbits learned about Gen. Alexander are that, during the war, he had two horses - Dixie and Meg. Dixie was a large horse and Meg a smaller one. He seemed to make the

Illustration of 'Cuss with the Spyglass' - Munson Hill, Falls Church, VA.

E. P. Alexander in later years.

right decision to ride each horse at the proper time, so his head or his leg wouldn't be taken off from artillery fire. He was known as "the cuss with the spyglass." A friend had gifted him a six-foot long telescope that was crafted to fit in his saddle. He learned how to use it without a tripod to keep it steady. He never used field glasses. He also used his spyglass at Munson Hill in Falls Church to see signals from E. Pliny, who rented a hotel room in Washington. Pliny would signal important information to him with a coffee pot reflecting the sun. The spy, Rose O'Neal Greenhow, was also involved in this operation.

Alexander also hired a 15-year old "ginger cake darkie," Charley, as a body servant; Charley accompanied him throughout the war. He rented Charley from his master, making payments for his service to a Richmond bank account. When the master never withdrew the funds, Alexander withdrew them, converted them to a 10-dollar gold piece and gave it to Charley after the war. When Gen. George Custer captured Alexander's baggage wagon at Petersburg, he lost his new frock coat, personal items and his sword.

Gen. Alexander is the author of two books – Military Memoirs of a Confederate (public edition) and Fighting for the Confederacy: The Personal Recollections of Gen. Edward Porter Alexander (unabridged private edition), published posthumously.

On June 9, 1902, Alexander was asked to be an honored guest at West Point for its Centennial. The New York Times stated that Alexander's speech was the best of the day. Famous guests on the speaker platform included Pres. Teddy Roosevelt and Gen. James Longstreet.

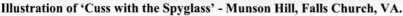

In Alexander's honor, one of Gettysburg's shield markers is positioned on the battlefield by the stone wall just south of the Millerstown Road on West Confederate Avenue. My daughter Lisa Tully gets credit for her never-ending search for markers for her Mom.

Gen. Alexander had several small strokes and died in Savannah, GA, on April 28, 1910. He is buried in Magnolia Cemetery in Augusta, Georgia. He has two markers – one at his grave site, and inclusion on a military marker to all the Confederate generals buried there.

Marker at Gettysburg describes Alexander's action there in 1863.
Photo by Lisa Tully

The Alexander grave marker in Magnolia Cemetery, Augusta, GA.
Photo by Janet Greentree

Brevet Lt. Col. Alonzo Hereford Cushing

This month's article is pretty newsworthy, as Brevet Lt. Col. Alonzo Hereford Cushing's bravery at the battle of Gettysburg on July 3, 1863, will now be finally recognized, and he will be awarded the Medal of Honor for his heroic efforts on Cemetery Hill. Pres. Barack Obama signed the order on August 26, 2014, more than 152 years after the battle.

Normally, the Medal of Honor recommendation must be made within two years after the act of heroism and be awarded within three years. The Medal of Honor is awarded for gallantry above and beyond the call of duty. An exception was made for then-1st Lieutenant Cushing. Family members, Wisconsin residents (his home state) and Civil War buffs have pushed for this exception for a long time. Cushing's Medal of Honor will be awarded posthumously, and is the longest time span between the actual event and the awarding of the medal.

The United States Congress made the following findings on Cushing: "(1) Alonzo H. Cushing was born in Delafield, WI, on January 19, 1841. (2) Alonzo H. Cushing

1st Lt. Alonzo H. Cushing at West Point, in 1861.

graduated from the United States Military Academy at West Point, New York, on June 24, 1861. (3) On July 3, 1863, First Lieutenant Alonzo H. Cushing commanded Battery A, 4th United States Artillery, Army of the Potomac, during the Battle of Gettysburg. (4) During the battle, First Lieutenant Alonzo H. Cushing was shot multiple times but refused to retreat. (5) First Lieutenant Alonzo H. Cushing continued to command his battery until he was shot and killed. (6) The Union victory at the Battle of Gettysburg was one of the key turning points of the Civil War. (7) The Secretary of the Army and the Secretary of Defense have determined that the actions of First Lieutenant Alonzo H. Cushing do merit the award of the Medal of Honor."

Cushing's grave is located at West Point. He is buried right next to General John Buford. See

At left, Pres. Barack Obama (behind, left) presents the Medal of Honor posthumously to Army First Lt. Alonzo Cushing for conspicuous gallantry at the 1863 Battle of Gettysburg. Shown accepting the medal on Nov. 6, 2014, is Helen L. Ensign of Palm Desert, Calif. (left) in a ceremony at the White House. Ensign is Cushing's distant cousin. With them were (third from left and at right, respectively) then-Army Secy. John McHugh and then-Veterans Affairs Secy. Robert McDonald.

the October 2011 *Stone Wall* for more information on Cushing's grave. Cushing's mother wanted the inscription "Faithful unto Death" etched in his marker. He is buried in Section 26, Row A, Grave 7 in the company of many fine Civil War generals.

Cushing was born in Wisconsin, but he was raised in Fredonia, New York. He is one of four brothers who served during the Civil War. Brothers Milton and William were in the Navy. Milton was a paymaster and is buried in Dunkirk, NY. William commanded several Union warships and is buried in the U.S. Naval Academy Cemetery overlooking the Severn River. His brother Howard was in the U.S. Army during the Civil War. He was later killed by Apaches in 1871 in the Arizona Territory.

Alonzo graduated 12th in his class from West Point in June 1861. Some of his classmates were George Armstrong Custer, Thomas Rosser, Felix Robertson, and Patrick O'Rorke. O'Rorke was killed defending Little Round Top, the day before Cushing, on July 2, 1863.

At left, Lt. Alonzo Cushing's marker at West Point, NY, is inscribed just as his mother had wanted - saying: "Faithful Unto Death." Below, Cmdr. William Cushing's grave marker at the U.S. Naval Academy in Annapolis, MD.
Photos by Janet Greentree

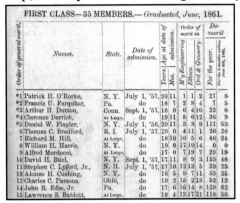

FIRST CLASS—35 MEMBERS.—*Graduated, June*, 1861.									
Order of general merit.	Names.	State.	Date of admission.	Years	Mos.	M'y Engineering.	Ethics.	Ord. & Gunnery.	For the year.	De-merit
*1	Patrick H. O'Rorke	N. Y.	July 1, '57	20	11	1	1	2	27	8
*2	Francis U. Farquhar	Pa.	do	18	7	2	8	4	7	5
*3	Arthur H. Dutton	Conn.	Sept. 1, '57	18	9	6	4	10	22	0
*4	Clarence Derrick	At Large	do	19	11	5	6	12	36	9
*5	Daniel W. Flagler	N. Y.	July 1, '56	20	11	3	3	9	117	53
6	Thomas C. Bradford	R. I.	July 1, '57	20	0	4	11	1	20	20
7	Richard M. Hill	At Large	do	18	10	10	5	6	46	24
8	William H. Harris	N. Y.	do	19	0	17	10	14	0	0
9	Alfred Mordecai	At Large	do	17	0	7	19	7	29	19
10	David H. Buel	N. Y.	Sept. 1, '57	17	11	8	9	3	153	48
11	Stephen C. Lyford, Jr.	N. H.	July 1, '57	17	10	12	13	5	39	25
12	Alonzo H. Cushing	N. Y.	do	16	5	9	7	11	53	25
13	Charles C. Parsons	Ohio.	do	19	2	15	2	13	52	12
14	John R. Edie, Jr.	Pa.	do	17	6	16	14	8	129	62
15	Lawrence S. Babbitt	At Large	do	18	4	13	17	21	118	56

One of the class assessments for Alonzo Cushing during his study at West Point.

I found two interesting pictures of Cushing (see bottom of this page). In one, he appears with other Army officers at Antietam in 1862. He saw action at Chancellorsville, where he was brevetted a major. In the other photo, Cushing is standing to the far left as part of Gen. Edwin Sumner's staff.

Cushing Park, named in his honor, is located in Delafield, Wisconsin. In the park, a huge obelisk is dedicated to the Cushing brothers. Cushing Elementary School in Delafield is also named for Alonzo.

A stone monument was placed on Hancock Avenue at the Angle in Gettysburg where he held his position on the fateful day of July 3, 1863.

Lt. Alonzo Cushing is shown here at back, center, with other officers in a photo taken at Antietam in 1862.

Cushing in undated photo with Gen. Edwin V. Sumner and staff: left to right: Lt. Alonzo H. Cushing; Capt. W.G. Jones; Maj. Laurence Kip, A.D.C.; Lt. Col. Joseph H. Taylor, A.A.C.; and Gen. Edwin V. Sumner.

Cushing was the commander of Battery A, 4th U.S. Artillery, Artillery Brigade, 2nd Corps, Army of the Potomac at Gettysburg, under General Winfield Scott Hancock. He faced the onslaught of 13,000 men coming towards his cannons on Cemetery Ridge. His position having been battered by Confederate artillery, his cannon was the last remaining working cannon at the Angle. "If one would clap their hands as fast as they could, the sound would be equal to the sharp gunfire coming towards him," says former National Park Ranger Scott Hartwig.

Only 22 years old, Cushing was wounded by enemy gunfire in the shoulder and the stomach. Holding his hand on his stomach with his intestines protruding from the wound, and

The monument on Hancock Ave. (and a close-up) at Gettysburg that marks the spot where Cushing was struck down. The view looks west from the monument to Lt. Alonzo Cushing. The monument to his Battery A, 4th United States Artillery; a 3-inch ordnance rifle (cannon) is just behind it, and the monument to the 71st Pennsylvania Infantry Regiment is in the upper right of the photo.

Photo above, left, by Lisa Tully

On the face of the monument shown in the rear of the far left photo, the official marker for Alonzo Cushing's Battery A, 4th United States Artillery. The marker is facing out toward the expanse that was the ground over which Pickett's Charge was executed.

Photo by Lisa Tully

Above, First Sgt. Frederick Fuger, later in life. Fuger held Cushing up, and despite being partially disemboweled, Cushing continued to fire his artillery piece. Fuger picked up firing when Cushing was shot through the head and died.

An 1882 William Tipton image showing the area occupied by Cushing's battery. During the bombardment preceding Pickett's Charge, his six guns were across the ground in the foreground. Following the initial bombardment, he moved two guns up to near where the man is standing on the stone wall. This is where Cushing was killed.

being held up by his First Sgt. Frederick Fuger, Cushing continued to fire. He was then struck in the mouth, with the bullet exiting the back of his head. It was then the brave lad died. The Confederates were within 100 feet of his guns at the time. Out of 110 men in his battery, 32 were injured and 6 died. Sgt. Fuger fired the last shot after laying Cushing on the ground. Fuger was also awarded the Medal of Honor.

If you look out across the field, just imagine what Cushing must have seen...and he still held his position after being told to go back.

My Gettysburg-resident daughter, Lisa, and her husband Paul get a shout-out of thanks for taking the picture of the monument on Hancock Avenue for me. She and Paul photo-bombed the first one they sent me! I have one I snapped of the monument (amongst the thousands of Gettysburg pictures I've taken over the years), but it would have been extremely hard to find it. Thanks again to my freelance team.

The Cushings, and Ellsworth, Wisconsin

The birthplace of the Cushing Brothers – Alonzo, William, and Howard, is memorialized in a city park in Delafield, Wisconsin. There is a huge 50-foot "Washington Monument" type marker in the park, with a bas relief of the Cushing brothers' faces. The monument was dedicated in 1915. The tribute to them reads as follows: "Alonzo, William, & Howard Cushing – Perhaps the most conspicuously daring trio of sons of one mother of any whose exploits have been noted in the places of history."

Above, left to right, the Cushing brothers - Alonzo, William and Howard. The trio have been immortalized in the history of Delafield, Wisconsin. The park where the monument is located is also named after the Cushings. A re-dedication of the monument has since been conducted by the local camp of the Sons of Union Veterans.

Above, left, the May 31, 2015 dedication of the Cushing monument in Delafield, WI. Above, right, a complete view of the monument.
Photo above/right by Janet Greentree

At left, Mrs. William (Kate) Cushing (center), at the 1915 dedication of the Delafield memorial to her husband and his two brothers, Alonzo and Howard. Alonzo's sister-in-law is shown here with her two daughters, Alonzo's nieces, Maria and Katherine. At right, the author is shown placing the U. S. flags at the monument to the three Cushings.
Photo at right courtesy of Janet Greentree

The marker further states: "Alonzo Cushing, born 1841, died 1863, Brevet Lieutenant Colonel, 4th U.S. Artillery, William B. Cushing, born 1842, died 1874, Commander, U.S. Navy, and Howard B. Cushing, born 1868, died 1874, 1st Lieutenant, 3rd U.S. Cavalry."

Alonzo died at the battle of Gettysburg, at the angle, holding off Confederates while being mortally wounded, until a shot to his face killed him instantly. William led the raid on the *CSS Albemarle* during the Civil War. Howard was an Indian fighter in Arizona, fighting the Apaches.

After the diligent work of Margaret Zerwekh, who once lived on the Cushing property in Delafield, a posthumous Medal of Honor was awarded on November 6, 2014, to Alonzo Cushing by President Barak Obama. Several Cushing family members, along with Ms. Zerwekh, were present for the ceremony in the White House. The Medal of Honor travels between Delafield, West Point, and Gettysburg.

For the third Civil War connection, the town of Ellsworth, Wisconsin is named for Col. Elmer Ellsworth, who was the first Union officer killed in the Civil War. He entered the Marshall House

in Alexandria to take down the Rebel flag when he was shot and killed by the owner of the hotel, James W. Jackson. Jackson was, in turn, immediately killed by a companion of Ellsworth.

Although Ms. Rebelle did not visit Ellsworth, it is worthy of a mention, as a Civil War related place. It seems that Ellsworth is famous for its cheese curds, and the company that produces them is called Ellsworth Dairy Cooperative.

Ms. Rebelle added eight Civil War generals to her list of graves visited and decorated. There would have been 16, but the cemetery gate was locked in Red Wing, MN, and the road to Ripon, WI, was closed for construction work.

Since we were out in the farmland of WI, my sister and I decided not to pursue trying to find another way into town. I missed six generals in St. Paul, MN; also, as we ran out of travel time.

There is always next time!

Above, left, Col. Elmer Ellsworth in regular Union Army dress, not the famous Zouave 'uni' he was known for wearing in performance before the war. Above, center, is an undated photo of him in Zouave garb. Ellsworth was very renowned before the war, putting on military reviews as a Zouave across the U.S.; when he became the first Union casualty, the nation was shocked. His funeral was held in the White House, as Ellsworth was a close companion to Abraham Lincoln. Ellsworth is buried in Hudson View Cemetery, Mechanicville, NY. Above, right, his grand monument was erected in 1874.

At right, in a photo taken on the 100th anniversary of Ellsworth's death that will today make historians' heads explode, is shown New York State Historian Nancy Cosselman exhibiting Ellsworth's sword while wearing his bullet-holed coat (see tear on left breast of the tunic).

Official Period News wire photo

Finding my Roots

My annual trip with my sister this year was a genealogy/family history trip to Ohio and Indiana to find out about our family's roots. Our parents were from the Columbus, Ohio area and our paternal grandfather was from Peru, Indiana.

Our maternal Civil War great-grandfathers, George Washington Baker, 23rd VA Cavalry, and Daniel Smethers, 18th U.S., Army of the Ohio, are buried in Gahanna and Westerville, Ohio, respectively. George came from the Augusta County area of Virginia. George Baker's son, William, married Daniel Smethers' daughter Laura. I've always wondered how that worked out.

George enlisted at New Market, Virginia on November 23, 1863, at age 19. His older brother John was in the 12th Virginia Volunteers. George was wounded at Woodstock in May 1864, and sent to Camp Chase in Columbus, Ohio. The family story goes that George and a Yankee confronted each other, but neither one wanted to kill the other, so they shot to wound. George was wounded in the hip and carried the bullet the rest of his life. John was captured at one of the many battles of Winchester and sent to Camp Chase as well. John was later sent to Johnson's Island. George was released on May 15, 1865, after signing the oath of allegiance.

Another family story was told that George met his wife while at Camp Chase in Columbus. It seems that it was customary

This precious photo, although unclear, is an incredible family treasure. Above: George Washington Baker family - 1900s: (L-R) George Washington Baker, Sivilla Souder Baker, Robert E. Lee Baker, David Baker, William Baker, Joseph Baker, Nettie Baker, George Walter Baker, & Alburtus Baker. Below: present Baker cousins - (L-R) Bob & Dan Cheadle, Janet Greentree, Kathe Fernandez, Gwen Green Martin, Bari Martin Huthmacher, Pat Perkins, Megan Perkins, & Cheryl Baker Harrison.

Photo courtesy of Janet Greentree

George Washington Baker

for young ladies to come and visit the camp and bring food to the prisoners. He fell in love with Sivilla Souder, and after being released, came back to Ohio to marry her. Her father said that if he would marry her, he would give him some land to farm.

George's farm was in Gahanna, Ohio. My mother lived on his farm when she was a little girl and remembered him talking about the Civil War. The site of the farm is now an upscale housing development. George and Sivilla had eight children

Through the internet, Ancestry.com and Facebook, several of George's descendants have contacted each other. We decided that we would all get together and meet each other for the first time while my sister and I were visiting. There were ten of us at the gathering. George's first son was named Robert E. Lee Baker (Bob & Dan Cheadle), William Baker (my sister Kathe Fernandez and I), Nettie Baker (Sue Ellen Kirkman, Gwen Green Martin, Bari Martin Huthmacher, Pat Green Perkins, Megan Perkins), and George Walter Baker (Cheryl Baker Harrison). The picture here shows us in the birth order behind our common ancestor, George Washington Baker's grave in Mifflin Cemetery, Gahanna, Ohio. What a great time we had together. It felt like we had been friends and family forever.

Our Union ancestor, Daniel Smethers, is buried in the Tussic Street Road Cemetery in Westerville, Ohio, right across the road from the 55+ acre farm he owned. His house is no longer standing, but the house of his son Frank Smothers (yes, they changed the name as they thought Smothers sounded better) is still standing. It, too, is surrounded by an upscale housing development. As a young child, I remember being in the house and the farm. The one thing that stuck out in my mind was that they had a pump in the kitchen for water. I remember playing with my cousin Norma Jean on the farm.

A visit to Mount Vernon, Ohio, to visit Norma Jean and her husband Bob Higgins turned out to be quite a fruitful visit. No one in my branch of the family had any pictures of Daniel Smethers. Norma Jean had several, so I finally got to see what my ancestor looked like. The picture here is of him in later life. Daniel was in the Civil War almost from the beginning. He signed up in New Albany, Ohio, on November 22, 1861. William Fetterman, of the Fetterman Massacre in 1866, in Montana, signed his enlistment papers. My sister and I visited Fetterman's grave at Little Big Horn National Cemetery in 2012.

Daniel Smethers

Daniel was wounded six times and injured his spine from a shell. He hurt his back on the way to Shiloh trying to pull a wagon out of the mud. He was sent back to Ohio to recuperate. He was discharged due to injury on January 18, 1864. I have 85 pages of his records from the National Archives. The papers show his battle with rheumatism, trying to get his pension increased, the signature of my Great Uncle Frank Smothers when Daniel died, and the birth of my grandmother Laura. It was very interesting reading for sure.

Peru, Indiana

Ms. Rebelle has talked about connections many times in her writings. Would you believe NPS Historian Emeritus Edwin Cole Bearss and I share a connection to Peru, Indiana?

My grandfather Albert Schrader was born in Peru in 1868, so there is no Civil War connection for him. Albert married my grandmother Ida Bauer in 1907 in Columbus, Ohio. We do not know how they met or how he got to Columbus to meet her. Albert was a cabinet maker for the Indiana Manufacturing Company, located in Peru. Albert and Ida had three children – Robert, Dorothy, and Alan (my father).

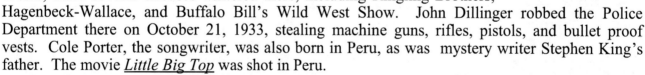

Albert Schrader

Peru has several claims to fame. It's known as the Circus Capital of the World, since several circuses wintered there, including Ringling Brothers, Hagenbeck-Wallace, and Buffalo Bill's Wild West Show. John Dillinger robbed the Police Department there on October 21, 1933, stealing machine guns, rifles, pistols, and bullet proof vests. Cole Porter, the songwriter, was also born in Peru, as was mystery writer Stephen King's father. The movie *Little Big Top* was shot in Peru.

For our purposes though, Ed Bearss' ancestor Daniel Bearss was one of the pioneers who settled the town when it was just a wilderness. Daniel married Emma Cole, a daughter of Judge

Albert Cole, another pioneer of the town. At one time, there was a Bearss Hotel. The building (shown at left) is still standing at East Main and South Broadway.

On March 25, 1913, an Easter flood hit Peru, caused by six inches of rain falling in a small amount of time. The Wabash and Mississinewa Rivers overflowed their banks, causing massive flooding in Peru, and all along the river towns. The Wabash, normally 400 yards across, expanded to four miles across. The water came down the streets at 20 miles per hour, destroying everything in its path.

My grandparents lived on East Third Street, three blocks from the river. (When we visited the Miami County Museum in town, the docent told us that people marked on their walls how high the floods were over the years.) Some stayed too long in their houses, hoping that they wouldn't have to leave. I fear that my Albert and his family were one of those families.

In 1913, Albert had a 5-year-old, a 4-year-old, and a twenty-two month-old (my father). Large row boats rescued the townspeople. My grandmother was in a rescue boat with the two older children, Robert and Dorothy. My grandfather was on the second floor of his house with the baby, my father. Albert threw my father out of the second-story window into the boat. Albert then crawled out on the porch roof, slipped, and hit his side on the sharply peaked roof. He was able to get into the boat. The survivors were taken to the Miami County Courthouse.

As you can see by the picture at left, the window was very small on the second floor and the picture shows the sharply peaked roof where he slipped. History is such a split-second in time. What if my father had not survived? What if my Baker and Smethers great-grandfathers had not survived the Civil War?

As a direct result of Albert's injury, he developed cancer and died on May 16, 1914, leaving my grandmother with three

Above, South Peru in the 1913 flood. At right, East 5th Street, Peru.

The Wabash River overflowed to drown Peru.

Schrader House - then and now. This is the house that Janet's grandfather tossed her father from into a boat to save him from the flood, and the roof on which he slipped and injured himself trying to slide down himself to the rescue boat.

Modern photos by Janet Greentree

This postcard was sent by Janet's paternal grandmother Ida Schrader to her sister Emma Drobisch, telling her about the flood in Peru in 1913, and how it affected her family. Janet's father was less than two years old at this time. It says: *"Received your letter this morning, will write later. The children are all better, with the exception of a bad cough. It will take us all summer before we get things cleaned up. This is a scene in South Peru, we were down Sunday afternoon. It is a most horrible looking place. Ida & Albert."*

small children. Her family urged her to give up her children for adoption, but she refused. She took in laundry, did sewing, took in boarders, and somehow survived for three years before she moved back to Columbus, Ohio, to be with her family. After selling her house in Peru, she ran boarding houses and three different hotels with restaurants in Columbus and Westerville.

Peru was a thriving town before the flood. It was home to 100 factories, 15,000 residents, circuses, a railroad, and a trolley service. Over 500 circus animals died in the flood. The Hagenbeck-Wallace headquarters were on the east side of town, between both rivers. The damage to Peru was $3,000,000 in 1913 money. The town never recovered to what it was before.

Albert (at left in photos below) is buried in the Mount Hope Cemetery off Logan Street in Peru. Directly across from his grave are buried the entire Bearss family, including Ed's parents, and his Medal of Honor-recipient cousin, Hiram Bearss (photo at right, below). Ms. Rebelle placed flags on both Omar Bearss' grave (Ed's father, center photo, below), and Hiram Bearss' grave. Ed's father was in the service in WWI and WWII. Cole Porter is also buried in Mount Hope, and is related to Ed Bearss through the Cole family.

Photos by Janet Greentree

My sister and I spent much time in the Miami County Courthouse in Peru, finding the death certificates of our family members, Albert's will, the deed to Albert's house, and looking at the large deed books with our great-grandmother's name deeding property to Albert and his brother.

We spent time at the library looking at the history of the town and found the funeral bill for Albert in a big book, as well as newspaper obituary of Albert's older brother John, who was Chief of Police at one time (before the Dillinger episode). Everyone who helped us was so happy to find our family members for us.

Miami County Courthouse in Peru.

Photo by Janet Greentree

In the space of a week, we also saw some Civil War places in Ohio, including a new statue of Gen. William Starke Rosecrans in Sunbury; a statue of Gen. Phil Sheridan in Somerset; Sheridan's boyhood home and the graves of his parents in Lancaster, Ohio.

In addition, we took in the homes of Gen. William Tecumseh Sherman and Gen. Hugh Boyle Ewing, two doors down, where Sherman lived after becoming orphaned. Also included were Camp Chase in Columbus; Spring Grove Cemetery in Cincinnati; and 19 new Civil War generals' graves, including one on my bucket list – Gen. Joseph Hooker – but that's another story.

Our Ohio family members and my cousins Alan (Dorothy Schrader's son) & Carol Norris made our trip so much fun. We found all of our family members' graves, explored all the places our ancestors lived in Columbus, along with the 'Civil War' and 'cemetery' road trips. Alan's cemetery map-reading skills were awesome in Green Lawn Cemetery in Columbus. Many thanks go out to them for their great hospitality.

Booth Home, Thomas Viaduct Bridge

Editor's note: this was one of the first trips Ms. Rebelle took with the assistance of GPS; it shows how new (at the time) technology can be a great aid in accomplishing historical research.

February 16th was another day on the road for Ms. Rebelle, Yankee Nan, and 'Ms. Lori' TomTom. We were rewarded with a beautiful blue-sky day, after so many gray ones this winter. It was a little nippy at times, but bearable. We have done two Booth Escape tours recently, and because of our upcoming Round Table tour, we wanted to find the boyhood home of John Wilkes Booth and the Booth family in Bel Air, Maryland. After checking several sources quite a while ago, it was determined that the house was privately owned and surrounded by trees. The only time one is able to view it is when the leaves are off the trees. One last check prior to departure revealed that the Booth house was recently bought by Harford County, Maryland, and is now the Center for the Arts. How fitting is that, with its most famous occupants having been the Booth family?!

The Booth home—Tudor Hall—in Bel Air, MD.

Photo by Janet Greentree

Ms. Lori was programmed for the destination of 17 Tudor Hall Lane, Bel Air, Maryland, and we were off. This time we didn't carry along numerous maps and map books highlighted with the directions, as usual. We just let Ms. Lori take us there. I must say, she did a fine job. It took a little less than two hours to get there from Springfield. She even kept working through the Baltimore tunnels. How is that possible? The screen went to black and white, but you could see the car going and the water overhead. Just amazing.

A long, curving lane leads down to the house. Beautiful, huge, stately trees line the driveway. There is a small pond off to the right, in front of the house. The house is in remarkable condition and looks exactly like pictures we've seen of it. It was deserted when we arrived, so Ms. Rebelle looked in the window. Yankee Nan decided to stay in the car. At the end of the entrance hall was a painting of Junius Brutus Booth. I truly wished we could have gone inside, but that wasn't meant to be on this trip. There is a Maryland historical marker on Route 22 stating that the house is "near here." Don't you just love the vague directions on those markers? It mentions that Junius Brutus Booth lived there and that his son, Edwin Booth, was born there on November 13, 1833. There was no mention of any other Booth children, nor John Wilkes. Nancy and I felt we were extremely lucky to come there when the house wasn't privately owned; there was no chain across the driveway, and it was so deserted. Both of us expected to have to peek at it from a distance but driving right up to it was awesome.

Junius first built a log cabin on the 137-acre property. In 1822, he moved the log cabin to the present-day location of the house and kept adding onto it for the next 30 years, until it looked like it does today. Logs in the basement are part of the original log cabin, but when he added porches and more rooms, no one suspected that the original log cabin was, indeed, part of the current house. Junius, and his second wife, Mary Ann Holmes, raised 10 children there. John Wilkes was next to the youngest. When his mother learned of the terrible deed John Wilkes did, she collected all his clothes, letters, and photographs and burned them in one of the fireplaces of the house. John's sister, Asia, rescued some of the items from the fire. Today, the house sits on 8½ acres of land, contains 18 rooms, and five fireplaces. Junius designed the house in the Tudor style, so that is how the name Tudor Hall came to be. John Wilkes' bedroom is on the second floor, with a balcony, so he could practice his craft. There is also a stage on the second floor where the family put on plays. John Wilkes scratched his initials in a windowpane to the left of the entryway, which can still be seen today. *Note to self: "Do the research first, so you could have checked out the initials!"*

Our next programmed stop was New Cathedral Cemetery in Southwest Baltimore. Ms. Lori took us through the city with no problem. She knows the one-way streets, and she knows the streets on which you are unable to turn left. We again ended up at the gate of the cemetery with no problems. My last remaining general in Baltimore, Lucius Bellinger Northrop, CSA, is buried there. This was our third visit to Baltimore to find generals. Even with maps, it took a little doing to find him. A Confederate flag was placed in front of his stone in his honor. He was from Charleston, SC. I wonder how he ended up in Baltimore. He died in Pikesville, Maryland, in 1894 and was a farmer after the war. He was the Commissary General of the Confederacy and a favorite of President Jefferson Davis. That must have been quite a job. There are other notables buried there: Henry Mears, who was Booth's undertaker; Dr. William Cole, a Confederate surgeon; George Kane, the police chief during the Baltimore President Street riots, and John Surratt, son of Mary Surratt. We found everyone but George Kane, who was supposed to be buried near Dr. William Cole. However, either because of the wind on the hills, vandals, or time, many of the tombstones were toppled over, which is truly sad. As we were leaving, we noticed - way off in the distance - a beautiful view of the skyline of Baltimore and the Key Bridge.

Our third programmed destination was G&M Restaurant in Linthicum, MD. Again, Ms. Lori took us there so easily. If you like crab cakes, this is the place to go. The crab cakes are at least 4" x 3" and absolutely chocked full of jumbo crabmeat. Being from 'Crab town,' a/k/a Annapolis, I love crab cakes, and this place by far has the best I've ever eaten. No other crab cake will be worthy after dining in this establishment. The manager said they could accommodate a group at lunch, so if the Round Table ever wants to do another Baltimore tour, this is the place to stop for lunch.

After lunch, Nancy suggested that we stop at Relay, Maryland, to see the Thomas Viaduct Bridge again, since the leaves were off the trees. This is definitely the time to go. Ms. Lori didn't recognize Relay though, so we programmed in the nearby town of Elkridge, and found it OK. The famous obelisk monument at the railroad track intersection can be seen from several angles through the trees. The last time we were there, I had no idea that it was so close to the bridge and tracks. The 15-foot obelisk was dedicated when the bridge was finished in 1835. The Thomas Viaduct Bridge over the Patapsco River is the oldest stone arch bridge in use today. It is 704 feet long, 60 feet high, and was once the country's largest bridge, and the first bridge built on a curve.

The bridge was designed by Benjamin F. Latrobe, Jr. It was made a National Historic Landmark in 1964, and was named for Philip E. Thomas, the first president of the B&O Railroad. During the Civil War, it was heavily guarded by Federal troops along its length. It was used as shelter for the Underground Railroad during the Civil War, as well. The 6th Massachusetts set up camp on Lawyer's Hill, overlooking the Viaduct. Gen. Benjamin Butler, USA, was in command to guard the bridge and control the rail traffic at Camp Essex.

Ms. Rebelle's Disclaimer: I do not sit on the board or have stock in TomTom. However, this trip was the most effortless trip through a city that I've ever done. Nancy, my excellent map-reader, could actually sit back and enjoy the trip this time. I love my Tom-Tom. No connection to G&M Restaurant either, but they sure have good food, and it's out in record time.

The Thomas Bridge Viaduct today (left), during the Civil War (center) and the dedication monument (left).
Modern photos by Janet Greentree

Booth Escape Route by Car or Ten New Things I Learned

Can you believe after three bus tours to this site, Ms. Rebelle actually wanted to do another Booth Escape Route tour by car? Not only that, Yankee Nan [Nancy Anwyll] agreed to go along. Since this seems to be my main focus now, I wanted to do this at as close to the exact time as possible to April 14th. So, Yankee Nan and I took off for that foreign country (to this non-Big City driver), Washington, DC, on April 12th, to start the tour.

Most of you know who I am, but in that foreign country, people of authority tend to think I look like a terrorist. Our first stop was 10th Street to take a picture of Ford's Theatre and the

Peterson House. To steady my camera, I brought along my monopod. I was busy setting up the shots when a policeman from Ford's came up to me and asked me what I was doing. Always being honest, I told the truth, and told him I was working on a documentary of the Booth Escape Route. Right away, he asked if I had a permit. It seems a common citizen cannot use a tripod on the street, and it wasn't even a tripod. Finally, I said it was just a dream, so he let me keep taking my pictures.

The next stop was Baptist Alley. We drove the car right down the alley leading to the backstage door of the theater. How cool is that?! There was a whole crowd of people there on a tour. Guess who their tour guide was?

Above, Baptist Alley, down which Booth fled on horse after murdering Abraham Lincoln. Below, the rear stage door on the right) that led to Booth's growing nightmare of escape, capture and death.
Photos by Janet Greentree

None other than Michael Kauffman, author of "*American Brutus*." How both Yankee Nan and I wished we could just hop on their bus. Their tour was through the Surratt Society. The front of the bus said, "John Wilkes Booth Tour." Since I've read so much about John Wilkes Booth's personality, somehow, I think he would really enjoy his notoriety, and the fact that, 154 years later, people are still interested in him and his escape.

Now comes the *real* terrorist threat assessment. The Washington Navy Yard seemed to be the best vantage point for taking a picture of the 11th Street/Navy Yard Bridge. This was the bridge that both Booth and Davy Herold crossed over into Uniontown, now known as Anacostia.

The epicenter of a national tragedy - Ford's Theatre (top photo) and (across the street from the theater) the Peterson House.
Photos by
Janet Greentree

I contacted three people at the Navy Yard. One of them was the head of Public Affairs. Again, I was honest about what I wanted to do. All three of them said it wouldn't be a problem. So, I presented my license, insurance card and my car registration to two young Marines at the gate. They didn't have me listed as a visitor and said they would have to call their Sergeant. It took forever for the Sergeant to appear. Yankee Nan and I knew we were in trouble, just by his demeanor when he came walking up, studied my license plate, and his tone of voice. Being honest didn't help one bit here. He said the bridge was right there if I wanted to take a picture of it – that is – outside of the Navy Yard. Needless to say, we didn't get in there.

We just crossed over the Navy Yard Bridge, went into Anacostia Park, and I got a decent picture there.

Yankee Nan and I both heaved a huge sigh of relief to be out of D.C. and back into Maryland. Yankee Nan had been studying internet topo maps trying to find Soper's Hill, where Booth and Herold met up. There had been some discussion on the tours as to exactly where it was. Just after going under the Beltway on Route 5, we turned right on Linda Lane, and right again on Old Branch Avenue. You go down a long hill, and that is Soper's Hill. Henson Creek is at the bottom. I remember reading that Herold "halloed" for Booth at the top of the hill there.

The 11th Street/Navy Yard Bridge leading out of Washington City, where Booth conned his way through the roadblock thrown up following the alerts of the president's assassination.
Photo by Janet Greentree

Above, the Surratt house, one half of the split scene of the plotting, outfitting, evidence-gathering and arrests in the assassination of Abraham Lincoln. Below, Huckleberry, the home of Thomas Jones, Confederate sympathizer and, some think, possibly another conspirator.

Photos by Janet Greentree

The Samuel Mudd house, left, where Booth stopped to have the staunch Southern doctor treat his broken shin bone. The two had met previously, when the plan to kill Lincoln was still a plan to kidnap the president. Dr. Mudd's attempt to convince the court that he did not know Booth were unsuccessful.
Photo by Janet Greentree

Then it was on to the Surratt House, and the other group's tour bus was already there. We got to talk to Michael Kauffman. That was awesome. We fought the raindrops both there and in Anacostia Park. Then the sun came out – for a time anyway. We went on to T.B. – the area named for Confederate sympathizer Thomas Brook. The ruins of his house sit at the intersection of Route 5 and Brandywine Road. Davy Herold spent the night there on his March visit to Southern Maryland. The nightshirt he wore is in the Surratt House Museum.

We decided to follow the Surratt Society's route and went to the Mudd House after a quick stop at St. Peter's Church, Dr. Samuel Mudd's home church. We found the grave of Edmund Spangler, one of the conspirators, who is buried in the Old St. Peter's Cemetery. The Surratt and Mudd Societies have placed a nice stone on his grave.

The cemetery is at the intersection of Brandywine and Gardiner Roads. The road must have been named for the Gardiner family. George Gardiner was a close neighbor of Dr. Mudd and sold Booth the one-eyed horse that he rode during his escape. George Gardiner's farm is at the intersection of Malcolm and Poplar Hill Roads.

When we got to the Mudd House, who should be there but the Surratt Society bus. The sky was a dark, deep cloudy blue from an impending rainstorm, which showered us again when we got to the Bryantown Tavern. It rained from there to the site of Oswell Swann's house. Swann guided Booth and Herold through the Zekiah Swamp. We stopped at Rich Hill, the home of Col. Samuel Cox, who aided them and sent them on to Thomas Jones, his adopted son, who hid them in the Pine Thicket for six days and nights. We actually found the Pine Thicket across from a house at 9185 Wills Street in Bel Alton. I have to give my cousin, Alan Norris (our Ohio Bull Run Civil War Round Table member), credit for this one. We didn't venture in the woods but were certainly close to where Booth

It didn't seem prudent to do a deeper investigation of the pine thicket without proper preparation - so this is just a glimpse into it.
Photo by Janet Greentree

and Herold were.

Huckleberry was our next stop – the home of Thomas Jones. We took the road down to the river where the Loyola Retreat is. With 95% certainty, I would say we found the road that leads down to Dent's Meadow where Booth and Herold got into the flat-bottomed 12-foot skiff to cross the Potomac. We

The road to the Potomac spot where Booth and Herrold boarded a skiff to cross into Virginia.
Photo by Janet Greentree

verified this by an old picture on a Civil War Trails sign about Dent's Meadow, across the street from Captain Billy's restaurant. Yes! We had a nice lunch at Captain Billy's again, and guess who appeared after we pulled up? The Surratt Society tour bus. This was the last time we saw them, however.

Now it was on to see Thomas Jones' other house, sitting 80 feet up on a bluff over the Potomac River near the Route 301 bridge. Zooming in on the house gave me a nice photo. It's a lovely house. It would have been nice to see it close up. We crossed the Route 301 Bridge into Virginia. We felt like we were shadowing Booth and Herold all day.

Thomas Jones' other home on the Potomac River.
Photo by Janet Greentree

Mrs. Quesenberry's house on Machadoc Creek was the next stop. We checked out Gambo Creek, where our Round Table bus had to turn around. Booth and Herold landed there on their second attempt at crossing the Potomac. We went on to Dr. Stuart's home Cleydael for more photo ops. From there it was on to Port Conway, which we are pretty sure we found, as well. There is a gravel road parallel to the northbound lane of Route 301 just before the Rappahannock Bridge that we followed. It goes down to the water across from Port Royal. There is a sign there: "Warning, keep out, snake sanctuary." We got a kick out of that,

Mrs. Quesenberry's house on Machadoc Creek was a Confederate safe haven Booth was seeking across the Potomac in Virginia - but the fugitives came up short by a mile. The Confederate agent wasn't home when they located the house, but when they later met up with her, she refused to help them obtain a horse or shelter.
Photo by Janet Greentree

Okay. Will do. The sign on the land associated with the area across from Port Royal catches the attention of all who would follow closely Booth's travel through the landscape of northern Virginia.
Photo by Janet Greentree

The sign (above) at right is located on the side of a divided highway, leading visitors down a beaten path to the site on the left - where, in the right bottom quadrant of the picture, a pipe can be seen sticking out of the ground. In front of that pipe is the doorstep of the Garrett Farm house, where Booth sought shelter, learning by this time not to request aid as himself - so he said he and Herold were returning Confederate soldiers. They were placed in the barn nearby and, soon, met their fate.

Photo on right, above, by Janet Greentree

but I suppose if you don't want people around, having a sign like that will do the job.

We checked out Port Royal and the Peyton-Brockenbrough House before heading to Bowling Green. We found the location of the Star Hotel at Bowling Green, next to the Caroline County Courthouse. The Star Hotel is now gone, but a new building which houses an insurance agency has taken its place. It's a charming little town.

Our last stop – the Garrett Farm site - where John Wilkes Booth was killed. It's always sad and a little creepy to go in there. Every time I go, something else of interest has been added. Someone has placed a small metal cross at the stone and pipe there. Thus ended our trip, closest to the actual time of year the escape occurred as possible.

What I have learned is this: Ms. Rebelle looks like a terrorist; you can't use a tripod or monopod in DC; I look too suspicious to get into the Navy Yard; but we found Soper's Hill; the house in T.B. where Herold spent the night; Ned Spangler's grave; George Gardiner's farm; the Pine Thicket; Port Conway - which is full of snakes - and Bowling Green, site of young 18 year old Private Willie Jett's squealing on Booth's whereabouts. It was an awesome day.

Inside John Wilkes Booth's Boyhood Home – Tudor Hall

On a gray, very foggy Sunday, April 25th, Ms. Rebelle and Yankee Nan (Nancy Anwyll) drove yet again to John Wilkes Booth's boyhood home in Bel Air, Maryland for a tour of the inside of the home. Four groups, including the Junius B. Booth Society, sponsored the tour. As you enter the foyer, there is a fireplace with a huge portrait of Junius Brutus Booth hanging above it.

There is a small parlor on the right, with portraits of Edwin and John Wilkes Booth. To the left is a bigger parlor with a bay window put in by one of the many people who have lived in the house since the Booths. On the other side of the foyer are a fireplace and a large room. This fireplace backs up to the one in the next room. The portraits of all the Booth children are on the mantle. A portrait of Mary Ann Holmes Booth, Junius Brutus Booth's second wife and mother of most of his children, hangs above the fireplace. When his mother learned of the terrible deed John Wilkes did, she collected all his

Greeting visitors to Tudor Hall is Junius Brutus Booth, scion of a family of actors—one of whom murdered the president of the United States.
Photo by Janet Greentree

Edwin (left) and John Wilkes Booth (right) Spend eternity side-by-side on the wall at Tudor Hall, although they were bitter rivals in life.
Photo by Janet Greentree

At left, the Mary Ann Holmes Booth is prominent over the children's pictures (shown below), as well as one of her as a saucy, much younger girl (see picture at right).

Photos by Janet Greentree

Marie Christine Adelaide Delannoy, Junius' first wife, from the New York Dramatic News, August 1, 1891.

Above, left to right, Junius, Jr.; Rosalie; Edwin; below, Asia; John Wilkes and Joseph Adrian, the youngest of the Booth children.

Photos by Janet Greentree

clothes, letters, and photographs and burned them in one of the fireplaces of the house. John's sister, Asia, rescued some of the items from the fire. Sadly, visitors can only tour the first floor; we did not get to go above to see the bedrooms.

Mary Ann Holmes was a beautiful flower girl at the Covent Garden Theatre in London when Junius Brutus Booth met her. Booth was married at the time to Marie Christine Adelaide Delannoy Booth and had a son, Richard Junius Booth, age two. In 1821, Mary Ann followed Junius to America, landing in Norfolk, VA, and later living in Charleston, South Carolina. They then lived on Exeter Street in Baltimore and bought the Hereford County, Maryland, property to build their dream house and retirement haven.

Marie Booth, left at home in London, was not aware that her husband was living for the many years of separation with another woman and that he had ten children with her. When she did find out in 1846, she came to America and harassed him, even to the point of throwing apples at him in the street and showing up at his performances to taunt him. Finally, they were divorced, and Junius and Mary Ann were married on John Wilkes' 13th birthday, May 10, 1851.

Junius first built a log cabin on the 137-acre property in Bel Air. In 1822, he moved the log cabin to the present-day location of the house and kept adding onto it. They raised their ten children there. Junius, age 56, died in 1852 on a riverboat on the Ohio River while touring, and never lived

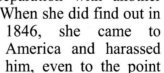

A staircase to the second floor is off limits to visitors - a shame, if you are a photographer that attracts orbs from time to time.

Photo by Janet Greentree

The pastoral setting of Tudor Hall belies the infighting, alcoholism and - finally - violence, that beset the family that dwelled there.

Photo by Janet Greentree

in the house as it looks today. Mary Ann and her youngest children lived there for the following seven years.

Since neither John Wilkes nor his youngest brother, Joseph, were interested in farming, Mary Ann rented out the farm in 1857. None of the Booth family lived in the house after 1857. Four of the Booth children died in the 1830s and were buried on the property. Later, their graves were moved to the family plot at Green Mount Cemetery in Baltimore, where most of the Booth family rests today, including John Wilkes, in an unmarked grave.

John Wilkes' sister Asia was married to John Sleeper Clarke and left the country after the assassination, never to return. Following her death, her body was brought back from England and interred in the Green Mount plot. The youngest child, Joseph Adrian Booth, became a doctor.

Left to right - the balcony on the second story of the house marks where John Wilkes' bedroom was; in center, the windowpane that contains the etched initials "JWB;" and, at right, the pretty side garden at Tudor Hall.

Photos by Janet Greentree

The house is solid brick with diamond-shaped pane windows and columns that are original to the house. The house was red brick when the Booths lived there, but it was whitewashed some time later. John Wilkes, who tattooed his initials, JWB, on his wrist, also etched his name in the windowpane to the right of the door. We were able to see the etching still today. The gardens on the left side of the house are beautiful. The balcony on the right side of the house was John Wilkes' bedroom.

Junius Brutus Booth's first wife, Marie, lived in Baltimore well after the divorce and is buried in New Cathedral Cemetery.

The Booth monument in Greenmount Cemetery, Baltimore, MD. It is surmised that the monument was replaced at least three times by Edwin Booth, he being the dissatisfied designer of the obelisk. It was created to honor his father Junius, whom Edwin was oddly devoted to, even though he was emotionally distressed by the years-long obligation that was required of him by his mother to caretake the elder actor. As a mere child, Edwin was consigned to keep Junius out of bars, or - failing that - keep him upright on stage and out of trouble after performances. Each year he was responsible for keeping the breadwinner of his family alive and earning (without gambling away his revenue), Edwin sank deeper into despair.

Edwin changed out the obelisk with each new inscription he found that might better express his father's genius. The current obelisk is the third one commissioned by Edwin Booth. Each time Edwin had the epitaph changed he required the construction of a new, but nearly identical stone. All the lettering on the monument is in bas relief except for the back, which lists some of the children of Junius and Mary who were buried there. It is believed that a younger relative crammed John Wilkes' name in amongst the names of the Booth children who died in childhood.

117

Gen. William Dorsey Pender, CSA

Maj. Gen. William D. Pender

Rather than drive north coming back from my Outer Banks vacation one year, Ms. Rebelle drove south, down to Manteo, and crossed the longest bridge in Virginia, the Virginia Dare Memorial Bridge (going west on Route 64) to the quaint southern town of Tarboro, North Carolina. Gen. George Washington slept in the town (so they say, as many other towns who like to boast that fact). His comment about Tarboro's welcome was that it was "as good a salute as could be given with one piece of artillery."

Tarboro is situated on the southwestern banks of the Tar River. The town has five 18th-century homes and more than 24 antebellum homes within its historic district. It is a lovely little town, and Ms. Rebelle wished she could have explored it more.

Of course, now you are all wondering what Ms. Rebelle's objective was in going to Tarboro, but I'm sure you suspect the motive. Maj. Gen. William Dorsey Pender, one of the six Confederate generals – Lewis A. Armistead, William Barksdale, Richard B. Garnett, Paul J. Semmes, and James J. Pettigrew (who died during the retreat) all were fatal casualties at Gettysburg in July 1863.

Gen. Pender is buried in the Cavalry Church Cemetery in Tarboro. His grave is unique, as it is surrounded by cannon balls, since he was in the artillery. A large cross is on the top and the words

Gen. Pender's grave in Calvary Church Cemetery, Tarboro, NC. Below, a close-up of the inscription on the stone.
Photos by Janet Greentree

"Patriot by Nature, Soldier by Training, Christian by Faith" are etched on the marker of his final resting place.

Dorsey, as he was known to his friends and family, was born on February 6, 1834 (he shares the same birthday with J.E.B. Stuart but is a year younger) on his family's plantation in Pender's Crossroads, Edgecombe County, North Carolina. His early education was at North Carolina's common schools. He worked as a clerk in his brother's store before going to West Point. At the young age of 16, he was accepted to West Point and graduated in 1854, 19th out of 46 in his class, where he excelled in math and cavalry tactics. Eight classmates (including Pender) who became generals during the Civil War would die during the conflict - Benjamin Davis (Brandy Station), James Deshler (Chickamauga), Archibald Gracie (Petersburg), John Pegram (Hatchers Run), Stephen Weed (Gettysburg), John Villepigue (died of disease in 1862), J.E.B. Stuart (Yellow Tavern), and Pender. Five other officers of that class also died during the Civil War. Classmates who did survive the war include: Oliver O. Howard, George Washington Custis Lee, Stephen Dill Lee, and Thomas Ruger.

Dorsey was described as being thin and handsome, with dark hair, an olive complexion, brown eyes, a neatly trimmed and pointed beard, and a sweet disposition, but with a strict sense of discipline. He was modest, gentle, and spoke little. When he did speak, he did so with a low and cultivated voice, featuring a Southern drawl, of course. He was most sensitive about his loss of hair and described himself to his wife in a letter as "quite bald." One of his men said that "He was one of the coolest, most self-possessed and one of the most absolutely fearless men under fire I ever knew."

After graduating in 1854 as second lieutenant in the 1st U.S. Artillery, he was sent to Fort Myers, Florida. His second assignment was with the 1st Regiment of Dragoons, and he was sent out west to New Mexico, California, Oregon, and the Washington Territory, where he fought the Apaches in the Indian Wars. He married on March 3, 1859, to Mary Francis Shepperd, a sister to his West Point classmate Samuel Shepperd and daughter of Congressman Augustine H. Shepperd. Three sons would be born of the marriage, the last one four months after Pender's death.

Mary F. Shepperd and William D. Pender on their wedding day, March 3, 1859.

Prior to the Civil War and the secession of North Carolina, he offered his services to the Confederacy. He was given the rank of captain. His first assignment was as a recruiting officer in Baltimore, Maryland. He missed the First Battle of Manassas but fought at Seven Pines, Seven Days Battles, 2nd Manassas, Harpers Ferry, Antietam, Fredericksburg, Chancellorsville, and Gettysburg.

Pender was wounded a total of five times. It's been said that if he wasn't wounded in a battle, something was wrong. His first wound was in the arm, at the Battle of Glendale. At Fredericksburg, he was wounded in his left arm but kept riding his horse, rallying his men while his blood ran down his arm and hand. At Chancellorsville, he received a minor wound from a spent bullet that killed an officer standing in front of him. At Second Manassas, he was knocked down from the explosion of a shell but refused to leave the field. He received a small cut on the top of his head and some of his hair had to be removed. His last wound was from a piece of shrapnel to his leg, at Gettysburg. Gen. Robert E. Lee wrote to Confederate President Jeff Davis that "Pender is an excellent officer, attentive, industrious and brave; has been conspicuous in every battle, and, I believe, wounded in almost all of them."

Gen. Pender was one of Lee's up-and-coming stars. He became a brigadier general at the young age of 28 on June 1, 1862, for his meritorious fighting at the battle of Fair Oaks. Pres. Davis, who rode from Richmond to watch the battle, came on to the field to promote Pender. You can't ask for more of a commendation than that. At Antietam, he was with A.P. Hill's Third Corps, coming up in a timely manner from a 17-mile march to save the Army of Northern Virginia's right flank. He was promoted to major general on May 27, 1863, at age 29.

He was with Hill's corps again when Gen. Lee came up through the Cashtown Pass at the battle of Gettysburg. Pender was camped at the Cashtown Gap. Pender's men marched down the Chambersburg Pike and took position on Herr's Ridge on July 1, 1863. Gen. A. P. Hill ordered Pender to support Gen. Henry Heth, but Pender kept his division in the rear. Pender's men attacked the Union position on Seminary Ridge about 4 p.m. Although the assault was very bloody and Gen. Alfred Scales' men were almost destroyed by Union artillery, Pender was able to force the Union troops back through Gettysburg.

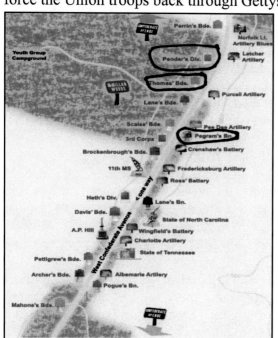

On July 2, 1863, Pender's artillery position was near the Lutheran Seminary south of the Hagerstown Road (now the Fairfield Road). Gen. Pender's luck ran out, as he was wounded in the thigh from a 2" square fragment of a shell fired from Cemetery Hill. He had just ridden from his Division Headquarters on West Confederate Avenue towards Gen. Edward Thomas' headquarters. He turned over his command to Gen. James H. Lane. For some unknown reason, Gen. Pender was wearing a colonel's uniform with three braid loops, three unwreathed stars, and the light blue pants of an infantry officer at the time of his fatal wounding. The general was evacuated to Staunton, Virginia, but died on July 18, 1863, after an artery in his leg ruptured. The surgeons amputated his leg, but he died shortly thereafter. His last words were: "Tell

The map at left shows the placement of Pender's Division in relation to the position of Thomas' Brigade and Pegram's Battalion at the Battle of Gettysburg.

119

my wife that I do not fear to die. I can confidently resign my soul to God, trusting in the atonement of Jesus Christ. My only regret is to leave her and our two children. I have always tried to do my duty in every sphere in which Providence has placed me."

Gen. Lee's words, when hearing of Pender's death, were as follows: "The loss of Major-General Pender is severely felt by the army and the country. He served with this army from the beginning of the war, and took a distinguished part in all its engagements. Wounded on several occasions, he never left his command in action until he received the injury that resulted in his death. His promise and usefulness as an officer were only equaled by the purity and excellence of his private life."

Gen. A.P. Hill reiterated: "On this day (July 2, 1863), also, the Confederacy lost the invaluable services of Major Gen. W.D. Pender, wounded by a shell, and since dead. No man fell during this bloody battle of Gettysburg more regretted than he, nor around whose youthful brow were clustered brighter rays of glory."

There is a marker for Gen. Pender's Third Corps along West Confederate Avenue, denoting all the men serving under him. The Gettysburg National Park Service has also marked witness trees in the park with small round metal tags. The former internet publication, the *Gettysburg Daily*, has identified tag #195 or tag #196 as the tree where Gen. Pender lay wounded. Pender's HQ was close to the Hagerstown (now Fairfield) Road. Gen. Thomas' HQ was close to the now McMillan's Woods Youth Camp. Gen. Pender was brought back to be placed at either

Above, the Pegram marker at Gettysburg, where two 'witness trees' stand - either one of which could have been the one Pender was laid against after his wounding.

Monument/tree photos by Lisa Greentree Tully

A closer look at the Pegram marker (above, left) and the nearby marker for Pender. At left, the marker for Thomas' Brigade.

The United States War Department, which operated Gettysburg National Military Park before the National Park Service took over in 1933, thought some of these "witness trees" to the battle were important enough to mark, and sometimes, protect. Small brass tags were placed in some of the trees, and lightning rods were also placed in some. The tree at right, above, was struck by lightening in 2010. The lightning struck the rod at the top of the tree, ran down the grounding cable and exploded the bark where the bare wood is visible.

the tree to the left of the Pegram marker (tag #196) or on the right (tag #195) .

Gen. Pender is the posthumous author of *"The General to his Lady: The Civil War Letters of William Dorsey Pender to Fanny Pender,"* published in 1965, 102 years after his death. A liberty ship, the *S.S. William D. Pender*, was named in his honor and saw service during World War II.

My dear Gettysburg daughter and husband, Lisa and Paul Tully, get a BIG 'thank you' for doing my site search and picture-taking for me. Lisa said it was a treasure hunt.

Paul recreated the moment of Pender's wounding, but I won't share that photo with you, although Lisa says it is the best one taken during the excursion.

I told her that every time she rides down West Confederate Avenue now, she will remember William Dorsey Pender, who was mortally wounded there.

Maj. Gen. Galusha A. Pennypacker, USA

What do the names Romeyn, Absalom, Milledge, Egbert, Goode, Lysander, Jubal, Speed, Isham, States Rights, Elkanah, Pleasant, Theophilus, FitzHugh, Evander, FitzJohn, Galusha, Carnot, Americus, Green, Otho, Erastus, Strong, and Gouverneur all have in common? They are the decidedly different first names of American Civil War generals. My two personal favorites are Galusha and States Rights.

Gen. Galusha A. Pennypacker also has the distinction of being the reason that many Pennypackers write me all the time from www.findagrave.com asking if their family members, buried in the National Cemetery in Philadelphia, are related to me. My only connection to the cemetery is that, when researching Pennypacker, I posted a picture of the cemetery gate, which auto defaults onto any family member's grave memorial page.

Gen. Galusha A. Pennypacker

Galusha A. Pennypacker was born on June 1, 1842, in Valley Forge, Pennsylvania. This date may or may not be true, however. Even the general himself tossed around different birth years. He was pretty much abandoned when he was 3-4 years old. He was the son of Joseph J. Pennypacker and Tamson Workizer Pennypacker. His father ran the Valley Forge Temperance House from 1843-1844. Unfortunately for Galusha, his Mom died in January, 1846, of smallpox at the age of 22. The family then moved to Philadelphia. After his wife died, Joseph left Galusha in the care of the Pennypacker family and joined the Mexican War as a wagon-master and aide-de-camp. He later settled in California, starting a newspaper called the Petaluma Argus. He married again, to Mary Coley, and had a daughter Lizzie. Joseph never returned to Pennsylvania and never saw his son again. One has to wonder if there was at least any correspondence between the two of them.

Galusha's equally dedicated cousin, Rebecca Lane Pennypacker Price, who was a renowned nurse during the Civil War.

After his schooling at the Classical Institute in Phoenixville, PA, Galusha volunteered at the Fame Fire Company and later, like his father, worked for a newspaper, the Chester County Times. He had thought of attending West Point when the Civil War broke out. He instead enlisted on August 22, 1861 at the age of 16 or 17, and served as Quartermaster for the 9th Pennsylvania Volunteer Infantry. He was promoted to major on October 7, 1861. The regiment saw action in South Carolina, Florida, and Georgia. He also served in Court Martial proceedings, and trained officers.

Above, left, illustration of the vast Union naval forces arrayed in the attack on Ft. Fisher, N C. Above, right, illustration of the ferocity of the fighting at the fort.

Galusha served under Gen. Benjamin Butler at Drewy's Bluff, Chester's Station, and Bermuda Hundred. He was wounded three times in his right arm at Bermuda Hundred. After recuperating, he fought at Deep Bottom, Weirbottom Church, and Petersburg. Leading a charge at Fort Gilmer, he was again wounded by a shell fragment in the right ankle, and his horse was shot from under him. His most severe wound was received at Fort Fisher, NC on January 15, 1865. He placed the 97th Pennsylvania Volunteers flag on the fortifications and was wounded again in the right hip and side. The upper portion of his pelvic bone was fractured. He was evacuated on a ship bound for Chesapeake Hospital. Sgt. Jeptha Clark, 124th Regiment, stayed with him until he got to the hospital.

His men murdered the Confederate who shot him. In 1911, Pennypacker stated: "The horror of it has never gone out of my mind to this day. I did see him – a big North Carolinian. I saw the man taking aim at me. He was about 20 feet away. I fell forward at the feet of the men who had fired. I kept my mind clear. I could see and hear, but could not move. I still could see the man who had shot me." Secretary of War Edwin Stanton watched the assault from a ship in Wilmington Harbor. He wrote to President Lincoln stating: "The conflict lasted for seven hours. The works were so constructed that every traverse afforded the enemy a new defensive position from which they had to be driven."

Pennypacker was awarded a Congressional Medal of Honor on August 17, 1891, for his actions at Fort Fisher. The citation reads: "Gallantly led the charge over a traverse and planted the colors of one of his regiments thereon, was severely wounded." A reporter asked him in his later years: "You carried the standard? You? The commander of the brigade?" The general replied: "I was a boy, boys do those things." He was brevetted to brigadier general, and later in

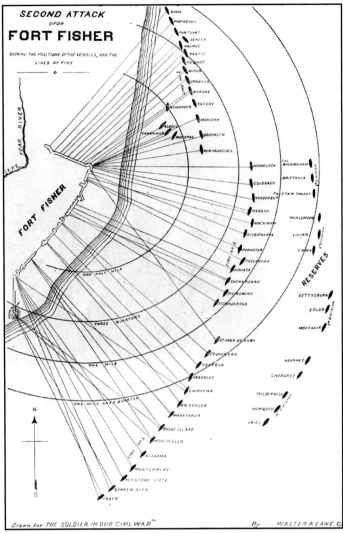

An interesting chart of the placement of Naval vessels in the second assault on Fort Fisher, NC, January 13-15, 1865.

Gen. Galusha Pennypacker's uniform coat, on display at the Chester County (PA) Historical Society.

March, 1867, he was brevetted a major general of the U.S. Army. To this day, Pennypacker is the youngest officer to hold the rank of general, at age 20.

Directly following the war, he practiced law in West Chester, PA, before going back into the Army with the rank of colonel in the 34th U.S. Infantry in 1867. He was assigned to Mississippi. In March, 1867, he was assigned to the 16th Infantry. After enduring all his wounds in the Civil War, he was involved in a train wreck where the train went off a trestle. He stated that he "was bruised all over, and had my wounded shoulder almost dislocated. I have suffered miserably, since. 'My time' hadn't come yet! I wonder when it will."

He served in the Army until 1871, when he took a year's leave of absence for his disabilities. It was then he and his surgeon, Dr. John Everhart of the 97th Pennsylvania Volunteers, toured Europe together. The general, who was one of eight boy generals of the Civil War, met the oldest general, Kaiser Wilhelm.

After returning to the states, he went back in the Army, and was stationed at Nashville, commanded the Military Department of the South, served at Fort Riley, Fort Davis, Fort McKavett and Fort Concho. In 1883, he retired from the army because of his wounds. Being in constant pain from his injuries, he tried therapy at Hot Springs, Arkansas. While he suffered from two other medical conditions, his death certificate states he died from a gunshot wound to the right hip. He died on October 1, 1916.

This half of a stereo view photo was a unique souvenir from Pennypacker's trip to Europe in 1872 on military business. A stereo view produces a 3-D image of twin images when viewed through a stereo viewer. This stereo half shows Pennypacker seated, with Dr. John Everhart standing on the right. The man standing at left is unidentified.

Pennypacker's house in Philadelphia, PA.

Pennypacker lived at 300 South 10th Street in Philadelphia until the end of his life. He was never married, and there are no direct descendants. Galusha was buried in the National Cemetery in Philadelphia in the Officers Section, grave 175. His date of birth on his marker shows 1844. He was raised a Quaker by his grandmother, and his funeral was performed with simple services by the Society of Friends.

A 97th PA Regiment monument was placed in West Chester, PA, commemorating the regiment. Gen. Pennypacker attended the unveiling in 1887. A very modern statue was later designed by Charles Grafly, entitled "Timeless Warrior," sculpted by Albert Laessle. The statue stands at 18th and Vine Streets in Philadelphia. It was unveiled on May 13, 1934.

Gen. Pennypacker was a member of the Society of Cincinnati, Loyal Legion, and the Historical Society of Pennsylvania. He was also a 5th cousin of Gen. George Armstrong Custer.

Gen. Pennypacker in later life.

At left, the "Timeless Warrior" statue in Philadelphia, PA, inspired by Pennypacker's military career; at right, Galusha's grave marker in the National Cemetery, Philadelphia, PA.

Gravestone photo by Janet Greentree

Maj. Gen. James William Forsyth, USA

How many of you have seen the picture below of Custer with his dog lounging in camp during the 1862 Peninsula Campaign? How many of you know who the officers are? These men are part of Gen. Fitz John Porter's staff. Of course, Custer is at the right, bottom. He was only a lieutenant at the time. The man seated on the left is Lt. William G. Jones. Two future generals are in the second row. To the far right is Wesley Merritt. At the far left is Ms. Rebelle's subject this month - James William Forsyth. The others are unidentified. Did you know there is another brevet general Forsyth? His first name was George. He and James were friends, as George was an aide-de-camp for Gen. Sheridan and James served under Sheridan as well. To distinguish between themselves, James called himself Tony and George called himself Sandy. George Forsyth would later say: "It would have been difficult to have found a more enthusiastic soldier in the whole corps than its popular and efficient chief of staff."

James William Forsyth (seated, left) poses during the 1862 Peninsula campaign with fellow officers, including (in front, right, George Custer).

This little tidbit of an article in the Cleveland Plain Dealer on October 18, 1867, entitled "A Wedding in 'High' Life" just called out to be mentioned first in profiling Tony. It says, in part: "The event of the season was the marriage last night at Trinity Church, when Gen. James W. Forsyth was united in the holy bonds of wedlock to Miss Lizzie, eldest of Hon. Wm. Dennison (governor of Ohio and Lincoln's Postmaster General). The church was filled to repletion long before the hour appointed for the ceremony – 8 o'clock – by a vast concourse of gentlemen and ladies anxious to see what the bride wore and how she deported herself under the, to her, novel situation. The bride......looked as all other brides do, very interesting, as she advanced down the aisle..... She was dressed in a robe of white satin, low-necked and short-sleeved. Over the dress she wore a white bertha (a deep collar of lace attached to a dress with a low neckline) trimmed with satin piping......The groom, attended by Gen. Sheridan and his brother officers, was dressed in full military uniform, as were all the officers present." Don't you just love the flowery and descriptive language of long ago? Then add Gen. Phil Sheridan to the mix!!!

Now to get to the nitty gritty of this man's life; it seems like most people don't know who he is. As my research has documented, he was sort of lost in time as to what he did during his life and, especially, during the

Above, left, Gen. James W. (Tony) Forsyth, keeping the hardtack warm, and above, right, both Forsyths (George at left, James at right) with Gen. Philip Sheridan (middle).

Civil War and after. James William Forsyth was born on August 8, 1834, in Maumee City, Ohio, south of Cleveland. He was the son of James Henry and Charlotte Templeton Jackson Forsyth. His mother's Jackson side were related to Andrew Jackson. He was one of eight children. His brother George was in the 100th OVI from Ohio and died as a POW at Libby Prison in Richmond. George was shot in the head and killed by a guard. He had been captured at Limestone Station, TN. That fact is even stated on his tombstone in Toledo, OH. His grandparents were from Detroit, MI, and his great-grandfather William Forsyth was from Blackwater, Ireland. William fought at the siege of Quebec under Gen. James Wolfe in 1759 in the French and Indian Wars.

Tony attended local schools in Ohio and was appointed to West Point in 1851 at age 16. He graduated 28th in his class as a 2nd lieutenant, attached to Co. D, 9th U.S. Infantry, in 1856. He and 10 of his classmates would achieve the rank of general, including: George Bayard, Samuel Carroll, William H. Jackson, Fitz Hugh Lee, Lunsford Lomax, Hylan Lyon, James Major, Orlando Metcalfe Poe, William Price Sanders, and Francis Vinton. After graduation, he was sent to San Juan Island, WA, serving under Capt. George Pickett. He also served at Fort Bellingham in the Washington Territory, and his 9th U.S. helped Pickett built the fort.

Sheridan and Forsyth (undated).

After making the rank of 1st lieutenant in 1861, he was sent East to command Union forces in the Civil War. He was assigned to the 64th Ohio Infantry. In 1862, he transferred to the Army of the Potomac and was assigned as an aide-de-camp to Gen. Joseph Mansfield. When Mansfield was killed at Antietam, Forsyth became provost marshal. In 1863, he was assigned to the western theatre again under Gen. Philip Sheridan as adjutant at Chickamauga. He stayed with Sheridan when he transferred to the Cavalry Corps and served as his chief of staff. He was brevetted to lieutenant colonel at Cedar Creek, colonel at Five Forks, and brigadier general in the Shenandoah Valley Campaign for gallant and meritorious services at the battles of Opequan, Fisher's Hill, and Middletown, VA. Forsyth was present at the surrender at Appomattox Courthouse on April 9, 1865.

After the Civil War ended, President Andrew Johnson promoted him to brigadier general on January 13, 1866. Forsyth would continue to serve with Gen. Sheridan, along with Gens. Wesley Merritt, Thomas Devin and George Custer. All would become well known as Indian fighters. In 1867, he was with Sheridan in Missouri as department secretary and inspector. He was appointed to the cavalry and fought the Comanche, Cheyenne, Arapaho, and Kiowa Indians during 1868-69. In 1870, he was sent to Europe to observe the Franco-Prussian War. He was with the 1st U.S. Cavalry in 1878 during the Bannock War. In 1885, he was the commander of Fort Maginnis, Montana, where the troops observed the Crow, Cree and Gros Ventres Indians. In July 1886, he assumed command of the 7th U.S. Cavalry (Custer's command) at Fort Meade, South Dakota. At Fort Riley, KS, he worked on organizing and developing a system of instruction for light artillery and cavalry. He organized the School of Application for Infantry and Cavalry while at Fort Riley.

Now for the biggest "did you know" of the whole story – did you know that James William Forsyth was in command of the 7th Cavalry at Wounded Knee on December 29, 1890? Ap-

The 7th Cavalry at Wounded Knee.

proximately 150-300 Lakota Sioux men, women, and children were killed. Twenty-five soldiers were killed and 39 were wounded. The 7th surrounded the Lakota, who were doing the Ghost Dance, led by Chief Big Foot in response to the death of Sitting Bull. Tensions were high and a shot was fired from an unknown source, killing a U.S. soldier. Fighting broke out and the brutal massacre occurred. Chief Big Foot was also killed in the melee. The soldiers were armed with Hotchkiss machine guns. Forsyth was also present the next day at the Drexel Mission Fight, also on

"Ghost Dance" that sparked the Wounded Knee massacre (artist's rendering).

the Pine Ridge Indian Reservation. Gen. Nelson Miles investigated Forsyth's actions. Forsyth was cleared of wrongdoing by the Secretary of War, but very much resented Miles' accusations. Gen. Miles stated: "I have never heard of a more brutal, cold-blooded massacre than at Wounded Knee." Even in 1920, Gen. Miles went to Washington, along with Sioux descendants, in an attempt to discredit Forsyth. He failed to achieve his goal. Wounded Knee was the only black mark on Forsyth's reputation in his life-long military career. He was much loved by his troops and fellow officers.

The Bismark Tribune, on April 3, 1891, stated in part: "Noted for a long line of meritorious services in the field, commander of the largest government post in the United States, colonel of the Seventh cavalry, made famous by Custer, and in command of the regulars at the battle of Wounded Knee, the most severe engagement with Indians in recent years, James William Forsyth has been a prominent figure in army circles during the past few months. His being relieved of his command by Gen. Miles while in the field after the battle of Wounded Knee,... for alleged cruelty in ordering his soldiers to fire on the women and children, was discussed the nation over. The investigation of the war department was followed by his reinstatement and the finding that "the evidence shows that great care was taken by the officers and men to prevent unnecessary killing of Indian women and children, and that Colonel Forsyth's conduct was well worthy of commendation." He at once resumed his place in command of Fort Riley, Kansas....... Colonel Forsyth is a man of fine personal appearance; his soldierly bearing and snow-white hair make him a marked figure in any gathering. He is a genial conversationalist, with an inexhaustible fund of reminiscence and anecdote. He is an excellent disciplinarian, and his regiment shows it."

Forsyth was promoted to brigadier general in December 1894 by President Grover Cleveland and commanded the Department of California. He was then promoted to major general in May 1897 by President McKinley while still in California. He retired after his appointment to major general and lived the rest of his life in Columbus, Ohio. He and his wife Lizzie had four children - Elizabeth (Bessy), Mary, Marion, and William, who fought in World War I.

The general died on October 24, 1906 at the age of 71 in Columbus, Ohio. He is buried in Section 56, Lot 55 in Green Lawn Cemetery in Columbus. The Cleveland, Ohio Plain Dealer's headline was "Gen. Forsyth is Called by Death." "James W. Forsyth, major general U.S.A., retired, died at his home in this city (Columbus) this evening. He was stricken with paralysis Monday night and never rallied. He had been in apparently good health up to the time he was stricken."

Forsythe's grave marker in Green Lawn Cemetery, Columbus, OH.

Photo by Janet Greentree

Travels to New York State

Ms. Rebelle, the Confederate at heart that she is, recently traveled into Yankee territory in New York state for a Thanksgiving visit with her son, Mark, and family. Mark is the son that has lived in the 'Land of Lincoln' for 19 years. The family has now moved to thaca, New York. With that change, Ms. Rebelle immediately began studying maps, planning the way up there. My New York map is now circled with 33 little orange circles noting all the cities and towns where Civil War generals are buried. My plan was to take off on my own to find "my guys," but my son expressed a desire to come along. I was very proud of him. He helped to find "my guys" in New York.

Ithaca sits at the mouth of Cayuga Lake, one of the Finger Lakes in New York. There are no bridges over the lakes, so you have to drive the entire length of them before going down the other side. Auburn, NY, is about 45 minutes north of Ithaca. Coming into that town, we saw a magnificent Victorian mansion with a statue of William Seward, Lincoln's Secretary of State, in front of it. It turns out that it was Seward Park, and the house belonged to the Seward family. Then it was off to Fort Hill Cemetery in Auburn on a very,

Above - William H. Seward, indispensable friend and cohort of Abraham Lincoln; below - Seward's statue, located near the Seward home.
Bottom photo by Janet Greentree

Above, the Seward home in Auburn, NY.
Photo by Janet Greentree

The gravesite of William H. Seward in Fort Hill Cemetery, Auburn, NY.
Photo by Janet Greentree

very cold day to find the Seward family; his son; Gen. William Seward, Jr.; Lt. Colonel Myles Keogh; Gen. Emory Upton; Brevet Gen. Andrew Alexander, and Harriet Tubman. One can look and study cemetery maps, but when you get inside the gates, it looks so very different. Some cemeteries have famous people's graves marked very well. Other cemeteries have no directions, no street names, and no section names. We took off on foot when we got to the general area of the Sewards' section, and Mark found the Seward family. They are all buried in a row.

William Seward, of course, is also famous for surviving the attack of Lewis Powell during the Lincoln assassination. His daughter, Fannie, and son Frederick, who were slashed by Powell, are buried there, as well. Seward was a governor of New York and then a U.S. senator before taking the Cabinet post under Lincoln. He stayed in his Cabinet post under Pres. Andrew Johnson and was later ridiculed for Seward's Folly, the purchase of Alaska.

Our next stop in the cemetery was really logistically fortunate, as Keogh, Upton and Alexander are all buried together in a semi-circle. Myles Keogh is a close second "want" for me, behind George Armstrong Custer, since I've been unable to get into West Point to find Custer's grave. Keogh was killed with Custer at Little Big Horn.

Keogh, an Irishman, was born in County Carlow, Ireland, in 1840. His maternal aunt, Mary

Lt. Col. Myles Keogh

Blanchfield, willed to him the family estate, Clifden Castle. Myles craved adventure, though, so at age 20 he joined the Papal Guard, donning the green uniforms of the Company of Saint Patrick. Secy. Seward began recruiting experienced European officers to serve with the Union during the Civil War. Keogh resigned his commission with the Company of Saint Patrick in 1862 and sailed to America with two friends, who were all given the rank of captain, through Seward's intervention.

Keogh served in the Valley Campaign, Port Republic, Antietam, Fredericksburg, Chancellorsville, Brandy Station, Upperville and Gettysburg, alongside Gen. John Buford. When Buford became ill with typhoid fever in the fall of 1863, Keogh stayed with him in Washington at the home of Gen. George Stoneman, until Buford died on December 16, 1863. The general died in Keogh's arms. After the funeral service at the New York Avenue Presbyterian Church in Washington, Keogh accompanied Gen. Buford's body to West Point, where he was buried alongside Lt. Alonzo Cushing, who died defending Gen. Buford's high ground at Gettysburg. Keogh was devastated by Buford's death and transferred out to the Western Theatre. The rest is history.

Keogh's body was found at the center of several troopers at Little Big Horn. He was stripped of his clothes, but not mutilated as other dead soldiers were, with one theory of why being because he wore the Agnus Dei (Lamb of God) figurine around his neck on a chain. His horse, Comanche, was the only survivor (man or animal) of the battle.

There always seems to be connections to those in our past, and Gen. Andrew J. Alexander

Gen. John Buford's staff during the Civil War - left to right: Bvt. Lt. Col. Myles Keogh; Maj. Gen. John Buford; Capt. P. Penn-Gaskell; Capt. C. W. Wadsworth; and Lt. Col. A. P. Morrow.

is no different. He was a Southerner, born in Kentucky. However, he chose to fight for the Union. He served under Gen. George B. McClellan, and later with Gen. George Stoneman. He received brevets for gallantry in the 1862 Peninsula Campaign for scouting, and for reconnaissance before and during the battle of Gettysburg. He was brevetted to brigadier general on March 13, 1865. Alexander had the honor of bringing Gen. Buford his major general's commission on his deathbed. He held Buford's hand as he signed the papers, making him a major general. Alexander became friends with Myles Keogh when he served under Stoneman and Buford.

In 1883, Alexander began to have serious health problems. On May 4, 1887, while on a train going to Auburn, New York, Alexander died unexpectedly at the age of 54. He and his very good friend, Myles Keogh, are buried side by side in Fort Hill Cemetery in Auburn, New York.

Stay tuned for the rest of my adventure in next month's issue.

At left, Ms. Rebelle stands by the grave monument to Lt. Col. Myles Keogh; at right, the monument marking the burial site of Gen. Andrew J. Alexander.
Photos courtesy of Janet Greentree

More Travels in New York State

We are still in Auburn, New York, at Fort Hill Cemetery.

Our next find was Major Gen. Emory Upton. Upton was a brilliant military strategist. His unit attacked the entrenched positions of Dole's Salient at the Battle of Spotsylvania Courthouse. The VI Corps Chief of Staff, Martin McMahon, told Upton that no one expected him to return from his attack, but, if he did, he should certainly expect a promotion to brigadier general. The plan used was Upton's, and he commanded four regiments of the twelve that were engaged. Rather than have his men fire uselessly at the entrenchments and be mowed down while reloading, he had them hold fire until atop the trenches, fire into the defenders at that point and spread out to reload while a second wave did the same. His tactics would have broken the Rebel line if Gen. Gershom Mott had supported him, as he had been ordered to. Grant recognized Upton's innovative firing tactic and supported his promotion.

Major Gen. Emory Upton

Upton was the author of a book published posthumously in 1904, *"The Military Policy of the United States."* This book actually was used as a guide for operations by the military. Upton included his tactic - used at Spotsylvania - where columns of infantry would assault a small portion of the enemy line without pausing to reload, thereby overwhelming the enemy and achieving a breakthrough.

Upton was born in Batavia, NY. He was the brother-in-law of Gen. Andrew J. Alexander, who is buried in the same semi-circle as Upton, along with Maj. Gen. Francis P. Blair, Jr., who is credited, while a politician, with keeping Missouri out of the Confederacy. More connections.

Gen. Upton's grave in Ft. Hill Cemetery, Auburn, NY.
Photo by Janet Greentree

He went to Oberlin College in Ohio; graduated from West Point in 1856, eighth in his class. He started his military career with Gen. Irvin McDowell; was an aide-de-camp to Gen. Daniel Tyler and was wounded in the First Battle of Bull Run in 1861. He also saw action at Blackburn's Ford, which the BRCWRT has visited many times. More action was seen at Fredericksburg, Gettysburg, Bristoe, Rappahannock Station, the Wilderness, Petersburg, Valley Campaigns, Wilson's Raid, and the Battle of Selma. He also arrested the Vice President of the Confederacy, Alexander Stephens, at the close of the war. Confederate Pres. Jefferson Davis was placed in Upton's custody after his capture. Upton escorted Davis by steamer to Savannah, GA.

During the Third Battle of Winchester, Upton was wounded in the thigh. Refusing to leave the field, he was carried on a stretcher while still directing his troops in the battle. Upton had the distinction of commanding in all three branches of the Army: the infantry, cavalry and artillery. The 25-year-old Upton remained in the U.S. Army after the Civil War, serving in various capacities. He also served as commandant of West Point for five years, from 1870-1875. In 1881, while in San Francisco, he committed suicide. Upton suffered from severe headaches, possibly caused by a brain tumor. He was also devastated by the loss of his young wife, 11 years earlier, in 1870.

Harriet Tubman, a remarkable figure of the Civil War.

Harriet Tubman is also buried in Fort Hill. She has connections to William H. Seward, a prominent abolitionist, who was profiled in the above article. Mrs. Tubman is known as the most famous guide of the Underground Railroad. She was nicknamed the 'Moses of her people.' She was never caught, nor did she ever lose an enslaved escapee under her protection to the Southern Militia, while guiding them to freedom. She was only five feet tall; her original name was Araminta Ross, and she was born enslaved on a plantation in Dorchester County near Cambridge, Maryland,

Araminta Ross, known to us as Harriet Tubman, claimed back her own humanity in escaping slavery, and - at the risk of her own life - restored to hundreds of other people their humanity, also.

in 1820.

Her father taught her knowledge of the woods, which later helped with her rescue missions. Grandparents on both sides came from Africa to America in chains. In 1849, when she heard rumors that she and other slaves were to be sold south, she bravely escaped by herself and reached Philadelphia. She found work in the North, saved her money and eventually freed more than 300 enslaved people, some her own relatives, through the Underground Railroad. By 1857, she had freed her entire family, including her aging parents.

Harriet Tubman-Davis' headstone in Ft. Hill Cemetery, Auburn, NY.
Photo by Janet Greentree

Abolitionists such as John Brown, William Seward, Susan B. Anthony and Ralph Waldo Emerson supported her work and helped her out financially. At one time, there was a $40,000 reward for her capture. During the Civil War, she served as a scout and spy for the Union Army in South Carolina. After the war, she moved to Auburn, New York, settling there permanently.

She remarried after the Civil War to Nelson Davis, a former enslaved man, who had served in the Union Army. Her first husband, John Tubman, did not follow her to freedom. Mrs. Tubman died of pneumonia at age 93 on March 10, 1913. Auburn held a military funeral for her. During World War II, a liberty ship was named the *Harriet Tubman* in her honor. In 1978, the U.S. Post Office issued a commemorative stamp honoring her as well. She has, since this article was written, been scheduled to be featured on the $20 bill, but that recognition has since been put on the shelf indefinitely.

Leaving Auburn and driving west, my son Mark and I drove to Waterloo, NY, to find Gen. Edward Payson Chapin. Waterloo, like Auburn, was full of beautiful Victorian houses. Gen. Chapin is buried in Maple Grove Cemetery. Since I had a hand-drawn map and a photo of his gravestone, I knew exactly where to go in this small cemetery.

Brig. Gen. Chapin was with the 116th New York Infantry and was killed at the Battle of Port Hudson, Louisiana, on May 27, 1863. He was promoted posthumously to brigadier general.

Chapin was born in Waterloo, studied law in Buffalo and became an attorney in 1852, practicing in Buffalo. He was also on a baseball team, the Niagaras, Buffalo's first semi-pro baseball team.

Gen. Edward Payson Chapin

Chapin fought in the Peninsula Campaign. He was first wounded on May 27, 1862, in the Battle of Hanover Court House. After going home to New York to recover, he led his unit to Baltimore, where they sailed to Ship Island, Mississippi. The unit reached New Orleans in December 1862. He served under Gen. Nathaniel P. Banks, defending against the Confederates on the Mississippi River.

On May 27, 1863, he was sent to be part of Gen. Christopher Auger's brigade in Port Hudson, Louisiana. There, on that day, Chapin received a mortal wound to the head and died.

The final chapter of Ms. Rebelle's New York visit will appear in next month's issue.

Above, left - Gen. Chapin's monument in Maple Grove Cemetery, Waterloo, NY, is in poor condition, so an added marker has been added to the burial site.

Wrapping Up Travels in New York State

Our next little trip was to Elmira, New York, to see if anything was left of the infamous Elmira Prison. The prison was located on the banks of the Chemung River in Elmira. There is nothing there except a very small park and a couple of historical signs telling briefly what happened on that site. Even though the prison was there for only a year, it had a 24% death rate, more than any other prison, north or south. Elmira Barracks was built at the beginning of the war as a recruiting facility. In July 1864, part of it was turned into a prison camp for Confederates.

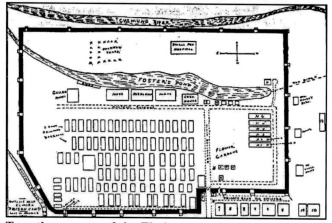

Top: the acreage of the Elmira camp is crammed full of tents in this undated photo. Just above: an illustration of the camp as it was envisioned. When Confederate Pres. Jefferson Davis would not take black soldiers as prisoners (meaning they were shot and killed as they offered themselves, disarmed, for capture), Pres. Abraham Lincoln refused to parole rebel prisoners to return home, thus making it inevitable for overcrowding to produce much suffering in military prisons.

As with every national cemetery, the Elmira National Cemetery is a place of rest for many generations of heroes who have given their last full measure of devotion to the United States of America.

Photo by Janet Greentree

All the prison buildings were located on the high northern banks of the river, but the prisoners were on the flood plain gravel by the Chemung River. An inspector of the prison stated that "the condition of the patients is pitiable, the diseases are nearly of all type, and much of the sickness is justly attributed to crowd-poisoning."

In January 1865 there were 1,738 prisoners on the sick list out of a total of 5,934 prisoners. Of the 5,934 so-called healthy prisoners, many were sick as well, and in need of better accommodations. By June of 1865, when the weather was better, the sanitary conditions at the camp improved. Thus, the mortality rate lessened. Foster's Pond (see map) was used as the prisoners' "sinks". The stench was extremely offensive and unhealthy for the men to be in such close quarters to the pond.

Finally, after the war ended, the prisoners who were healthy enough to travel by train were sent to City Point for exchange. There were only 1,200 men well enough at that time to travel by train. Thus, Confederate soldiers named the camp 'Hell-mira.'

Also in Elmira is the National Cemetery and Woodlawn Cemetery where Mark Twain, a/k/a Samuel Clemens is buried. While Mark Twain did live during the Civil War (1835-1910) and fought for a short time for the Confederacy, he didn't have too much of a connection to the Civil War. Amusingly, he often noted that his "resignation" from the Rebel army ensured Union victory.

Twain owned a Victorian house (which now features a fairly modern garage) in Elmira that is now a Christmas gift shop. We thought that was just sad. We also wondered whether Mark Twain had a car, or did he keep his buggy in that garage. Another famous person in Woodlawn Cemetery is Hal Roach of silent

Above: Mark Twain's charming Victorian home in Elmira, NY, is now used as a retail enterprise. Above, right: The great Mark Twain's grave marker at Woodlawn Cemetery in Elmira, NY, and, at right: a second marker at the site. To quote Twain on the subject of death: "I do not fear death. I had been dead for billions and billions of years before I was born, and had not suffered the slightest inconvenience from it."

Photos by Janet Greentree

film fame, who also was from Elmira. Roach produced and directed silent films, as well as the Laurel & Hardy pictures and "The Little Rascals" films that were popular in the 1930's and 40's. The inscriptions notes his service in the armed forces: Lt. Col. - US Army - World War II.

The last stop made as I headed back to Virginia was looking for Gen. James Nagle, who is buried in in the Presbyterian Cemetery in Pottstown, PA. Pottstown is just southeast of Route 81.

Driving into town, there were mountains on each side of the highway, but the town itself looked pretty flat. My trusty Lori TomTom (GPS) found the cemetery okay, but it was on the side of a mountain. The street going up to it and coming back down looked like San Francisco's Lombard Street. So - bad knees and all - I grabbed my trusty map and a photo of his marker and entered the cemetery. There were several markers like his, but his was at the very top of the

mountain, of course. So, General Nagle, Ms. Rebelle made the extreme sacrifice for you.

Nagle was born in 1822 in Reading, PA, but moved to Pottstown in 1835. His father was a drummer in the Continental Army during the Revolutionary War. Nagle's profession before the Civil War was that of a paperhanger and painter.

Nagle enlisted in the Army in 1842 and fought in the Mexican War. He served at Fort Monroe, Hatteras Island and Newbern, North Carolina. He was assigned to Gen. Jesse Reno, in the Department of North Carolina.

Nagle was at Second Manassas, Ox Hill and Antietam (Burnside's Bridge). Gen. George B. McClellan said Nagle saved the day at Burnside's Bridge. He served in Kentucky until May 1863. Later, he guarded the approaches to Baltimore.

Nagle died in Pottsville in 1866 from heart disease.

Gen. James Nagle; at right: Nagle's grave monument.

Photo by Janet Greentree

AWOL in New York

According to our trusty Bull Run Civil War Round Table Field Trip Leader, Kevin Anastas, Ms. Rebelle was AWOL for the Chancellorsville tour in June, so she was unable to take the photos for the PowerPoint show planned for the next meeting. Ms. Rebelle went north again into Yankee territory to visit her son in Ithaca, New York. In the process, she has gained a 'flag girl' who likes to help her grandmom, my little six-year old granddaughter, Katerina (now quite a young lady).

The first stop on my way north was at Binghampton, NY, to find Union Gen. John Cleveland Robinson, who is buried there in Spring Forest Cemetery. It took two times around the grounds, together with the caretaker (who came along to help, after the fact) to find him.

Robinson was born in Binghamton in 1817 and died there in 1897. He attended West Point but was dismissed for disciplinary reasons in 1838; nevertheless, he went on to become a major general in 1865. He fought in battles in the Peninsula Campaign; 2nd Manassas; Fredericksburg; Chancellorsville; Gettysburg; the Wilderness, and Spotsylvania. Robinson was awarded a Medal of Honor for actions at Spotsylvania, where - severely wounded in the left knee - he

Left: Gen. John Cleveland Robinson; right: his grave in Spring Forest Cemetery, Binghamton, NY.

lost his leg to amputation, thus costing him field command. After the war, he ran the Freedman's Bureau in North Carolina and later became a lieutenant governor of New York.

My son Mark and my granddaughter Katerina traveled with me to Penn Yan, NY, to Lake View Cemetery to find the grave of Union Gen. John Morrison Oliver. I must say, I was interested in the strange name of the little village of Penn Yan. It was named for Pennsylvania Yankees who settled the town. The village is on Keuka Lake. Heading into the cemetery, we were armed with a

map, but it was a little off as to where the general was buried. I said to Katerina, "Give us a sign, Gen. Oliver." Right then, a groundhog came out of the ground and was walking across the cemetery. We went to look at the groundhog, and there was the general's grave! Katerina placed a flag on the grave for me.

Oliver was born in Penn Yan in 1828 and died in Washington, D.C. in 1872. His early career was that of a pharmacist. Joining up at the onset of war, he started out as a private, but rose to a brevet major general of Volunteers. He was at Bull Run but was detached at Fairfax Courthouse during the advance to Manassas. Most of the battles he fought in were with the Army of the Tennessee – Shiloh; Corinth; Vicksburg;

Above, left: the grave marker (pointed out by a groundhog) of Gen. John Morrison Oliver, shown above, right.
Gravestone Photo by Janet Greentree

Atlanta; Sherman's March to the Sea, and Bentonville. He went on to lead the attack on Fort McAllister. In addition to his first career as a druggist, he later became a lawyer, was a post office superintendent in Little Rock and then retired to Washington, D.C.

Next was a visit to Syracuse, NY, and Oakwood Cemetery, where three Union generals are buried – Henry Alanson Barnum, John James Peck and Edwin Vose Sumner. Sumner was my

Left to right: Gen. Henry Alanson Barnum; Gen. John James Peck and Gen. Edwin Vose Sumner. All three are buried in Oakwood Cemetery in Syracuse, NY. The rural/garden-type landscape of the cemetery is a challenge to drivers, as the pathways are unrefurbished since the days of carriages.

biggest find on this trip. I must say that Oakwood ranks second for having the worst roads I've encountered in a cemetery. Of course, the roads were made for carts, not cars, and it's a wonder my car didn't get stuck. The *worst* cemetery for roads is Oak Hill, right here in Georgetown.

Barnum was born in 1833 in Jamesville, New York, and died in 1892 in New York City. He was a brevet major general during the Civil War. He also received the Medal of Honor. Barnum had a varied career and was even left for dead at Malvern Hill in 1862. The surgeon said the wound he had sustained was mortal; his body was abandoned and fell into the hands of the

Gens. Barnum and Peck's grave markers - typical of the Oakwood Cemetery's Victorian character. Gravesites are often marked again with a simple identifier stone, in addition to the main monument.

Photos by Janet Greentree

Confederates. He did get back to Union lines, went on medical leave and was treated in New York and recovered.

He served with Gen. George B. McClellan in the Peninsula Campaign; was at Fairfax Station; Edwards Ferry; Ely's Ford; later with the Army of the Tennessee at Wauhatchie, and Lookout Mountain. Barnum received his Medal of Honor in 1889 for duty in Chattanooga on November 23, 1863. The citation reads: "Although suffering severely from wounds, he led his regiment, inciting the men to great action by word and example until again severely wounded." Gen. George Thomas ordered him to convey the flags captured by the 149th New York and other regiments to the War Department in Washington. He was later in Savannah, being the first to lead his brigade into the captured city. He was wounded several times during his service. In his post-war career, he was a New York state prison inspector.

John James Peck was born in 1821 in Manlius, NY, and died in 1878 in Syracuse. His father, John W. Peck, served in the War of 1812. Peck graduated from West Point in 1843 with classmate Ulysses S. Grant. Peck was 8th in his class of 39 Cadets. Peck, like a lot of the general officers in the Civil War, fought in the Mexican War under Zachary Taylor. Later, he was assigned to Winfield Scott. When the Civil War began, he left his profession as bank cashier (he was one of the founders of the Burnett Bank of Syracuse) and was soon appointed a brigadier general in the Union Army.

Peck started his career right here in VA, commanding a brigade defending the Chain Bridge in Arlington, VA, and the northern defenses of D.C. at Tenleytown, then known as

134

Tennallytown. He served under McClellan in the Peninsula Campaign; the battles of Williamsburg; Fair Oaks; the Seven Days battles, and Malvern Hill. He was also in command of all the Union troops in Virginia south of the James River. During Longstreet's 1863 Tidewater Campaign, both generals focused on the town of Suffolk, VA. During the siege of Suffolk, Peck's 13,000 men repulsed Longstreet's 30,000 men.

He received serious injuries in this campaign and was forced on sick leave. He later was with the Department of North Carolina in New Bern. After the Civil War, he was president of the New York Life Insurance Company.

Now came the trek to find Gen. Edwin Vose Sumner. It was a good thing the ground was dry the day I attempted the drive; otherwise my car would have been stuck in the mud for-

Gen. Edward Vose Sumner, top step, at left, was the one of the oldest battlefield commander in the Civil War - Alonzo Cushing is second from right. Sumner is shown here with his staff at headquarters in Warrenton, VA.

ever. The ruts in the dirt road were very deep. Sumner's grave is up on top of a hill overlooking Syracuse University.

Sumner was born in Boston, MA, in 1797 and died in Syracuse in 1863. He was 64 years old when the Civil War started. He was the oldest battlefield general on either side in the Civil War. Sumner's nickname was "Bull" or "Bull Head," due to his loud, booming voice and the story that a musket ball once bounced off his head.

Sumner entered the army in 1819. He served in the Black Hawk War and various Indian campaigns. In 1838, he was a cavalry instructor at the Carlisle Barracks. He was brevetted for bravery at the battle of Cerro Gordo in the Mexican War. Later, he became involved in the events of Bleeding Kansas.

In 1861, he was assigned by Gen. Winfield Scott to accompany President-elect Abraham Lincoln to Washington. In November 1861, Sumner was promoted to major general. Based on his seniority, he was selected as one of four corps commanders by President Lincoln. Sumner participated in the Peninsula Campaign; the Seven Days Battles; Williamsburg; Glen Dale; Antietam, and Fredericksburg.

After Gen. Joseph Hooker's appointment to command the Army, Sumner was relieved at his own request. He was appointed commander of the Department of the Missouri.

While traveling to his daughter's home in Syracuse, Sumner suffered a fatal heart attack on March 21, 1863.

This trip brings my total to 313 generals' graves located -- 151 Union and 162 Confederates. On a recent trip to Monticello in Charlottesville, I added Confederate Gen. George Wythe Randolph, a grandson of Thomas Jefferson. Randolph is buried right next to Jefferson.

The charming Katerina Greentree was on hand to help find and honor Gen. Sumner in Oakwood Cemetery, Syracuse, NY.
Photo by Grandmom Janet Greentree

135

Back to New York - One Confederate and One Yankee

It's a good thing Ms. Rebelle's son moved to New York State. It opened up a whole new area in which to find "my" generals. There are 114 generals buried in New York. My total for New York now is only seven, but there will be many more visits to see my son, and more opportunities to visit those who peopled history. Of course, there are 28 at West Point, my all-time "great gets."

This trip found one of eight Confederates buried in New York: Brig. Gen. John Wesley Frazer, CSA. He was born in Hardin County, Tennessee, on January 6, 1827, and died at the age of 79 in New York City on March 31, 1906, after suffering complications from being struck by a fire truck while crossing 23rd Street in the city.

Frazer was appointed to West Point from Mississippi and graduated in 1849. Before the Civil

John Wesley Frazer

War, he was stationed at Fort Columbus, NY, San Miguel, CA; Fort Monroe, VA, and Forts Simcoe and Colville, Washington. He was a delegate to the Montgomery, AL, convention in February 1861 that organized the Confederate States of America. When hostilities began, Frazer resigned his commission from the U.S. Army and became a captain in the Confederate Army, being assigned to the 8th Alabama.

He served in several different units during the war – the 28th Alabama; 55th Georgia; 62nd & 64th NC, and Rains' Battery. In 1862, Frazer led the 28th Alabama in the Battle of Shiloh. He was commissioned a brigadier general on May 19, 1863, commanding the Fifth Brigade of the Army of East Tennessee, and was sent to guard the Cumberland Gap. Frazer was ordered to guard the Gap at all costs by Gen. Simon Bolivar Buckner. A three-day battle of the Gap shortly ensued, somehow accomplished without bloodshed.

Gen. Ambrose Burnside convinced Frazer to surrender on September 9, 1863; Frazer believed he was outnumbered by a considerable margin, and so, capitulated. The Confederates were shocked to see the small size of the force to whom they surrendered. Frazer surrendered 2,026 men, 2,000 small pieces of artillery, ammunition, provisions, 200 horses and mules, 50 wagons, 160 cattle, 12,000 pounds of bacon, 2,000 bushels of wheat, and 15,000 pounds of flour. According to the Official Record, "General Frazer had the opportunity to flight, retreat, or evacuate from the Cumberland Gap and save his command from a long imprisonment and death." Jefferson Davis endorsed the report, stating that Frazer's surrender "presents shameful abandonment of duty."

After Frazer's capture, he was sent to Johnson's Island, Ohio, for imprisonment. During his stay there, he organized an escape. The escape failed. He was then moved to Fort Warren in Boston Harbor for the remainder of the war. However, during his time at Johnson's Island, many Northern women who were sympathetic to the South began writing the prisoners held there. One was Miss Kate Tiffany from Utica, New York. Frazer looked her up after the war and married her in 1870. She became an invalid and died in 1892, with her husband caring for her for many years.

After the war, the general was a planter in Memphis and Arkansas, and

Illustration of the Battle of Cumberland Gap, TN, KY and VA, September 7-9, 1863.

then moved to New York City where he became a business-man. Gen. Frazer is buried in the village of Clifton Springs, New York. He is buried further north than any other Confed-erate Civil War general except Gen. Camille de Polignac, bur-ied in Frankfort-on-Main, Germany. It's always interesting to see where people end up. Through my research, I discovered that his granddaughter lived in Clifton Springs, so I believe that is why he is buried there.

My next stop was the town of Geneva, New York, near the west side of Cayuga Lake (one of the Finger Lakes in New York) to search for Brig. Gen. James Hughes Stokes, USA. Gen. Stokes was born on July 11, 1816, in

Confederate Gen. Frazer's grave in Yankee-land - Clifton Springs, NY.
Photo by Janet Greentree

Above: Gen. James Hughes Stokes.

Maryland. There is some discrepancy about the exact location. Sources note ei-ther Hagerstown or Havre de Grace. He graduated 17th in his class from West Point in 1831, just ahead of Montgomery Blair (18th) and George C. Meade (19th).

After West Point, he was as-signed to the artillery and fought the Creek and Seminole Indians. Later, he was assigned to quartermaster du-ty. He resigned from the Army in 1843 and became a businessman and railroad executive.

When the Civil War began, Stokes was in St. Louis. He re-entered the Army and was assigned to Gen. Nathaniel Lyon. The Union was concerned that the large amount of military stores and equipment in St. Louis would be seized by se-cessionists. Stokes was in charge of moving the 20,000 muskets and powder to Alton, Illinois. In 1862, he became the captain of the Chicago Board of Trade. Stokes saw action in the western theatre – Perryville; Murfreesboro; Chickamauga, and Missionary Ridge, with Gen. John Basil Turchin's Cavalry. Stokes was commended for his gallant and efficient service against the enemy. He went back to the Quartermaster Department and was appointed brigadier general in July 20, 1865. Stokes mustered out shortly after that on August 24, 1865. After the war, Stokes worked in the real estate business in New York City, and died there on December 27, 1890, at the age of 77.

Gen. Stokes' gravesite in Geneva, NY.

Photo by Janet Greentree

As my view of Lake Cayuga disappeared under November snow showers, my son called to say

it was time for his Mom to come home and stop running around finding graves!

At left: illustration of the Battle of Per-ryville, KY, October 8, 1862, the culmina-tion of the Confeder-ate Heartland Offen-sive (Kentucky Cam-paign).

Myles Keogh, William Seward & Me

Ms. Rebelle cannot seem to stay away from anything to do with Myles Keogh, so here she is again in Auburn, New York, at Fort Hill Cemetery to visit Keogh's grave. Since going to Little Big Horn last year, I felt that Myles Keogh should have a 7th Cavalry flag on his grave to commemorate his brave efforts at Custer's Last Stand. I scoured the Internet and stores selling flags trying to find a 7th Cavalry flag. There were none available. I did find a large one, but at 2' x 3', it was way too big to put on someone's grave.

Lt. Col. Myles Keogh in resplendent uniform, undated.

The only possible thing to do was to try to make one of my own to place on his grave. I printed a copy of the flag on 8 x 10 photo paper, placed it on poster board, and encased it in plastic with dowels to hold it up and "a lot" of Scotch tape. "Rest in peace Myles Keogh – Ms. Rebelle" was written on the back. When I got to Keogh's final resting place, other people had left mementos there as well, including a picture of him in his 1872 uniform with a fancy helmet; flowers; flags; and a Rosary, hung on his monument. He's buried between his two good friends - Generals Emory Upton and Andrew Alexander. It felt really good to leave the flag there for him. Three American flags were placed there, surrounding the 7th Cavalry flag.

Ms. Rebelle's 7th Cavalry guidon (with crossed swords), placed with reverence at the grave of Myles Keogh.
Photo by Janet Greentree

William Henry Seward's House in Auburn, NY

May 16th was the date of my visit to Auburn, which happened to be the 212th anniversary of William Seward's birth in 1801 in Florida, New York. Seward is also buried in Fort Hill Cemetery near Myles Keogh. Another American flag was left for him in tribute. Since May 16th was his birthday, all fees were waived to enter and tour his beautiful mansion at 33 South Street.

All I could think of while touring this exquisite house was how much the Round Table would enjoy seeing this. The house was owned and built originally in 1816 by Elijah Miller, a Cayuga County judge and the father of Seward's wife, Frances. He must have been extremely wealthy, as the house was absolutely opulent. Seward's sister Cornelia, a classmate of Frances, introduced Frances to Seward. Our tour guide said Seward was interested in two women, but picked Frances and, in doing so, moved up in the world. The judge gave his permission for them to marry, but

The home of Sec. of State and former senator and governor William Seward, in Auburn, NY.
Photo by Janet Greentree

At left and right: William Seward, early and later in life. Following the Powell attack, Seward was never photographed showing the enormous scar left on his right cheek.

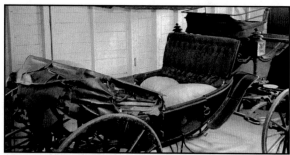

The carriage Seward was riding in when it turned over, causing Seward's jaw to be broken and wired. But that was not the worst thing that happened to the Secretary of State that day.

The fabulously Victorian library in the Seward house, Auburn, NY.

required that the two of them live in the house before the marriage. The Sewards married October 20, 1824, and had six children: Augustus (1826-1876), Frederick (1830-1915), Cornelia (1836-1837), William, Jr. (1839-1920), Frances (Fanny) (1844-1866), and an adopted daughter, Olive (1841-1908).

His son Augustus was paymaster of the Army in the Civil War, as his mother didn't want him in the line of fire. Son William, Jr., was a brigadier general.

Photos were not allowed to be taken in the house, but there are several available on the Internet to share with the Round Table. One of the most interesting things on display was the carriage that Seward was riding in on April 14, 1865, when he had his carriage accident and was confined to bed. Five men were injured that night during John Wilkes Booth conspirator Lewis Powell's vicious knife attack on Seward: Seward, his sons Augustus and Frederick, his nurse Sgt. George Robinson, and messenger Emerick Hansell. Hansell was paralyzed permanently from the stabbing. The small museum upstairs has a piece of the bed sheet that was on the bed at the time of the attack.

All five men, including Seward, survived the attack. Frederick had to wear a skull cap the rest of his life because of how the blows of the knife made his head misshapen. Seward's wife Frances died two months later on June 21, 1865, from a heart attack, due to the anxiety she suffered from the attack. Their daughter Fanny died from tuberculosis two years later in 1866.

The house was the only one ever owned by Seward. All the furnishings in the house belonged to the family. On display are mementoes from his 44-year political career. There are many beautiful antiques in each room. The drawing room has a large painting of their daughter Fanny, showing her with one glove on her hand, holding flowers pointing downward, with lilies and clouds in the background. This symbolism represents the fact that she sat for the portrait but died before it was finished. There was a small chair nearby that had a hand-cranked music box under the seat.

His library is magnificent. There are books in most every room. He had the complete Official Records, which looked to be very old. There was a bust of Lincoln in one window and a bust of Seward in the other. Seward was a short

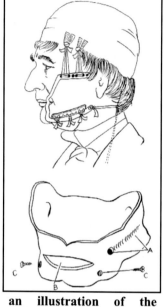

Above - an illustration of the apparatus holding Seward's jaw together after the carriage accident also served to protect his jugular vein when, later that night, Lewis Powell attacked him with a huge Bowie knife during the Lincoln assassination spree. Below, Fanny Seward as a girl; Fanny was in the room with her father during the attack on him. Fanny, throwing herself in front of the bed where Seward lay helpless, struggled with Powell and detained him long enough for others in the house to run to their aid, saving Seward's life.

man at 5'4", and always sat for his pictures. There is a picture of him with his daughter Fanny, and he is seated. There are several pictures around the house of the famous Lincoln cabinet picture. The dining room was very large, and several china pieces belonging to the Sewards were on the table.

A curving stairway leads up to what Seward called his diplomatic gallery. He has many pictures of people he met while being Secretary of State, as well as from his later travels. He numbered all his pictures. Abraham Lincoln's picture is No. 66, and Seward numbered his No. 66 ½, to show how close he was to the president. The suit he wore when he met Queen Victoria is displayed in a cabinet upstairs. There are four bedrooms upstairs.

The picture gallery upstairs at the Seward house; many of the luminaries Seward met as secretary of state, as well as through his travels overseas after the Civil War, are featured in this gallery.

On display upstairs, too, are items from Alaska, which Seward facilitated the purchase of in 1867. Also on display was a gold ring that the tour guide said was one of five made from the golden spike finishing the transcontinental railroad in 1869 at Promontory Summit, Utah. He told us that one was given to President U.S. Grant, one to each of the presidents of Union Pacific and Central Pacific Railroads, one to the minister giving the invocation, and one to William Seward. When researching the golden spike, this story does not come, up but the ring is definitely there.

Actor David Strathairn, who portrayed William Seward in the movie "Lincoln," visited the house to soak in the atmosphere prior to filming, per the tour guide.

Above, the high Victorian dining room at Seward's house; below, the "opulent" drawing room, where guests gathered.

After graduating from Union College with a law degree, Seward entered into a law partnership with his father-in-law, Judge Elijah Miller. William was the 12th governor of New York, from 1839- 1842. He was a U.S. senator from New York from 1849-1861. Seward was favored to win the nomination for president in 1860 but lost to Lincoln. Seward was Secretary of State under Presidents Abraham Lincoln and Andrew Johnson, from 1861-1869.

Both Seward and his wife were involved in the abolitionist movement. Frances operated a safe room in their home for fugitive slaves. Seward traveled extensively around the world in 1870-1871. On October 10, 1872, he died in his downstairs office on a green velvet couch, which is still in the room.

David Strathairn as William Seward in the movie "Lincoln."

Black Knight of the Confederacy - Gen. Turner Ashby

One of the benefits of belonging to the Stuart-Mosby Historical Society is going on their biannual bus trips. Don Hakenson has been guiding these tours since September 2000, when he took over from the late Jim Moyer. He and president Eric Buckland had a spectacular tour on September 22, 2018. We visited quite a few safe houses where Mosby's Rangers evaded the pursuit of the Union Army. Don and Eric were able to get us inside some of these fabulous old

The mounting step at Wolf Crag, used by Turner when riding off or returning to the house.
Photo by Janet Greentree

houses. In addition to the safe houses, we visited the home of Turner Ashby, Wolf Crag Farm, Markham, VA. The owners of the house graciously let all of us come inside and even served Virginia's famous ham biscuits and sweet tea to us (with a shot of bourbon, if you so desired). We also were able to see the house where Ashby was born, just a short distance down the road from Wolf Crag. We saw that Ashby's mounting stone for his horse-riding is still in the yard.

Above: Wolf Crag, the home of Turner Ashby, Jr., in Markham, VA. Below: Rose Bank Plantation house, where Ashby was born.

Photo by Janet Greentree

Turner Ashby, Jr. was born on October 23, 1828, at Rose Bank Plantation to Turner Ashby, Sr. and Dorothea Green. He was the third of five sons and the fifth of nine children. His father fought as a colonel in the War of 1812. His grandfather, Jack Ashby, served as a captain in the Revolutionary War. His father died when Turner was young. His mother hired a tutor for him and eventually sent him to Major Ambler's school. Turner Ashby is the only Civil War general that I have run across that was home-schooled, for the most part.

Young Turner was an excellent horseman; he competed in tournaments, and very rarely lost the competitions. He even competed once as an Indian chief and rode without saddle or bridle.

As a young man, he ran a mill on his father's property. He formed a cavalry company with his friends, called the Mountain Rangers. Some of their duties were to keep order among the laborers on the Manassas Gap Railroad. The railroad ran right by his home at Rose Bank. When John Brown executed his raid at Harpers Ferry, the Mountain Rangers went to Charles Town during Brown's trial and execution, to keep order.

Just prior to the war, Ashby tried running as a Whig for the state legislature, but didn't win the seat. Later, in the war, his company became the 7th Virginia Cavalry, Co. A, Ashby's Brigade, at Harper's Ferry. His unit was assigned to Gen. Thomas J. "Stonewall" Jackson at Harper's Ferry. Their assignment was to guard the fords

Gen. Turner Ashby, Jr.

across the Potomac River, as well as bridges from Harper's Ferry to Point of Rocks, MD. Jackson ordered the Rangers to blow up Dam No. 5 on the C&O Canal.

Ashby's brother, Richard, was killed early in the war, in June 1861, while skirmishing with Union troops along the Potomac River. Turner became obsessed with revenge for his brother's death after he heard rumors that his brother had been bayonetted while trying to surrender.

Ashby was appointed lieutenant colonel of the 7th VA Cavalry by Gen. Joseph E. Johnson on July 23, 1861. When Col. Angus McDonald left the

Illustration of Gen. Ashby's cavalry raiding Union supply wagons.

regiment, Ashby assumed command. He would then organize Chew's Battery, the first Confederate horse artillery. The 7th VA was called upon to screen Johnston's army at First Bull Run. In October 1861, he was back in Harper's Ferry, fighting the battle of Bolivar Heights against Gen. John W. Geary for control of the armory. Ashby lost to Geary. The 7th, by the spring of 1862, had grown very large, to include 27 infantry and cavalry companies.

Ashby and Jackson disagreed with the way the 7th was commanded. Jackson tried to strip Ashby from the cavalry command. Ashby threatened to resign, and Jackson backed down. On May

The Kemper house, where Ashby's corpse was brought and laid out for viewing. In the upper photo, man leaning against side of house is at window where people could view Ashby's body.

23, 1862, Ashby received his promotion to brigadier general and received his general's star from Jackson's aide, Sandie Pendleton, at the Taylor Hotel in Winchester. Pendleton's comment to Ashby was: "I hope that it will make you more careful." Unfortunately, the Confederate Congress never approved the promotion before his untimely death on June 6, 1862.

Ashby fought in Jackson's Valley Campaign; the First Battle of Kernstown; the First Battle of Winchester; Harrisonburg, and Port Republic. The day before First Winchester, Ashby and one of his captains rode through that town in Union uniforms, which had been occupied by the Union Gen. Nathaniel Banks. Ashby's command was the rear guard at Harrisonburg against Gen. John C. Fremont.

On the fateful day of June 6, 1862, Ashby's forces were attacked by the 1st New Jersey Cavalry at Good's Farm. His horse, Tom Telegraph, was shot from under him. Ashby proceeded on foot but after a few steps was shot through the heart, dying instantly. His last words were: "Charge men! For God's sake. Charge."
Ashby was taken to the Frank Kemper house in Port Republic. His body was prepared for burial and was put by a window in the house, so visitors could view his body. He was originally buried in the University of Virginia Cemetery in Charlottesville, VA. In October 1866 his body was reinterred at the Stonewall Cemetery in Winchester, VA, next to his beloved brother Richard. The marker says: "The Brothers Ashby." A marker was erected on the spot where he died at Chest-

nut Ridge, south of Harrisonburg.

His friend, Henry Kyd Douglas, said of him: "His face was the kind that cannot be photographed. Riding his black stallion, he looked like a knight of the olden time, galloping over the field on his favorite war horse." His battle regalia included a spyglass, gauntlets and a fox-hunting horn - all things a Virginia-born gentleman would have on his person. He only rode pure white or pure black horses.

A civilian in the valley named Thomas A. Ashby (no relation) described him as follows: "Dressed now in Confederate Gray, with gilt lace on his sleeves and collar, wearing high top-boots with spurs and a broadbrimmed black felt hat with a long black feather streaming behind, his appearance was striking and attractive. He stood about five feet eight inches in height and probably weighed from

The monument marking the graves of "The Brother's Ashby."

Photo by Janet Greentree

150-160 pounds. He was muscular and wiry, rather than robust or rugged. His hair and beard were as black as a raven's wing; his eyes were soft and mahogany brown; a long sweeping mustache concealed his mouth, and a heavy and long beard completely covered his breast. His complexion was dark in keeping with his other colorings."

At the time of Ashby's death, "Stonewall" Jackson was in the Frank Kemper house at Port Republic interviewing the captured Sir Percy Wyndham. Ashby's body was brought into the house by his saddened men. Jackson told his men to take Sir Percy out of the house and spent a long time alone with Ashby.

Later he would say of Ashby: "As a partisan officer, I never knew his superior; his daring was proverbial; his powers of endurance almost incredible; his tone of character heroic, and his sagacity almost intuitive in divining the purposes and movements of the enemy."

An very descriptive obituary from the *Lynchburg Republican*

Illustration of Gen. Ashby riding Tom Telegraph who, unfortunately, was shot out from under Ashby at Good's Farm.

states in part: "He lay there as if a gentle slumber had fallen upon him, his physiognomy indicating resolution, determination, and firmness - heavy black eyelashes and moustache, prominent forehead, slowing quick perception and thought, dark complexion, and an honest Virginia face...."

After the services in the chapel, the remains of Gen. Ashby were conveyed to the university cemetery and committed "earth to earth, ashes to ashes, and dust to dust. Col. T.G. Randolph and the professors of the university assisted in the ceremony. The grave was covered by the cavalry, and they fired several volleys over it, and there he will remain in this classic ground until the last tramp shall summon all to the general judgment."

A marker notes the spot at Post Republic where Turner Ashby died.

Photo by Janet Greentree

143

Gen. G. Moxley Sorrel, CSA

Moxley Sorrel has yet another unusual name from the Civil War. His first name was Gilbert, but he was called Moxley, his mother's maiden name. He is intricately linked to another Civil War general, William Whann Mackall, also a Confederate. On one of Yankee Nan (Nancy Anwyll) and my excursions, we visited the Greenwich Presbyterian Church Cemetery in Greenwich (Prince William Co.), VA. The church was founded in 1802 by Moxley's grandmother, Aminta Douglass Moxley. There to - our surprise - were many Sorrel and Mackall graves. All the Sorrels were born in Savannah. We remarked that it was as if the Sorrels came up to Virginia to die. But, after much research, Ms. Rebelle found that Moxley's father had a summer home in Greenwich called *The Lawn*. The house burned down in 1924, but was later reconstructed. Moxley's sister Aminta married Gen. Mackall. She is buried in Greenwich, but he is buried in McLean (VA) Presbyterian Church Cemetery. Now comes much more intrigue.

Moxley was born February 23, 1838 in Savannah, GA, the son of one of the wealthiest men in Savannah – Mathurin Francois

At left: Gen. William W. Mackall, whose family intertwined with that of Gen. Moxley Sorrel.

Above: Gen. G. Moxley Sorrel; at left, his father, Francis, whose mother was a free black woman. Francis "passed" as white; Gen. Moxley's grandmother, Eugenie de Sutre, was never spoken of in the family.

"Francis" Sorrel and his wife, Matilda Aminta Douglass. Moxley's father was born in Saint Domingo on the Mirigoane Plantation, in the West Indies (now Haiti) to Antoine Sorrel and a free black woman, Eugenie De Sutre, who died a week after giving birth to Francis. Eugenie was Antoine's second wife. Antoine was born in France and was a French military colonel. Antoine abandoned his child. Francis lived with Eugenie's relatives in Port au Prince. Francis was light-skinned and passed for white. Francis was left out of his father's will, as well. No one in the Sorrel family descendants ever talked about Eugenie. Brothers Richard and Henry Douglass, sugar

The Sorrel-Weed House, Savannah, GA, where Moxley grew up. It is supposedly one of the most haunted houses in America.
Photo by Jackie Shepherd

and coffee traders, took Francis in, and sent him to Baltimore to work for them. He later was sent to Savannah and started a mercantile company, Douglass and Sorrel, with Richard. In 1825, he started his own company, becoming extremely wealthy himself. He was a shrewd businessman, and, by the years following the Civil War, he had accumulated $40,000 in gold.

Francis' first wife was Lucinda Douglass (the niece of Henry Douglass), the sister of Matilda, who died after contracting yellow fever while caring for neighbors who also had the disease. Eleven children were sired by Francis (three from Lucinda and eight from Matilda). Francis was listed as a merchant in the 1850 census with real estate worth $48,000 and as owning slaves.

Young Moxley grew up in the Sorrel-Weed House (Shady Corner) at Bull and Harris streets (6 West Harris Street) in Savannah. The house is still standing and is open for tours/ghost tours. It is purported to be one of the most haunted houses in Savannah. In 1859, Francis sold the house to Henry Weed and moved to the townhouse next door at 12 West Harris Street.

In 1860, Moxley's mother, after discovering her husband was having an affair with a slave named Molly, committed suicide by throwing herself headfirst off a second-floor balcony. His mother suffered from depression and had also just lost two of her children. Molly lived in the carriage house on the property, which is also said to be haunted. Molly was found hanged shortly after her mistresses' suicide. It was not clear whether she hanged herself, or if someone else did it. Since she was the property of Francis, there was no police inquiry.

Chatham Academy in Savannah, GA, where Moxley was educated.

Francis was friends with Robert E. Lee, who visited the house in 1861 and 1862 during the Civil War. Gen. Lee would also visit the house in 1870 and continue to do so up until his death in October of that year. Moxley had met Lee at the train station and showed him around the city, beginning their friendship.

Moxley was educated at the Chatham Academy in Savannah, GA. He was working as a banking clerk at the Central Railroad when the Civil War began. His house was across the street from the Olgethorpe Barracks. He watched all the activity at the barracks and wanted to become a soldier himself. He joined the Georgia Hussars as a private and participated in the capture of Fort Pulaski. His father arranged for a letter of introduction from Col. Thomas Jordan, staff aide to Gen. P.G.T. Beauregard.

Moxley was assigned to Gen. James Longstreet on July 21, 1861, at the battle of Bull Run/First Manassas as a volunteer aide-de-camp. Later, he would write in his book Recollections of a Confederate Staff Officer, "....approaching the ford, shot and shell were flying close overhead, then feeling a bit nervous, my first time under fire, I began to enjoy the folly that had brought me into such disturbing scenes." Longstreet wrote: ("...that) his young aide came into the battle as gaily as a beau, and seemed to receive orders which threw him into more exposed positions with particular delight."

Illustration of the shelling of Ft. Pulaski, Savannah, GA.

Sorrel came up the ranks, quickly becoming adjutant-general under Longstreet and then lieutenant colonel by June 1863. He fought in the Peninsula Campaign, 2nd Bull Run, Antietam, Fredericksburg, Gettysburg, Chickamauga, the Wilderness, Spotsylvania, Cold Harbor and Petersburg. He served under Longstreet until October 1864 when, at age 26, and at the suggestion of Gen. Lee, he was made a brigadier general. During the battle of the Wilderness, Longstreet was severely wounded and Moxley led four brigades against the Union.

Moxley was assigned to Gen. William Mahone after 1864. He was in charge of a brigade consisting of the 2nd, 22nd, 48th, and 64th regiments and 2nd and 10th battalions of Georgia infantry in A.P. Hill's Corps. While in the Petersburg area, he was wounded in the leg. Shortly after, at Hatcher's Run, he endured a severe chest wound, resulting in a punctured lung, at Hatcher's Run. His older brother Francis, who was a surgeon in the Confederate Army, helped with Moxley's convalescence. Moxley recuperated and was returning to his command when the Confederates surrendered at Appomattox.

After the war, Moxley went back to Savannah and became the superintendent of the Central Railroad of Georgia. Seven years later, he became the general manager of the Ocean Steamship Company, which had routes between Savannah, New York and Liverpool.

On November 14, 1867, at Woodville Plantation, Baldwin Co., GA, Sorrel married Kate Amelie DuBignon. The Sorrels had one daughter.

Under "local and personal news" in several newspapers, Gen. Sorrel was mentioned as follows: The *Savannah Daily Advertiser* reported that he and General Joseph Johnson were judges at an immense gathering at the base ball park in May, 1871.

The *Savannah Daily Advertiser,* in November 1871, listed him and Gen. Bushrod Johnson as honorary managers for the Industrial Association of Georgia Citizens Ball. *The Morning News of Savannah* in May 1890, reported that Sorrel "will leave this morning on the Chattahoochee for New York, where he will spend the summer months, and will give his personal attention to the business of the company at that end of the route. The general feels a very just pride in the magnificent fleet of steamships of which he is the manager, and to his never ceasing care and energy is due much of the popularity of the line."

Above: the mausoleum holding Sorrel and his wife; at left: panel marker describing the military service of the deceased.
Photos by Janet Greentree

In January 1891, the *Morning News* also reported that "Ohioans See the Sights, The Buckeye Visitors Given the Freedom of the City…. The next stop was at the Ocean Steamship wharves. Gen. G. Moxley Sorrel, who was one of the escorts, invited the visitors and the committee aboard the Chattahoochee, which had just began loading. A number of the Ohioans had never seen an ocean steamer before…." *The Morning News of Savannah*, also in January 1891, reported that "Gen. G. Moxley Sorrel, general manager of the Ocean Steamship Company, has given his personal attention to getting this handsome exhibit ready…. The company was shipping models of the steam ships Savannah and the City of Augusta to St. Augustine, FL."

Gen. Gilbert Moxley Sorrel died in Roanoke, VA, at the Barrows, the home of his older brother Francis. *The Times-Picayune* of New Orleans reported as follows: "Gen. G. Moxley Sorrel, aged 64, of Savannah, GA., died at the home of his brother, near Roanoke, last midnight. General Sorrel entered the Confederate army in Savannah as volunteer aid[e] on Longstreet's staff at the outbreak of the civil war. He was promoted several times for gallantry, and in the third year of the war was made a brigadier general on Longstreet's staff…."

Gen. Sorrel died August 10, 1901, and is buried at Laurel Grove Cemetery in Savannah, GA.

As a side note, Gen. Orlando Poe camped at the Greenwich Presbyterian Church in August 1862, before 2nd Bull Run/Manassas.

146

Maj. Gen. John Alexander "Black Jack" Logan

Did you know that 11 presidents have lain in state in the Capitol Rotunda? Did you know that there were 18 other people to lie in state in the Capitol Rotunda? Did you know that there was only one Civil War general to lie in state in the Capitol Rotunda? By now I'm sure you have guessed that it was Gen. John Logan. He lay in state on December 30th and 31st, 1886, before being buried in the U.S. Soldiers' and Airmen's Home National Cemetery in Washington, D.C. He was in good company, with other non-presidents Henry Clay, Thaddeus Stevens, Charles Sumner, and Pierre L'Enfant, to name a few.

Maj. Gen. John A. Logan

The reason General Logan had this privilege was that he issued General Order No. 11 from the Headquarters, Grand Army of the Republic, Washington, D.C., on May 5, 1868, which reads as follows:

"I. The 30th day of May, 1868, is designated for the purpose of strewing with flowers or otherwise decorating the graves of comrades who died in defense of their country during the late rebellion, and whose bodies now lie in almost every city, village, and hamlet churchyard in the land. In this observance no form or ceremony is prescribed, but posts and comrades will in their own way arrange such fitting services and testimonials of respect as circumstances may permit.

"We are organized, comrades, as our regulations tell us, for the purpose, among other things, of preserving and strengthening those kind and fraternal feelings which have bound together the soldiers, sailors, and marines who united to suppress the late rebellion. What can aid more to assure this result than by cherishing tenderly the memory of our heroic dead, who made their breasts a barricade between our country and its foes? Their soldier lives were the reveille of freedom to a race in chains, and their death a tattoo of rebellious tyranny in arms. We should guard their graves with sacred vigilance. All that the consecrated wealth and taste of the Nation can add to their adornment and security is but a fitting tribute to the memory of her slain defenders.

"Let no wanton foot tread rudely on such hallowed grounds. Let pleasant paths invite the coming and going of reverent visitors and fond mourners. Let no vandalism of avarice or neglect, no ravages of time, testify to the present or to the coming generations that we have forgotten, as a people, the cost of free and undivided republic.

"If other eyes grow dull and other hands slack, and other hearts cold in the solemn trust, ours shall keep it well as the light and warmth of life remain in us.

"Let us, then, at the time appointed, gather around their sacred remains and garland the passionless mounds above them with choicest flowers of springtime; let us raise above them the dear old flag they saved from dishonor; let us in this solemn presence renew our pledges to aid and assist those whom they have left among us as sacred charges upon the Nation's gratitude – the soldier's and sailor's widow and orphan.

"II. It is the purpose of the Commander-in-Chief to inaugurate this observance with the hope it will be kept up from year to year, while a survivor of the war remains to honor the memory of his departed comrades. He earnestly desires the public press to call attention to this Order, and lend its friendly aid in bringing it to the notice of comrades in all parts of the country in time for simultaneous compliance therewith.

The first Decoration Day ceremonies at Arlington National Cemetery, May 31, 1868.

"III. Department commanders will use every effort to make this order effective.

"By Command of: JOHN A. LOGAN, Commander-in-Chief"

Yes, General Logan began the custom which prevails to this day of Decoration Day, later changed to Memorial Day. This reverence shown to our soldiers and sailors, who died for our country, earned him the honor of lying in state in the Capitol Rotunda after his death.

John Logan as a lawyer, 1855.

John Alexander Logan was born on February 9, 1826, in Murphysboro in southern Illinois, in a triangle of land at the confluence of the Ohio and Mississippi Rivers, known as Egypt. He was the son of a wealthy southern Illinois doctor, John Logan and his wife, Elizabeth Jenkins Logan. The senior Logan was a friend of Abraham Lincoln.

Dr. Logan first schooled young John at home, and he later studied at Shiloh College. He graduated from the University of Louisville in 1851 with a law degree. He had a very successful law practice and got interested in politics as a Democrat; he was elected county clerk in 1849. He served in the Illinois House of Representatives from 1853-54, and again in 1857. He was a prosecuting attorney in the Third Judicial District of Illinois. Logan worked on passing a law to prohibit African Americans, including freedmen, from settling in the state of Illinois.

When the Civil War began, he was an Illinois Congressman and observing at First Bull Run with a Michigan unit. He picked up a rifle and started fighting. He was one of the last men to leave the field on July 21, 1861. He went back to Washington and resigned his Congressional seat on April 2, 1862. He entered the Union Army as a colonel of the 31st Illinois Voluntary Infantry. It is here that he got the name 'Black Jack,' because of his dark eyes, swarthy complexion, black hair, and long black drooping mustache. Logan was mostly in the Western Theater of the Civil War, fighting with General U. S. Grant.

Logan was wounded at Fort Donelson and had a horse shot out from under him in the Battle of Belmont. He was appointed brigadier general on March 21, 1862, and major general on November 29, 1862. He was the first to enter the city of Vicksburg after the siege in July 1863. He commanded the Army of the Tennessee after the death of Gen. James B. McPherson and commanded the entire Union Army at the Battle of Atlanta. Gen. William T. Sherman replaced him with Gen. O.O. Howard. Logan felt this was a personal slight to him, since Howard was a West Point graduate and he was not. Logan was considered a "political" general.

Illustration depicting Gen. Logan at the Battle of Dallas, GA, May 26-June 4, 1864.

He went on to commanded the XV Corps in Sherman's Carolina Campaign and was with him when Gen. Joseph Johnston surrendered in North Carolina in 1865. He was again given command of the Army of the Tennessee on May 23, 1865, and led them in the Grand Review in Washington, D.C.

After the war, he went back to politics, but as a Republican. He won election to the House of Representatives in 1866. In 1868, he was part of the impeachment trial of President Andrew Johnson. He was elected a senator on March 4, 1871.

The Blaine-Logan ticket, presidential campaign of 1884.

148

A Thomas Nast cartoon lampooning Blaine and Logan; Blaine, whose bluster toward England was seen as a tactic to garner Irish-American votes, can't do the deed, and Logan, who is ridiculed for massacring the English language.

As a senator, he was part of the effort to stop the action to overturn the Court-martial of Maj. General Fitz John Porter.

In 1884, he ran on the Republican ticket as vice president, with James G. Blaine as the candidate for president. Grover Cleveland won the election. Logan was still representing the people of Illinois when he died on December 26, 1886.

He married Mary Simmerson Cunningham in Gallatin, Illinois, on November 27, 1855. They would have three children, but only the youngest two survived to adulthood. His son, John Alexander Logan, Jr., posthumously received the Medal of Honor during the Philippine-American War. Logan and Mary lived at a rented house at 1114 G Street, N.W. in Washington, D.C. The house is now located in the Mount Pleasant neighborhood of

Logan with his wife Mary Simmerson Cunningham Logan, son Manning Alexander Logan and daughter Mary Elizabeth "Dollie" Logan, in about 1870.

Washington. They later purchased a house on what is now Logan Circle, which features an equestrian statue in tribute to the general. After he died, Mary was unable to make payments on the house, and the general's friends from Chicago raised enough money for her to pay off the house. He also has a statue in Chicago at Grant Park. Several counties across the country have been named for him, as well. There is a Gen. John A. Logan Museum in his hometown of Murphysboro, Illinois.

Logan's house in Murphrysboro, IL .

In December 1886, Gen. Logan's arms swelled up and his legs were in pain. The doctors thought it may be rheumatism. The symptoms subsided, and then he relapsed on December 24th, dying at 3 p.m. on December 26th. It was the general opinion of the doctors that his wounds from the Civil War were also responsible for his demise. (Note: His marker at the U.S. Soldiers' and Airmen's Home National Cemetery shows his death date as December 27, 1886.)

Gen. William Tecumseh Sherman lamented in 1886 that "I am an older man than Grant, McClellan, Hancock, and Logan, who in the past year have been taken suddenly, almost without premonition." Sherman was asked to be a pallbearer at Logan's funeral.

At left: the tomb of Gen. John A. Logan at the U.S. Soldiers' and Airmen's Home National Cemetery, Washington, DC. At right: the statue of the general at Logan Circle, Washington, DC.

Photos by Janet Greentree

The General in the Field & General William McComb

This article is a big thank you, albeit a little late, to our Bull Run Civil War Round Table member, Mike Block, who made it possible for me to find Gen. William George Mackey Davis,

CSA, buried in the Tacketts Burroughs family cemetery on the Ott Farm in Remington, VA. Other than my maps, my "bible" is the book *"Generals at Rest,"* written by Richard and James Owens (father & son).

On a side note here, my first copy of this book completely wore out from carrying it around cemeteries. In the back of the book, the Owens give directions for hard to find graves. Davis' grave is one of them. I can't tell you how many times Yankee Nan (Nancy Anwyll) and I have driven down Route 29, bypassing Remington, and wondering about the location of the general in the field. We tried several times ourselves to find him, but the directions in the book never quite matched up with what we were seeing as we drove on down the road.

Above, left: Gen. William G. Mackey Davis, who signed up at age 50; above, right: the general later in life.

Mike Block was so kind to contact Larry & Lory Payne, fellow cemetery gravers, and members of the Southern Fauquier Historical Society for help. Mike also brought his wife, Caryn, along too. It turns out the general is buried on a turf farm in Remington, off Sumerduck Road. Another interesting grave in the plot was that of Charles E. Mills Davis of the 43rd Virginia Cavalry, Mosby's command, who was the general's son.

Gen. Davis was born on May 9, 1812, in Portsmouth, VA. I was unable to determine how, but by some turn of fate, he ended up in Tallahassee, Florida, where he was a practicing attorney. He was held in high esteem by the legal community in Florida.

On January 1, 1862, at age 50, he raised the First Florida Cavalry at Camp Mary David, and was commissioned the colonel of the unit. The unit's mission was to watch the coast and Union troop movements to prevent them from penetrating the interior of Florida. The Governor of Florida, John Milton, was opposed to cavalry commands and insisted all Florida needed was artillery and infantry.

On March 25, 1862, Col. Davis and his unit were sent to East Tennessee to Gen. Albert Sidney Johnston's command. Davis patrolled the mountains of East Tennessee. On November 4, 1862, he was commissioned a brigadier general. Davis mustered out on May 5, 1863, due to

Gen. Davis' grave marker "in the field" in Remington, VA.

age and health reasons. He did, however, command blockade runners out of Wilmington, NC, after resigning.

Davis went back to practicing law in Jacksonville, FL, after the war. Later he moved to Washington, DC, to practice law. He died in Alexandria, VA, on March 11, 1898.

General William McComb, CSA

Gen. McComb was born in Mercer County, PA, on November 21, 1828. His family moved to Clarksville, TN, in 1854. McComb, before the war, erected a flour mill in Cumberland County and had various manufacturing businesses. When the Civil War began, McComb chose to serve the Confederacy, in spite of his Northern birth. He enlisted as a private in the 14th Tennessee Infantry in May 1861. The unit was formed at Camp Duncan. McComb was soon elected 2nd lieutenant and rose through the ranks to brigadier general on January 20, 1865. The 14th was part

Gen. William McComb

of Gen. James Archer's brigade in General A.P. Hill's Light Division of the Army of Northern Virginia.

McComb was wounded in several battles, including Gaines' Mill; Antietam and Chancellorsville. In August 1863, he took command of Gen. Wilcox's old Alabama brigade. He commanded that unit through the Overland Campaign and the Siege of Petersburg. Gen. McComb was paroled at Appomattox Court House.

After the war, he lived in Alabama and Mississippi but eventually settled in the Gordonsville area of Virginia. He was a farmer for fifty years. The general died on his plantation in Gordonsville on July 12, 1918. He is buried at the Mechanicsville Baptist Church near Boswell's Tavern in Louisa County, VA. He was one of the last 10 surviving Confederate generals. His obituary in the New Castle, PA, newspaper lists him as having been 90 years old, serving all four years in the Civil War, with wounds to both legs.

Gen. McComb's gravesite in the yard at Mechanicsville Baptist Church, VA.
Photo by Janet Greentree

One Lone Civil War General in New Mexico

Ms. Rebelle and her sister, both being retired, have been bitten by the travel bug. Our latest trip at the end of September was to New Mexico and Colorado. The main purpose of the trip was to see the beautiful golden aspens in color in Colorado. Along the way though, there had to be a stop to find the only Civil War general buried in the whole state of New Mexico – Union Brigadier General Gustavus Adolphus Smith.

Gen. Smith was born December 26, 1820, in Philadelphia, PA. After living in the states of Maryland and Ohio, he settled in Decatur, Illinois. His occupation before the war was that of a carriage manufacturer. After Fort Sumter, Smith was one of the first to volunteer in Illinois. On September 1, 1861, he became the colonel of the 35th Illinois Infantry.

Smith was severely wounded at the Battle of Pea Ridge, Arkansas. His horse was shot from under him, a bullet struck the sword he held in

Gen. Gustavus Adolphus Smith.

his hand, his belt was shot off, he received a shot in the shoulder, and a piece of shrapnel struck his head, giving him a skull fracture. He was carried off the field, thought to be mortally wounded. He did recover, however, but his wounds were not fully healed until 1868.

Gen. Smith's grave marker in the Santa Fe National Cemetery, Santa Fe, NM.

Smith was commissioned a brigadier general in September 1862, but was unable to fight in the field, so the commission expired. Later, in February 1865, he was given a brevet brigadier general rank for commanding the 155th Illinois. His unit guarded the Nashville & Chattanooga Railroads.

After the war, in 1870, Smith was the collector of internal revenue in New Mexico, a job given to him by his friend, Pres. Ulysses Grant. Smith died in Santa Fe, NM, on December 11, 1885. He was originally buried in Fairview Cemetery in Santa Fe but was reinterred at the Santa Fe National Cemetery. His tombstone says: "Colonel G. A. Smith, Illinois."

Clara Barton Tour

Ms. Rebelle, and fellow Bull Run Civil War Round Table member, Gwen Wyttenbach, signed up for the Fairfax Station Railroad Museum tour on March 28, 2009, given by round table member Bill Etue. Bill's very capable assistant was his wife, Rebecca Marti. They are quite a team. Bill would read the text on one page, and Rebecca would give him the text for the next page, so he didn't have to turn pages. Gwen and I were impressed.

Clara Barton, confident, courageous and competent at all she undertook.

We started the tour at the Museum, and boarded our bus for the ride downtown to see Clara Barton's office at 7th & E Streets, or 448 ½ Seventh Street, N.W. Waiting to let us in was Richard Lyons, who while working as a GSA carpenter in the building in 1996, saw an envelope hanging out of the attic ceiling above Clara's room. Out poured a plethora of Clara's papers. That must have been such a thrill for Richard.

We climbed up 42 steps in a very narrow building that led to Room No. 9 that was her office. It was definitely like walking back in time. Although the building had been used over the years, you could definitely see the time frame of the past with the wallpaper and the old banisters on the stairs. Richard tells the story that as he entered the room, he looked around, and felt a tap on his shoulder. He turned around but no one was there. Then he looked up to see the envelope. In addition to the envelope, he saw a metal sign "Missing Soldiers Office, 3rd Story, Room 9, Miss Clara Barton." Letters and artifacts belonging to Miss Barton were in that space. Richard also found a blouse with a bullet hole in it that he later discovered was worn by her at Antietam. Clara lived at this residence all during the war. She moved there in 1860 while working at the Patent Office two blocks away. It later served as her office. She had a privacy wall built at the back of the office for her bedroom. The wallpaper is still on the

Above, left, the 7th Street (front) entrance to the famed Missing Soldiers Office run by Clara Barton. Above, right, the staircase leading to the second-floor office.
Photos by Janet Greentree

wall. On the door, with the No. 9 still intact, is the mail slot that Clara herself carved in the door for her mail. She got lots and lots

Ms. Rebelle points to the mail slot that Clara carved into the door of her office and private rooms upstairs at the Missing Soldiers Office.
Photo courtesy of Janet Greentree

Richard Lyons experienced the greatest of historical finds - the lost location of Clara Barton's Missing Soldiers Office in downtown Washington, DC.

It's a miracle that this iconic sign, at left, was salvaged from the abandoned office building that had been the location of Clara Barton's great undertaking.
Photo by Janet Greetntree

Barton's house in Maryland, Glen Echo, was spare inside, but useful as home and office for the Red Cross, the organization she started to respond to threats to the well-being of the public.
Photo by Janet Greentree

Above, the desk where Clara Barton spent long days building the Red Cross to provide assistance in the event of community disaster, as she had used her Missing Soldiers Office assist after the national disaster of the Civil War. Below, the bedroom in which she died on April 12, 1912.

Photo by Janet Greentree

of mail from families trying to find their missing loved ones after the war.

Clara was the first woman appointed to run a U.S. Government Office. She was appointed by Pres. Abraham Lincoln in March of 1865 to be in charge of the search for 62,000 men missing from the Union Army. No Confederates? She called her office the "Office of Correspondence with the Friends of the Missing Men of the United States Army." The men of the period didn't take too kindly to a woman running an office and were very unkind to her, even to the point of spitting on her. She prevailed, and spent 1865 -1868 looking for the missing soldiers. She was given $15,000 and a small staff to get the job done. She accounted for about 22,000 men, although some were dead.

Clara had an interesting life. She was born on Christmas Day of 1821 in North Oxford, MA. She was the youngest of five children in a middle-class family and was educated at home. Clara stayed home from school for two years to care for her brother David, who fell from a barn roof. Perhaps it was this experience that made her become a nurse.

She started teaching school at the age of 15. The science of phrenology was becoming popular at that time. Clara's mother had a "reading" for Clara and had the bumps on her head measured. Dr. Franz-Joseph Gall read her head. He declared that she was destined to become a school teacher. Clara was extremely shy and a very slight young lady. Nevertheless, she did become a school teacher. After her mother died and her siblings moved away, she went to Bordentown, NJ (are you reading this, John De Pue?). She taught at the Pauper School, later named Barton's Pauper School. The school was so popular that even the children in private schools wanted to go to Miss Barton's school. The 1851 New Jersey School Board didn't believe a woman could run a school, so the job of principal was given to a man. This man made $350 more a year than she did for the same work. She had been told she was making the same as the men in the school. She quit teaching, came to Washington, D.C. and got a job as a clerk at the Patent Office, making $1,400 a year. Later, the

Clara Barton later in life.

Secretary of the Interior didn't think women should be working in the government, so her job was reduced to a copyist. She then made a penny for each ten words she copied. The Civil War began, and the rest is history.

Her brother David became the Quartermaster of the 18th Army Corp. This is interesting to me, as this is the unit my Union ancestor, Daniel Smithers, served with (are you reading this, Yankee Nan?). David was sent to Hilton Head Island and Clara followed along to tend to the sick. Here she met Col. John J. Elwell, a married man from Ohio, and they began an affair. That surprised both Gwen and me, as we had never heard anything about that before. The affair ended; Clara never married.

After lunch at the Irish Inn, a former biker bar but now an upscale restaurant, we toured Clara's house at Glen Echo. That is another story in itself. She started the Red Cross in 1881. The Red Cross built the house at Glen Echo for her, and she finally moved into the premises in 1897. At first, it was a warehouse for her supplies. It's a very utilitarian house. There were no ceilings, so she tacked gauze on the beams. There is a large second and third floor, but at that time there were no stairs. Clara climbed a ladder up to the second floor to her bedroom at the age of 76.

The house is filled with awards and mementos of her service with the Red Cross. Her desk is there, and several original pieces of her furniture. Clara died there in her bedroom in 1912. She is buried in Oxford, Massachusetts. The house sits next to the former Glen Echo Amusement Park.

The park is now a center for the arts. Ms. Rebelle's first date with her former husband was at Glen Echo many years ago. I certainly didn't know then that Clara Barton's house was next door. It was rather strange to be there again. Bill Etue told a funny story about landing a job selling cotton candy at the park, trying to impress a girl. In the former bumper car pavilion before touring the house, we were treated to a little three-character play about Clara's life. It was very well done.

Clara Barton's Glen Echo home features many examples of the red cross motif, as in this parlor window.

Photo by Janet Greentree

Bill Etue's tours are wonderful. This is my second tour with him. He gives everyone a nice booklet printed out with your name on it. He takes you to nice restaurants. It was a very good tour. Thanks a lot, Bill.

Editor's note: Since this article was written, Bill Etue (left) has passed on to his eternal reward, but he left in the hearts of many a fond remembrance of the historic places and people that energized him to be one of the best public historians of our acquaintance.

Clara Barton's gravestone in the Brush Hill Cemetery, Oxford, MA.

Gen. Godfrey Weitzel, USA

Have you all heard the quote "Like Grant took Richmond?" Did Grant take Richmond? Unfortunately, not, but the general listed above, the 6'4" Godfrey Weitzel, did on April 3, 1865, at 8:15 a.m. Our Gen. Grant never stepped foot into Richmond until after the Civil War ended.

Gen. Godfrey Weitzel

There are two historical markers honoring Gen. Weitzel – No. SA 40 located at the Osborne Pike (Rt. 5) and New Market Road, and No. SA 41 located at E. Main Street & Nicholson Street in the Richmond area. As his troops marched towards town, musicians played Yankee Doodle. Not only that, but Weitzel led the all-black 25th Army Corps into the burning city. Weitzel is credited with raising the Union flag over Richmond, but it was actually done by his aide, Lt. Johnston de Peyser. The flag was raised over the Virginia Capitol building.

Richmond mayor, Joseph C. Mayo, traveled along the Osborne Pike to find a Union commander to surrender the city to. He found Majors Atherton Stevens and Eugene Graves, who took his note to Gen. Weitzel. The surrender was accepted at City Hall by the general. Weitzel's first order was to quell the fires set by the Confederates, to save the city. By then, only about 20,000 people remained in the deserted city, about half of which were the enslaved people. Gen. Weitzel sent a telegraph to Gen. Grant on April 3rd stating: "We took possession of Richmond at 8:15 a.m. I captured many guns and cannons. The rebels evidently left in great haste. The city is on fire in two places. I am using every effort to put out the fire." Within 24 hours, Weitzel's message was quoted in every Union newspaper.

His headquarters on the evening of

The burning of Richmond, VA, April 3rd, 1865.

April 3rd was Jefferson Davis' White House of the Confederacy, located at 12th and Clay Streets in Richmond. Davis' housekeeper was instructed to surrender the house for the occupancy of the commanding officer of the federal troops who would occupy the city. Gen. Weitzel was that man. The next day, President Abraham Lincoln and his son, Tad, traveled to Richmond. Lincoln, himself, would sit in the chair of Jefferson Davis in his office in the mansion. Gen. Weitzel had planned to meet Lincoln when he arrived, but Lincoln appeared early. Weitzel said: "I was therefore very much surprised to hear, just about the time I intended to get into my [carriage], that the president was already at my quarters. I drove over as hastily as possible and found the report correct." Weitzel queried the president as to what should be done with the citizens of Richmond. Lincoln replied: "If I were in your position, General, I think I would let them up easy, let them up easy." Later, when Godfrey heard his friend FitzHugh Lee was at the Lee house, he sent his purse to the residence, offering FitzHugh any sum that might be needed to secure the safety and comfort of the Lee family.

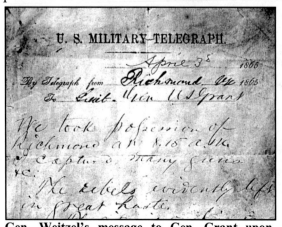

Gen. Weitzel's message to Gen. Grant upon capturing Richmond.

Gottfried Weitzel, later known as Godfrey, was born on November 1, 1835, in Winzlen, Germany, to

Pres. Abraham Lincoln depicted entering Richmond, where formerly enslaved people surrounded and exuberantly cheered him.

Ludwig and Susanna Krummel Weitzel. His place of birth would be changed later to Cincinnati, Ohio, by his parents' wishing to fit into the "Over the Rhine" neighborhood in Cincinnati. Godfrey did not reveal this fact until late in his life. His parents changed his name to Godfrey to be more Americanized, as well. His father served in the German military, but wanted to achieve a better life by immigrating to America. They emigrated when Susanna was pregnant with their younger son, Lewis. Ludwig also changed his name to Lewis to fit in. Godfrey's father operated a grocery store in the Tenth Ward. He became a city commissioner and served on the local school board. Both Godfrey and Lewis would be educated in the local schools and attended the "new" Central High School located in the basement of the German Lutheran Church on Walnut Street. Godfrey finished at the top of his class and was appointed to West Point by Ohio Congressman David Tiernan Disney. Young Godfrey had just passed his 15th birthday when he reported to West Point. He was the youngest cadet on campus.

At West Point, Godfrey would be known as Dutch. His roommates were Cyrus Comstock and Francis R.T. Nicholls. Robert E. Lee became superintendent of West Point when Godfrey was in his second year. Lee took interest in Godfrey, who was a top engineering and math student at the "Point." Godfrey spent much time at Lee's house and became friends with FitzHugh Lee.

Godfrey Weitzel finished 2nd in his class (as did Robert E. Lee in 1829) out of 34 cadets in 1855. Weitzel's roommate, Cyrus Comstock, was first in his class. Comstock became a Union brevet major general and Nicholls a Confederate brigadier general.

Gen. Godfrey Weitzel and staff - Capt. Lewis Weitzel is third from left.

Photo by Matthew Brady

Godfrey married Louisa C. Moor of Cincinnati on November 3, 1859. After only three weeks of marriage, tragedy would strike Louisa when her dress caught fire while preparing Thanksgiving dinner. Her husband tried to extinguish the flames, but she suffered severe burns and died within hours of the incident. On January 6, 1865, he married Louise Bogen. The Weitzels had three children, with only one surviving to adulthood.

Weitzel's first assignment was to help improve the defenses of New Orleans under Gen. P.G.T. Beauregard. In 1859, Weitzel returned to West Point as an Assistant Professor of Civil and Military Engineering. In 1860, he was assigned to the Corps of Engineers in Washington, D.C. His unit served as bodyguards during the inauguration of President Abraham Lincoln. When the Civil War began, he was sent back to Ohio and served under Gen. George B. McClellan, constructing defenses in Cincinnati and Washington. He was attached to Gen. Benjamin Butler as chief engineer of the Department of the Gulf. In New Orleans, he was promoted to brigadier general in August 1862, and was made acting mayor of New Orleans. His knowledge of the area helped Admiral David Farragut sail his gunboats past Confederate forts guarding the Mississippi River south of New Orleans. He commanded the XIX Corps under Gen. Nathaniel Banks during the siege of Port Hudson. Port Hudson fell five days after Vicksburg on July 9, 1863. From May to September 1864, he was chief engineer under Gen. Butler, targeting the Confederate capitol at Richmond. He was engaged at Swift's Creek, Drury's Bluff, the Bermuda Hundred Campaign, and Deep Bottom. From September 1864, he commanded the XVII Corps. On November 7, 1864,

Weitzel's Alpena Lighthouse, Lake Huron's Thunder Bay in Michigan.

he was appointed major general of volunteers and assumed command of the XXV Corps, which consisted of U.S. Colored Troops. After Richmond, he was assigned to Gen. Alfred Terry and fought at Fort Fisher. Towards the end of the war, Gen. Grant assigned him to command all Union troops north of the Appomattox River. Gen. Weitzel spoke to his men as follows: "Let history record that on the banks of the James, 30,000 freemen not only gained their own liberty, but shattered the prejudice of the world, and gave to the land of their birth peace, union, and glory."

After the war, Weitzel was given what he called his most difficult assignment – being sent to Texas to evict the French, who had occupied Mexico. He was in command of the District of Rio Grande until 1866, when he mustered out and reverted to his regular army rank of lieutenant colonel in 1882.

If you read Ms. Rebelle's article in the April 2019 *Stone Wall*, you will see that Weitzel was closely aligned with Gen. Orlando Poe working on engineering projects in the Great Lakes area. He and Poe both worked on the Stannard Rock and Spectacle Reef Lighthouses. Weitzel worked on the Falls of the Ohio on the Indiana side. He also designed a massive lock at the St. Mary's Falls Canal at Sault Saint Marie. The lock was named the Weitzel Lock in his honor. In 1876, he designed a unique rear range light 2,300 feet from the Saginaw River in Bay City, Michigan called the Saginaw River Lighthouse In 1881, he designed the 515-foot building lock at the Soo Canal, the largest canal lock in the world at that time. In 1897, he built a crib (wooden pier-like device filled with sand and sunk to hold the foundation of the lighthouse) for the Alpena Light.

Weitzel was then sent to Philadelphia to be in charge of engineering projects in the Pennsylvania area, and was Chairman of the Commission Advisatory to the Board of Harbor Commissioners. Unfortunately for Weitzel, he caught typhoid fever in Philadelphia. He was living near the University of Pennsylvania, and it was thought that the fetid water of the Aramingo Canal, five miles away, was to blame for his malady. He died in that city on March 19, 1884, at the age of 49 at his home at 102 South 36th Street, of complications after a month of being ill with typhoid fever. His body was taken back to Cincinnati for burial in Spring Grove Cemetery. The general is buried in the Moor family plot in Section 28, Lot 3, Grave 6. His wish was for a small funeral, but the city of Cincinnati wanted to honor him for his service and conducted one of the largest funerals for the general in many, many years. His service was held in the English Lutheran Church, which was packed with mourners. Thousands lined the streets to the cemetery. The general was survived by his wife Louise, their daughter Irene, his mother Susanna, and his brother, Ohio State Senator Lewis Weitzel. The U.S. Army, in tribute to the general, named one of the major streets in Arlington National Cemetery - Ord & Weitzel Drive. In the past history of the cemetery, there was a gate with Ord and Weitzel's names on it. It was later removed for cemetery expansion. Gen. Weitzel was acknowledged to be one of the best engineers in the U.S. He was always found where difficult work was being performed.

The *Cincinnati Commercial Gazette* honored Weitzel as follows: "In private life he was one of the most diffident and unassuming men. He was quiet in all his ways, and plain and practical in the discharge of all his duties. In his death the army and the Corps of Engineers loses one of its most capable officers, and society one of its best citizens."

Gen. Weitzel's grave marker at Spring Grove Cemetery, Cincinnati, OH.

Photo by Janet Greentree

KIA - Two Confederate Generals Who Died Too Young

With no disrespect for our new Yankee editor, Nadine Mironchuk, Ms. Rebelle has been up north way past the Mason-Dixon Line for much too long and has ignored her Southern generals.

One of the beautiful homes in Charleston, SC; this is in the White Point Gardens neighborhood.
Photo by Janet Greentree

It's time for us to go south down to Charleston and Columbia, South Carolina. What absolutely beautiful cities they are, full of Southern gentility, ornate beautiful old houses, gorgeous flowers, good Southern food, and many monuments. Yankee Nan (Nancy Anwyll) and I did this trip in June 2004. Charleston is a lovely city to walk around and enjoy the sights. The porches/piazzas are definitely part of its charm, with many houses having their entrance on a side porch.

Charleston loves Gen. Pierre Gustave Toutant Beauregard. We saw a beautiful painting of him and his sword in one of the city's buildings. It was mighty hot in Charleston in June, so Nancy and I spent part of each evening in White Point Gardens enjoying the breezes from the Battery.

Gen. Micah Jenkins, CSA

Micah Jenkins was only 28 years old when he was killed by friendly fire at the Wilderness on May 6, 1864. He was born on December 1, 1835, on Edisto Island, South Carolina, located between

Gen. Micah Jenkins

Charleston and Beaufort. His father was a wealthy cotton grower and sent his 15-year-old son to the South Carolina Military Academy, now called The Citadel. The Citadel looks very much like the Virginia Military Institute in Lexington, VA. Micah graduated at the top of his class in 1854. In 1855, he founded the Kings Mountain Military School in Yorkville, SC. He stayed at the school until 1861, when the Civil War began. Jenkins began his Civil War service by recruiting the 5th South Carolina Infantry Regiment on April 13, 1861. Jenkins fought at the 1st Battle of Manassas under David Rumph Jones. He made brigadier general on July 22, 1862, becoming one of the "boy" generals of the Confederacy, assigned to Gen. Richard H. Anderson.

Portrait of Gen. P.G.T. Beauregard.
Photo by Janet Greentree

The Citadel military school in South Carolina.
Photo by Janet Greentree

Jenkins was extremely religious. He took his Bible and prayer books with him everywhere and frequently could be found reading them on the battlefield.

At the Battle of Seven Pines in May 1862, Jenkins was wounded in the knee, the first of four wounds he would incur. Capt. W.B. Smith of the Palmetto Sharpshooters said of him at Seven Pines: "After we had driven back four fresh lines of battle General Jenkins drew his lines back a short way and formed a new line, someone said to him 'just look at them coming at the double quick.' Jenkins replied: 'We shall meet them at the double quick.'" Leading his men on horseback through the entire battle, Jenkins fought five charges by five lines of battle and whipped every one of them.

At Gaines Mill in June 1862, Jenkins' brigade engaged the 16th Michigan, captured their colors and took a large number of prisoners. Jenkins presented the flag to the Governor of South Carolina. In June 1862, at Frayser's Farm with Longstreet, he was wounded by shrapnel after his

An illustration of the wounding of Gen. James Longstreet and fatal wounding of Gen. Micah Jenkins by friendly fire.

horse was shot out from under him, his personal aide was shot beside him, his saddle shot, his horse's bridle cut in half, and his sword hit three times.

At the 2nd Battle of Manassas in August 1862, he was wounded in the abdomen. He was sidelined for two months recuperating and missed being with his brigade during the Battle of Antietam in September 1862. Jenkins was assigned to Gen. George Pickett at the Battle of Fredericksburg in December 1862 but was not engaged. He fought in the Siege of Suffolk with Gen.

James Longstreet in 1863 and became a favorite of the general. In the fall of 1863, he was assigned to the 1st Corps of the Army of Northern Virginia and sent to Tennessee in command of Gen. John Bell Hood's division. There he fought at the Battle of Chickamauga on September 20, 1863. Jenkins led his brigade to victory against Federal cavalry at the Battle of Kimbrough's Crossroads. He fought at Campbell Station and the Siege of Knoxville. His health deteriorated in the spring of 1864, with carbuncles between his shoulder blades attributed to undernourishment.

His health was still suffering at the battle of the Wilderness on May 5, 1864, but he insisted on being present. An ambulance had to transport him to the battlefield. Later, while riding at the head of the column with Gen. Longstreet near the Brock Road trenches, men from the 12th Virginia under Gen. William Mahone, mistook them for Federal troops and opened fire. Both generals were wounded, Jenkins mortally, with a shot to the head. The ball lodged in his brain. He lived for about six hours and died that evening. Gen. Longstreet suffered from his wounds for the rest of his life.

Jenkins was married to the former Caroline Jamison, daughter of Gen. D. F. Jamison, who was one of the founders of The Citadel. He left four young children. Originally buried in Summerville, South Carolina, he was moved to Magnolia Cemetery in Charleston in 1881. Jenkins Hall at The Citadel is named after him.

Gen. Longstreet said of Jenkins: "He was one of the most estimable characters of the army. His taste and talent were for military service. He was intelligent, quick, untiring, attentive, zealous in discharge of duty, truly faithful to official obligations, abreast with the foremost in battle, and withal a humble, noble Christian. In a moment of highest earthly hope, he was transported to serenest heavenly joy; to that life beyond that knows no bugle call, beat of drum or clash of steel. May his beautiful spirit, through themercy of God, rest in peace! Amen!"

Gen. Jenkins' grave monument, Magnolia Cemetery, Charleston, SC.
Photo by Janet

Gen. Maxcy Gregg, CSA

We now venture to Columbia, South Carolina to find the grave of Gen. Maxcy Gregg. Columbia is the state capitol and has a magnificent state house with six bronze star markers denoting where the building was hit by artillery on February 19, 1865. Thirty monuments are located on the lawn, including Gen. Wade Hampton, with 12 bronze plaques commemorating the battles Hampton fought in at the bottom of his equestrian monument.

Gen. Gregg was mortally wounded at the battle of Fredericksburg (on Ms. Rebelle's future birthday, December 13th), and died two days later on December 15, 1862. Gen. Gregg is buried in Elmwood Cemetery in Columbia.

Gen. Maxcy Gregg

The capitol building in Columbia, SC, shows the cannon ball damage done during the Civil War with bronze stars attached to the façade (circled).
Photo by Janet Greentree

Maxcy Gregg was born August 1, 1814, in Columbia, SC. His father was Col. James Gregg, a distinguished attorney in Columbia. He was the grandson of Esek Hopkins, a commodore in the Continental Navy. Gregg graduated from South Carolina College, now known as the University of South Carolina, with a degree in law. He practiced law with his father for a time and then went into the army and fought in the Mexican-American war as a major in the 12th U.S. Infantry. Gregg had many interests, including botany, ornithology, languages, astronomy, and even owned his own private observatory. He carried an antique scimitar from the Revolutionary War.

In 1858, as an ardent supporter of secession, he wrote a pamphlet entitled, "An Appeal to the States Rights Party of South Carolina." In 1860, when South Carolina seceded from the union, Gregg helped organize the 1st South Carolina Volunteers and was made their first colonel. He became a brigadier general and served in A.P. Hill's Light Division. He fought at the battle of Gaines Mill, 2nd Manassas and Lee's Maryland Campaign. Prior to 2nd Manassas, he was stationed at Centreville, Fairfax Courthouse, and commanded infantry in Vienna. He also fought at the battle of Ox Hill – another local connection.

When fighting at Antietam, he was wounded in the thigh by the same bullet that killed Gen. Lawrence O'Bryan Branch. He discovered the ball in his handkerchief the next morning at breakfast. His brigade reached the field in time to save the Confederate right.

[Note: The remains of one of his men were unearthed at Ox Hill in 1985 during the construction of townhouses. Dubbed "South Carolina's Unknown Soldier," the remains were reinterred with appropriate ceremony at Columbia's Elmwood Cemetery on November 22, 1986.]

At the battle of Fredericksburg, both Confederate Gens. Gregg and Thomas Cobb were killed. Gregg was hit with a rifle ball that entered his side and passed through his spine. He lingered in agony for two days and then died on December 15, 1862. Gen. A.P. Hill, in whose command he served during the entire war, stated: "A more chivalrous gentleman and gallant soldier never adorned the service which he so loved."

Prior to Gen. Stonewall Jackson's death he said of Gregg: "General Gregg was a brave and accomplished officer, full of heroic sentiment and chivalrous honor. He had rendered valuable service in this great struggle for our freedom, and the country has much reason to deplore the loss sustained by his premature death."

Gravesite monument of Gen. Gregg, Elmwood Cemetery, Columbia, SC.
Photos by Janet Greentree

Trail markers (left) note the place where Gregg was killed at the Battle of Fredericksburg.
Photo by Janet Greentree

Springfield - Worth a Second Look

As my non-Civil War friends tend to say, I always find something Civil War to include on any trip I take, and this year's Thanksgiving trip was no different. This year, Ms. Rebelle got back into her tradition of going to see her son Mark and family who live a little northeast of St. Louis in Collinsville, Illinois. Mark is a good son and always takes his Mom somewhere she might enjoy, and of course, he knows I am a Civil War Nut. He calls me a Civil War 'Geek,' but that's OK. So, this year, we all pile in the car – Mark, his wife Wendy, my granddaughter, Sarah, her boyfriend Cory, and her almost four-year-old little sister, Katerina. We take off for Springfield, Illinois, which was a little over an hour from their house. Yes, Springfield, Illinois. I know you all know what that town is about.

Our last visit there was in 1979, which was the year the whole family took a thirty-day cross-country trip and stopped there to see the sights. Mark's and my memories of Springfield have definitely become clouded with the passing of time. Both of us remember walking downstairs to see Lincoln's tomb. It's been on ground level since 1930. Oh, well.

Our first stop is Lincoln's House at 8th and Jackson Streets. We remember parking on the street in front of his house, but now the whole area is blocked off, and no cars can drive on the street. There is a Visitors Center in front of the house where you go to check in and then exit into the compound. In fact, the whole street has been restored to look as it did during the time when Lincoln lived there. This was the first house he ever owned, and he lived there for 17 years before leaving for Washington. The house is owned by the National Park Service, and there is no fee to enter the house. We had a little talk by a very knowledgeable Park Ranger across the street, and then were led in a small group into the house. I absolutely love walking in history. It was just as exciting to go in there this time as it was in 1979.

The Springfield, IL, house of Attorney and Mrs. Abraham Lincoln.
Photo by Janet Greentree

You are allowed to walk into the rooms versus just looking through the doorways. A narrow pathway of carpet leads your way through the rooms. You are also allowed to take photos – yes! The antiques are beautiful. There are a lot of things in the house that were owned by the Lincolns. Mary's music box is one thing, and Lincoln's shaving mirror hanging very high on the wall is another. A lot of the furniture is theirs as well. My son always thought his Mom had pretty wild taste in the 70s, but Mary Todd Lincoln was way, way beyond me. Her taste was high style in those days. The wallpaper was very, very busy, as was the carpeting. We wondered what happened if you got sick in that house and everything started spinning. The look on Sarah's face was definitely worth the picture I took of her looking at the wallpaper.

We toured the upstairs, where there were several bedrooms – a guest room, Lincoln's bedroom (adjoining Mary's), the boys' room, and a servant's room. Lincoln's bed was six-feet-nine-inches long, according to our tour guide. It definitely didn't look that long, but he says he's

The law office where Abraham Lincoln set out on one of the most unique lives in American history.
Photo by Janet Greentree

measured it before. In addition to the busy wallpaper and the busy rug, the bedspread was another busy pattern. Mary had her own "porta -potty" in her room. Out back, there was a three-hole privy with small barrels for seats. Somehow, I just can't imagine my whole family going out there together to use the potty at the same time. We saw Mary's small kitchen where, for the first time

Top photo: the grandiose mausoleum that Lincoln said he particularly did not want was erected for his remains by a grateful public who could not contain their desire to honor the great man. Bottom photo: the sarcophagus marking Lincoln's place of repose.

Photos by Janet Greentree

in her life, she learned to cook, and cooked for her family. Since they had servants, I imagine she got some help.

Our next stop was Oak Ridge Cemetery, where the Lincolns are buried, except for Robert Todd Lincoln, who is in Arlington Cemetery. My son's family is not into cemeteries at all, so to get them to go to one is really an accomplishment. The cemetery itself isn't big, but Lincoln's monument is quite large, and on a large piece of land. The base of the monument has four sculptures on it, which were cast from 65 Civil War cannon donated for that purpose. There is a large statue of Lincoln in the center, and what I call the 'Washington Monument' type of monument (an obelisk), behind him. There is a bust of him in front, with a very shiny nose, like the Patrick O'Rourke bust on Little Roundtop in Gettysburg. O'Rourke's nose gets rubbed all the time for good luck. It looks like visitors here like to do the same thing, as Lincoln's nose was very shiny.

Very nicely, I asked if I could find just one Civil War general for my collection, even though there are about three there in Oak Ridge. Mark said 'OK,' and we were off to find Gen. John Alexander McClernand. Ms. Rebelle put out her Union flag this time, since he's definitively Union. Unfortunately, his marker is almost unreadable from the elements. Then on the way out, I spotted the famous Oak Ridge mausoleum where Lincoln's body was first interred – another awesome photo op.

After that, we went to the historic section of town where we found the train station from which Lincoln left for Washington, and where the train brought him back, after the long funeral train ride. We saw the old Illinois State Capitol. It is right across the street from the Lincoln and Herndon Law Offices. Then it was on to the fairly new Abraham Lincoln Presidential Library and Museum, located at 212 North 6th Street. This was so well done. It follows Lincoln's life from a small boy, all the way through his funeral. It has a map showing the route of the funeral train going from Washington by way of just about every major city in the east and mid-west. There is even a replica of his coffin surrounded by flowers, with the drape above it, which everyone has seen in photos.

The tour started off with a very interesting theatre experience. There were lots of magical things happening. None of us were sure how they did it at all and would like to see it again. The

A more humble site was originally designated as the resting place of the president, but a plan by a counterfeiter's friends to kidnap the body for the criminal's freedom, which failed, convinced authorities to keep Lincoln's remains "hidden," until being placed in the grander tomb in 1901.

Photo by Janet Greentree

museum has lots of artifacts, visuals for children as well as adults, and a tremendous time-line map, which shows every single battle of the war and the list of casualties, which grows and grows and grows. It was called "The Civil War in Ten Minutes."

I thoroughly enjoyed every minute of the trip. My son's family enjoyed it, too. Even Katerina had fun playing in Abraham Lincoln's leaves in his backyard. The city is not big so it's easy to get around. Everything is well-marked with signs showing where to go. The traffic was good, too, for Springfield being the capitol of Illinois.

Katerina, Me, and Abraman Lincoln

No, no, no, that's not a typo on our 16th President's name up there. That's just what my little (then) four-year-old granddaughter, Katerina, calls him. She's been able to recognize 'Abraman' Lincoln since last year, when we all went to Springfield, Illinois. At that time, she got to play in Mr. Lincoln's leaves at his home in Springfield. This year, she got to stand next to his statue and see how tall he really was.

For my annual Thanksgiving visit to see my son and family this past November, we went to Alton, Illinois, the site of the Lincoln-Douglas Debates on October 15, 1858. Alton sits on the confluence of three rivers: the Mississippi, the Illinois and the Missouri.

Ms. Rebelle and grand-daughter Katerina measure themselves against the Lin-coln-Douglas Square statue of Abe Lincoln in Alton, IL.
Photo courtesy of
Janet Greentree

In 1995, the city made the site of the debates 'Lincoln Douglas Square.' It's located at the intersection of Broadway and Market Streets, just across the street from the beautiful 4,600 cable-stay Clark suspension bridge going west into Missouri. The site of the debates was in front of City Hall; however, the building was destroyed by fire in 1923. As you look at the photo included here, notice the stone wall behind us. That is the east wall of City Hall, and it was saved to be part of the Square.

In 1837 pre-Civil War Alton, Elijah Parish Lovejoy, an abolitionist and newspaper editor, was killed while protecting his presses from a pro-slavery mob. Mr. Lovejoy's press was thrown in the river. This event was a precursor of the war to come.

Alton had a history during the Civil War. It was a hotbed of politics, as well as the site of a Union Prison. The prison, which had previously closed in 1860, was reopened per Union Gen. Henry Halleck, and the first prisoners were detained there on February 9, 1862. Many Confederate men [11,764] passed through the gates of Alton prison in the next three years.

The spot in Alton, IL, where the Lincoln-Douglas debates took place in October, 1858.
Photo by Janet Greentree

In all, seven Lincoln - Douglas debates were held, one in each of the Congressional districts of Illinois. The main issue of the debates was whether slavery would be allowed in the new territories of the U.S. At first, Lincoln was kind of a political groupie, as he would appear at various of Stephen Douglas' speeches and then rise to speak after Douglas was finished. By doing this, he became well-known around the country.

Later, he challenged Douglas to a series of debates, and Douglas accepted. There were debates in Ottawa (9,000 spectators), Freeport (15,000), Jonesboro (1,500), Charleston (15,000), Galesburg (15,000), Quincy (15,000), and the last one in Alton, Illinois.

The spectators arrived by foot, on horseback, carriage, wagons, steamers, and the railroad. The charge for a round-trip steamboat ride from St. Louis was $1.00. The Chicago and Alton Railroad offered half-price fares from Springfield and other locations. Around 5,000 people attended the

At right, an illustration of the pro-slavery crowd setting fire to Lovejoy's building and printing press; Lovejoy's murder disturbed Lincoln, felt it would have a shocking effect, unleashing further violence, which would contribute to the dissolution of the Union. Far right, a memorial to Lovejoy in Alton.

Alton debate. It was the first one that Mrs. Mary Lincoln and her son Robert attended.

The National Park Service has the whole text of the Alton debate on the Internet. Here are some of Lincoln's more interesting statements.

"First, in regard to his doctrine that this Government was in violation of the law of God, which says that a house divided against itself cannot stand, I repudiated it as a slander upon the immortal framers of our Constitution."

"We had slaves among us, we could not get our Constitution unless we permitted them to remain in slavery, we could not secure the good we did secure if we grasped for more; and having by necessity submitted to that much, it does not destroy the principle that is the charter of our liberties. Let the charter remain as our standard."

Stephen Douglas depicted in debate with Abraham Lincoln, at Alton, IL.
Photo by Janet Greentree

"I shall very readily agree with him that it would be foolish for us to insist upon having a cranberry law here, in Illinois, where we have no cranberries, because they have a cranberry law in Indiana, where they have cranberries. I should insist that it would be exceedingly wrong in us to deny to Virginia the right to enact oyster laws where they have oysters, because we want no such laws here."

"And I understand as well as Judge Douglas, or anybody else, that these mutual accommodations are the cements which bind together the different parts of this Union that instead of being a thing to "divide the house" – figuratively expressing the union – they tend to sustain it; they are the props of the house tending always to hold it up."

"There was never a party in the history of this country, and there probably never will be, of sufficient strength to disturb the general peace of the country. Parties themselves may be divided and quarrel on minor questions, yet it extends not beyond the parties themselves."

"There are the two principles that have stood face to face from the beginning of time; and will ever continue to struggle. The one is the common right of humanity and the other the divine right of kings."

I don't know about you, but I can hear Mr. Lincoln in my mind saying those words in his folksy way of talking. After Alton, we drove down the Great River Road (see photo below) to Pere Marquette Park, passing great white cliffs on the way. I tried to get Katerina to believe there were Indians up on the cliffs looking at us, but she didn't buy it *(smart girl!). Ms. Rebelle needs to explore more of Illinois in the future.

Alton Military Prison, IL, where Confederate prisoners were kept during the Civil War. It held over 11,000 prisoners from 1862 to 1865. The prison had earlier been closed because of dire conditions, but the 1863 stop to prisoner exchanges made it critical to reopen.

In photo at left: Samuel Breckenridge (on right) of Murfreesboro, Tennessee, returned to Alton in 1937, the last living survivor of the infamous prison. He recounted how he hid overnight in 1863 inside a coffin that was delivered to the cemetery the next day. Breckenridge was not in it when it reached its final destination - he climbed out during the transport of the coffin and was able to return to the South. At his 1937 visit, he picked out a stone from the ruins of the prison to be shipped to his home for later use as his tombstone.

164

The Angel of Marye's Heights – Richard Rowland Kirkland

Most of us looking at the picture of Sgt. Richard Rowland Kirkland's marker in Camden, South Carolina, will have a moist eye or two. It surely makes you wonder who placed the canteen on his grave and how long it has been there. Sgt. Kirkland is not a Civil War general, but he did a good humanitarian and brave act at the battle of Fredericksburg on December 13, 1862.

Sgt. Richard R. Kirkland

Ms. Rebelle is now in Camden visiting the Quaker Cemetery at Camden & Meeting Streets, looking for the graves of Civil War Gens. Joseph Brevard Kershaw, John Dolby Kennedy and John Bordenave Villepigue. Mary Todd Lincoln's brother, Dr. George Rogers Clark Todd, is also buried there with his wife, Martha Lyles. While walking around the cemetery, the grave of Sgt. Kirkland was spotted with the canteen hanging on the side of his monument. He is buried very close to Gen. Kershaw.

The Angel of Marye's Heights was born August 20, 1843, in Flat Rock, Kershaw County, SC, the fifth son of John and Mary Kirkland. He was slender, but muscular at 5'8" and 150 pounds. When the Civil War began, Kirkland enlisted shortly thereafter, even before his older brothers, and was assigned to Company E, 2nd South Carolina Volunteer Infantry under John Dolby Kennedy. He was transferred at a later date to Company G and received a promotion to sergeant. His unit was at the siege of Fort Sumter. He saw action at 1st Manassas; the battles of Savage Station; Maryland Heights; and at Antietam, where many of his friends from Kershaw County were killed.

In a nod to the humanitarian actions taken by Sgt. Kirkland at the Battle of Fredericksburg, a visitor to his grave in Quaker Cemetery, Camden, SC, hung a canteen from the gravestone.
Photo by Janet Greentree

At the battle of Fredericksburg, December 13, 1862, Kirkland's unit was at the stone wall at Marye's Heights. After the battle, many of the soldiers were able to walk to the field hospital, but the severely wounded were left on the icy field in near zero temperatures in front of the stone wall. Over 8,000 Union soldiers had been shot. Many were still alive, but in dire need of water and attention to their wounds. The cries of the men went on for hours and hours. Neither North nor South ventured out onto the field for fear of being shot. During the day of December 14th, Sgt. Kirkland could stand the cries no more. He approached Gen. Joseph B. Kershaw at his headquarters at the Martha Stevens house to ask permission to bring water to the wounded. Gen. Kershaw denied the request, but later granted it. Kirkland asked if he could show a white handkerchief, but the general would not agree to that request.

Kirkland gathered all the canteens he could find, filled them with water, and hopped over the stone wall. At first shots rang out, but when both sides saw what Kirkland was attempting to do, the shots ceased. He crossed the stone wall back and forth several times administering to the wounded men, giving them water, encouragement, and arranging their blankets over them. It was here than he earned the sobriquet of the "Angel of Marye's Heights." After ninety minutes of this heroic deed, both sides rang out with shouts of approval.

Kirkland went on to fight at the battle of Chancellorsville and fought at Gettysburg in both the Peach Orchard and the Wheatfield. During the battle of Chickamaugua, charging up Snodgrass Hill on September 20, 1863, a rifle ball hit him in the chest. Knowing the wound was mortal, he said: "No, I am done for. You can do me no good.

"Save yourselves and tell Pa goodbye and I died right. I did my duty. I died at my post." He was only 23 years of age at the time.

Richard Kirkland was returned home to Camden for burial. In 1909 his remains were removed to Quaker Cemetery in Camden, SC. In tribute to the bravery and humanity of Sgt. Kirkland, a statue erected by the State of South Carolina was dedicated to him; it was unveiled in 1965 by the artist Felix DeWeldon, in front of the stone wall at Fredericksburg. The inscription reads: "At the risk of his life, this American soldier of sublime compassion, brought water to his wounded foes at Fredericksburg."

His obituary, dated October 16, 1863, reads as follows: "Fell, in the battle of Chickamaugua, Sergeant R.R. Kirkland, in the 23rd year of his age. In the very beginning of the war the deceased volunteered in the 2nd Regiment and participated in every battle in which Kershaw's Brigade was engaged in Virginia, from the battle of Bull Run to the late battle of Chickamauga, where he fell mortally wounded. Many gallant heroes have fallen, but not a more generous or gallant spirit has been sacrificed on our country's altar since the beginning of the war, than that of the one for whom this is intended as a feeble tribute. He was one of those who, knowing his duty was willing to discharge it, be the consequences what they might. He shunned no hardships, he shrunk from no danger. His was a steady course, making the path of the duty the road which he was won't to travel. As a friend, as a comrade, as a soldier, as a son, his equals were rarely found; as a friend there was none more true, none more constant, in their attachment, none who would make greater sacrifices for those he relied upon as friends; as a comrade, he was kind and obliging – ever ready to share an equal part with those amongst whom he was thrown; as a soldier, he was brave, calm and collected amidst danger, ever ready to go, at a word, to the post

The statue depicting the actions of Sgt. Kirkland at Marye's Heights is there to evoke the sympathetic feelings that the story itself had done for more than a century-and-a-half.
Photo by Janet Greentree

Nathan Greene's "For I Was Thirsty," also a modern visual telling of the story of Sgt. Kirkland.

assigned him; as a son, he was dutiful, obedient and kind. His form once animate, now lies encircled in the cold silent grave. No more will we meet his cheerful countenance, ever lit up with a smile; no more will his comrades stand side by side with him in fierce battle storm or set around the campfires together. Young and gallant soldier rest in peace; fate has decreed that you should not reap the reward of your toils; but your name stands recorded upon the long list of victories already sacrificed upon the altar of your country's liberty."—A Friend.

Confederate Maj. Gen. Joseph Brevard Kershaw

Gen. Joseph B. Kershaw

Since Gen. Kershaw's 2nd South Carolina Volunteer Infantry soldier, Capt. Richard Rowland Kirkland, was profiled last month, it is only fitting that his commander be the subject of this month's article. For all of you out there who are writers, no one has ever written a biography of Gen. Kershaw. The general is buried in Camden, SC, in the Quaker Cemetery nearby Capt. Kirkland.

Standing 5'10", with deep blue eyes, blonde hair and a drooping mustache, Joseph Brevard Kershaw came from a third-generation family in South Carolina. Kershaw County, formerly Kershaw District, was named for his family. His paternal grandfather, plus two brothers, emigrated from England in 1748. His maternal grandfather served on Francis Marion's staff.

Kershaw's father John was a mayor of Camden; state legislator; member of Congress, and judge. His mother was Harriett DuBoise, who came from another distinguished South Carolina family. Kershaw was born January 5, 1822, in Camden, one of eight children of the couple. Both the Kershaw and DuBoise families had ancestors who fought in the American Revolution. His grandfather, Joseph Kershaw, was the most famous of the family to fight in the Revolution, losing his fortune in the process.

Kershaw went to school in Camden, and also to the Cokesbury Conference School in the Abbeville District. He did not go to college but read the law and passed the bar in 1843. He married Lucretia Douglass in 1844. Joseph joined the Palmetto regiment in the Mexican War and was elected first lieutenant in the DeKalb Rifle Guards. He contracted a fever in Mexico and returned home to Camden a very sick man. Kershaw resigned his commission and his wife nursed him back to health.

Kershaw was elected to the State Legislature in 1852 and 1854. He became active in the Militia in 1859 and participated in the Charleston Convention, which led to South Carolina seceding from the Union. He was in Charleston, on Morris Island, during the siege at Fort Sumter. Joseph organized the 2nd South Carolina Regiment and was named its colonel in 1861. His regiment was sent to Virginia, assigned to Gen. Milledge L. Bonham. They fought at Henry House Hill at 1st Manassas and played a major role in breaking the Union lines and chasing the Yankees back to Washington.

After Gen. Bonham resigned, Kershaw was appointed brigadier general. His unit fought at 2nd Manassas, South Mountain and Antietam. He took over at Fredericksburg after the death of Gen. Thomas Cobb. They also fought at Chancellorsville; Gettysburg; Chickamauga; The Wilderness; Spotsylvania Court House; Cold Harbor; First Deep Bottom, and Sailor's Creek.

On June 30, 1863, Kershaw spent the night in Greenwood, PA, 15 miles outside of Gettysburg on the Chambersburg Pike. On July 1, 1863, Kershaw was part of McLaws' Division in Longstreet's First Corps. Kershaw's men lined up early at 10 a.m. but were not able to march until 4 p.m. that day. It took them 8 hours to march the 12 miles to Gettysburg. Once they got to Marsh Creek, after a long day of marching, the men dropped to the ground exhausted and slept.

On July 2nd, they were at the Black Horse Tavern

The Advance Position Marker for Kershaw's Brigade is located on the west side of Brooke Ave. at Rose Woods on the Gettysburg battlefield. The road is a loop that originates and ends at Sickles Road.

Soldiers of Kershaw's Brigade lie in preparation for burial near the Rose Farm on the Gettysburg battlefield.

on Fairfield Road but realized they could be seen from Little Roundtop and had to re-route. They then moved north and west on Herr's Ridge, going east to Willoughby Run and Pitzer's School House.

Arriving at Gettysburg, his position was at the stone wall to the right of the Rose Farm, advancing to the fight at the Peach Orchard where Gen. Sickles incurred more than fifty percent casualties. His left wing of the 3rd South Carolina was engaged at the Wheatfield. On the third day, his unit was not engaged. Following the battle, Kershaw's brigade retreated through Falling Waters, Maryland and crossed the Potomac River on July 14th, 1863.

He then commanded a division in Longstreet's Corps at Chickamauga, fought at The Wilderness, Shenandoah Valley Campaign, Cedar Creek, and was promoted to major general on June 2, 1864. At Sailor's Creek, three days before Gen. Lee surrendered at Appomattox, he was captured, along with eight other generals – Richard Ewell, Dudley DeBose, Eppa Hunton, Montgomery Corse, Seth Barton, James Simms, Meriwether Lewis Clark, Sr., and Custis Lee. Kershaw was taken to Gen. Custer, who shared blankets with him. Years later, hearing of the disaster at Little Big Horn and Custer's death, Kershaw recalled fondly Custer sharing his blankets with him. Kershaw was held in Fort Warren in Boston Harbor and was released in August, 1865.

He returned to Camden, where he resumed his legal career, becoming a judge and was elected to the State Senate in 1865, being chosen as President of the Senate. When his health began to fail, Kershaw was appointed as postmaster of Camden, a position he held until his death in Camden on April 12, 1894.

His obituary reads: "Gen. Joseph B. Kershaw died in Camden, S.C. yesterday. He was born in that place on Jan. 5, 1822. He was educated in South Carolina academies and was admitted to the bar in 1843. He was a member of the State Senate from 1852 to 1857. He organized the Second Regiment of South Carolina at the outbreak of the war, and commanded it at the battle of Bull Run. He was made brigadier general Feb. 13, 1862, and commanded a brigade in McLaw's division throughout the Peninsula campaign. His command led the attack of Longstreet's corps at Gettysburg, where he lost more than half his brigade. After engaging in the battle of Chickamauga and the siege of Knoxville he returned to Virginia in 1864 as Major General, and commanded a division in the final campaign of Lee's army. He held the Northern forces in check at Spotsylvania until the arrival of Gen. Lee, was at Cold Harbor in Gen. Early's valley campaign, and in the rear of Lee's army at Sailors' Creek, where he surrendered April 6, 1865. He was imprisoned at Fort Warren until July 1865, when he resumed his law practice in his native city. He was a member of the State Senate 1865-6, serving in the latter year as President. In 1870, he prepared for the Conservative Convention the resolutions that were adopted by that body, recognizing the constitutional amendments as accomplished facts and entitled to obedience. In 1877, he was elected Judge of the Fifth Circuit Court of the State. This office he held for sixteen years. He was recently appointed Postmaster of Camden. The State Legislative at its last session elected him to prepare a history of South Carolina troops in the war."

Gen. Kershaw's grave stone in Quaker Cemetery, Camden, SC. Photo by Janet Greentree

Dr. Charles Augustus Leale

At our May BRCWRT meeting, Dr. Gordon Dammann spoke about Civil War medicine and mentioned Dr. Charles Augustus Leale, the man who put his finger in Abraham Lincoln's head after John Wilkes Booth shot him on April 16, 1865 at Ford's Theatre. He also mentioned the

Dr. Charles Augustus Leale

report submitted by Dr. Leale, which is shown below. In case you are squeamish, note that there are some gory medical details included. The 22-page report was written in Leale's own hand but copied for him by a copyist.

"Having been the first of our profession who arrived to the assistance of our late President, and having been requested by Mrs. Lincoln to do what I could for him I assumed the charge until the Surgeon General and Dr. Stone his family physician arrived, which was about 20 minutes after we had placed him in bed in the house of Mr. Peterson opposite the theatre, and as I remained with him until his death, I humbly submit the following brief account.

"I arrived at Ford's Theatre about 8¼ p.m. April 14/65 and procured a seat in the dress circle about 40 feet from the Presidents Box. The play was then progressing and in a few minutes I saw the President, Mrs. Lincoln, Major Rathbone and Miss Harris enter; while proceeding to the Box they were seen by the audience who cheered which was reciprocated by the President and Mrs. Lincoln by a smile and bow. The party was preceded by an attendant who after opening the door of the box and closing it after they had all entered, took a seat nearby for himself. The theatre was well filled and the play of 'Our American Cousin' progressed very pleasantly until about half past ten, when the report of a pistol was distinctly heard and about a minute after a man of low stature with black hair and eyes was seen leaping to the stage beneath, holding in his hand a drawn dagger. While descending his heel got entangled in the American flag, which was hung in front of the box,

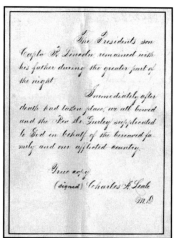

The signature page of Dr. Leale's report of having treated Pres. Lincoln.

causing him to stumble when he struck the stage, but with a single bound he regained the use of his limbs and ran to the opposite side of the stage, flourishing in his hand a drawn dagger and disappearing behind the scene.

"I then heard cries that the 'President had been murdered,' which were followed by those of

A rather comical depiction of the assassination has John Wilkes Booth appearing to fly and Lincoln standing and holding the place of the fatal wound.

'Kill the murderer' and 'Shoot him,' etc, which came from different parts of the audience. I immediately ran to the Presidents box and as soon as the door was opened was admitted and introduced to Mrs. Lincoln when she exclaimed several times, 'O Doctor, do what you can for him, do what you can!' I told her we would do all that we possibly could. When I entered the box the ladies were very much excited. Mr. Lincoln was seated in a high backed arm-chair with his head leaning towards his right side supported by Mrs. Lincoln who was weeping bitterly. Miss Harris was near her left and behind the President.

The President's box at Ford's Theatre, with bunting of the type that snagged Booth's boot and caused him to crack the small shin bone of his leg upon leaping from the box and landing awkwardly on the stage.

Ford's Theatre and the street across which Lincoln was carried that terrible night of April 14th, 1865.

While approaching the President I sent a gentleman for brandy and another for water.

"When I reached the President he was in a state of general paralysis, his eyes were closed and he was in a profoundly comatose condition, while his breathing was intermittent and exceedingly stertorous. I placed my finger on his right radial pulse but could perceive no movement of the artery. As two gentlemen now arrived, I requested them to assist me to place him in a recumbent position, and as I held his head and shoulders, while doing this my hand came in contact with a clot of blood near his left shoulder. Supposing that he had been stabbed there I asked a gentleman to cut his coat and shirt off from that part, to enable me if possible to check the hemorrhage which I supposed took place from the subclavian artery or some of its branches. Before they had proceeded as far as the elbow I commenced to examine his head (as no wound near the shoulder was found) and soon passed my fingers over a large firm clot of blood situated about one inch below the superior curved line of the occipital bone. The coagula I easily removed and passed the little finger of my left hand through the perfectly smooth opening made by the ball, and found that it had entered the encephalon. As soon as I removed my finger a slight oozing of blood followed and his breathing became more regular and less stertorous. The brandy and water now arrived and a small quantity was placed in his mouth, which passed into his stomach where it was retained.

"Dr. C. F. (Charles) Taft and Dr. A. F. A. (Albert King) now arrived and after a moments consultation we agreed to have him removed to the nearest house, which we immediately did, the above named with others assisting. When we arrived at the door of the box, the passage was found to be densely crowded by those who were rushing towards that part of the theatre. I called out twice "Guards clear the passage," which was so soon done that we proceeded without a moments delay with the President and were not in the slightest interrupted until he was placed in bed in the house of Mr. Peterson, opposite the theatre, in less than 20 minutes from the time he was assassinated. The street in front of the theatre before we had left it was filled with the excited populace, a large number of whom followed us into the house.

As soon as we arrived in the room offered to us, we placed the President in bed in a diagonal position; as the bed was too short, a part of the foot was removed to enable us to place him in a comfortable position. The windows were opened and at my request a Captain present made all leave the room except the medical gentlemen and friends. As soon as we placed him in bed we removed his clothes and covered him with blankets. While covering him I found his lower extremities very cold from his feet to a distance several inches above his knees. I then sent for bottles of hot water, and hot blankets, which were applied to his lower extremities and abdomen.

"Several other Physicians and Surgeons about this time arrived among whom was Dr. R. K. Stone who had been the President's Physician since the arrival of his family in the city. After having been introduced to Dr. Stone I asked him if he would assume charge (telling him at the time all that had been done and describing the wound,) he said that he would and approved of the treatment. The Surgeon General and Surgeon Crane in a few minutes arrived and made an

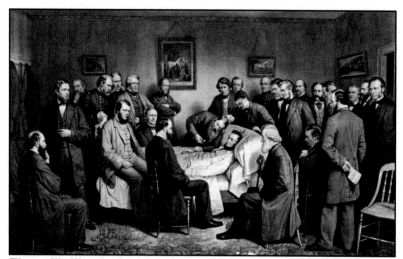

The unlikelihood of 26 people (with wife Mary Lincoln held apart from her dying husband) being able to fit into the small room in which Lincoln died was not a constraint to the popularity of this famous 1875 print of the death of the President by Alexander Hay Ritchie.

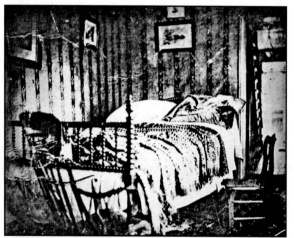

Pres. Lincoln's deathbed, photographed by Julius Ulke, April 15, 1865

One of the pages of Dr. Leale's report that describes his part in the treatment of Pres. Lincoln following his fatal wounding.

examination of the wound.

"When the President was first laid in bed a slight ecchymosis was noticed on his left eyelid and the pupil of that eye was slightly dilated, while the pupil of the right eye was contracted. About 11. p.m. the right eye began to protrude which was rapidly followed by an increase of the ecchymosis until it encircled the orbit extending above the supra orbital ridge and below the infra orbital foramen. The wound was kept open by the Surgeon General by means of a silver probe, and as the President was placed diagonally on the bed his head was supported in its position by Surgeon Crane and Dr. Taft relieving each other.

"About 2 a.m. the Hospital Steward who had been sent for a Nelatons probe, arrived and examination was made by the Surgeon General, who introduced it to a distance of about 2½ inches, when it came in contact with a foreign substance, which laid across the track of the ball. This being easily passed the probe was introduced several inches further, when it again touched a hard substance, which was at first supposed to be the ball, but as the bulb of the probe on its withdrawal did not indicate the mark of lead, it was generally thought to be another piece of loose bone. The probe was introduced a second time and the ball was supposed to be distinctly felt by the Surgeon General, Surgeon Crane and Dr. Stone.

After this second exploration nothing further was done with the wound except to keep the opening free from coagula, which if allowed to form and remain for a very short time, would produce signs of increased compression: the breathing becoming profoundly stertorous and intermittent and the pulse to be more feeble and irregular.

"His pulse which was several times counted by Dr. Ford and noted by Dr. King, ranged until 12 p.m. from between 40 to 64 beats per minute, and his respiration about 24 per minute, were loud and stertorous. At 1 a.m. his pulse suddenly increasing in frequency to 100 per minute, but soon diminished gradually becoming less feeble until 2.54 a.m. when it was 48 and hardly perceptible. At 6.40 a.m. his pulse could not be counted, it being very intermittent, two or three pulsations being felt and followed by an intermission, when not the slightest movement of the artery could be felt. The inspirations now became very short, and the expirations very prolonged and labored accompanied by a guttural sound. At 6.50 a.m. The respirations cease for some time and all eagerly look at their watches until the profound silence is disturbed by a prolonged inspiration, which was soon followed by a sonorous expiration. The Surgeon General now held his finger to the carotid artery, Col.

Above, left: Mary Lincoln, the distraught survivor of that evening at Ford's Theater; at right, the man who ruined Mary's life, and condemned the South to years of continued misery, with Conf. Gen. Joseph E. Johnston calling the act "a disgrace to the age."

Crane held his head, Dr. Stone who was sitting on the bed, held his left pulse, and his right pulse was held by myself. At 7.20 a.m. he breathed his last and "the spirit fled to God who gave it.

"During the night the room was visited by many of his friends. Mrs. Lincoln with Mrs. Senator Dixon came into the room three or four times during the night. The President's son Captn R. Lincoln, remained with his father during the greater part of the night. Immediately after death had taken place, we all bowed and the Rev. Dr. Gurley supplicated to God in behalf of the bereaved family and our afflicted country."

Young Dr. Leale was only 23 years old at the time of the assassination. He was in charge of the Wounded Commissioned Officers' Ward at the U.S. Army Hospital in Armory Square in Washington City. He had only graduated from medical school at Bellevue Hospital Medical College in New York City six weeks before. He lived at 511 10th Street, NW, Washington City. While walking down Pennsylvania Avenue for some air on April 14, 1865, he stopped at the White House and heard President Lincoln give his last public address. Leale decided to go to the theatre that night. A seat in the orchestra was requested by him, but he was placed in a dress circle seat near the front and 40 feet away from the president's box. His quick actions saved President Lincoln and allowed him to live nine hours until the next morning April 15, 1865. Mary Todd Lincoln requested he be given a place of honor at Lincoln's funeral for his quick thinking and medical service to the president. He tied a piece of crepe on his sword that was carried during the funeral and never removed it.

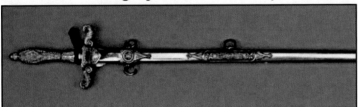

Dr. Leale wore this sword while serving in the honor guard for Lincoln's body when it lay in state at the White House. With the 2006 bequest of Helen Leale Harper, Dr Charles Leale's granddaughter, the sword is on view at the Smithsonian Museum of American History, Washington, D.C.

Charles Augustus Leale was born March 26, 1842, in New York City. His father was ship Captain William Pickett Neal; William drowned when he was 23 years, old leaving Charles' mother Anna Marie Burr Neale a widow. She subsequently married Dr. George Wilson, who later gave Charles the money he needed to attend McGill University in Montreal. Charles was exposed to the medical profession by his step-father, who ran the U.S. Marine Hospital in Portland, Maine.

After graduating from Bellevue, he served at the U.S. Army Hospital at Elmira, NY. He tended both Union and Confederate soldiers. Dr. Leale studied the heart and lungs under Dr. Austin Flint and gunshot wounds and surgery under Dr. Frank H. Hamilton.

Dr. Leale didn't say much about his role in the assassination until 1909, when he spoke about it in front of the State of

The registration noting Dr. Leale's membership in the New York chapter of the Military Order of the Loyal Legion of the United States, the veteran's group for officers of the Civil War.

New York Military Order of the Loyal Legion of the United States. He described his somber mood following the president's death: "I left the house in deep meditation. In my lonely walk I was aroused from my reveries by the cold drizzling rain dropping on my bare head, my hat I had left in my seat in the theatre. My clothing was stained with blood, I had not once been seated since I first sprang to the President's aid; I was cold, weary and sad. The dawn of peace was again clouded, the most cruel war in history had not completely ended."

Dr. Leale held Lincoln's hand the entire evening. Even though Lincoln was grievously wounded, Leale felt he could hear and sense what was going on around him. Including Dr. Leale, there were three other doctors – Taft, Crane, and Stone - who also each put their finger in Lincoln's brain. Drs. Stone & Barnes also put a Nelaton probe in Lincoln's head. Leale was among 23 people who were present in the Peterson boarding house when Lincoln died on April 15, 1865 at 7:22 a.m. The others that were in the room included Gov. Farwell, Secretaries McCulloch, Wells,

Denison, Stanton, Senator Sumner, Generals Farnsworth, Halleck, Auger, Usher, Meigs, Speed, Vice President Johnson, Judge Otto, Speaker Colfax, Drs. Strong, Taft, Barnes, Crane, Mrs. Lincoln, Robert Lincoln, Major Hay, and Rev. Dr. Gurley.

The Copcutt Mansion, now St. Casimir's church rectory, in New York City.

He continued to serve in the military until 1866. He traveled to Europe to study Asiatic cholera. In 1867, he married Rebecca Medwin Copcutt in the Copcutt Mansion in New York City. Together, they had six children. His son Medwin became a doctor and his son Loyal became a lawyer. Dr. Leale served for 20 years as trustee of the New York Institution for the Instruction of the Deaf and Dumb. He also started clinics for the poor children on New York City. He retired from medicine in 1928, at the age of 86. When asked about that

At left, Dr. Leale in later years; at right, the gravesite marker of Dr. Charles and Mrs. Rebecca Leale, Oakland Cemetery, Yonkers, NY.
Photo at right by Janet Greentree

The 1893 three-story collapse of floors at Ford's Theatre.

historic night, he said: "I have tried to avoid everything that tended to make vivid to me again the experience of that night." He died on June 13, 1932, and was one of the last people alive who witnessed the Lincoln assassination. Lincoln's son Robert preceded Leale in death.

Dr. Leale died of infirmities of old age. He was living at 1261 Madison Avenue, New York City at the time. His funeral was held at the Protestant Episcopal Church of the Heavenly Rest on 5th Avenue and 90th Street, NYC on June 15, 1932. He is buried in Oakland Cemetery in Yonkers, NY.

A strange fact surfaced when researching this article. According to a Boston newspaper, the day when Edwin Booth was buried in Mount Auburn Cemetery in Cambridge, MA, on June 9, 1893, Ford's Theatre collapsed while under renovation, killing 28 people and injuring 68. You just can't make this stuff up.

Maj. Gen. William "Extra Billy" Smith, CSA

This article is dedicated to the late Dave Meisky who so greatly reenacted and effortlessly portrayed Gen. Extra Billy Smith. Dave died on October 24, 2019, in Buena Vista, Virginia. Dave had the Southern accent already going for him and always carried his blue umbrella as did Extra Billy. Dave was a member of Lee's Lieutenants and participated in many events, including a tete-a-tete with Gen. Richard Ewell (Chris Godart) at one of our Round Table meetings. Extra Billy was born on September 6, 1797, making him the oldest Confederate Civil War general. The Union's oldest Civil War general was George Sears Greene, but he was born in 1801, so Extra Billy had three years on Greene. They both also faced off at Culp's Hill at Gettysburg. Smith was born at Office Hill Plantation, Marengo, King George County, Virginia, to Caleb Smith and Mary Ann Waugh Smith (his cousin). His maternal grandfather was also named William Smith and was wounded in Lord Dunmore's war fighting for Virginia against the Shawnee and Mingo Indians. His paternal grandfather Thomas Smith fought in the Revolutionary War and spent the winter at Valley Forge (with George somebody – oh, OK – George Washington). Caleb and Mary's joint ancestor was Sir Sydney Smith, a British admiral, who fought in the American and French Revolutions. Napoleon Bonaparte was quoted as saying of Admiral Smith: "That man made me miss my destiny."

Above, (left to right): Chris Godart (Gen. Richard Ewell) and Dave Meisky (Gen. William "Extra Billy" Smith) take a moment to plan strategy at a past meeting of the Bull Run Civil War Round Table. At right: the man himself - Gen. William "Extra Billy" Smith.
Photo at left by Janet Greentree

Smith was educated at private schools in Virginia and later at the Plainfield Academy in Connecticut. He returned to Virginia to read for the law and was admitted to the bar in 1818 in Culpeper. In 1820, he married Elizabeth Hansbrough Bell and had eleven children. Four of their children died in infancy or as young adults. Smith's house in Culpeper was located at 302 North Main Street, which is now a post office. There is a historical marker on the corner of North Main and West Spencer Streets. The house was so large it encompassed an entire city block. The house was also three blocks from General A.P. Hill's house on Main Street. Smith's house was torn down in 1931 to build the post office, but the pillars were sold to A.W. "Jim" Hawkins, who installed them at the entrance of the

Above: Extra Billy's house in Warrenton, VA; At right: Woodland United Methodist Church in Culpeper, VA where the pillars from Smith's house have been repurposed.

Photos by Janet Greentree

Woodland United Methodist Church at 14280 Woodland Church Road in Culpeper. The church is still standing and in use, with Extra Billy's pillars welcoming parishioners. As you read the paragraph below, it is a little more than interesting that a post office was erected at the former site of his home in Culpeper.

In 1827, Smith earned his soubriquet "Extra Billy" for the mail lines he established, going from Washington City to Warrenton. Soon, he expanded the route to Culpeper. Eventually, his route went all the way to Milledgeville, Georgia. He was awarded the contract by Pres. Andrew Jackson. Smith fortified his routes with numerous spur routes, but always charged "extra" for doing so. Hence his nickname - Extra Billy - which stuck with him for the rest of his life.

From 1836-1841, he served in the Senate of Virginia, from the Piedmont District. He served one term in the 27th Congress, from March 1841 to March 1843. He then moved to Fauquier County. He was elected as governor of Virginia in 1845 without his knowledge. The *Richmond Times Dispatch* stated that "while walking down Main Street in Warrenton..., Smith was told by a friend he had just been elected governor by the legislature. I replied I hoped it was not so for I at once saw that I would have to give up my profession and as the governor's salary would barely support a family in a very moderate way, I would at the close of my term be utterly destitute."

Extra Billy was correct about being destitute at the end of his term. The year 1849 had him moving to California to find his fortune in the Gold Rush. He was also president of the first Democratic Congress in California in 1850. In 1853, he was elected to the U.S. House of Representatives. He was reelected from 1855-1859. He returned to Virginia a wealthier man than he was when he left, from his many dealings in the Gold Rush business. He was elected to the 33rd Congress and reelected three times. He then resigned to join the Confederate Army. Even while fighting for the Confederacy, he was elected governor of Virginia in 1863. Biographer John W. Bell stated: "Smith never left his command for a single day to do any political campaigning."

Extra Billy participated in the Battle of Fairfax Courthouse in June 1861. Participated is a broad word, as he sat on the porch of the Joshua Gunnell House in Fairfax City firing his single-barrel gun. A newspaper article in the *Richmond Times Dispatch* stated "Extra Billy was there at the time and did his fighting from the hotel porch, with a long single-barrel gun, picking the tube and putting on caps as coolly as if he were hunting robins, with bullets striking the walls around him." When Captain John Quincy Marr, the first Confederate officer to be killed in the Civil War died, Extra Billy took over command of the troops. At the advanced age of 64, he requested a commission in the Confederate Army. He was appointed colonel of the 49th Virginia Infantry three days before 1st Bull Run/Manassas. He was offered a commission as a brigadier general first, but declined stating he was: "wholly ignorant of drill and tactics." He fought under Gen, P.G.T. Beauregard at 1st Manassas/Bull Run. He fought at the Seven Days Battle, where he was described as having a characteristic coolness and fearlessness. He was known for expressing

Above, left, Fairfax Courthouse during the Civil War; above, right, an illustration of the battle of Fairfax Courthouse, including portraits of sitting governor and Confederate colonel William "Extra Billy" Smith, who took over command of the troops under Capt. John Quincy Marr, the first Confederate officer to be killed in the Civil War, just prior to 1st Manassas.

contempt for West Point graduates (West P'inters) for their formal tactics. He was also known to go into battle with a tall beaver hat and his blue cotton umbrella.

He also fought at Seven Pines (wounded); 2nd Bull Run/Manassas; Sharpsburg/Antietam (wounded); Fredericksburg, and Gettysburg. Smith marched with the Army of Northern Virginia through York, PA, the week before Gettysburg. He fought with the 49th VA, 31st VA, and the 52nd VA on Culp's Hill and has a shield marker there noting his position. The marker is very close to Spangler's Spring. The marker states: "July 3. The Brigade having been detached two days guarding York Pike and other roads against the reported approach of Union Cavalry was ordered to

The Smith's Brigade marker near Spangler's Spring, commemorating "Extra Billy's" showing at Gettysburg, PA.
Photo by Janet Greentree

Culp's Hill to reinforce Johnson's Division. Arriving early formed in line along this stone wall receiving and returning fire of Infantry and sharpshooters in the woods opposite and being subjected to heavy fire of Artillery. It repulsed the charge of the 2nd Massachusetts and 27th Indiana Regiments against this line and held its ground until the Union forces regained their works on the hill. It then moved to a position further up the creek and during the night marched to Seminary Ridge where it rejoined Early's Division. July 4. Occupied Seminary Ridge. After midnight began the march to Hagerstown. Present about 800 Killed 12 Wounded 113 Missing 17 Total 142"

Maj. Robert Stiles stated that Extra Billy was in great form as they moved near the Potomac on the way to Gettysburg. Stiles said: "I heard a great cackling and shouts of laughter at the head of the column….and riding forward to see what it meant, found Gen. Smith dismounted in the road, surrounded by a bevy of pretty girls, every one of whom he was kissing, despite very vigorous sham resistance, and, as he performed the ceremony in each case, he would comfort his blushing, laughing victims by the reflection – never mind, my dear, it's all right, you just tell your father Extra Billy did it, and he'll say it's all right."

Gen. Smith took over the governorship of Virginia on January 1, 1864. Richmond falling in April 1865 caused Smith and the state government to retreat to Lynchburg and then Danville. After the surrender in Appomattox, Gen. Henry Halleck put a $25,000 reward on Extra Billy's head, calling him the Rebel Governor of Virginia. No one was able to collect the award. Extra Billy negotiated his own surrender, gave up the governorship on May 20, 1865, and was paroled on June 13th. At age 80, he served one term as a delegate from Fauquier County.

Extra Billy returned to his home Monte Rosa, a big yellow house at 343 Culpeper Street in Warrenton, VA. The house is still standing and was later named Neptune Lodge. There is a narrow cart path called Monte Rosa to the right of the house, which goes down to his massive barn/stable located behind the house. The house and barn are privately owned, however.

Extra Billy had the unique distinction to be the first two-term governor of Virginia and is one two governors (Gov. Harry Byrd) to have a statue on the Capitol grounds in Richmond. It wasn't until Gov. Mills Godwin was inaugurated a second time that Godwin joined Extra Billy's club. Gov. Godwin even mentioned Extra Billy in his inauguration address in 1974. Smith's statue was unveiled in 1906. The inscription says, in part: "A Virginian of Virginians…A man of strong convictions…When the storm of war burst, his voice was in his sword."

Gen. Beauregard said of Smith at the battle of 1st Bull Run/

The statue of Gov. Extra Billy at the state capitol in Richmond, VA.
Photo by Janet Greentree

The Gen. William "Extra Billy" Smith that we at the Bull Run Civil War Round Table will always remember - Dave Meisky - enjoying the connection many Civil War reenactors feel when presenting the personalities that peopled the war and made it the near-fatal episode in American history that might have broken the country forever. At the last Remembrance Day ceremonies in Gettysburg, Dave's friends and colleagues in the reenactment community held a special service for him at the Gettysburg National Cemetery.

Photo by Janet Greentree

Manassas: "Col. William Smith was efficient, self-possessed and brave, and the influence of his example and his words of encouragement were not confined to his immediate command."

Gen. Jubal Early said of Smith at the battle of Antietam: "I found Colonel Smith standing by

Gov./Gen. William "Extra Billy" Smith's grave marker in Hollywood Cemetery, Richmond, VA.
Photo by Melanie Greentree

himself on a limestone ledge. I rode up to him and said: Colonel, get your men together and reform your regiment as soon as possible; the enemy may come back again. He answered: "General is he gone? Yes, I said, but he may come back again, and we must be in a condition to receive him. Then he replied: "Yes will observe, General, that I am very badly wounded, and can't do anything more." Smith had blood streaming from his left shoulder, and he was also shot in the leg. Early said: "He was very seriously wounded, and I saw he was unable to move, though he was standing up. He was subsequently carried from the field in a hapless condition and was confined with his wounds for a considerable time. He was as brave a man as I ever saw, and seemed almost insensible to fear."

Extra Billy was sitting on his piazza of Monte Bella on the evening of May 16, 1887, when he took a chill. He died at the age of 89 on May 18, 1887, in Warrenton. A service was held at his home and then he was transported by rail to Richmond where he lay in state at the Capitol Rotunda. Then Governor (General) Fitz Hugh Lee met the funeral cortege. Edward Valentine, the great sculptor, did a death mask of him after the viewing. Col. Alexander Payne of the Black Horse 4th Virginia and Col. Robert Stribling of Stribling's Battery, both Delegates, gave speeches for Extra Billy. He is buried along Midvale Avenue in Hollywood Cemetery in Richmond, Virginia.

A big 'huzzah' goes out to my daughter, Melanie Greentree, who now lives in Richmond, for the beautiful, blue-sky day picture of Extra Billy's grave and mausoleum in Hollywood Cemetery.

Union Gen. Johann August Ernst von Willich

Never did Ms. Rebelle think she would be writing about a Communist who was a Civil War general in the Union Army, but here he is. I found Gen. Johann August Ernst von Willich's grave in Elm Wood Cemetery in St. Mary's, Ohio last year. He's buried in Section F, Lot 42. St. Mary's is located on Route 33 going northwest out of Columbus, and is nearly at the Indiana state line. He dropped some of his names along the way through the war, and was mostly known as August Willich.

August (I'm sure it must be pronounced Auuu-guust) was born in Braunsburg, East Prussia, on November 19, 1810. Like some other of our featured generals, he was orphaned at the age of three. His father was a captain of the hussars during the Napoleonic Wars. August and his older brother were sent to live with Friedrich Schleiermacher, a theologian. Schleiermacher's wife was a distant relative to Willich. At the age of 12, he entered the Potsdam Academy as a cadet. He graduated in 1828 as a second lieutenant and later served as captain of the 7th Royal Artillery Brigade. In 1846, he resigned from the army. His letter of resignation was not accepted, and he was arrested and court martialed. After he was acquitted and allowed to resign, he became a commander during the German Revolution of 1848.

Two images of Gen. Johann A. E. von Willich

He and Karl Schapper became the leaders of the left faction of the Communist League. Two of his friends at that time also became Civil War generals: Franz Sigel and Carl Schurz. He left Prussia at that time, immigrating to Switzerland and then England; learned a trade as a carpenter; and, along with Schapper, became the leader of an anti-Karl Marx group. Willich and French Revolutionary Emmanuel Barthelemy plotted to kill Karl Marx because they felt he was too conservative. Willich first publicly insulted Marx and then challenged him to a duel, but Marx refused to fight. Marx let his associate Conrad Schramm fight the duel, with Willich and Barthelemy acting as Willich's second. Schramm was shot, but survived.

Advertisement Willich used to raise a German-American regiment during the Civil War.

In 1853, August came to the United States and worked at the Brooklyn Navy Yard. He later worked for the coastal survey. In 1858, he moved to Cincinnati, Ohio, and became the editor of the German Republican (Der Cincinnati Republikaner), which was printed in German for the many German immigrants living in Ohio.

In 1861, at the start of the Civil War, he recruited German immigrants to form the 9th Ohio Infantry ("Die Neuner"). Most all of them came from the Cincinnati area called "Over the Rhine." His recruiting efforts enabled the Union Army to enlist 1,500 German immigrants. The 9th served in western Virginia and saw action at Rich Mountain and Carnifex Ferry.

Later that year, Indiana Governor Oliver P. Morton, a supporter of Abraham Lincoln, commissioned Willich as the colonel of the 32nd Indiana, also called the "First German." Willich's men were drilled in German. His men called him Papa, because of his care and concern for them. When time permitted, he had brick ovens constructed for his men so they would have access to fresh bread.

The 32nd Indiana fought at Rowlett's Station, Shiloh (on the 2nd day), Perryville, and Stones River, where he was captured when his horse was shot out from under him. He was sent to Libby Prison in Richmond. After four months, he was released and exchanged for Confederates in May, 1863. In Willich's own words about his march through Southern states as a prisoner - being insulted and taunted - he said: "the only ones who accepted us, cooked for us, or did us favors at every opportunity were the slaves;" and he said "that the Union Army were their liberators." After release from Libby Prison, he stopped in Cincinnati prior to rejoining his troops, and addressed 3,000 German immigrants at the city's German center, Turner Hall.

Illustration shows that Gen. Willich was very demonstrative in encouraging his men to stand the test of battle.

Willich was known for his leadership ability. He was fond of playing La Marseillaise during battles. At the battle of Shiloh, when his men became unsteady, he stood in front of them with his back to enemy, and took his men through the manual of arms. The men then launched a bayonet attack.

He was promoted to brigadier general in July, 1862, and fought under Gen. Don Carlos Buell at the battle of Perryville. In the XX Corps, he fought in the Tullahoma Campaign, Chattanooga Campaign, and his 32nd Indiana captured Orchard Knob. He said to his men: "My poys, you kills me mit joy, you kills me mit joy." The 32nd was the first to reach the top of Missionary Ridge.

The 32nd was under Gen. Sherman in the Atlanta Campaign. Sherman had a policy that no alcoholic beverages would be allowed on the campaign. Gen. Willich spoke to Gen. Sherman and told him that if the 32nd was not allowed to have their beer ration, it would seriously deteriorate their morale. Sherman acquiesced, and granted his request to continue his men's beer rations.

Willich was wounded in the shoulder at Resaca and sent back to Cincinnati, where he was promoted to brevet major general. He had various administrative duties in Cincinnati and Covington, and Newport, Kentucky. On October 21, 1865, he resigned from the army to return to civilian life. He lived in Cincinnati at 1419 Main Street, and the house still stands, although I am unable to find a picture of it. He became auditor of Hamilton County, Ohio.

He returned to Germany in 1870 and volunteered his services to the Prussian Army during the Franco-Prussian War. Being 60 years old in 1870, the Prussian Army declined to take him. Willich then decided to go to college at the University of Berlin and earned a degree in philosophy. He returned to the United States to live in St. Mary's, Ohio, where an old comrade, Major Charles Hipp, had suggested he live.

No longer a Communist, he turned to literature to fill his remaining year, and organized a Shakespeare Club in St. Mary's. Papa Willich died on January 22, 1878 at age 67.

Gen. Willich's grave marker in Elm Wood Cemetery, St. Mary's, OH, is a slightly unusual stacking of tablets describing Willich and his accomplishments.

Gen. Albert Gallatin Jenkins, CSA

So, who do you think had the best beard in the Civil War? There is Strong Vincent and Ambrose Burnside rocking sideburns; George Crook with a separated beard that he sometimes tied

Gen. Albert Gallatin Jenkins

Alberta Jenkins, actress daughter of the general.

separately; James Longstreet had a pretty long and thick beard; Lafayette Laws; John Bell Hood; Maxcy Gregg; Alpheus Williams, and Gustavus DeRussy, to mention a few. My favorite after George Crook is Albert Gallatin Jenkins, with his very long, skinny beard. Albert Gallatin Jenkins was one of the generals I found on a trip to find Gen. John McCausland in West Virginia. He is buried in Spring Hill Cemetery in Huntington, WV, and McCausland is close by in the Smith Family cemetery in Henderson, WV.

Jenkins was born on his family's plantation, called Greenbottom, in Cabell Co., western Virginia, on November 10, 1830. His parents were Dr. William Jenkins and Janetta McNutt. His father had built and lived in the Greenbottom house since 1835. The farm consisted of 4,441 acres along seven miles of the Ohio River. Dr. Jenkins practiced medicine in St. Louis, MO, before moving to western Virginia. The Greenbottom house is still standing on the Ohio River Road, Lesage, WV.

Young Jenkins attended Jefferson College in Canonsburg, PA, between the ages of 14-18. When he graduated in 1848, he studied law at Harvard and was admitted to the bar in 1850. Albert married Virginia Bowlin on July 15, 1858. They had four children – James Bowlin, Alberta, Margaret, and George. While researching Jenkins and looking for photos of him, I found more pictures of his daughter, Alberta, who was an actress, than pictures of the general.

Jenkins was a delegate to the 1856 Democratic Convention. He represented his district in western Virginia in the 36th and 37th Congresses. When the Civil War began in April 1861, he resigned his seat in Congress and stood with the Confederate cause. He started out as a captain from Cabell and Mason Counties. His company became a cavalry command known as the Border Rangers. Jenkins' rangers defended the Kanawha Valley in western Virginia and trained on the grounds of Greenbottom. He and 50 of his rangers captured several

Greenbottom (alternately referred to as Green Bottom), the Jenkins plantation, and where the then-militia captain commanded cavalry training at the start of the war. Above, left, is how it looked until 2006, when West Virginia began a restoration of the plantation house back to its original state. After spending $3 million on restoration (shown at right), the property has yet to be sold and has remained boarded up and empty since 2012, when the project ran out of money.

Photo above, left, by Janet Greentree

prominent citizens of Point Pleasant, getting the attention of the public. He fought several battles in western Virginia, including Scary Creek, in a fight against Col. George S. Patton; Hawks Nest (near Piggot's Mill), and Guyandotte, capturing all the papers, books, and rolls of the Union Army located there.

Taking time out from the army, he served as a congressman from February 18, 1862 to August 6, 1862. He re-entered the army when he was commissioned a brigadier general. Still in western Virginia, he fought at Cheat Valley, destroying the B&O Railroad, Rich Mountain and Buckhannon, capturing 5,000 rifles and supplies. He also destroyed Weston. While in Ripley, he

A marker notes the locale of Gen. Jenkins' raid into Ohio, at Racine.

took $5,525.00 from a paymaster of the Union Army. After fording the Ohio River on September 4, 1862, he planted the Confederate flag on Ohio soil. He captured the town of Racine, OH, and forded back across the Ohio River into western Virginia. Gen. Robert E. Lee requested his presence in the Shenandoah Valley in late 1862 and put him in charge of foragers and couriers in the Valley, reporting to Lee's headquarters.

Jenkins went back to western Virginia in 1863, fighting at Hurricane Bridge, where he ordered the Union bridge guard to surrender. After five hours of fighting, Jenkins withdrew his men and went on to Point Pleasant.

In June 1863, Jenkins was assigned to the Gettysburg Campaign under Gen. Robert E. Rodes. The Confederates made their way north through Winchester and Berryville, and then attacked Martinsburg. Gen. Jenkins demanded the surrender of Martinsburg. After five hours, the town reluctantly was made to surrender. Gen. Jenkins crossed the Potomac River at Williamsport, MD, bringing the troops onto northern soil, where his men seized large numbers of horses from the Union troops. They continued on to Greencastle, PA, where he commandeered the residence of the editor of the newspaper, *The Repository*.

Moving on to Chambersburg, he waited for the arrival of Gen. Rodes' division, but had to withdraw. He reoccupied Chambersburg on June 22, 1863, and realized the town had hidden all their supplies from the Confederates. He ordered the citizens of Chambersburg to feed his men. Jenkins' cavalry went on to Shippensburg, Carlisle, Harrisburg, and Mechanicsburg. He occupied the Rupp house in Mechanicsburg from June 28-30, 1863. Unbelievably, there is a Confederate marker there to Gen. Jenkins, located at 5115 East Trindle Road at Jenkins' headquarters. As a side note, the marker was created by Rick Robison of Codori Memorials, who is my daughter's neighbor in Gettysburg. His wife Kim was a Codori.

The Rupp House (shown far left) in Mechanicsburg, PA, which Jenkins occupied in June 1863, with large marker in the foreground. At right: historical marker notes Rupp House history, also. The stone marker was removed July 7, 2020.

Gen. Lee then called Jenkins back to Gettysburg, where Jenkins was wounded on July 2nd on Barlow's Knoll, with his horse shot from under him while guarding Gen. Richard S. Ewell's left flank. Jenkins was unable to continue fighting, but his men later were with Gen. J.E.B.Stuart on the East Cavalry Field.

A marker (pictured at right) dedicated to Gen. Jenkins is on the Confederate side of the East Cavalry Field, behind the Rupp Barn. Gen. Rodes praised Jenkins as one of nine Confederates who had won distinction in the Gettysburg Campaign. Jenkins recuperated from his wound until the fall of 1863. He was then in West Virginia (statehood, 6/20/63) at Calahan's Station, and at Franklin in Pendleton County. By May 1864, he was appointed Commander of the Department of Western Virginia, with his headquarters in Dublin. His final battle was at Cloyd's Mountain against Gen. George Crook, where he suffered a mortal wound. He died in Dublin on May 24, 1864, at age 34.

In an article published by the *Huntington Herald* on June 22, 1900, writer E. F. Chapman wrote the following about General Jenkins: "That General Jenkins was a brave man is fully attested by the circumstances of his death. During the battle of Cloyd's Mountain his brigade was charged by two Ohio regiments of Federal troops…and repulsed…. The General headed the 45th Virginia and, with drawn sword, was encouraging the men to stand and cover the retreat of the other regiments of the brigade. They too fled, leaving the General alone when he was shot from his horse and picked up by the Federal troops. He was taken to the house of Mr. Cloyd (or Guthrie) and all possible done to aid his recovery, but he died on the above date."

His death was also reported as follows: "The widow and three children of General Albert Gallatin Jenkins of the

Gen. George Crook, Jenkins' nemesis at Cloyd's Mountain, VA, and a man clearly in the running for most peculiar hirsuteness.

Gen. Albert Gallatin Jenkins' gravestone in the Confederate plot in Spring Hill Cemetery in Huntington, WV. He was initially buried in New Dublin Presbyterian Cemetery. After the war, his remains were reinterred at his home in Greenbottom, near Huntington, West Virginia. He was last reinterred here in Huntington.

Photo by Janet Greentree

Confederate Army, reached Charleston, VA, on the 1st inst., under a flag of truce, a chaplain accompanying them there. Gen. Jenkins was wounded three times at the fight with Gen. Crook at Cloid Mountain, near Dublin. The wound causing his death was in the arm near the shoulder; amputation was necessary and was made. He was removed to a place near Dublin, where his family joined him, and was doing well until one night the artery, which had been incautiously taken up began to flow, and once those in attendance discovered it, he had bled so profusely that recuperation was impossible. He was 35 years of age, and owned a splendid property in Virginia, on the Ohio, a few miles below the Kanawha, valued at $300,000." His age was reported incorrectly, as he was only 34.

Lancaster, PA - Where Reynolds Rests

Christmas was over; the tree taken down; the ornaments and decorations were put away; no more broken ankles, so it was time to get on the road again. On Saturday, January 12th, Ms. Rebelle was on the road with Yankee Nan, a/k/a Nancy Anwyll. Our final destination was the Lancaster Cemetery in Lancaster, PA, to find the grave of the first Union general killed at Gettysburg – Gen. John Fulton Reynolds, USA. It turns out that Gen. Reynolds is buried right next to his brother, Rear Adm. William Reynolds, USN. Buford's words (or was it Sam Elliott's words, referring to the imminent clash between armies at Gettysburg), kept ringing in my ears – "It's the devil to pay, John." It was a thrill to find Reynolds' grave. The graves are very near the entrance, and very easy to find.

The great John Reynolds, one of the many saviors of the first day at Gettysburg, in his best general's dress.

But, of course, since we never go straight through to anywhere, there were stops at other places to find two more Civil War generals, one buried in York, PA, and the other in Columbia, PA. Our first stop was York, where Gen. William Buel Franklin, USA, is buried in Prospect Hill Cemetery, on the outskirts of York. This was my second attempt to find him, and this time I succeeded, with Nancy's outstanding map-reading skills. The cemetery has nice markers now, showing the locations (with photographs) and outlines of the graves of the famous people buried there.

We took Route 83 up to York from outside of Baltimore. There are lots of rolling hills and horse farms. After getting on Route 30, going towards Lancaster, we sidetracked 'Ms. Lori' Tom Tom and took Route 462, the old Lincoln Highway, into Wrightsville. Lori's not too happy when I do this, but eventually she stops telling me to "make a U-turn," and adjusts to what I am doing. She definitely has a mind of her own. She's never gotten mad at me, which I kind of expect her to do.

Wrightsville was called Wright's Ferry in the 1700s, named for a ferry that crossed the Susquehanna River. The ferry was operated by John Wright, and later his son, John Wright, Jr. The ferry consisted of two dugout canoes fastened together with carriage and wagon wheels. In 1834, a covered bridge - the world's longest covered bridge - was built across the river, connecting Wrightsville to Columbia, PA. The bridge was 5,690 feet long, 30 feet wide, and had 54 stone piers.

Left to right—Nancy ("Yankee Nan") Anwyll and Ms. Rebelle pay their great respect to the reposing Gen. John F. Reynolds, at Lancaster Cemetery, Lancaster, PA.
Photo courtesy of Janet Greentree

Now comes the Wrightsville and Columbia Civil War connection. In 1863, Gen. Robert E. Lee was intent on crossing into Pennsylvania and instructed Gen. Richard S. Ewell to take Harrisburg, if he were able. On June 27, 1863, on the way to Carlisle, Ewell captured the county seat of Cumberland County without a fight. On June 28, 1863, Gen. John Brown Gordon was in York County, advancing on Wrightsville, and was instructed to capture the wooden bridge there. This one bridge was the only way across the Susquehanna for 25 miles, either north or south of Wrightsville. The local militia and volunteers placed explosives on the center part of the bridge to blow it up, but the charges failed to detonate.

They had already soaked the center section with kerosene and oil. They then set the bridge on fire to prevent the Rebs from getting across into Columbia, and Lancaster County. However, the winds spread the fire into the town of Wrightsville. Several buildings and homes were lost as a result of this. In the spirit of unity, though, both sides formed a bucket brigade from the river to the town to stop the fires. You can see the pilings from the old bridge next to the new one. Actually, this bridge is still the "old" bridge, as the new, more modern bridge now crosses just west of it on Route 30. The water is very shallow in the Susquehanna, and in times of drought, you can walk across the "river." The armies then converged at that small, south central Pennsylvania college town where a historic three-day battle occurred.

Above, an illustration of the battle for the bridge from Wrightsville to Columbia, over the Susquehanna River, as Confederate troops made their way toward the Battle Gettysburg. At right, the existing bridge.

Columbia was also part of the 'Underground Railroad,' established to transport slaves to northern states and on to Canada, by way of the bridge. Columbia is also the home of the National Watch and Clock Museum, with its collection of Civil War timepieces. The town was considered for the capital of the country in 1789, which was endorsed by Gen. George Washington. The vote was one short, and as they say, the rest is history. Gen. Thomas Welsh, USA, is buried in Columbia, at Mount Bethel Cemetery. This now brings my count of Civil War generals' graves to 285, with the Rebs still maintaining a lead of 23 on the Yankees.

After touring around Bird-in-Hand, having a nice Amish lunch, topping it off with some awesome shoofly pie, cruising by Amish farms and buggies, we were off for home again. Ms. Lori started directing us home without me even telling her that was where we were going. I think she thought it was time to go. She had already announced our destination. She had our ETA right on target for home. What an amazing little toy my children gave me for Christmas. Now if I could only program cemeteries into her memory.

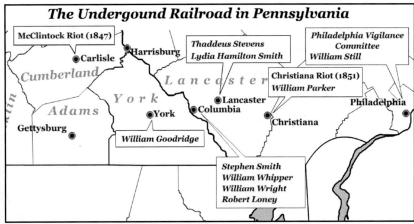

The Undergound Railroad in Pennsylvania

Sen. Thaddeus Stevens, perhaps the most vocal abolitionist in Congress, lived in Lancaster, PA, with his housekeeper (and some say common law wife) Lydia Hamilton Smith, who was one-quarter African-American. When Confederate troops marched through the area in late June 1863, Gen. Jubal Early personally gave the order for the troops to burn the ironworks owned by Stevens.

Is Union Gen. Alvan Cullem Gillem
Rolling Over in His Grave?

I'm sure you are all asking yourselves "why did Janet give this article such a strange name?" Stick with me, and I'll let you know.

This article is written as a continuation and/or addendum to Nancy Anwyll's article last month about our Tennessee trip in May. You see, there was a whole second part of that trip, in addition to the wonderful and informative time we had with the Greater Boston Civil War Round Table and the Bearss "twin," Jim Ogden, at Chicamauga and Chattanooga. After we left our Boston friends, we took off for the University of the South at Sewanee to find the graves of Civil War Gens. Francis Asbury Shoup, CSA, and Edmund Kirby-Smith, CSA. They were the second and third graves on our (well, really my) agenda in Tennessee. The first one was Union Gen. William Price Sanders, in the Chattanooga National Cemetery. From Sewanee, we were off to Murfreesboro and the Stone's River Battlefield; but, of course, there was Gen. Joseph Benjamin Palmer, CSA, buried in Evergreen Cemetery in Murfreesboro. We saw the Hazen Monument, which sits right up against a railroad track and a factory. The whole monument is enclosed by a brick wall enclosing graves and is one of the oldest Civil War monument erected. Outside of the wall, there were three more graves. Upon closer look, they were the graves of Colored Troops.

Our next stop was Franklin, and - you guessed it - another Civil War general buried in the McGavock Confederate Cemetery in front of Carnton Plantation. The general was Johnson Kelly Smith, CSA. Six Southern generals were laid out on the porch at Carnton, after they were killed in the battle of Franklin. We toured all the Civil War places we could find in Franklin, including Winstead Hill, the Carter House and Fort Granger.

Then it was on to Nashville, with the help of a wonderful book called "Guide of Civil War Nashville" by Mark Zimmerman, put out by the Battle of Nashville Preservation Society. The book had nice maps showing the location of all the Civil War sites in and around Nashville. Well, guess what, there are two cemeteries in Nashville – Old City and Mount Olivet – where twelve – count them – twelve Civil War generals are buried. Herein lies the rub. Wouldn't you think they would all be Confederate generals buried in Nashville? No, just not so. In my haste to put out my

flags on each of their graves, Gen. Alvan Cullem Gillem, USA, got a Confederate flag in front of his marker. I didn't realize this until I got home and started marking down all the generals found on the trip. I must say, I feel really bad about this, and sincerely hope he's not rolling over in his grave from the disrespect of a Virginia woman visiting in Tennessee. At least we visited his grave.

After Nashville came Hendersonville, TN, where Gen. Daniel Smith Donelson, CSA, is buried. Fort Donelson is named for him. Then there was a little side trip to find Johnny Cash, June Carter Cash and her parents, all buried in Hendersonville. Other than Civil War generals, the Cash and Carter family are my first really famous graves. Then we started

Gen. Alvan Cullem Gillem, USA, taught Ms. Rebelle an invaluable lesson about Civil War research, and has inspired her to become more closely acquainted with lives and achievements of her honorees. At left, the teeny-tiny Confederate flag left at Gillem's gravesite.

crisscrossing Tennessee and stopping in all the little towns where Civil War generals were buried. All in all, we visited 21 cemeteries, from southwest VA, NC and TN, finding 34 Civil War generals. From the big ones like Ewell, Cheatham, Zollicoffer, Grumble Jones, to lots of lesser knowns, it was great being able to stop, put a flag on their graves, and pay tribute to the men who fought in the Civil War, which all of us study so much about.

L to r: brothers Dave (president) and Al Smith (trip coordinator), of the Civil War Round Table of Greater Boston, who are responsible for the best North-South relations since the United States was founded.
Photo by Nadine Mironchuk

You're probably wondering - how did I get involved in such a hobby? It started the first time I saw Hollywood Cemetery in Richmond, VA, and I still think it is the most beautiful one around. That's how I met the Boston Civil War Round Table. They were doing a trip to Richmond, and going to all the places I wanted to see; I called up the president, Dave Smith, and asked if I could join them. So, since 1997, like they say, the rest is history - I've been the only Rebel on a busload of Yankees who all talk funny. They are a great, great bunch and lots of fun.

I found out that Col. John Singleton Mosby was buried in Warrenton, VA, so my youngest daughter and I went there and found his grave. Shortly thereafter, www.findagrave.com was profiled in the paper. Then I started sending the webmaster there photos of the graves I had found.

A variety of photos and bios on historical people are placed by volunteers on Findagrave, assisting researchers; for instance, this photo of Gen. Gillem's grave monument was contributed to the Web site by Daniel Sheron.

Mosby was my first that was posted on the site. Now I have over 500 photos on the site. Through these postings, other people have written me about their interest in doing this, as well. I believe I'm one of the first few women who began this type of research posting; most people do their own families, for the benefit of other family members. They send me maps and directions, and we all help each other out.

One of my friends showed Nancy and me the grave of Confederate Gen. John McCausland, which is on the very top of a mountain in West Virginia. That was quite a hike. We even ended up meeting his grandson, Smith McCausland. It's really an interesting hobby, and I have books of photos of all the Civil War generals' graves I've found. Did you know there are 425 CSA generals and 583 Union generals? My collection only includes 96 Union and 154 Confederates, so I have a long way to go.

Before going on a trip anywhere, I always check to see if a Civil War general is buried nearby. My trip to Oregon last Thanksgiving to visit my daughter included a trip to Washington state to find the only two buried there – Robert H. Milroy and John W. Sprague.

I have lots of "wants" yet – Winfield Scott Hancock in Norristown, PA; George G. Meade and others in Philly, and Joseph Hooker in Cincinnati. So, if anyone would like to join me, or needs a map to find a Civil War general somewhere, I have lots and lots of maps and directions.

Then there's the time Nancy and I got locked in Green Mount Cemetery in Baltimore, in a less than nice neighborhood - but that's another story.

Fort Vancouver, Washington

Ms. Rebelle went off to the Pacific Northwest the first week of June and managed to find some Civil War-related sites to share with you. My youngest daughter, Melanie, lives in Portland, OR, so in addition to a road trip around the state, she took me to Fort Vancouver in Vancouver, Washington, to see Officers Row and the Fort.

An illustration of Fort Vancouver in 1845.

Fort Vancouver was part of the Hudson Bay Company, if you can believe that. It was also known as Columbia Barracks, Fort Vancouver, or Vancouver Barracks. Dr. John McLoughlin was sent to find a location for the fort, around 1825. He was the Fort's first manager and would later be called the "Father of Oregon." The site he selected was close to the Willamette River (pronounced Wil-LAM-ette), where the land was flat, and there was access to the greater Columbia River. In 1849, the U.S. Army established a post just north of the Fort, and it was the first military post in the Pacific Northwest. It was used for trading, so no money changed hands. The Fort was named for Capt. George Vancouver and is located on the northern bank of the Columbia River. In its heyday, it housed over 600 people from 30 Indian tribes, to Hawaiians, French-Canadians, English, and the Scots. It became the Vancouver National Monument in June 1948. The stockade was reconstructed at that time, as well as several other buildings. Some knowledgeable docents tell the history of the Fort for visitors.

In 1879, the name of the post was changed to Vancouver Barracks, and is still known as that today. It continues to house some of the U.S. Army. We saw the barracks and parade field. Pearson Airfield is located there as well, and is one of the oldest operating airfields in the U.S.

There are three houses of interest on Officers Row. World War II Gen. George C. Marshall occupied one of them. The other two houses were the homes of Gens. U.S. Grant and Oliver O. Howard. Grant didn't actually live in the house, but he did live in a log cabin on the same site, and it is incorporated in the present-day house.

U.S. Grant's desk that is kept upstairs in a restaurant, formerly a building at Fort Vancouver, Washington.

Photo by Janet Greentree

The houses are magnificent old structures. Gen. O.O. Howard's house was named for him, having been the home's first inhabitant. Grant was stationed at the Fort in the 1850s as a Quartermaster. He spent 15 months as the regimental Quartermaster of the post. His house was called the Quartermaster's Ranch and was a large two-story home with a porch on three sides and high ceilings. The house was made in New England and shipped around Cape Horn in sections. When he returned to the Fort in 1879, after his presidency, the present-day house was built in his honor. His house is the oldest building remaining on Officer's Row. For a time, it was the Officers Club, but now it is a restaurant. A nice young man gave us a tour and showed us Grant's desk upstairs. Ms. Rebelle got to sit at his desk.

Grant was sent there in 1852 with the 4th Infantry Regiment when he was a 30-year old brevet captain. In addition to his duties as quartermaster, he found time to try to go into business for himself on the side. He and his fellow officers tried several things, but like most of Grant's business ventures, they didn't pan out. He tried cutting up the ice on the Columbia River and shipping it to San Francisco, but it melted en route. He tried to send cattle and pigs to San Francisco, but that, too, failed. One of the docents told us about his stab at a potato garden. He tried very hard to grow potatoes but didn't succeed in that venture, either. The Columbia River flooded his garden and his potatoes rotted. He did start growing his beard at the Fort. Grant missed his family terribly, and his time at the Fort was the start of his drinking to compensate for not being with his beloved wife, Julia, and the children. He did have one "first" to his credit. Grant, and future Gen. Rufus Ingalls, were the first people to walk across the frozen Columbia River in January 1853.

The first thing I do when going to a new place is research to see who of interest is buried there. I came across two of the 16th New York Cavalry who captured John Wilkes Booth and Davy Herold at the Garrett Barn in Port Royal, Virginia. I imagine the large sum of money ($1,683.70) each of them received made the trip across the country to the Pacific Northwest easier to accomplish. They are not buried in the same cemetery, but both are in Portland. It's just fascinating to me that both of them ended up there. It makes you wonder if they knew the other were there.

Pvt. John W. Millington, Company H, 16th New York Cavalry, is buried in the Grand Army of the Potomac Cemetery. He was born on February 27, 1843, in New York and died on November 11, 1914. He enlisted in Plattsburg, NY, as a private. He was one of the two men who carried John Wilkes Booth out of the burning Garrett barn. His gravestone, as are many others in the cemetery, is flat to the ground. It was a little difficult to find, but one of my 'Findagrave' friends met us there and showed us the spot.

Pvt. John W. Millington's grave stone in the Grand Army of the Potomac Cemetery in Portland, OR. Photo by Janet Greentree

Pvt. Emory Parady, also in Company H, 16th New York Cavalry, is buried in Lincoln Memorial Park. This cemetery is huge and on many, many acres of land. I had a map, but the grounds' sections weren't clearly marked, so a stop at the office was a must. A nice gentleman led the way to the Columbine Section, where Parady is buried. His tombstone reads in part: "Member of the 16th New York Cavalry, One of Twenty-Six Enlisted Men Who Captured John Wilkes Booth, the Assassin of President Abraham Lincoln." Parady was born in New York in 1844 and died on March 14, 1924, in Port-

The grave marker of Pvt. Emory Parady, located in Lincoln Memorial Park, Portland, OR.
Photo by Janet Greentree

land. Pvt. Parady interviewed Davy Herold when he surrendered at the Garrett Barn. He was a shoemaker after the war.

This one is for our (Bull Run Civil War Round Table) Ed Wenzel. Fort Stevens guarded the mouth of the Columbia River, and is named for our Gen. Isaac Stevens, who was killed at the Battle of Ox Hill, or Chantilly. The Fort is located in Warrenton, Oregon. This was my second venture there. Gen. Stevens was named the first governor of the Washington Territory in March 1853. Fort Stevens was open for 84 years, from the beginning of the Civil War to the end of World War II. The museum at the park has a collection of Civil War items. The only Civil War enclosed earthworks on the West Coast are located at the site, as well as gun batteries. There is a magnificent shipwreck on the beach, the Peter Iredale, which my daughter and I enjoyed photographing.

So, there are Civil War adventures outside of our Virginia. You just have to look for them. I must say that Oregon is a most diverse and beautiful state. It's pretty much only populated in the western third of the state. There aren't many towns or roads in the heavily forested eastern part of the state. We drove down to Crater Lake, where there was snow on the ground (that was the week it was 97 degrees in Virginia), and so much fog shrouded the area that we never saw the lake. We saw the Painted Hills, the Columbia River Gorge, lots of waterfalls, Mount Hood (snow there too), many mountains, prairies, beaches, and at least a million pine trees. At one point, the terrain was absolutely flat, and you could see 360 degrees to the horizon. My daughter and I had quite an adventure together.

Union Gen. Oliver Otis Howard

This past October, after leaving the beautiful state of Maine and the coastal town of Bar Harbor, Ms. Rebelle and her sister drove into New Hampshire, getting to see their first view of the peak of the fall foliage. We travelled Route 26 north from Maine to Errol, NH, through Grafton Notch, Umbagog State Park, then took Route 16 south along the Androscoggin River, through Pinkham Notch to Conway, NH. At Conway, we went west along Route 112, the Kancamangus Highway, to Lincoln, NH. Now you know I would have to find some Civil War reference in the towns we visited. It's always a toss-up as to whether you pick the right time to catch the peak of the fall foliage, but we did luck out, driving through New Hampshire, Vermont and New York. I would seriously recommend that route for the sheer beauty of the countryside. The leg from Conway to Lincoln was my absolute favorite of the trip.

From Lincoln, we headed west through Vermont, stopping in Montpelier for the grave for Gen. Stephen Thomas before ending up in Burlington, VT. Burlington fronts on Lake Champlain. Gen. Oliver Otis Howard, USA, is buried there in Lakeview Cemetery, Pine Grove Section 1, Lot 40. The cemetery also fronts on Lake Champlain. Ms. Rebelle, armed with her map showing the sites of the three generals buried there, found Gen. Howard very illusive to locate. His main marker is flat to the ground. He does have a small elevated marker, and after driving around the relatively small cemetery at least 3-4 times, we finally found Howard's grave.

Gen. Oliver O. Howard, above - during the Civil War and at left, late in life, displaying military and veteran honors.

The other two Union generals buried there are George Jerrison Stannard, who has a statue there, and Williams Wells, who has a big rock on his grave. I love the easy to find ones!

Howard was born in Leeds, ME, on November 8, 1830. His father was a farmer who died when Oliver was only 9 years old. Howard graduated from Bowdoin College in 1850 at the age of 19. He then went to West Point and graduated fourth in his class of 46 in 1854. Other illustrious graduates of that class included James Deshler, Archibald Gracie, Jr., Custis Lee, Stephen Dill Lee, John Pegram, William Dorsey Pender, Thomas H. Ruger, J.E.B. Stuart, John Bordenave Villepique, and Stephen Weed. He was commissioned a brevet second lieutenant of ordnance. His first assignments were at Watervliet Arsenal near Troy, NY, and then he was a temporary commander of Kennebec Arsenal in Augusta, ME. During the Seminole wars, he was sent to Florida, where he converted to evangelical Christianity. Howard seriously considered resigning from the Army to be a minister, but when the Civil War began, he remained in the Army. One of his nicknames was the "Christian general." At the beginning of the Civil War, he was appointed colonel of the 3rd Maine Infantry and saw action at the First Battle of Bull Run. He was given the rank of

The two grave markers in place at Gen. O.O. Howard's gravesite in Lakeview Cemetery, Montpelier, VT.
Photos by Janet Greentree

189

brigadier general on September 2, 1861. He then joined Gen. George B. McClellan in the Peninsula Campaign.

While commanding his brigade at Fair Oaks on June 1, 1862, Howard was wounded twice in his right arm. The arm had to be amputated. Thirty-one years later, he would receive the Medal of Honor for his bravery at Fair Oaks. His citation reads: "Led the 61st New York Infantry in a charge in which he was twice severely wounded in the right arm, necessitating amputation." His friend, Gen. Philip Kearny, who had lost his left arm, joked that both of them would be able to shop for gloves together. Howard recovered and was promoted to major general in November 1862, commanding the XI Corps, replacing Gen. Franz Sigel. Many of the corps were German, spoke no English, and were resentful of their new general. At the battle of Chancellorsville, Howard earned another nickname: "Uh-Oh Howard" for letting "Stonewall" Jackson flank him, after being warned by Gen. Joseph Hooker of the danger. Although Howard was the senior general at Gettysburg, Gen. Winfield Scott Hancock was assigned field command over him, after the death of John Reynolds on July 1, 1863.

After Gettysburg, Howard's corps was transferred to the Army of the Cumberland in Tennessee. His corps fought in the Battle of Chattanooga, Missionary Ridge, and forced the retreat of Gen. Braxton Bragg. Howard led the right wing of Gen. William Tecumseh Sherman's March to the Sea.

When the Civil War ended, Howard became commissioner of the Freedman's Bureau, playing a major role in Reconstruction. He initiated programs for rations, courts, schooling, and medical care for the former slaves of the South. In 1867, he played a major role in founding Howard University, a school for black students, in Washington, D.C. He served as president of the university from 1869-1874.

In 1874, he was sent to the Department of the Columbia in Fort Vancouver, WA, where he fought the Nez Perce and Chief Joseph. (Ms. Rebelle went to Fort Vancouver in 2008 and saw his quarters there on Officer's Row. The house was built in 1878 to Howard's specifications at a cost of $6,938.20.) Howard was also superintendent of West Point from 1881-82, served as Commander of the Department of the Platte from 1882-84 and the Department of the East at Fort Columbus on Governors Island, New York Harbor, which became his last assignment. He retired from the Army in 1894, with the rank of major general. In 1895, he founded the Lincoln Memorial University in Harrogate, TN, for education of the "mountain whites."

Tributes to Gen. Howard include a bust of him at Howard University; an equestrian statue on East Cemetery Hill in Gettysburg; a dormitory named for him at Bowdoin College in Brunswick, ME; Howard High School of Technology in Wilmington, DE; Howard County in Nebraska, and the Howard School of Academics and Technology in Chattanooga, TN.

Gen. Howard is also the author of several books: "Donald's School Days" (1878); "Nez Perce Joseph" (1881); "General Taylor" (1892); "Isabella of Castile" (1894); "Fighting for Humanity, or Camp and Quarterdeck" (1898); "Autobiography" (1907); and "My Life and Experiences among Our Hostile Indians" (1907). The general died in Burlington, VT, on October 26, 1909.

Gen. Howard's statue at Gettysburg, where he commanded with poor results; however, having lost an arm earlier in the war at Fair Oaks, he received the Medal of Honor. Howard, devoted to seeing the Reconstruction period following the war be a success for the newly-freed enslaved people of the South, and is the founder of the historically black college, Howard University. He served as its president.
Photo by Janet Greentree

"Road Trip" and/or: Civil War Sites in the Valley

Ms. Rebelle recently went on a very happy and proud road trip up the Valley Pike to Blacksburg, VA, to attend the graduation of her first grandchild to graduate from college, Jack

Tully. At this same time, Jack was commissioned in the U.S. Air Force as a 2nd Lieutenant. His first duty station will be in Pensacola, FL. Some of you may remember Jack when he and his sister Ashley joined me on one of our Bull Run Civil War Round Table tours to Culpeper. The picture included here shows them "under arrest" in the Culpeper County Courtroom in 2004.

Since I was traveling in the beautiful Shenandoah Valley of Virginia, there was no way I was not going to also stop at some Civil War sites. My first stop was the Virginia Military Institute to visit Gen. Thomas "Stonewall" Jackson and his cannons 'Matthew,' 'Mark,' 'Luke' and 'John.' My next stop was at Lee Chapel (Washington & Lee University), to at last be able to photograph Lee's Recumbent statue there. The last several times I have been there, photos were not allowed. My last photo of it was with a non-digital camera, prior to 2003. The statue is now behind a new locked gate; now gone are Civil War Confederate flags that had surrounded his monument. The beautiful statue was commissioned by Lee's wife Mary, portraying him at rest on the battlefield. Edward Valentine was the sculptor.

Top photo: gallant Lt. Jack Tully, USAF, shown here at his graduation from the Virginia Military Institute, didn't seem so charming above, left, with his sister Ashley, touring the Culpeper, VA, County Courtroom in 2004.

Photos by Janet Greentree

On the way back, I stopped in Harrisonburg, VA, to find the grave of boy Maj. Joseph White Latimer, CSA, buried in Woodbine Cemetery. Latimer was mortally wounded on Benner's Hill at Gettysburg on July 2, 1863. He was wounded in his right arm after being given an order to withdraw his cannons from Benner's Hill. His horse fell on him, mangling his right arm, and it was amputated at the Daniel Lady Farm on the Hanover Road. He was first moved to Winchester, VA, and then to the E.T. Warren family home in Harrisonburg, VA, which was being used as a hospital. Gangrene set in his wound and his condition worsened. Maj. Latimer died there on August 1, 1863, at the age of 19, nearly a month prior to his 20th birthday. His mother tried going to assist him in his recovery but was unable to get to him. Latimer's sash is on display not far up the road in New Market, at the VMI Museum.

Joseph White Latimer was born on August 27, 1843, in Oak Ridge, Prince William County, VA, to Samuel H. Latimer and Charlotte Barron Latimer. The 1860 census lists his father as being

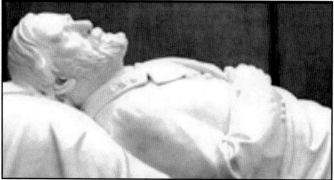

"Recumbent Lee," at Lee Chapel - Washington & Lee University in Lexington, VA, with its iron gate serving as an impediment to photographers.

Photos by Janet Greentree

191

a farmer, owning land worth $5,000. Young Joseph left home and entered the Virginia Military Institute on July 27, 1859. There he studied artillery tactics under the master, Thomas Jonathan Jackson, a/k/a "Stonewall."

Latimer left VMI in September 1861, after the Civil War had begun. He had been serving as drill master for the Corps of Cadets in the Spring of 1861. Entering the Confederate Army, he served in Hampden's Light Artillery, later to become the 38th Battalion, VA Light Artillery. He was elected captain on July 30, 1862, and promoted to his final rank of major on April 4, 1863. He was made an Honorary Graduate of the Class of 1863 of VMI on July 2, 1869.

Prior to his death, he fought under Gen. Richard S. Ewell in the Shenandoah Valley Campaign; 1st Winchester; Cedar Mountain, and Fredericksburg. Ewell referred to him as a "young Napoleon." He was later assigned to Maj. Richard Snowden Andrews' Battalion under Gen. Edward "Allegheny" Johnson. After Andrews was wounded at the Battle of Stephenson's Depot (Winchester), Latimer took command of the artillery battalion.

Joseph Latimer as a cadet at VMI.

At the Battle of Gettysburg, Latimer commanded the artillery on Benner's Hill, which was not an advantageous position, since it was open and exposed to the enemy. His 20 pieces of artillery endured fire from approximately 41 cannons on Cemetery Hill, Culp's Hill and Stevens Knoll for an hour-and-a-half. His request to move the guns to a more favorable position was granted. Unfortunately, as mentioned above, it was at this time that he was severely wounded in his arm when his horse was shot, killed and fell on him, pinning him to the ground. His artillery losses consisted of two limbers blown up, 27 horses killed or permanently disabled, 10 men killed and 40 men wounded. His battalion had fired 1,147 rounds.

There are several markers along Benner's Hill referring to Latimer and the artillery battalion, as well as several cannon markers. None show the site where Maj. Latimer's wounding took place. In the 1914 issue of "The Bomb," the yearbook of VMI, a salute to Maj. Latimer appears, reading as follows: "Headquarters Corps of Cadets, Virginia Military Institute, Harrisonburg, VA, May 13th, 1914 – Order No. 176. 1. Pursuant to the instructions of superior authority, the corps of cadets of the Virginia Military Institute will fire a salute of three volleys over the grave of Major Joseph White Latimer, V.M.I. 1861. Before this is done, however, it is proper that the corps should hear a brief statement of the services of this distinguished Confederate officer and eleve [lofty student] of the Institute. 2. Joseph White Latimer, the "Boy Major" whose portrait hangs in the hallway of our library, was perhaps one of the most illustrious soldiers that ever went

An illustration of Maj. Joseph Latimer commanding artillery on Benner's Hill at Gettysburg, PA, July 2, 1863.

forth to the field of war from the martial halls of the Virginia Military Institute. Without a Cooke to write his history, posterity has limned his historic features upon the canvas of immortality along with those of Pelham and Pegram and Poage and Haskell and Dearing and Chew and Thompson and Cutshaw and the rest of those brave and daring young artillery officers who contributed so much blood and valor to the fame of Lee and Jackson. Among the many men who have gone from the walls of the Institute to try fortune upon the field of battle, no more illustrious figure presents itself than that of Joseph White Latimer, the 'Boy Major of the Confederacy.' Upon the occasion of the march of the cadet corps from Lexington to New Market last May, to participate in the fiftieth anniversary of the battle fought May 15th, 1864, the city of Harrisonburg was reached on the 13th. Here in the beautiful Woodbine Cemetery lies the body of Joseph White Latimer. Here the Corps paused in its march down the Valley to do homage to an illustrious graduate of the Institute. In this secluded spot that May morning, with the emblems of life present in all of their true color, three hundred cadets of this distinguished man's Alma Mater stood at attention as the following order was read to them and the assembled throng, after which a salute of three volleys was fired."

His death announcement in the *Rockingham Register* of August 14, 1863, reads as follows: "The Boy Major.... A young officer of no ordinary merit and promise died at Mrs. Warren's, in this place, on Saturday last. We allude to Major Joseph W. Latimer, of Prince William County, familiarly spoken of by his fellow officers as "the boy Major" for he was under 20 years of age when he died. When the war began, he was in the Lexington Military Institute. He entered the army as Second Lieutenant, and rapidly advanced until, at Gettysburg, he commanded a

Above, left, Latimer's uniform sash is on display at the Virginia Military Institute in Lexington, VA. At right, Latimer's grave monument in Woodbine Cemetery, Harrisonburg, VA. Below, a close-up of that monument.
Photo of sash and partial monument by Janet Greentree

battalion of artillery in General Ewell's corps. In this battle he lost an arm. He reached this place, on his way to Richmond, when he was arrested by a disease, produced by his wound, which in a few days terminated his short, but useful and honorable career."

His 2nd Corps staff officer Campbell Brown said of him: "Latimer was idolized by his own men and the infantry of his division as well. The latter called him the 'Boy Major' and sometimes cheered him as he passed – a distinction they conferred on very few." It was also written that he was "one of those born soldiers whose promotion is recognized by all to be consequence of their own merit."

It was an honor to put a flag on Maj. Latimer's grave.

193

Maj. Gen. Joseph Hooker

Yes, as stated in last month's article, Union Maj. Gen. Joseph Hooker was on Ms. Rebelle's bucket list, strange as that may seem. My trip to Spring Grove Cemetery in Cincinnati, Ohio, netted my grave collection 13 new generals in one cemetery. There was a break to be had with the Fighting McCooks, as three of them were buried in one family plot. Spring Grove is the biggest cemetery I have ever been in, covering 733 acres of ground. The graves are located very far apart.

Gen. Hooker's grave sits up on a hill overlooking Geyser Lake, with a terrific view of the city. His sarcophagus is made of polished Scottish granite and is very impressive. He and his wife's name are both etched on the front, but are not very readable anymore. The general died on a trip to Garden City, NY, on October 31, 1879. He was in poor health after the Civil War and suffered a stroke on October 15, 1868 (exactly three months after his wife died), leaving him partially paralyzed. The cause of death was listed as apoplexy.

Gen. Hooker's gravesite in Spring Grove cemetery, Cincinnati, OH.
Photo by Janet Greentree

Colorized photo of Gen. Joseph Hooker shows him nearly bursting with "self confidence," shall we say.

He was born in Hadley, Massachusetts, on November 13, 1814. He first attended Hopkins Academy in Massachusetts, and later graduated in 1837 from West Point, 29th in his class. Fifteen future generals were in the class of 1837 – nine Union and six Confederate – including (for the Union): Lewis G. Arnold, Henry W. Benham, Alexander Dyer, William. French, John Sedgwick, John B.S. Todd, Israel Vogdes, and Thomas Williams. Future Confederate generals included: Braxton Bragg, Arnold Elzey Jones, William. Whann Mackall, John Pemberton, and William. H.T. Walker.

Site of Captain Joseph Hooker's Farm at Greenwich, Mass., 1765 to 1810. (Now included in the limits of Enfield.)

Home of the Hooker Family in Westford, Mass., from 1736 to 1765. (Now standing.)

Hooker served in both the Seminole and then Mexican Wars. He resigned from the army in 1853, went west and tried his hand at farming, land development and politics. He lived in Sonoma County, CA, where his house still stands at 414 1st Street East, Sonoma. When the Civil War began, he returned to the Army as a brigadier general. He fought at the battles of Williamsburg; Peninsula Campaign; Antietam; Fredericksburg; Chancellorsville; Chattanooga and Atlanta Campaigns. He was wounded at Antietam. He was made a major general at the Battle of Williamsburg, and was given command of the Army of the Potomac after Fredericksburg. Lincoln relieved him of command just prior to Gettysburg. Hooker returned to service in November 1863 in Tennessee, with a victory at Lookout Mountain. While in Chattanooga, he purchased a horse that he called Lookout.

Hooker was the third general that President Lincoln tried out as commanding general of the Army of the Potomac. On January 26, 1863, becoming somewhat dissatisfied with Hooker's performance, Lincoln wrote the following letter to him: "I have placed you at the head of the Army of the Potomac. Of course I have done this upon what appears to me to be sufficient reasons. And yet I think it best for you to know that there are some things in regard to which, I am not quite satisfied with you. I believe you to be a brave and a skillful soldier, which, of course, I like. I also believe you do not mix politics with your profession, in which you are right. You have confidence in yourself, which is a valuable, if not an indispensable quality. You are ambitious, which, within reasonable bounds, does good, rather than harm. But I think that during Gen. Burnside's command of the Army, you have taken counsel of your ambition, and thwarted him as you could, in which you did a great wrong to the country, and to a most meritorious and honorable brother officer. I have heard, in such way as to believe it, of your recently saying that both the Army and the Government needed a Dictator. Of course it

Gen. Joseph Hooker (above at Lookout Mountain, TN, and (left) on his horse, named Lookout.

was not for this, but in spite of it, that I have given you the command. Only those generals who gain success, can set up dictators. What I now ask of you is military success, and I will risk the dictatorship. The government will support you to the utmost of its ability, which is neither more nor less than it has done and will do for all commanders. I much fear that the spirit which you have aided to infuse into the Army, of criticizing their Commander, and withholding confidence from him, will now turn upon you. I shall assist you as far as I can, to put it down. Neither you, nor Napoleon, if he were alive again, could get any good out of an army, while such a spirit prevails in it. And now, beware of rashness. Beware of rashness, but with energy, and sleepless vigilance, go forward, and give us victories. Yours very truly, A. Lincoln."

"The President, General Hooker and Their Staffs at a Review in the Army of the Potomac," published in *Harper's Weekly* in May 1863.

Those are very powerful words to receive from your Commander in Chief. This letter was written after Hooker described Burnside as a "wretch…of blundering sacrifice." Burnside countered that Hooker was "unfit to hold an important commission during a crisis like the present."

There are several interesting things about Gen. Hooker. His sobriquet "Fighting Joe Hooker" (which he hated) came after the battle of Williamsburg, from a reporter's error, when his article stated "Fighting – Joe Hooker" and the dash was left out. Even Gen. Robert E. Lee referred to him as "Mr. F.J. Hooker." The word "hooker" was attached to those ladies of the night who followed the armies around, but it had only an unfortunate resemblance to his name, not used because it was his name. The term "hooker" was used as far back as 1845, describing the prostitutes surrounding the shipyards and ferry terminals in the Corlear's Hook area of Manhattan. Gen. Hooker was known as a ladies' man as early as the Mexican War. He married very late in life, at the age of 50, to Miss Olivia Augusta Groesbeck, age 40, on October 3, 1865.

The general's wife was a member of the prominent Cincinnati family of John and Mary Groesbeck. Even though she has been described as a general favorite in society, renowned alike for her beauty and intelligence, I can find no photos of her. The couple met at a ball at Burnet House, a grand hotel in Cincinnati, while Hooker was stationed there after the war. They were married at her residence at 178 West 77th Street in Cincinnati. Per the Cincinnati Inquirer: "The general was dressed in full military uniform, wearing the celebrated diamond-hilted sword

Burnet House, a grand hotel in Cincinnati, OH, where Gen. Hooker met his wife-to-be.

presented him by the citizens of California." The paper further stated "This is, we believe, the first time the gallant Hooker has been known to surrender." They traveled extensively in Europe, beginning on their honeymoon trip, and their touring lasted for the next few years. In 1868, Olivia died of consumption at their residence in Watertown, MA. There were no children born from the marriage.

Always looking for obscure interesting things to share with you, I came across Gen. Nelson Miles' account of what happened when Hooker was shell-shocked at the Chancellor House in Chancellorsville in 1862. Gen. Miles was speaking at the dedication of the Hooker statue in front of the Boston State House in Massachusetts in 1903. He states in part: "I was seriously wounded at the battle of Chancellorsville, and was carried into the house where Hooker had his headquarters. A shell struck the house and set it on fire, and every one realized that the place had to be deserted. As the shell crashed through the house, one of the falling timbers struck General Hooker, knocking him down. As I was being carried out by two comrades, I saw General Hooker going from the other side of the building, limping, scarcely able to walk, and with his clothes covered with dust. And yet the hero was undaunted, and was endeavoring by his presence, by his act, and by his determination, to hold the position and to hold the confidence of the army. He was at that moment disabled, but was so heroic that he would not leave the field, and remained when others might have gone to the rear."

The Chancellor House - before and after the battle.

Hooker's men loved him. He gave them better food; made camp sanitary changes; improved the quartermaster system; monitored company cooks; made hospital reforms instituted a new furlough system adopted corps badges for identification during battle; tried to stem desertion; added more preparatory drilling, and also brought in strong officer training. At a dedication called "Hooker's Day," on May 7, 1895 in Hooker's hometown of Hadley, MA, Gen. Daniel Sickles made a few remarks (in part) after presenting a portrait of Gen. Hooker to the town. "Our loyalty to the memory of Hooker is a sentiment in which affection and admiration are blended. His comrades loved him because he gave them confidence in themselves; because he made them soldiers. They loved him because he was so proud of them, and jealous of their honor and fame. We admired him as the intrepid brigade and division commander whose plume was always to the front of battle. We admired his fearless bearing, his picturesque figure in the saddle, at the head of a column or in the line of battle – the type of a soldier who shared every peril to which his command was exposed. We admired his thorough knowledge of his profession – from the duty of a soldier to the responsibility of a commander."

Hooker's statue in Boston replaced one of Gen. Nathaniel Banks that had stood at the same spot. Above the door to a nearby entrances to the State House is a sign "General Hooker's Entrance." Somehow I think he would like that.

Gen. Hooker's statue in front of the Massachusetts State House in Boston.
Photo by Janet Greentree

Brig. Gen. Richard Brooke Garnett, CSA

Ms. Rebelle seems to be on a roll here with generals who died at the Battle of Gettysburg, so here is another one for you. Gen. Garnett has a couple of amazing historical connections, which I will get into later.

Richard Brooke Garnett was born at his family's plantation, Rose Hill, in Essex County, VA, on November 21, 1817. He had a twin brother, William Henry, who died on August 4, 1855 at the

Gen. Richard B. Garnett

age of 37 in Norfolk, Virginia. Even using my genealogy search tools, I have been unable to find out anything about William. It's always interesting that so many of these ranking men came from big families, most likely outshining their siblings; you don't hear much about their brothers' service unless they became staff members, etc.

His father was William Henry Garnett and his mother Anna Maria Brooke. First interesting connection: His father was descended from an indentured servant who arrived in Jamestown in 1610. What a true success story for his family to own a plantation in later years.

Like many of our generals, Garnett attended West Point along with his cousin Robert Seldon Garnett (although not his brother) and graduated with the class of 1841. There is some contention that pictures purported to be of Richard B. Garnett are instead those of his cousin Robert Seldon Garnett. Robert Seldon also has the distinction of being the first Confederate general to be killed in the Civil War, at Corrick's Ford, western Virginia, on July 13, 1861.

Richard was commissioned as a second lieutenant in the 6th U.S. Infantry. His service included military posts in Florida during the Seminole Wars; Fort Laramie; the Utah Expedition; Mexican War, and California. In May 1855 he had attained the rank of captain but resigned his commission in May of 1861 to return to Virginia to serve with the Confederacy.

Before we get into the Civil War, the second connection evolves. Richard was stationed at Fort Laramie in Wyoming when he married an Indian woman in 1855, named Looking at Him Woman,

daughter of Chief Crow-Feather. Looking at Him Woman may or may not have been previously married to John Baptiste Boyer, a French-Canadian hunter, trapper, and blacksmith. This earlier union did produce a son, Mitch Boyer/Bouyer, who you may know as one of Gen. George A. Custer's Indian scouts at Little Big Horn. Mitch Boyer died along with Custer at the Little Big Horn massacre in 1876.

The union/marriage between Looking at Him Woman and Garnett produced a son as well, William Garnett, a/k/a Billy Garnett or Billy Hunter, born on April 25, 1855, in Laramie, WY. Billy Garnett and Mitch Boyer were half-brothers. Once Richard Garnett left Fort Laramie, he never saw his son again. After Garnett left, Billy's mother went back to John Baptiste Boyer, but later married a man named John Hunter, so that is why Billy went by Garnett and/or Hunter.

At left, Mitch Boyer, Gen. Garnett's step-son by his Native American wife and her former partner, a French Canadian hunter. At right, William Garnett, Gen. Garnett's own son with wife Looking at Him Woman.

Garnett's first assignment in the Civil War was with the artillery of Cobb's Legion. He was promoted to brigadier general on November 14, 1861, and commanded the Stonewall Brigade. In

March 1862, at the battle of Kernstown, Garnett was surrounded on three sides by 9,000 men from Gen. James Shields' infantry division. The division was almost twice the size of Garnett's unit. Rather than stay and be slaughtered, Garnett chose to retreat. This infuriated Gen. Thomas "Stonewall" Jackson so much that he accused Garnett of coward-ice and disobeying orders. Jackson's position was that he should have request-ed permission to retreat. Jackson had him arrested for neglect of duty on April 1, 1862, and relieved him of command. This was devastating to Garnett. Gen. Robert E. Lee stepped in and suspended

BATTLE OF KERNSTOWN
MARCH 23, 1862

General James Shields with 7,000 Federals defeated Stonewall Jackson with 3,500 Confederates. Jackson's object was to create a diversion which would prevent troops being sent to McClellan for the attack on Richmond. He arrived south of Kernstown in early afternoon Sunday, March 23, and attempted to turn the Federal right flank. To counter this, Colonel N. Kimball who succeeded to command after Shields was wounded March 22nd, advanced Colonel E.B.Tyler's brigade. Savage fighting followed for possession of the stone wall separating Jackson's and Tyler's troops. Seeing that Tyler was hard-pressed, Kimball rushed reinforcements from his and Sullivan's brigades. The Federals turned the Confederate right, and General R.B.Garnett with his ammunition running short fell back without Jackson's orders, exposing Colonel S.V. Fulkerson and forcing his withdrawal. Colonel J.S.Burks reached the field in time to check the Federal attack and cover the Confederate retreat from the field. This was Jackson's only defeat.

The battle of Kernstown, Winchester, VA, was the scene of continued humiliation for Garnett - having had to retreat under the scrutiny of "Stonewall" Jackson, who was nearly court martialed.

Photo by Janet Greentree

the proceedings because every officer was needed for Lee's Northern Virginia Campaign. Garnett was hard-pressed to get over the embarrassment of what happened to him at Kernstown.

He next commanded Pickett's Brigade under Gen. James Longstreet, when Gen. George Pickett was injured. He fought at Antietam and Fredericksburg. He missed Chancellorsville, as he was with Gen. Longstreet at Suffolk. When Jackson was killed at Chancellorsville, Garnett re-turned to Richmond for the funeral and served as one of Jackson's pall bearers.

Garnett's brigade under General Pickett did not arrive in Gettysburg until the afternoon of the second day, July 2, 1863. Garnett was ordered by Gen. Lee the next day to fill the center of the line, commanding the 8th, 18th, 19th, 28th, and 56th VA. Gen. James L. Kemper was on the right

The shield marker denoting the posi-tion of Garnett's Brigade at the Bat-tle of Gettysburg, PA, on July 3rd, 1863, where the troops took part in the ill-fated Pickett's Charge.
Photo by Lisa Greentree Tully

and Gen. Lewis Armistead behind. Their lines curved to the left, arriving at the copse of trees. All the generals were ordered to walk (to avoid being easy targets), but Garnett had been kicked by his horse, Red Eye, had a fever, and was wearing his heavy great coat, and so was mounted. Most likely his insist-ence on riding instead of walking was to clear his name of the stain of cowardice from the Kernstown Court Martial. He chose to ride Red Eye, even though everyone told him he would be a sitting target for the Union's guns. General Armistead said to him: "This is a desperate thing to attempt." Garnett replied: "Yes, it is. But the issue is with the Almighty, and we must leave it in His hands."

Gen. Garnett managed to get within 20 paces of the stone wall on the Emmitsburg Road. He was wearing a brand new coat with his general's star and braid. Was he a victim of Alonzo Cushing's guns, along with Gen. Armistead - as related in my previous story (see February, 2015 Stone Wall). Some surviving witnesses said he was shot in the waist area. Others say he was shot in the head while waving his black hat. Was his body cut in half and blown up, as rumored? His body was never recovered. From the black cloud and smoke of powder explod-ing, his horse emerged rider-less, surviving a deep slash to the shoulder, and ran back to Confederate lines. A shield monu-ment to Garnett is on West Confederate Avenue, on the right side, two monuments down from the Lee Monument.

Pvt. James W. Clay, 18th VA, Co. G stated: "General Garnett was killed while leading his brigade in Pickett's charge across the field and up the slope between the two contending battle lines. Immediately after the great artillery duel, during which many of the enemy's guns were silenced, orders came for the general advance of Pickett's division, but it was not until we had covered nearly the entire distance between the two lines that the General received his death wound." "…The last I saw of General Garnett he was astride his big black charger in the forefront of the charge and near the stone wall, just beyond which is marked the farthest point reached by the Southern troops. The few that were left of our brigade advanced to this point." "…The horse in its mad flight jumped over Captain Campbell and me."

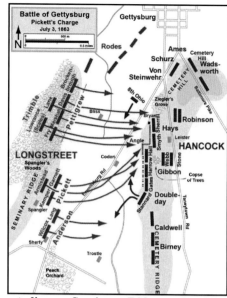

At left, Garnett's position in the Confederate line on Seminary Ridge outlined in orange; at right, Garnett's brigade fighting toward the stone wall on Cemetery Ridge, positioned in Pickett's division.

Another interesting tidbit concerns Garnett's sword. Thirty years later, Confederate Gen. George H. "Maryland" Steuart found Gen. Garnett's sword in a second-hand shop in Baltimore. The sword was engraved: "R.B. Garnett, U.S.A." Gen. Steuart purchased the sword, intending to give it to Garnett's descendants. Unfortunately, Steuart died in 1903. Steuart's nephew gave the sword to Garnett's descendant, the wife (no name was given) of Col. John B. Purcell in Richmond, VA.

Garnett's sword - redeemed from a second-hand store and returned to the Garnett family by a fellow Confederate general, three decades after the battle.

When the Gettysburg dead were disinterred from the fields of battle and sent back to Hollywood Cemetery in Richmond, it is presumed that Garnett's body was among them. A marker was erected in tribute to Gen. Garnett. The inscription reads as follows: "Among the Confederate Soldiers' Graves in this area is the probable resting place of Brigadier General Richard Brooke Garnett C.S.A. who was killed in action July 3, 1863, as he led his Brigade in the charge of Pickett's Division on the final day of the battle of Gettysburg. First buried on the battlefield, General Garnett's remains were likely removed to this area in 1872 along with other Confederate dead brought from Gettysburg by the Hollywood Memorial Association. Requiescat in Peace Richard Brooke Garnett, 1817-1863."

A Confederate of Medal of Honor was bestowed on Garnett by the Sons of Confederate Veterans in 1985.

Montana

Does Montana have Civil War significance? Well, there's Little Big Horn, where Gen. George Armstrong Custer and his men were killed - many of whom served in the Civil War. There is Helena, where there is a large equestrian statue of Union Gen. Thomas Francis Meagher in front of the Capitol; also in Helena is the grave of Union Gen. Benjamin Franklin Potts. There is also Fort Belknap, named for Union Gen. William W. Belknap, and former Forts Custer (George Armstrong Custer), Keogh (Myles Keogh), Logan (John Logan), and C.F. Smith (Charles F. Smith).

The equestrian statue of Gen. Thomas F. Meagher in front of the Montana state capitol building.
Photo by Janet Greentree

Thomas Francis Meagher

Thomas Francis Meagher, son of Thomas Meagher, was born on August 3, 1823, in Waterford, Ireland. The elder Meagher was a wealthy merchant who retired to enter politics. Young Thomas was educated at Catholic boarding schools. At age 11, he was sent to Clongowes Wood College in County Kildare for further education. He excelled at oratory, and when he was 15 years old, he was the youngest medalist of the Debating Society. He left Ireland for the first time to study in England at Stonyhurst College in Lancashire.

His professors had quite a time trying to rid Thomas of his thick Irish brogue. He later spoke with an Anglo-Irish upper-class accent.

Returning to Dublin in 1843, he decided to study for the bar, but became involved with the Repeal Association, which supported the repeal of the Act of Union between Great Britain and Ireland. He and John Mitchel, William Smith O'Brien and Thomas Devin Reilly formed the Irish Confederation in 1848. O'Brien and Meagher traveled to France to study revolutionary events there. They returned to Ireland with a new flag – a tricolor of green, white and orange, given to them by a French woman who was sympathetic to the Irish cause. It is similar to the present-day flag of Ireland. After the Battle of Ballingarry in August 1848, Meagher and O'Brien, along with Terence MacManus and Patrick O'Donoghue, were arrested and tried for sedition. They were sentenced to be hanged, drawn and quartered. Their death sentence was commuted, and they were all sent to Van Diemen's Land, Tasmania, Australia.

Gen. Meagher during his service in the Civil War.

Capt. Meagher, of the New York 69th Militia, Co. K (the "Irish Zouaves") - The *Irish American*, August 17, 1861.

Meagher was sent to Campbell Town and his friends were sent to other locations. He married Katherine Bennett on February 22, 1851, while in Tasmania. In January 1852, Meagher planned an escape to the U.S. He did manage to escape, but Katherine stayed behind, as she was pregnant with their first child. Unfortunately, the child died before his father even got to New York City. Katherine came to America to be with her husband for a short time but ended up going back to Ireland in poor health and pregnant with their second child. Meagher never met his son, who lived with his relatives. Katherine died in May 1854. Soon thereafter, Meagher married Elizabeth Townsend.

When tensions were mounting before the U.S. Civil War, Meagher originally supported the South. His friend John Mitchel had settled in the South. Finally, the friends split over their allegiance, and Meagher joined the Union Army. In September 1861, he made a speech at the Boston Music Hall for the Irish to join the Union Army. He recruited Irish men for Company K of the 69th Regiment of the New York Militia. His ad read, "One hundred young Irishman – healthy, intelligent and active – wanted at once to form a company under the command of Thomas Francis Meagher." The regiment was assigned to Gen. Irvin McDowell's Army of Northeastern Virginia. After 1st Bull Run, Meagher returned to New York to form the Irish Brigade. He was commissioned a brigadier general on February 3, 1862, during the Peninsula Campaign.

His first battle as a general was Fair Oaks, where he was defeated, but where his Irish Brigade gained a reputation as fierce fighters. For a time, he was given a regiment of non-Irish men, but said he would only command Irishmen. The Irish Brigade sustained large losses at Antietam on the Bloody Lane. During the battle, Meagher fell off his horse, and there were rumors of him being drunk, but actually, his horse had been shot. Meagher led 1,200 men into battle at Marye's Heights at Fredericksburg, but there were only 280 men left in his unit the next day. He resigned on May 14, 1863, after the Battle of Chancellorsville.

His 69th Irish Brigade fought at the Angle at Gettysburg, but Meagher wasn't there. His resignation was rejected in December 1863, and he was sent to the Western theatre. He resigned again on May 15, 1865. Pres. Andrew Johnson appointed him secretary of the Montana Territory in 1865, and he later became acting territorial governor of Montana. On July 1, 1867, while traveling on a steamboat near Fort Benton, Montana, he fell off the boat into the Missouri River. His body was never recovered. There are two schools of thought on his death. Some say he was drunk and fell overboard. Others say that he was sick with an intestinal problem and accidentally fell overboard. There is no battle marker for Meagher. He does have the statue in Helena and a monument at Fort Benton, alongside the Missouri River. He also has a monument at Antietam.

Benjamin Franklin Potts

Benjamin Franklin Potts was born in Carroll County, Ohio, on January 29, 1836. He attended Westminster College but ran out of funds to complete his education. He taught school and read the law under Ephraim R. Eckley, who later became a U.S. Congressman. Potts was a Democrat, supporting Pres. James Buchannan. After passing the bar exam in Canton, OH, he started his law practice in Carrollton. He was a member of the Ohio delegation to the 1860 Democratic National Convention in Charleston, S.C. where he supported Stephen A. Douglas for president against Abraham Lincoln.

Gen. Benjamin F. Potts, above - during the Civil War, and - at right - later in life.

Potts was mustered into service in the Civil War on August 29, 1861, as the captain of the 32nd Ohio Infantry. He served at Cheat Mountain; Greenbrier River; McDowell, the Shenandoah Valley in pursuit of Stonewall Jackson; Cross Keys; Port Republic; Winchester, and Harpers Ferry. His company was part of the largest surrender (at Harpers Ferry) of the U.S. Army, until World War II.

Potts was sent to Camp Douglas in Chicago, inactive under terms of his parole. After being exchanged, he refitted the 23rd Ohio for service again. They fought at Vicksburg; the Atlanta Campaign; Port Gibson; Raymond, and Champion Hill, where his unit captured an eight-gun Confederate battery. Most of his war service was in the Western theater. He was also with Sherman's 'March to the Sea' taking Savannah, GA. He received his rank of brigadier general in January 1865. He marched in the Grand Review of the Army in Washington, D.C., following the return of the troops.

After the war, he returned to Carroll County, OH, to practice law and resume his political career. He changed to the Republican Party and was elected to the Ohio State Senate in 1867. In 1870, Pres. Ulysses Grant appointed him governor of the Montana Territory, where he served until 1883. Gen. Potts died in Helena, MT, on June 17, 1887, where he is interred in the Forestvale Cemetery. His grave is on the same row as Montana native, actress Myrna Loy.

Gen. Potts' grave monument in Forestvale Cemetery, Helena, MT.
Photo by Janet Greentree

To add a postscript to my Myles Keogh/Little Big Horn article in the November 2012 issue of *The Stone Wall,* my sister and I met a young male descendant of Curly, who was a Crow scout for Gen. Custer. He told us where to find Curly's grave at the Custer National Cemetery at Little Big Horn. There are several Indian scouts (Goes Ahead, White Man Runs Him, White Swan, and Two Whistles) buried there, as well

Movie screen idol Myrna Loy is resting near Gen. Potts at Forestdale Cemetery.
Photo by Janet Greentree

as Maj. Marcus Reno (reinterred from Glenwood Cemetery, Washington, D.C.), Lt. J..J. Crittenden and Capt. William Fetterman (of the Fetterman Massacre on December 21, 1866, a decade prior to the battle of Little Big Horn).

Ms. Rebelle's Union ancestor, Daniel Smothers, was in the same 18th U.S. Army of the Ohio, with Fetterman. Lucky for us, Great-Grandfather Daniel went back to Ohio after the Civil War to farm and wasn't at Little Big Horn.

Above, left, Gen. George A. Custer's Army Scout Curly; center, his descendant - a battlefield guide; and Curly's grave at of the National Cemetery at Little Big Horn in Montana.
Center/right photos by Janet Greentree

Grave of Gen. Marcus Reno, National Cemetery, Little Big Horn.
Photo by Janet Greentree

L to r: sisters Kathe Fernandez and Ms. Rebelle at the grave of Capt. William Fetterman.
Photo courtesy of Janet Greentree

L to r: Crow Scouts White Man Runs Him; Two Whistles and Goes Ahead.
Grave photos by Janet Greentree

Gen. John Frederick Hartranft

Gen. John F. Hartranft is interesting to me for three reasons: he read the order sentencing the Lincoln conspirators to be hanged; he led the charge over Burnside Bridge at Antietam, and his cemetery marker in Montgomery Cemetery in Norristown, PA, is riddled with bullet holes. Hartranft shares space in Montgomery Cemetery with three other Civil War generals: Winfield Scott Hancock, Adam Slemmer and Samuel Zook. Unfortunately, there are bullet holes in other markers, as well, and the top of Gen. Slemmer's marker has been knocked over. Sadly, Hancock's mausoleum has a chain link fence around it. The late Brian Pohanka was instrumental in cleaning

up the cemetery, and a small garden dedicated to him is just inside the gate.

Late historian Brian C. Pohanka has been honored for his preservation of various historical sites, including Gen. Winfield Scott Hancock's gravesite in Montgomery Cemetery in Norristown, PA.

Photos by Janet Greentree

John F. Hartranft was born in Fagleysville in New Hanover Township, PA, on December 16, 1830, the only child of Samuel and Lydia Hartranft. He attended Marshall College in Mercersburg, PA, and then transferred to Union College in Schenectady, NY, receiving a degree in civil engineering in 1853. Hartranft returned home to Norristown after working for a short time for the railroad, to assist his father in his stagecoach, inn and real estate businesses. He was elected deputy sheriff of Norristown in 1854. He also worked for the Norristown Fire Company and was admitted to the bar in 1860. He married Sallie Douglas Sebring. They had six children, with only three surviving to adulthood.

At the beginning of the Civil War, Hartranft raised a regiment of 90-day volunteers, and served as colonel of the 4th Pennsylvania. The unit's 90 days were up on the night before July 21, 1861, in Manassas, where they refused to fight, walked off the field and returned home to Norristown to the deep embarrassment of Hartranft. He stayed in Manassas and volunteered to fight with fellow Pennsylvanian William Buell Franklin. For his efforts, he was awarded the Medal of Honor on August 26, 1886. His citation reads as follows: "Voluntarily served as aide and participated in the battle after expiration of his term of service, distinguishing himself in rallying several regiments which had been thrown in confusion."

The house in Fagleysville in New Hanover Township, PA, that Hartranft was born in, on December 16, 1830

He next raised a three-year regiment, the 51st Pennsylvania, serving as its colonel. His men called him "Old Johnny," even though he was only in his thirties. He drilled his men incessantly, but he also played baseball with them. When their enlistment was up, Hartranft gave a stirring speech about the Union cause, and many of the men signed up again. His unit fought at Roanoke Island; New

Burnside's Bridge, battle of Antietam, on September 17, 1862, was the scene of carnage for the Union troops, although the battle was a victory for the North.

Bern; Newport News, and joined up with Burnside's IX Corps, where they fought at 2nd Manassas and South Mountain.

Hartranft led the charge across Burnside Bridge at Antietam, losing 120 men in the fight against the Confederate right flank. The 51st was subsequently transferred to the Western Theatre, seeing action at Vicksburg, Campbell's Station and Knoxville. His unit then went back to the Eastern Theater and the Overland Campaign, fighting at the Wilderness and Spotsylvania. His unit was one of the few to fight in both the Eastern and Western theaters.

He was promoted to brigadier general on May 12, 1864. Commanding the 1st Brigade, 3rd Division of the IX Corps, his unit saw action at Peebles Farm, Richmond and Peters-

Two portraits of Gen. John F. Hartranft, as a civilian and, later in life, as a veteran officer.

burg. His last battle was Fort Stedman, where his unit captured the fort. Hartranft lived by his words: "The more I have made of myself, the better I can help my fellows."

Gen. Hartranft, front and center in each of the above photos; in photo at left, he is joined by his staff officers at Fort McNair, Washington, DC; in the photo at right, with his staff at an 1888 veterans reunion.

After the war ended, Hartranft was in charge of the Old Capitol Prison and was provost marshal at the Lincoln assassination trial. He was especially kind to Mrs. Mary Surratt, the first woman ever executed by the federal government. He personally led the four accused to the gallows. One Alexander Gardner picture shows Gen. Hartranft reading the order of execution for Mrs. Surratt, Lewis Paine, Davy Herold, and George Atzerodt. He also read last rites to them before they were hanged.

Above, left, is Alexander Gardner's iconic photograph of the hanging of the Lincoln assassination conspirators at the Washington Arsenal on July 7, 1865. In photo above, right, Gen. Hartranft (left) reads the orders of execution of prisoners Mary Surratt, Lewis Paine, Davy Herold, and George Atzerodt.

Also, see August/September, 2009, *Stone Wall* article about Lt. Col. William Henry Harrison McCall, who was an aide to Gen. Hartranft and who stood just behind Hartranft, to the left, on the gallows. The picture of Hartranft and his staff was taken at the Washington Arsenal. The gentleman on the far right was the executioner of the four Lincoln conspirators, Capt. Christian Rath. He can be identified as the man in the white coat on the gallows.

Hartranft returned to Norristown after the war, serving as Auditor General from 1867-1873. In 1872, after becoming a Republican, he was elected the 17th Governor of Pennsylvania, serving two terms, until 1879. He was preceded by Gen. John Geary as governor. During his administration, he was a strong advocate of education, banking regulation, commerce and industry, National Guard reorganization, African American suffrage, the workingman's rights, and fought the Simon Cameron political machine and the Molly Maguires. He also revised the Commonwealth of Pennsylvania's Constitution in 1873. One obscure fact I found was that Hartranft's inauguration in 1873 cost the Commonwealth of Pennsylvania $4,974.19.

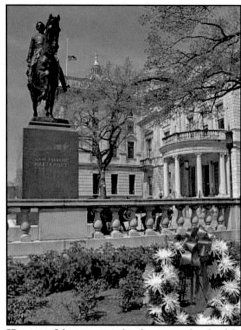

Hartranft's war service is recognized with a statue of him outside the state capitol in Harrisburg, PA.

He served as the 5th commander of the Grand Army of the Republic, from 1875-1877. In June 1876, at the Republican National Convention, he was almost nominated for president, but the nomination instead went to Rutherford B. Hayes. Hayes served in the same corps with Hartranft during the Civil War.

After his term as governor ended, Hartranft was appointed Postmaster of Philadelphia and Collector for the Port of Philadelphia. He also served as commander of the Pennsylvania National Guard.

Hartranft's gravesite at Montgomery Cemetery in Norristown, PA.

The general died at his home in Norristown on January 21, 1879, a victim of the kidney disease, from which he had suffered since 1873. The Pennsylvania National Guard provided the obelisk for his grave. On the south side of the Capitol in Harrisburg is a large equestrian statue of the general. The street leading to Montgomery Cemetery is named Hartranft Avenue, although the street address for the cemetery is 1654 Dekalb Street. A section in North Philadelphia is known as the Hartranft section, a street in South Philadelphia is named for him (as well as a residence hall at Penn State University), and also a street in Pittsburgh.

New Bull Run Civil War Round Table member Sam Laudenslager is the 2nd great grandson of Gen. Hartranft, on his mother's side. He also tells me that many of Hartranft's 51st Regiment are buried in Montgomery Cemetery, too.

The obelisk raised to Gen. Hartranft in the family area of the cemetery honors both his public and military service to the Commonwealth of Pennsylvania, and the United States.

Photos by Janet Greentree

Lt. Gen. John Clifford Pemberton, CSA

Gen. John Clifford Pemberton was like a man without a country. He was Northern born, but after marrying a woman from Virginia, he fought for the Confederacy. He was disliked by the

Gen. John C. Pemberton

North and not well-liked in the South, even though he became a lieutenant general. There were even protests after his death by the families of Gen. George Meade, Adm. John Dahlgren, and Thomas McKean (a signer of the Declaration of Independence) as to whether he should be allowed to be buried in his hometown of Philadelphia, in Laurel Grove Cemetery, where many Union veterans had been interred. The general's family won out, but he was buried in an obscure section of the cemetery, in 1881. He is buried in Section 9, Lot 53, with no mention on his monument that he was a Confederate general. A flat, in-the-ground plaque was added later, which states: "John C. Pemberton, Lt Gen General Staff, Confederate States Army, Aug. 14, 1814 - July 13, 1881." He is the only Confederate general buried in Laurel Hill, and in the State of Pennsylvania.

Pemberton was born on August 10, 1814, in Philadelphia, PA, to John and Rebecca Clifford Pemberton. His 4th great-grandfather was Phineas Pemberton, one of the early settlers of Pennsylvania and a friend of William Penn. Israel, his 3rd great-grandfather, owned Clarke's Hall, later known as Pemberton House and Gardens. James, his 2nd great-grandfather, was a Quaker merchant, manager of the Pennsylvania Hospital and founder of the Pennsylvania Abolition Society. James and Israel Pemberton were his 2nd great-uncles. Both James and Israel were exiled to Virginia, since they opposed the Revolutionary War. His grandfather Joseph's house has been reconstructed in Philadelphia between South 4th and South 3rd Streets, on Chesnut Street. As an interesting side note, his nephew, Dr. John Stith Pemberton, is the inventor of Coca Cola.

These bronze plaques were issued by the U.S. government in the 1970's - a perfect example of the ambivalent feelings many had in objecting to Pemberton's interment in Laurel Hill Cemetery in Philadelphia, PA.

Photo by Janet Greentree

John Clifford Pemberton was in college at the University of Pennsylvania when he decided he would like to pursue a career as an engineer. His father had connections to Pres. Andrew Jackson, which helped him secure an appointment to West Point. Ironically, he was the roommate and best friend of George G. Meade. Meade graduated two years before Pemberton, in 1835. John graduated with the class of 1837, ranking 27th out of 50 in his class. His classmates included future Confederate generals Braxton Bragg, Jubal Anderson Early, Robert Chilton, William Whann Mackall, and William Henry Talbot Walker; plus Union generals Lewis Arnold, Henry Benham, Alexander Dyer, Arnold Elsey, William French, Joseph Hooker, John Sedgwick, Eliakim Scammon, John Blair

Illustration of West Point in the 1840's, when Pemberton attended the military academy.

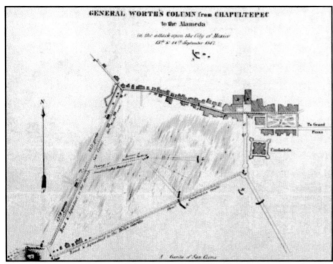

A map of Gen. William J. Worth's approach to Chapultepec in the Mexican War; Pemberton and Worth clashed at first, but their relationship improved to the point where the two could work together to achieve success in their push toward victory. Worth served then as Pemberton's aide-de-camp.

Smith Todd, Israel Vogdes, and Thomas Williams.

He started his army career as an officer of the 4th Artillery, serving in the Second Seminole War. He served garrison duty at Fort Columbus, NY; Trenton, NJ; Fort Mackinac; Fort Brady, Buffalo, NY; Fortress Monroe, and Carlisle Barracks. He later served with Zachary Taylor in the Mexican War, where he fought in the battles of Palo Alto, Resaca, and Monterrey. He was appointed a brevet captain for "Gallant Conduct in the Several Conflicts at Monterrey" on September 23, 1846. He also fought at Vera Cruz, Cerro Gordo, Churubusco, Molina del Ray, Chapultepec, and Mexico City. He was aide-de-camp to Gen. William J. Worth and a staff member, along with Ulysses S. Grant, a future adversary. He became one of the original members of the Aztec Club in 1847.

On January 18, 1848, in Norfolk, VA, he married Martha Thompson. Many historians believe that his marriage to a Southern woman is the reason he sided with the Confederacy. He was passing through Baltimore when the Pratt Street Riots took place in April 1861. He resigned his commission from the U.S. Army, even though his Northern family opposed his decision, as well as did Gen. Winfield Scott. His two brothers fought for the Union.

An illustration of the Battle of Champion Hill on May 16, 1863, in which Gen. Ulysses S. Grant pushes Pemberton's army back into the fortifications of Vicksburg, creating the opportunity to employ the siege of the city that ended with Pemberton's surrender of control of the Mississippi River.

He was appointed a lieutenant colonel in the Confederate States of America. He rose quickly through the ranks and was promoted to brigadier general on June 17, 1861. His first command was the Department of Norfolk. He was promoted to major general on January 14, 1862, commanding the Departments of Georgia and South Carolina. He was an unpopular general because of his abrasive personality. Confederate Pres. Jefferson Davis removed him from his command and sent him west. He was appointed lieutenant general on October 10,

1862, and his assignment was to defend Vicksburg. Davis' instructions were: "consider the successful defense of those States as the first and chief object of your command."

He faced his former Mexican War comrade, Ulysses S. Grant, and more than 70,000 Union soldiers during the Vicksburg Campaign. Even though Gen. Joseph E. Johnston advised Pemberton and his 50,000 men to sacrifice the city, he held on for six weeks. A vote in writing was proffered from his four division commanders, asking if they

Plaque describing the battle for Vicksburg, MS, including combined casualty figures of 1,302 killed, 3,486 wounded and 3,448 missing.

Photo by Janet Greentree

Shown above - an illustration of Gen. Grant and Gen. Pemberton discussing the surrender of Vicksburg to Union forces. At right: shown greeting each other, left to right, are: Hon. J. C. Pendleton III and Col. U. S. Grant III as they meet on May 22, 1937, at the scene of surrender talks between their grandfathers that were held 74 years earlier on July 3rd, 1863.

thought the city could be evacuated after 45 days of siege; all four of them voted no, leading to the prospect of surrender. He first asked Grant for an armistice. Grant being Grant, he refused to consider any terms but unconditional surrender. Pemberton surrendered 2,166 officers, 27,230 men, 172 cannon, and around 60,000 muskets to Grant on July 4, 1863. He was a held as a prisoner of war until his exchange on October 13, 1863, and he then was returned to Richmond. He spent eight months there without an assignment. Gen. Braxton Bragg thought about using his expertise, but his officers did not want Bragg to take him on.

Pemberton resigned as a general officer on May 9, 1864. Pres. Davis gave him a rank of lieutenant colonel, serving as commissioner of artillery. He commanded the defenses of Richmond and was later inspector general of artillery. He held the latter position until he was captured in Salisbury, NC, on April 12, 1865.

The Willis-Cowan house at 1018 Crawford Street, Vicksburg, MS, was his headquarters in Vicksburg; it was situated high enough for him to see the entire shelling and siege. It is owned now by the National Park Service and is open to the public.

Pemberton chose to live in Virginia after the war. Most research I have found shows he lived

Gen. Pemberton's gravestone in Laurel Hill Cemetery in Philadelphia, PA.

Photo by Janet Greentree

on a farm around Warrenton, VA. There have even been reports that it was Airlie. Ms. Rebelle even went on a field trip to Airlie to check it out, but the house in question was built in 1899. The 1870 census showed that he lived in "Center Township" and had an Upperville post office box. When looking up Center, VA, Google Maps outlined an area around Warrenton including Airlie and Auburn, bordered by Routes 29, 17, & 15. So, he lived in this general area of Fauquier Co., VA, but picked up his mail in Upperville. His land was valued at $5,000 and his wife's possessions were valued at $2,000. He left Virginia in 1876, moving back to Pennsylvania with his family.

Lt. Gen. John Clifford Pemberton died in Penllyn, Montgomery Co., PA, on July 13, 1881. His death certificate listed him living at 1947 Locust Street, Philadelphia, PA. His occupation was listed as "gentleman." Questions of his loyalty to the Confederate cause linger until this day. His war record proves he did not waiver in his devotion to his adopted South. Even though he surrendered Vicksburg, a statue of him is located there, along with a marker.

Maj. Gen. August Valentine Kautz, USA

When doing research on my generals, it is absolutely amazing what comes up for them.

Auuuguuust – the German way of saying his name - had three wives. Two of his wives were interesting, too. In addition to fighting in the Civil War, he was one of the judges of the military tribunal for the Lincoln Conspiracy Trial. He was stationed all over this beautiful country of ours.

Maj. Gen. August V. Kautz

A diarist for most of his life, Kautz's notes span from 1853-1895. He wrote about his life as a military man, his health, the weather but nothing about the current world situation. He was also a scrapbooker from 1884-1891, keeping noteworthy newspaper articles and his letters to various people, including Gen. William Tecumseh Sherman. The Library of Congress has possession of his diaries and scrapbooks.

August was born on January 5, 1828, in Ispringen, the Grand Duchy of Baden, Germany. His parents immigrated to America in 1828, when August was just a baby, settling in Baltimore, MD. In 1832, the family moved to Georgetown, OH, near Cincinnati. He was educated in the Georgetown schools.

In 1846, Kautz enlisted as a private in the 1st Ohio Infantry and served in the Mexican War until 1847. Unlike other Civil War generals who went to West Point before the Mexican War, August entered West Point afterwards and graduated with the class of 1852, ranking 35th out of 43. Twelve future Civil War generals would graduate in that class, including: George Burgwyn Anderson, George Blake Cosby, George Crook, John Horace Forney, George Lucas Hartsuff, Milo Smith Hascall, John Parker Hawkins, Alexander McDowell McCook, Henry Warner Slocum, David Sloan Stanley, and Charles Robert Woods.

After graduation, he was sent to Vancouver Barracks in the Washington Territory. He fell in love with the area and eventually retired there. It sometimes feels like I am following these generals around. My youngest daughter, Melanie, lived in Oregon for several years. On one of my visits to see her, we went to Vancouver Barracks.

While stationed at Fort Steilacoom in July 1853, August took his first wife, a 15-year-old Indian girl, Tenas Puss (Little Cat) in a Nisqually ceremony. She was the daughter of Nisqually Chief Lashimere. This is the second person profiled here who has who married an Indian woman. Gen. Richard Brooke Garnett was the first one I came across. Ms. Rebelle wonders if this was a common practice back then. Together, they had two sons, Nugan and Augustus. August and Little Cat were not allowed to live at the fort, but resided at a nearby Indian camp. While stationed at Fort Steilacoom, he was wounded twice in the Rogue River Wars in 1855.

During his time in the Pacific Northwest in July 1857, he was said to be the first person to climb Mount Rainier. He traveled with Dr. Robert O. Craig, an Army post doctor, and Indian guide Wapowety of the Nisqually. The group subsisted on dried meat and hard bread. At 10,000 feet, the Indian guide would not go any further up. He and Dr. Craig continued on. Kautz reached the rim of the summit crater at 14,411 feet, but not the mountain's highest point. In another 13 years, two other climbers would reach the summit. Kautz Creek,

At left - Vancouver Barracks is only one of the pleasant locations to visit in Washington state. At right - the heavy military presence of the U.S. Army in Washington territory.
Photo by Janet Greentree

209

Kautz Cleaver (an archeological term), and Kautz Glacier were named in his honor. Wapowety Cleaver was named for the Indian guide.

Kautz was transferred in 1858 to Camp Semiahmoo near the U.S./Canada border. He was transferred again on April 25, 1859, to Washington, DC. His wife Little Cat did not want to leave and live so far away from her people. August never saw his wife again. He made her promise that the boys would be educated and grow up amid the surroundings of civilization. Little Cat kept her promise, and the boys were educated at the Union Academy with James Pickett, son of Gen. George Pickett. Kautz sent letters and money to his sons, but did not see them again until they were adults. Eventually, Little Cat remarried. This information came from a newspaper article in the *San Francisco Call Bulletin* of October 25, 1895, noting the death of Gen. Kautz. The title of the article was: "Chief Lady at Post, The Aboriginal Wife Bore Two Sons Who Have Grown to Manhood, Recognized by their Father, Educated and Married, They Have Showed Themselves to be Reputable Citizens." (Keep this in mind, as there is another interesting newspaper site at the end of this article.)

Tenas Puss (Little Cat) - the first Mrs. Lt. Gen. August V. Kautz.

Kautz took a leave of absence and traveled Europe from 1859-1860.

When the Civil War began, he returned to Washington, D.C. and was made the captain of the 6th U.S. Cavalry, serving in the defenses of Washington. In September 1862, he was made the colonel of the 2nd Ohio Cavalry Volunteer Regiment and sent to Fort Scott, KS. The following year he commanded Camp Chase in Columbus, OH. He took part in the capture of Confederate Gen. John Hunt Morgan. He was under Gen. Benjamin Butler's command from April 1864 - March 1865 and fought at the battle of Ream's Station and Wilson's Raid. In March, 1865 he commanded a Division of Black Troops marching on the Capitol at Richmond on April 3, 1865.

The depiction above of the Conspirator's trial shows the table (right, rear) at which the judges, including Kautz, sat for the duration of the testimony.

Following the end of the Civil War and the assassination of Pres. Abraham Lincoln, he was appointed as one of the Judges of the Military Tribunal for the Lincoln Conspirators. Last May, Ms. Rebelle joined the Greater Boston CWRT for their annual Four Days in May tour. The group did all things "Booth" and through our tour guide, Kate Ramirez, we were allowed to go into Grant Hall at Fort McNair in Washington, D.C., where the trial of the conspirators was held. The building is occupied by offices except for the top floor, where the trial was held. The room is set up as it was for the trial. It was such a thrill to be in the building. Several sketches of the proceedings are available, but the conspirators are not shown hooded as they were in the trial. One has to wonder why the artist omitted that grim, but obvious detail. The courtroom is only open a couple of times a year.

On September 14, 1865, Gen.

The table in Grant Hall at Fort McNair where judges of the Military Tribunal of the Booth Conspirators sat is set with each member in their place, as they were 153 years ago.

Photo by Janet Greentree

210

Kautz married his second wife, Charlotte Delamater Tod. She was the daughter of Ohio Governor David Tod. She died in 1868.

After the war, he stayed in the U.S. Army and was appointed lieutenant colonel of the 34th U.S. Infantry. He served in New Mexico; the Department of the Arizona; California; and Nebraska, until he retired on January 5, 1892. Kautz wrote several books while stationed at Indian posts including: *Customs of Service for Non-Commissioned Officers and Soldiers, as Derived from Law and Regulations, and Practicing in the Army of the United States,*" "*The Company Clerk: Showing How and When to Make Out all the Returns, Reports, Rolls, and Other Papers,*

Military commission members who tried and convicted the Lincoln conspirators - (from left to right): Lt. Col. David R. Clendenin, Col. C.H. Tompkins, Brig. Gen. Thomas M. Harris, Brig. Gen. Albion P. Howe, Brig. Gen. James Ekin, Maj. Gen. Lew Wallace, Maj. Gen. David Hunter, Maj. Gen. August V. Kautz, Brig. Gen. Robert S. Foster, John A. Bingham, Henry L. Burnett and Brig. Gen. Joseph Holt (Library of Congress).

and What to do with Them," and "*From Missouri to Oregon – 1860: The Diary of August Kautz.*"

Gen. Kautz married his third wife, Fannie Markbreit, in 1872 in Cincinnati, OH. August was transferred to Fort Whipple in Arizona. Their first child, Austin, was born at the Fort. Gen.

The third Mrs. Lt. General August V. Kautz - Fannie Markbreit.

George Crook, former West Point classmate, opened his large home at Fort Whipple for the couple. Their second child, Francisca (Frankie), was born in 1875. Their third child, Navarra, was born in 1882.

The third Mrs. Kautz was very active socially in all the activities at the fort. She attended card parties, musical soirees, night hops, suppers, and flirted with all the young men. She loved being the center of attention. She loved acting and singing, and started the Fort Whipple Dramatic Association. She had a makeshift stage erected in Gen. Crook's club room. The Prescott newspaper *The Weekly Arizona Journal* gave her rave reviews for her acting and singing. When Gen. George A. Custer and his men were slaughtered at Little Big Horn, Fannie organized a musical benefit for the widows and orphans of the 7th Cavalry. This quote from the same newspaper of May 11, 1877, is about a party at Fort Whipple attended by Kautz and his wife: "Mrs. General Kautz was superbly attired in an elegant black silk, with demi-trained lace bertha and tunic. Her costume was rich, and one of the more expensive. This lady has so wonderfully preserved the freshness of her beauty that it is difficult to realize that she is a mother of several intelligent children." (Modern women would take offense at this.).

When the Kautz' left Fort Whipple in 1878, the same paper stated: "Mrs. Kautz, by her genial and kind disposition, ladylike deportment, magnificent hospitality and open heartedness in assisting in every good work of charity as well as amusement, has won for herself the hearty good will and esteem of this community."

After leaving Fort Whipple, Gen. Kautz had four more assignments. His fifth and last assignment took him back to Fort Vancouver. The Kautz family retired in Seattle, WA, where the general died on September 4, 1895. Fannie Kautz died at her youngest daughter Navarra's house on August 11, 1913. Both are buried in Arlington National Cemetery in Section 2, Lot 992.

Gen. Kautz' grave marker at Arlington National Cemetery in VA.

Photo by Janet Greentree

Maj. Gen. Cadwallader C. Washburn, USA

Here are a few questions for you. Have you ever eaten Cheerios, Lucky Charms, or Wheaties? Have you ever enjoyed Haagen Dazs ice cream? Have you ever eaten a Nature Valley bar or Yoplait yogurt? Have your children ever played with Play Doh, a Nerf ball, or played Monopoly? If the answer is yes to any of the above questions, you have Civil War Gen. Cadwallader Colden Washburn to thank for that privilege. Gen. Washburn had quite a life before the Civil War and quite a life afterwards. He started the company that is now known as General Mills in Minnesota.

Cadwallader C. Washburn, a/k/a C.C., was born on April 22, 1818, in Livermore, Maine. Livermore was originally part of Massachusetts. The Washburn family is so well connected and

famous that when you search the internet for the "Washburn Family," information comes up on *this* particular family.

C.C.'s great grandfather Israel was in the Massachusetts legislature, as was his son Israel II. Israel III was a Massachusetts state representative and father of Cadwallader. Ten children were born to Israel III and his wife Martha Benjamin Washburn – seven boys and three girls. All seven boys served politically in state government, U.S. Congress, industry, U.S. Navy, or in a diplomatic capacity.

The oldest son, Israel IV, was governor of Maine during the Civil War, as well as a member of Congress. Algernon was a banker and opened the Bank of Hallowell. Elihu was a Congressman from Illinois, Secretary of State under President U.S. Grant, and minister to France. Charles was a Commissioner to Paraguay. Samuel was the Acting Master of the U.S. Navy during the Civil War and fought in the battle of Drewy's Bluff on the *U.S.S. Galena*. William was a

Maj. Gen. Cadwallader C. Washburn

representative and senator from Minnesota. That is quite a family. This family did not lack in unusual names either. C.C. and his brothers and sisters were also fourth cousins, once removed, to Charles Sumner.

U.S.S. Galena

All seven brothers witnessed Lincoln's inauguration in 1861. When President Lincoln was assassinated on April 14, 1865, C.C.'s brother Elihu accompanied the body during the long train ride to his graveside in Springfield, Illinois. He served as a pallbearer at the ceremony in Springfield.

Elihu was also the only civilian to be present when arms were stacked at Appomattox, and stood with Gen. Joshua Lawrence Chamberlain. Gen. Grant had provided a cavalry escort so Elihu could witness the surrender.

Then there is Cadwallader. C.C. attended school in Wiscasset, Maine. He would later teach there from 1838-1839. In the year 1839, he moved to Davenport, Iowa, where he taught school, worked in a store and did surveying. His brother Elihu set up a legal practice in Galena, IL, which influenced C.C. to read the law and become an attorney in Mineral Point, Wisconsin. He set up the Wisconsin Mining Company in 1844 with Cyrus Woodman.

In 1855, they started Washburn's and Woodman's Mineral Point Bank. In 1853 Washburn built a mill on the Chippewa River in Waubeck, WI. In 1855, C.C. ran for Congress as

Illustration of St. Anthony's Falls - Minneapolis, MN.

a Republican, winning three terms in the 34th-36th Congresses, representing the 2nd Congressional District of Wisconsin from 1855-1861.

In 1856, even before the city of Minneapolis was incorporated in 1867, he saw the 16-foot St. Anthony's Falls in that area and knew the power it could generate for industry. He bought 89 acres to start his mills.

Washburn bought into the Minneapolis Mill Company and his brother William managed the company. Several of his cotton mills, sawmills, grist and flour mills, and woolen mills operated along the Mississippi River.

When talk about a Civil War began, Washburn had just moved to LaCrosse, WI. His family were ardent abolitionists and had always been strongly opposed to slavery. He went to Washington, D.C., as a delegate for the peace conference held there. He entered the Union Army as a colonel of the 2nd Wisconsin Volunteer Cavalry on February 6, 1862.

He advanced quickly, being made a brigadier general on July 16, 1862, and then major general on November 29, 1862. His appointment was signed by none other than President Abraham Lincoln. Lincoln and the Washburn family had been friends for a long time.

Portrait of a prosperous Washburn later in life.

Washburn commanded the XIII Corps, beginning with the Vicksburg Campaign. Gen. Grant said of him: "Washburn was one of the best administrative officers we have." Washburn also commanded three divisions of the XVI Corps during the siege of Vicksburg. He commanded the 1st Division of the XIII Corps in Texas, along with Gen. Nathanial P. Banks, and led the fight against Fort Esperanza in November 1863.

C.C. served in administrative functions in Mississippi and Tennessee. While he was in Memphis, Confederate Gen. Nathan Bedford Forrest unsuccessfully tried to capture him and other Union Generals. He resigned from the Army on May 25, 1865.

Washburn's B Mill.

After the war, he returned to LaCrosse, WI. He was elected for two terms, representing Wisconsin's 6th Congressional District from 1867-1871. He worked as the chairman of the Committee on Expenditures for Public Buildings. In 1871, his fellow Wisconsiners urged him to run for governor. Washburn was elected, and served from 1872-1874. As Governor, he brought in reforms for government control of telegraphs, railroads, and libraries. Unfortunately (well … maybe), he didn't win re-election in 1873. There were still things he needed to accomplish in

An illustration of what the 1878 mill explosion looked like — the event was undoubtedly a catastrophe for Washburn.

his life.

Earlier in this busy life, on January 1, 1849, he married Jeannette Garr. Both were 30 years of age at the time. Jeannette gave birth in 1850 to their first daughter, Nettie, but their happiness was short-lived, as Jeannette began to show signs of a mental illness after Nettie's birth. Their second daughter, Fanny, was born in 1852.

Jeannette continued to sink deeper into mental illness, and had to be hospitalized in the Bloomingdale Asylum in Brookline, MA. She remained there until her death in 1909 at age 90. Their children were raised by their grandparents on the East Coast.

While still in Congress in 1866, Washburn built the Washburn "B" Mill. The mill was so large, naysayers said it would never make a profit. In 1874, he built an even larger mill (Washburn "A" Mill) seven stories high. This mill was destroyed in a fire and huge explosion in 1878, but was later rebuilt. The explosion occurred at night, saving 200 daytime workers. Only 18 workers were killed in this catastrophe. He facilitated new safety technologies, including better ventilation to make his mills safer. Feeling devastated about the loss of men and his mill, he started an orphanage for children without question or distinction to age, sex, race, color, or religion.

In 1880, the Washburn Crosby Company entered several grades of its flour into a contest held in Cincinnati, OH, called the International Millers' Exhibition. Their flours won the gold medal. Some of you may have used his flour - which is called Gold Medal Flour.

On May 14, 1822, at age 64, Civil War general, miller, entrepreneur, politician, and philanthropist Cadwallader Colden Washburn died while seeking medical treatment in the springs of Eureka Springs, Arkansas. His body was brought back to LaCrosse, WI, and buried in Oak Grove Cemetery with a very, very large obelisk as his marker. His net worth at his death was estimated to be between $2-3 million. He left money to his daughters, other members of his family, and a large bequest to the city of LaCrosse. The city built a large public library with his kind bequest. His money also funded the orphanage he started for the children who lost parents in the mill explosion. The orphanage today is known as the Washburn Center for Children.

His Madison, WI, residence, Edgewood, was endowed as a Catholic Girls school. The largest sum went to take care of his mentally ill wife, Jeannette, residing in Massachusetts.

Oak Grove Cemetery has a Civil War Veterans section with a large monument of a soldier. Graves hold not only Wisconsin soldiers, but also soldiers from Ohio, Massachusetts, Iowa, and other states. The city of LaCrosse also has a marker for Gen. Washburn in a rest area at 2323 Lakeshore Drive.

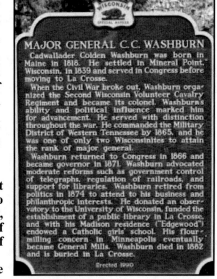

MAJOR GENERAL C.C. WASHBURN
Cadwallader Colden Washburn was born in Maine in 1818. He settled in Mineral Point, Wisconsin, in 1839 and served in Congress before moving to La Crosse.
When the Civil War broke out, Washburn organized the Second Wisconsin Volunteer Cavalry Regiment and became its colonel. Washburn's ability and political influence marked him for advancement. He served with distinction throughout the war. He commanded the Military District of Western Tennessee by 1865, and he was one of only two Wisconsinites to attain the rank of major general.
Washburn returned to Congress in 1866 and became governor in 1871. Washburn advocated moderate reforms such as government control of telegraphs, regulation of railroads, and support for libraries. Washburn retired from politics in 1874 to attend to his business and philanthropic interests. He donated an observatory to the University of Wisconsin, funded the establishment of a public library in La Crosse, and with his Madison residence ("Edgewood") endowed a Catholic girls school. His flour-milling concern in Minneapolis eventually became General Mills. Washburn died in 1882 and is buried in La Crosse.
Erected 1990

At left, Washburn's monument in Oak Grove Cemetery. Photo by Janet Greentree. At right, the marker put up in honor of Gen. Washburn in the city of LaCrosse, WI.
Photos by Janet Greentree

Cemeteries Containing
Civil War Generals

Civil_War_Generals

★ Generals In Book (80)

✚ Other Notables (21)

◉ Generals in Cemeteries (1075)

STATES

☐ STATES